MW01129987

CONFEDERATE
COMMISSARY
GENERAL

LUCIUS BELLINGER NORTHROP
(1811–1894)

COMMISSARY GENERAL, C.S.A., 1861–65

THE ONLY KNOWN PHOTOGRAPH,
TAKEN BY ORDER OF FEDERAL AUTHORITIES, JULY 1865.

CONFEDERATE COMMISSARY GENERAL

LUCIUS BELLINGER NORTHROP
AND THE
SUBSISTENCE BUREAU
OF THE
SOUTHERN ARMY

JERROLD NORTHROP MOORE

FOREWORD BY
LYNDA L. CRIST

 WHITE MANE PUBLISHING CO., INC.

This White Mane Publishing Company, Inc. publication
was printed by
Beidel Printing House, Inc.
63 West Burd Street
Shippensburg, PA 17257 USA

In respect for the scholarship contained herein, the acid-free paper used in this book meets the guidelines for permanence and durability of the Committee on Production Guidelines for Book Longevity of the Council on Library Resources.

For a complete list of available publications
please write
White Mane Publishing Company, Inc.
P.O. Box 152
Shippensburg, PA 17257 USA

Library of Congress Cataloging-in-Publication-Data

PRINTED IN THE UNITED STATES OF AMERICA

TABLE OF CONTENTS

LIST OF ILLUSTRATIONS

FOREWORD

BY LYNDA LASSWELL CRIST

Lucius B. Northrop's very name is synonymous with curmudgeon in the history of the Civil War. Contemporary critics of the "pepper doctor from Charleston" found him both incompetent and obstinate, if not actually criminal in his administration of the Confederate Commissary Department. Someone surely was responsible for hungry soldiers and prisoners: Northrop was the obvious choice. Usually maligned, when he is noticed at all in Civil War histories, the commissary general made an inviting scapegoat, blamed for national failings and the object of irrational hostility.

Born into Charleston society, related by marriage to the Cherokee, well-educated in the military and medicine, a Roman Catholic, fatherless at an early age, lame, a vegetarian, Northrop could not escape private insecurities, yet he rose to a monumental task during the Civil War and gave it his all. In the process he sacrificed his lifelong friendship with President Jefferson Davis and, in the waning days of the war, lost his very livelihood.

Like his friend, Northrop never asked for the job he held in the Confederacy, but accepted it from a sense of duty. He and Davis had been kindred spirits for thirty years, having known each other as cadets at West Point and on the frontier as officers of Dragoons. Davis valued Northrop's honesty, efficiency, his dedication to the task at hand, and probably his stubbornness and lack of personal ambition. Unfortunately for both of them, political savvy and diplomatic skills were also lacking. It was not nearly enough to be a skilled organizer and to do one's job. The Confederate commissariat demanded miracles.

Northrop was no miracle-worker. He was a realist who anticipated a long war, planned accordingly, and held his ground against the likes of P. G. T. Beauregard and Joseph E. Johnston without care for the consequences. According to one journalist, he "cared not a fig, individually, for such puny assaults." Other generals were critical, too, and they all outranked the commissary general. Many had powerful friends in Congress and were heroes of the cause.

The feuds with Beauregard, whom Northrop called a charlatan, and Johnston, whom he believed a liar, began early, at First Manassas and in the destruction of the Thoroughfare Gap depot. While most agreed that the destruction of vital stores at Thoroughfare laid "the heaviest hand on the Confederate Army of Northern Virginia for the rest of the war," the blame was variously assessed. Northrop's battles with Beauregard and Johnston, also

Davis' nemeses, were dredged up again and again for decades afterward, with great bitterness on all sides.

Northrop had his defenders in the first year or two of the war, even among newspapermen, who leveled charges instead at regimental commissaries and praised the South Carolinian for his "superhuman exertions." Although some later alleged that local commissary agents were profiting from impressment and price-fixing, Northrop's personal integrity was never questioned. He "lived like a Spartan," and he and his family suffered from a lack of basic necessities, along with most other folk.

Northrop's efforts were more often than not stymied by the lean, complex Treasury Department and the non-cooperation and deficiencies of Southern railroads. His differences with Secretary of the Treasury C. G. Memminger were basic and immutable, as were the railroad problems. From the start, Northrop sought to understand and take full advantage of existing food supply networks and to establish others. His agents roamed the South, trying to anticipate the size and movements of every army. All such efforts were doomed by shrinking territory, depreciated currency, lessening manpower, and the destruction of transportation, communication lines, and farmland.

By late 1863 he must have known (in the words of his biographer) that the central government "had failed, was failing, and would probably continue to fail." Still, he clung doggedly to his goals: to centralize purchasing and supply, to buy according to the ruling market, and to press for nationalization of the railroads. His plans and methods were visionary and most of his key staff appointments were brilliant, yet he failed to win support in Congress, among the generals, and in the public prints. Government insiders found him irascible, even "down" and "dark," but the few who commented also knew he worked night and day. And they believed he was ahead of his superiors in devising ways to meet the spiraling food crisis.

Northrop's position was a magnet for criticism; the faint praise accorded him in 1861 led inevitably to damnation. Even if all his procedures had been faultless, the perception was the opposite because the army traveled on very hungry stomachs much too frequently during the war. Refusing to answer his critics because important information might thus be revealed to the enemy, Northrop also was by nature secretive and strong-willed. He was not inclined to deflect criticism—and perhaps was prohibited from doing so. Instead, he composed official reports and long endorsements, "splutter[ing] . . . in his angular chirography at a furious rate." And he would not resign, equating resignation to desertion. He remained loyal to Davis even after they were estranged over the controversial issues of trade through the lines and blockade-running.

Over these questions and others, Northrop found himself bound by constitutional and state rights strictures while facing the daily and very practical matter of feeding soldiers and their stock. The story of how he managed so well for so long is a focused administrative history of a Confederate bureau, filling a great gap in Civil War historiography. It is also a mightily human story of perseverance and devotion to duty.

Northrop's central role in the operations of all the Southern armies made him a witness whose published recollections would have been invaluable. Lacking those (though urged by Davis to write), we have instead the two old friends' postwar letters, many penned while Davis was compiling his own history of the Confederacy. Northrop unburdened himself in the 1870s and 1880s, confiding opinions and reminiscences to his old ally.

Did Northrop act with "energy, fidelity, and good conduct," as Davis frequently asserted? Were his goals impossible dreams, given the challenges and resources of the new nation? Did he deserve to be "the most cussed and vilified man in the Confederacy"? Was he simply "a rather good, if 'crusty, routine' executive, who was forced to resort to harsh methods"? After reading his story and the chronicle of the Commissary Department, can any reader give an unqualified yes or no?

PREFACE AND ACKNOWLEDGMENTS

The subject of army subsistence at first nibble seems to promise only a crumb of Confederate history. In reality it is a vast and virtually endless subject, reaching into nearly every corner of the Old South and the story of its bid for independence. Yet the entire documentation is no longer there—largely because of the burning of Subsistence Bureau records in the conflagration of Richmond in 1865.

Working at it on and off for nearly ten years has taught me to accept some limitations. The lack of any extended account by a close participant or observer about the Subsistence Bureau leaves an emptiness on the personal side that can be filled in only here and there. The administrative side is less incomplete—because of the *Official Records of the Union and Confederate Armies* drawing together a selection of surviving papers, and because of a further large number of unpublished documents in the National Archives and other collections. Even then there are gaps, which are amongst the reasons why the subject has been neglected for so long.

The curve of this story is inevitably downward to failure. Problems occur, then they recur and recur with ever mounting severity. And so, despite the fragmentary character of some survivals, others show the same intractable problems returning and returning. The frustrations they created can thus be noted more and more briefly, however painful and protracted they were in life. My method is to portray each problem on its first appearance as fully as its importance seems to warrant and knowledge permits: hence for instance the detailed coverage of events surrounding First Manassas, from which flowed so much of what happened afterwards. When the same and similar problems recur, the reader will soon recognize them. But this is not a book for browsing: the end will convey little without the beginning and middle.

If there seems a heavy emphasis on the commissariat in Virginia, that is where the sharpest problems lay throughout the war. Granted that generals elsewhere complained as loudly as Lee, the evidence shows them feeding better than he did and often at his expense. The matter of food in Virginia is therefore central to the story of Northrop and his Bureau. Supplies and transport being what they were, the Confederate West could usually feed itself—with the Commissary General's help or in spite of it. For Lee in Virginia, the Subsistence Bureau became a lifeline in the most literal sense. When it failed, Lee failed, and the war ended.

The commissariat is a neglected field in military studies. One of the very few general works on the subject in English was written nearly a century ago by a British officer. Had it been available forty years earlier, Northrop —and perhaps more significantly his superiors—could have read:

> If we take the question of supplies, and look at it from its various points of view, we shall have no doubt in admitting that it affects the condition of an army and its mobility more than the weather or the state of the roads.

Yet the two matters of subsistence and transport are ultimately entwined:

> All officers should recollect that every ounce of food forwarded to the front advances the object of the campaign, and that for this purpose there is as much need to call in aid the transport of the country (bad as it may appear) as to draw largely on the food-supply contained in the theater of war. ...
>
> In his "Precis de l'art de la guerre," Jomini gives it as his opinion that the art of provisioning a numerous army, above all in an enemy's country, is one of the most difficult. Schellendorf and other writers seem to think that the problem of how to feed an army in the field is one that has not yet been solved, and one that is never likely to be solved.[1]

This basic lesson of subsistence-in-transport was learned quickly by the Confederate Commissary General, but hardly at all throughout the entire war by his superiors in government, and only occasionally by Southern generals in the field. Here as usual Robert E. Lee was first and best; yet even Lee's insights in this area, as will be seen, were too little and too late. The insights of Lee's military colleagues east and west ranged mostly from less to none.

The basic reason for the widespread failures in Confederate transport was the novelty of the railroads. This War was the first large conflict for which railroads were available. Almost nothing of their use had figured in the prior experience of most of the commanders. That was equally true in the North, but there a wealth of resources allowed the filling of many more conflicting requisitions. In the South, with resources much scarcer, military imagination did not in general fill the lacuna of military experience.

Of all the high Confederate officers, perhaps only the War Department Bureau chiefs were in a position to acquire comprehensive railroad experience quickly enough. Northrop's greatest achievement as Commissary General may have been that he acquired this experience as if by sheer insight from almost his first day in office—certainly from his first day in Richmond. His greatest failure was his inability to persuade any superior officer to share his vision.

* * *

Because of the statistics that do survive, nothing would have been easier than to make this book a half-acre tomb of numbers. The numbers

---

[1] Colonel George Armand Furse, CB, *Provisioning Armies in the Field* (London: William Clowes & Sons Ltd., 1899), 2, 20, 14. Antoine Henri Jomini (1779-1869), a Swiss soldier under Napoleon, published his "Treatise on Military Operations" in 1804. Paul Bronsart von Schellendorf (1832-1891) was a soldier and minister of war who helped reform the Prussian army in the 1880's. His most famous work was "The Duties of the General Staff" (1875; English translation 1905).

were undeniably important, and I hope to have included enough of them to show what that importance was. Despite our American obsession with numbers, however, I don't believe most people then or now find that games of statistical hockey produce more substantial truth than the study of personalities. So I have aimed at a truth of wider interest—to put it no higher.

In this approach, every reader will see the depth of my debt to the two great books by Douglas Southall Freeman, *R. E. Lee* and *Lee's Lieutenants*. Before Freeman's advent, there was no comprehensive history of these subjects. When he finished, that history was in place—written with a rare grace and understanding. Freeman's precept for the biographer is one I have tried to adopt:

> When biography becomes defense, it descends to special pleading and forfeits all confidence. The facts must speak for themselves. The duty of the biographer is discharged when he has arrayed them in their proper place and order. The informed reader who follows the successive steps of Lee's *[and I would add Northrop's]* planning must himself be the judge of the fairness of these criticisms; but the reader, at the same time, must examine all the circumstances in their relation to the desperate leadership of a desperate cause.[2]

It has been my misfortune to have to deal with a subject which revealed a rare blind spot in Freeman's understanding. He himself admitted— not a hundred pages after the paragraph just quoted—that he did not understand the springs of Northrop's character and actions. He called Northrop a "strange man" of "gloomy contrariness" and an "enigmatic code" of behavior. Then Freeman wrote of Northrop: "He is, in fact, one of the few functionaries of the period whose letters, read after seventy years, irritate if they do not outrage the historian."[3] Irritation and outrage should not invade the historian's thought, as Freeman himself would surely have agreed on reflection, and those emotions are hardly ever found elsewhere in his writings. By the time he came to write *Lee's Lieutenants*, in fact, there are signs that irritation had receded as his understanding even of Northrop had grown.

Almost every writer on the War from the 1860's onward has excoriated Northrop for obstinacy, rigidity, even stupidity in failing to feed his army well enough. Yet despite being one of the best-hated men in the Confederacy, Northrop held his post for nearly the entire length of the war, from March 1861 to February 1865. The usual explanation is still that he was the favorite of Jefferson Davis. Yet Davis was not a dictator. If Northrop was hopeless as claimed, Davis could not have shielded him from the onslaughts of the generals, the repeated investigations of the Confederate Congress, the farmers whose crops he impressed, and the armies who—in the East at any rate—were repeatedly on short rations through the last two years of the war.

---

[2] *R. E. Lee* (New York: Scribner, 1934), II, 410.

[3] Ibid., 494-95.

Gradually and with growing astonishment I have come to realize that the continuing abuse of Northrop persisted basically because no substantial examination had ever been made of Northrop's Subsistence Bureau. The allegators were basically reflecting the accusations of the politically motivated anti-Davis press in Richmond during the 1860's.[4]

The objurgations stop short in one matter. No responsible person seems ever to have accused Northrop of dishonesty or willful corruption. Granted that incorruptibility is a pearl beyond price in a Commissary General, did that alone keep him in office for nearly the entire war?

*   *   *

The origin of this book was family interest, but not I hope family hagiography. Its subject was the brother of my great-grandfather. Yet the two families had so entirely lost touch that I did not discover any of Lucius Northrop's direct descendants until the book was half complete. It began for me as simply the case of an old family relation who played a noticeable part in his country's history at a crucial time, but was still without an adequate account of what he had done or not done. It seemed that if such a study was to exist, I would have to write it. In no way a military scholar, I had at least extensive experience in handling historical materials and their use in biography. So I began to ask for help.

The generous aid I met from the beginning and on every hand has been the best encouragement. My first and greatest encourager has been Lynda Crist, editor of *The Papers of Jefferson Davis*. I approached her because of the sixty-year friendship with Davis—the greatest of Northrop's life. And history has repeated itself to this extent: both she and her coeditor Mary Dix saw the possibilities, as well as the difficulties. A full record of their real and practical help at every stage would fill many pages. Instead, I will here record my certainty that the present book would not have been realized in publishable form were it not for their good actions. It is impossible to place a value on that kind of understanding and sympathy.

Lynda Crist and her staff opened the way for me to approach the extensive archives. Here I must cite a special debt to the late Sara D. Jackson, who brought her unrivalled experience to bear on the retrieval of documents in the National Archives which I might not have found for myself in a year of searching there. Brian Dirck used his knowledge of Confederate administrative documents to look out many unpublished papers of clear importance but dim visibility on microfilm.

Amongst other archivists, those in Charleston and Charlottesville have placed me deeply in their debts. Stephen Hoffius and other friends at the South Carolina Historical Society have led me into obscure corners to illumine Northrop's early life and heritage. The best surviving collection of Northrop's private correspondence is preserved in St. John's Cathedral Di-

---

[4] A fair sample of such shallowly informed opinion about Northrop can be found in the well-regarded recent single volume history, *Battle Cry of Freedom,* by James McPherson (Oxford University Press, 1988).

ocesan Archives, where Father William Burn was generous and imaginative in turning the wheels of access. This book would have been very much less in every private aspect of Northrop's life without his help; and I add a heart-felt word of thanks to the ladies of the Diocesan Schools Office upstairs. At Charlottesville, A. Robert Kuhlthau garnered records from the Albemarle County Historical Society archives to illuminate Northrop's later years to a degree I would not have thought possible.

Other friends and colleagues have generously helped the writing of this book in many ways. It gives me much pleasure to record debts of gratitude to Frank Vandiver for invaluable advice and encouragement on an earlier draft; Sims Kline of Stetson University, who extended the rich resources of the University Library to me from the beginning of this project; Robert Elliott and the members of the James F. Hull Camp, Sons of Confederate Veterans; the late Frank Rankin, Historian General of the Military Order of Stars and Bars; George Heilborn; Mr. and Mrs. C. J. Myers; the late R. G. Emblem; Dr. William Morgan; Dr. Frederick Wagner, Professor emeritus and historian of the Thomas Jefferson Medical University; T. Kelly Fitzpatrick, archivist of Mount Saint Mary's College, Emmitsburg; the archivists of Georgetown University; Waverly Winfree and the staff at the Virginia Historical Society in Richmond; and archivists of the other collections from which I have drawn information.

Secondary sources are cited when they have given real help. This has been less often than I wished. When general histories of the War—even recent ones—mention Confederate subsistence at all, their remarks are usually based so entirely on one or two papers as to render the sketch more or less misleading. Two honorable exceptions are E. Merton Coulter's *The Confederate States of America* (Louisiana State University, 1950) and Herman Hattaway and Archer Jones's *How the North Won* (Univ. of Chicago, 1983).[5] Grateful acknowledgments to these authors and a handful of others will be found in the footnotes. Specific acknowledgments of permissions to publish will be found in footnotes and illustration credits.

The only previous writer known to me who tried to write a connected history of Confederate subsistence is Richard Goff. His *Confederate Supply* (Duke Univ., 1969) is not bad so far as it goes; but his attempt to combine the histories of all the supply bureaus in two hundred and fifty pages leaves many matters without explanation. Biographies of the generals are uniformly partial (in both senses) when they glance at subsistence.

In tangent fields I have been lucky to find one good secondary source in each. *The Railroads of the Confederacy* (Univ. of North Carolina, 1952; *rpr* Broadfoot, 1987) by Robert C. Black presents the whole subject with splendid comprehension. Jeffrey Lash's recent study of J. E. Johnston, *Destroyer of the Iron Horse* (Kent State, 1991) added several points, but it does not give a whole picture of anything.

---

[5] Curiously the same authors' *Why the South Lost the Civil War* (Univ. of Georgia, 1986) seems to contain not a word about food.

Southern farming is deftly sketched in Paul Gates's *Agriculture and the Civil War* (Knopf, 1965): his excellent pages on the Confederacy raise the wish he had devoted an entire book to it. Again there has been no real successor. In the field of trade through enemy lines, it is a pleasure to record the valuable help given by the work of Ludwell Johnson, the only scholar who seems to have approached the field. On blockade running, I have learned much from Stephen R. Wise's *Lifeline of the Confederacy* (Univ. of South Carolina, 1988).

Confederate finance has been more frequently served over the years, beginning with J. C. Schwab's invaluable and finely written *The Confederate States of America: a Financial and Industrial History* (Yale, 1913). Despite Schwab's success, monetary policy remains one of those obstinately unpalatable subjects for all but its devotees, and several later entries in the field are more careful than enlivening.

For military strategy and tactics, Edward Hagerman's *The American Civil War and the Origins of Modern Warfare* (Indiana Univ., 1988) makes a brave attempt to survey the complex field. When he comes to subsistence, Hagerman grasps several general truths more clearly than most; but he is finally betrayed by the partialities of his secondary sources. He does not really discuss any Northrop policies or actions—which he wrongly concludes were "improvised"—and suggests that the Subsistence Bureau "reorganization" of 1863 was imposed from above instead of implementing much of what Northrop had long asked for.

A note of general indebtedness must be recorded to the knowledge and insights of a profound scholar of the older generation, Charles W. Ramsdell—especially his *Behind the Lines in the Southern Confederacy* (L.S.U., 1944, *rpr* Greenwood, 1969). His observations, even casual ones, over many fields have repeatedly sent me scurrying toward some previously overlooked source or indicated some line of thinking that would not otherwise have been mine.

To try to come at a picture of Confederate subsistence as a whole, however, I have had no choice but to rely on primary sources—original letters and reports published and unpublished, and eyewitness accounts written at the time and later by participants at every level. This is reflected in the footnotes. I have not troubled the reader with every secondary author who agrees or disagrees with a conclusion reached herein. If I have done my work, the reader will see how I got there. The citation of a secondary source usually indicates the possibility of some worthwhile further reading.

* * *

One of the richest rewards for writing this book has come in the discovery of cousins previously unknown. It is a keen pleasure to record their names in the order they introduced themselves and each other: Frederic Bellinger of New Hampshire; Susan Pender Bellinger of Charleston; the Hon. Judge Edward S. Northrop, his sons Edward Middleton Northrop and Peter Northrop, Mr. and Mrs. Geoffrey Fielding (granddaughter of L. B. Northrop's eldest daughter), Mrs. Fielding's aunt, the late Claudia Bellinger Didier, and her cousin Arthur B. Steuart, all of Baltimore; Henry Coles of Charlottesville; Mary Northrop Hunt (granddaughter of Northrop's younger son), and Lillian Wilson (great-granddaughter-in-law of Northrop's elder son), of Florida. One and all they have brought intelligent and imaginative help to this project without the faintest suggestion of a wish to influence its outcome. Beyond that lies the special electric sympathy that inheres in family links.

The real founder of this book is my mother, Mary Letitia Northrop Moore, the great-niece of L. B. Northrop. It was her interest in history and genealogy that first awakened my own, and throughout the writing I have enjoyed the benefits of her memories, insights, and reflections. So it is with the greatest gratitude that I dedicate this book to her.

Jerrold Northrop Moore
September 1995

ABBREVIATIONS

CDA = Charleston Catholic Diocesan Records, St. John's Cathedral, Charleston, S.C.

Davis Papers = *The Papers of Jefferson Davis*, various editors (Baton Rouge: Louisiana State University Press, 1971 *ff*

f(f) = Frame number(s) in microfilm

Journal of Congress = *Journal of the Congress of the Confederate States of America, 1891-1865* (7 vols., Washington: Government Printing Office, 1904-1905)

M-437 = NA, RG 109, Letters Received by the Confederate Secretary of War (Government microfilm publication M-437)

M-474 = NA, RG 109, Letters Received by the Confederate Adjutant and Inspector General (Government microfilm publication M-474)

M-523 = NA, RG 109, Letters Sent by the Confederate Secretary of War to the President (Government microfilm publication M-523)

M-524 = NA, RG 109, Telegrams Sent by the Confederate Secretary of War (Government microfilm publication M-524)

M-618 = NA, RG 109, Telegrams Received by the Confederate Secretary of War (Government microfilm publication M-618)

NA = National Archives, Washington, D.C.

NYPL = New York Public Library

OR = *The War of the Rebellion: A Compilation of the Official Records of the Union and Confederate Armies* (70 vols. in 128, Washington: Government Printing Office, 1880-1901)

r = Reel number in microfilm series

RG = Record Group in National Archives
(N.B.: the RG number is not used with microfilm publication citations.)

Rowland   = Dunbar Rowland, *Jefferson Davis: Constitutional-*
                   ist (10 vols., Jackson: Mississippi Department of
                   Archives and History, 1923)

SHSP   = *Southern Historical Society Papers*

Tulane   = Tulane University, New Orleans, Louisiana Histori-
                   cal Association: Jefferson Davis Papers

Va. Hist. Soc.   = Virginia Historical Society, Richmond, Virginia

CHAPTER 1

ORIGINS

Lucius Bellinger Northrop was born in Charleston, South Carolina on September 8, 1811. His parents combined two heritages as distinct as could be found among old American families. His mother's emigrant ancestor was Edmund Bellinger (1657-1707)—descended from an English forebear who in 1475 first distinguished his patronymic from the parent family Bellingham. Edmund Bellinger arrived in the Carolinas in 1686, held several offices there, and returned briefly to England in 1698 to confer with the philosopher John Locke about the Carolina constitution. In 1700 Bellinger was made a Landgrave: four "Baronies" were granted to him, amounting to nearly fifty thousand acres in coastal lands below Charleston.

During ensuing centuries the Bellinger Baronies were much divided. The Ashepoo Plantation on the Ashepoo River, thirty miles west of Charleston, was occupied by Lucius Northrop's immediate ancestors. His maternal grandfather was John Bellinger of Ashepoo (1745-1809), second son of the third Landgrave. John Bellinger was a veteran of the American Revolution, having served in the 1st South Carolina Regiment under Charles Cotesworth Pinckney. In later years he kept a stud of race horses at Ashepoo, and was known as "Jockey John".

His wife was Rebecca d'Oyley, of another distinguished Carolina family; her immediate ancestors included Pinckneys and Brewtons. The elder son of "Jockey John" and Rebecca was John Skottowe Bellinger (1777-1842), who studied medicine at the University of Pennsylvania under the most celebrated doctor in eighteenth-century America, Benjamin Rush. In 1808 Dr. J. S. Bellinger moved his family to a plantation named "Pine Forest", 75 miles northwest of Charleston in the Barnwell District, near the present town of Bamberg—where other Bellingers, Pinckneys, and Bulls (cousins of the Bellingers) established themselves on nearby plantations.

Jockey John's daughter (who was to become Lucius Northrop's mother) was born on December 28, 1787, probably at Ashepoo. She was "the beautiful and stately" Claudia Margaret Bellinger.[1] The background of the man she was to marry, Amos Northrop, was in total contrast.

The Northrops had lived in Connecticut since the early 1630's. They were low-church Protestants, and were mostly small farmers. Then in the fifth generation two sons were sent for university education to Yale College. In the case of the younger son Joel (Lucius Northrop's grandfather) the experience changed the family pattern. Joel Northrop (1753-1807) graduated from Yale in 1776. One of his classmates was the son and namesake of the Rev. Samuel Bird, a powerful but controversial evangelical preacher in New Haven, and a passionate Revolutionary patriot. Bird's eldest daughter Mabel attracted the interest of Joel Northrop, and they were married in 1777.

By then Joel was serving in the Continental Army at a military hospital in Danbury as surgeon's mate. Afterwards he assumed the title of "Doctor", practicing in and around New Haven. He was (according to recollections gathered from surviving eyewitnesses in the middle of the nineteenth century) a great character—a man of huge physical energy, and a financial speculator of striking but temporary success. Perhaps this trait caused jealousy in his neighbors. He was recalled as doctoring horses as well as humans— among whom he was "... best remembered by a few old persons for his large practice in a certain class of contagious disease... Desirous, it is said, of more business, he rented his house on the Derby road [in Orange, Conn.] to a select company from New York, and thus greatly enlarged the demand for his peculiar skill." Yet he was an affectionate father, and it was thought that the deaths of two favorite children brought on his own demise.[2]

Of Joel Northrop's surviving children, the eldest became "a hatter, then farmer, eminent for integrity and piety".[3] Later he was steward of a school in Cornwall, Conn., charitably founded for the education of deserving young Indians and other minorities. (This circumstance cast a sensational influence on Lucius Northrop's military career years later.) Joel Northrop's second son went to sea and was lost in 1812. The fourth, Samuel (also a graduate of Yale, where he held the title of "Bully" for the Class of 1811[4]) fought as an army captain in the War of 1812 and survived to marry, but died childless at forty. The youngest son remained in New Haven as a carpenter with a large family.

Joel Northrop's third son, Amos (named after his grandfather and great-grandfather) was the father of Lucius. Amos Northrop (1784-1812) seemed to be cut out of different cloth from many of his family. A young man of

[1] Isabel C. Paterson, Laura Bellinger Jones et al., *Builders of Freedom and their Descendants* (Augusta, Ga.: Walton Printing Co., 1953) 93-95, 107-108.

[2] E. E. Beardsley, DD, "The Parsonage of the 'Blue Meeting House'", in *New Haven Colony Historical Society Papers*, I (1877), 105-119: and Henry Bronson, MD, "Medical History and Biography: Joel Northrop", in *New Haven Colony Historical Society Papers*, II (1878), 378-380.

[3] A. Judd Northrup, *The Northrup-Northrop Genealogy* (New York: Grafton Press, 1908), 1-4, 9, 26-27, 60-61; and John Gilmore Smith, "The Passing of Bishop Northrop", in *The Charleston Sunday News*, August 8 ff. 1920 passim.

[4] William L. Kingsley, ed, *Yale College: a Sketch of its History* (New York: Holt, 1879), II, 468,477.

great intelligence and charm, he attracted distinguished companions everywhere throughout his short life. At Yale he gained the friendship of his classmate John C. Calhoun (1782-1850). When they graduated together in 1804, young Calhoun suggested that Amos go to South Carolina (Calhoun's native state) to study law in Charleston.

From the moment of his arrival Amos Northrop found success. He studied law in the office of the leading lawyer in Charleston, Langdon Cheves (1776-1857), whose private practice was even then bringing in $20,000 a year. Yet Cheves had his eye on politics. Already a member of the South Carolina House of Representatives, he became a presidential elector for James Madison in 1808, and in December of that year was made Attorney General of South Carolina.[5] A year later Cheves took young Amos Northrop into partnership, with a view to the junior assuming control of the firm.[6] In 1811 Cheves was elected to the United States Congress, where he was to have a long and distinguished career.

The star pupil of Cheves and Northrop, and the man who would succeed to the firm, was Robert Young Hayne (1791-1839). Hayne would later debate with Daniel Webster in the United States Senate on the issue of Nullification—the South's claim to be able to nullify any Federal law it did not approve. Hayne would become Governor of South Carolina when Nullification reached a crisis—an early rehearsal for the Confederate War.[7]

These were the figures among whom Amos Northrop moved in Charleston. There (as a contemporary wrote)

> ... by a continued course of honorable action, he had acquired the love and esteem of all who knew him. ... His intellectual endowments were of the first order—his range of thought was extensive, and his conclusions admirably correct. Not satisfied with facts, he sought far into the nature and reason of things... and the mere suggestion of a difficulty was with him a sufficient motive for its solution. ...
>
> He differed from others in one important particular—his actions were not the result of feeling, education, or habit, but they proceeded from principle—what the world no doubt attributed to the goodness of his disposition or his high sense of honor, his friends well knew arose from settled rules of action. He was a Christian from reflection and conviction...[8]

(The last paragraph, except for "goodness of disposition", might have been describing his son Lucius.)

To crown his success in Charleston, Amos Northrop married Claudia Margaret Bellinger at St. Paul's Episcopal Church (Coming Street) on April 25, 1809. Three years later, at the age of twenty-eight, he was nominated to the

---

[5] W. B. Edgar, N. Louise Bailey et al., *Biographical Directory of the South Carolina House of Representatives* (University of South Carolina, 1977), IV, 111-115.

[6] MS agreement, entirely in the hand of Northrop, dated December 5, 1809, signed only by Northrop (South Carolina Historical Society MS 12-44-2).

[7] Edgar, op cit, 271-74. See also Theodore D. Jervey, *Robert Y. Hayne and his Times* (New York: Macmillan, 1909).

[8] *The Charleston Times*, September 29, 1812.

South Carolina House of Representatives. Before he could take his seat, he fell victim to the late summer malaria so lethal in the Low Country for those not accustomed to it from birth or earliest years, and after an illness of four days he died on September 27, 1812. He was eulogized in a long obituary in *The Charleston Times*:

> United to an amiable woman, the faithful partner of all his joys, the soother of his sorrows, he had adopted as his own the parent [Rebecca d'Oyley Bellinger (1761-1823)] and friends of her whom he had chosen. Blest by Providence with two promising children, his domestic happiness was complete.
>
> By the integrity of his character, the excellence of his heart, the strength of his understanding, and the purity of his manners, he had drawn around him a large circle of valuable friends. ... Who can doubt that his industry, ability, and patriotism would have promoted the happiness of his constituents, and led him to higher stations of honor and usefulness?[9]

Allowing for the fulsome style of the day, that was still the portrait of an impressive young man. Could he ultimately have attained eminence equal to Cheves, Hayne, Calhoun? Nothing is more futile than forecasting what might have been; and the strength of Amos Northrop's principles might have blocked preferment at many junctures. Still the possibility exists that had he lived, he might have gained distinction beyond what either of his sons achieved in their longer lives.

When their father died, the eldest child, Mary, was only two, and Lucius was barely a year old. Yet genetic inheritance cannot be discounted. The chief fact we know of Mary's character is her strength of purpose: she was the first of her family to become a convert to Roman Catholicism, and all the Northrops followed her—her mother, her brothers and their families. Catholicism had first appeared in the Bellinger family when two maiden aunts became converts about 1830.[10] By then Mary Northrop, after an upbringing by a Catholic nurse and education at a convent in Paris, had married her first cousin Dr. John Bellinger (1804-1860). She bore a large family and would have made a longer mark, though hardly a deeper one, had she not died in her thirties. Her widower became Lucius Northrop's greatest friend in Charleston.

Lucius inherited something of his father's principles and practicality. That was to emerge at the beginning of the War in the way he organized the entire Subsistence Bureau from nothing, and later developed an elaborate system of reporting commissaries who could tell him by means of fortnightly counts the locations of nearly every cow and pig and barrel of flour throughout the Confederacy. The practicality also emerged in Lucius's constant urging—against the wish and will of Jefferson Davis—that the Confederacy could feed itself only by trading through enemy lines, and in his finding the means to do it. But Lucius had almost none of his father's magnetic charm, and that lack was to prove costly to him.

---

[9] Ibid.

[10] J. J. O'Connell, *Catholicity in the Carolinas and Georgia* (New York: Sadlier, 1879, *rpr* Reprint Co., Spartanburg, 1972), 181.

Charm and magnetism were the portion of the posthumous son Claudian, born November 10, 1812, six weeks after his father's death. Claudian was educated at the South Carolina College in Columbia, and almost immediately gained election to the State House of Representatives. He was recalled by a college underclassman as "a brilliant, meteoric fellow, who didn't half fulfill the expectations of his friends; he didn't achieve any great reputation for solidarity, but he was an eloquent, good talker...".[11]
A fellow member of the Legislature recalled Claudian thus:

> He represented young Charleston and was generally regarded as extremely promising. He was a striking example of a very clever man spoiled by being pushed forward too early in life. He was excessively vain, he liked to be a party in duels, wished to be considered as a judge in points of honor, and at the same time desired to wear the laurels of genius. ... But his manners were pleasant and people generally liked him, pardoned his little outbursts of vanity.[12]

In later years Claudian fathered a large family, became a passionate poet and pamphleteer for the Southern cause, and died in 1865, a casualty of the War.

Both of Amos Northrop's sons were gifted, but each inherited an incomplete portion of their father's strengths. No doubt both missed the father's living example. Lucius, who grew up especially close to his mother, developed early in life a defensive and obsessive need to demonstrate his own rightness and righteousness at every moment.

The mother, Claudia Margaret Northrop, showed her own strength. "The characteristic of her life" (as John Bellinger observed to Lucius on the day of her death in 1855) "was that she scorned a sham."[13] Her conversion to Catholicism at the age of fifty-two speaks volumes. She was a great reader. Lucius was to recall this in writing of his own gentle daughter who died young in 1878: "She read with more profit and appreciation than any of her connections, or other lady except my mother, who was her antitype."[14] Thirty years after his mother's death, when he himself was past seventy, Lucius demanded: "Is it justice to me that such a *moral* tie should be severed? Only, unless an endless restitution follows." Her memory meant more to him, he said, than his living wife and children.[15]

His early upbringing with his sister and brother seems to have been divided between Charleston and his mother's old home, the plantation at Ashepoo. At the end of his life, in the bitterness of Southern defeat and Yankee reconstruction, Lucius wrote to Jefferson Davis (by then his friend of nearly sixty years): "...the only *spot* within this hateful nation for which I

---

[11] James Marion Sims, *The Story of My Life* (New York: Appleton, 1884), 104-5.

[12] "The Memoirs of Frederick Adolphus Porcher", in *The South Carolina Historical and Genealogical Magazine*, LVI (1945), 201.

[13] Quoted in Northrop's letter of March 9, 1885 to Davis (Dunbar Rowland, ed., *Jefferson Davis: Constitutionalist*) (Jackson, Miss: Mississippi Dept. of Archives and History, 1923) [hereinafter cited as Rowland], 10 vols., IX, 351.

[14] June 28, 1878 to Davis (Rowland, VIII, 221).

[15] March 9, 1885 to Davis (Rowland, IX, 351).

have an attachment is at Ashepoo, St. Bartholomew's Parish, S Ca, where little negroes and alligators thrived, where I played with the former, and we talked of the latter, in days which have no recollections but sincerity and goodness in the only one over me then. My wish to see her again grows on me with age."[16]

There was of course a black nurse. In later years Lucius quoted her: "'God knows' as my old Mom Paul used to say to every question."[17] And again: "'Patience is a great virtue.' My grandmother used to impress that on my nurse. She misunderstood it and used to tell me 'Patience devert you.' I could not see the fun in it, and lost the benefit of the lesson until taught the true meaning by experience painfully acquired."[18]

The boy's education up to the age of fifteen was summarized by his teacher: "... he has attended to the following branches of education: Arithmetic, Algebra as far as Cubic Equations, Geography, & the Latin Language, in which he has read Virgil, Horace, Cicero and part of Livy, in all which branches I believe him well versed as far as specified; his conduct, while under my observation, was such as to merit my approbation."[19]

That statement was sent in January 1827 with a letter of recommendation for Lucius to be admitted to the U.S. Military Academy at West Point. Such had been his mother's constant desire for several years. The first letter in this file, written the day after Lucius's twelfth birthday, contains her appeal to John C. Calhoun, then Secretary of War in Washington:

Charleston
9th September 1823

The interest which you Sir, expressed for my young family when last I saw you, encourages me now to claim your attention for the benefit of one of its members.—My eldest son has attained the age of twelve years.—The advice of several of my friends, and the result of every inquiry which a mother's anxiety could suggest, have inclined me to believe that the instruction he might receive, and the regulations to which he would be subject, in the Academy at West Point, would be most advantageous to him.—Having also understood that the situation must be secured for him at his present age, I have determined to address myself directly to you, not without a hope that the remembrance of former friendship m[a]y induce you to exert your influence in behalf of my child...

As early an answer Sir, as you can favour me with, will greatly relieve the suspense of

> Yrs & c
> C M Northrop[20]

---

[16] March 20, 1887 (Museum of the Confederacy, Richmond: Jefferson Davis Coll.).

[17] August 30, 1880 to Davis (Rowland, VIII, 491).

[18] May 29, 1879 to Davis (Rowland, VIII, 395).

[19] National Archives Record Group 94 [hereinafter cited as NA, RG 94] Adjutant General's Office: U.S. Military Academy, Cadet Applications, 1823/29: Certificate signed: "John B Gray, Teacher, Charleston, So C".

[20] *The Papers of John C. Calhoun* (University of South Carolina, 1975), VIII, 262-63.

Calhoun replied that the application had been placed on file and that a candidate for West Point must be at least fourteen and preferably older. He continued: "It will afford me great pleasure to contribute as far as I am able to the fulfillment of your wishes respecting your son, or to manifest in any other way the lively interest I entertain for the welfare of yourself and your family."[21]

In November 1825 Mrs. Northrop sent formal application to Secretary of War James Barbour requesting her son's admission to West Point in 1827, and enclosing a certificate from Lucius's teacher. A few weeks later her brother wrote from his plantation (in the Barnwell District of South Carolina) to the son of his old teacher, U.S. Treasury Secretary Richard Rush. A year later their cousin Joseph Bellinger,[22] a former member of the State Legislature and U.S. Congressman, added two letters to the file. One, to the Secretary of War, described the young candidate as "fifteen years and three months old, well grown, rather likely, possessing great courage and manliness; and as to his knowledge of the Latin, few boys of his age equal him. He is also a pretty good Arithmetician, and has made some progress in Algebra. He certainly is every way qualified to enter that Institution, and promises great usefulness to his Country." Bellinger added that the boy's chances might be helped by the fact that his mother now had residence in Barnwell—"where I think there has been few or no favours of this kind conferred... Should you make this appointment, you would render great service to a widow who is in slender circumstances, with several children to maintain and educate."[23]

(The perception of "slender circumstances" may have been relative. In addition to her house in Charleston served by six slaves, her brother had established her Barnwell property contiguous to his own. The U.S. Census of 1830 lists her household there with twenty-eight slaves [recorded just below her brother, with eighty].[24] Her daughter Mary was married by 1830. Claudian, then fourteen, was to follow his father to the Bar. Yet the experience of the Ashepoo and Barnwell plantations gave both Northrop sons an experience of farming: in their later lives each of them was to take to agriculture and its management with apparent familiarity.)

Joseph Bellinger wrote a similar letter to Henry Clay. Clay forwarded it to the Secretary of War with his "particular recommendation". A week later came a brief testimonial from Robert Y. Hayne, referring to a fuller recommendation written more than a year earlier. The applications were successful, and Lucius Northrop was appointed to West Point on July 1, 1827, two months before his sixteenth birthday.

---

[21] op. cit., 275

[22] 1773-1830. Fifth Landgrave. Presidential elector in 1808, Member of the Fifteenth Congress. Resided at his plantation "Aeolian Lawn" (close to Dr. Bellinger's "Pine Forest" in the Springtown section of Barnwell), and had houses at Ashepoo and Charleston (*Builders of Freedom*, 96, 107).

[23] NA, RG 94, Cadet Applications 1823/29.

[24] 1830 Census: Charleston, p. 163 ("M. Northrop"); Barnwell Dist. p 161 ("C.V. Northrop").

CHAPTER 2

SOLDIERS AND INDIANS

Lucius was a commanding figure. One description runs: "6 feet 2 inches tall, straight as an arrow, erect as a column, and a very Cincinnatus."[1] His granddaughter modified that description: "My father states that ... he was not quite six feet tall."[2] It was still noticeable stature for the time, and Lucius began early to make his mark at West Point. During his first year he had an opening encounter with a senior cadet who was later to become the greatest friend of his life: "Jefferson Davis became acquainted with Lucius B. Northrop at West Point, the latter being one of the youngest cadets. One day an officer of duty insulted young Northrop, and the fiery South Carolinian resented it with a blow. It was Davis's duty, as captain of the corps of cadets, to report the matter, but he had noticed the unprovoked insult, and admired the spirit with which the young cadet promptly resented it, and he passed the matter over. From that moment Davis and Northrop became friends...".[3] The friendship did not become close until the two were thrown together in the army five years later.

Lucius Northrop graduated from West Point twenty-second in his class of thirty-three, on July 1, 1831. He was brevetted Second Lieutenant in the U.S. Seventh Infantry, stationed at Cantonment Gibson in Cherokee Indian territory (about thirty miles southeast of the present city of Tulsa, Oklahoma). Gibson—soon to be designated a Fort—had been built in 1824 on the left bank of the Neosho (or Grand) River, two and a half miles above its confluence with the Arkansas. The construction was on a square plan: a single story except for two blockhouses at diagonal corners, all of rough logs, with a well house in the center.

---

[1]   Quoted in *The Northrup-Northrop Genealogy,* 268.

[2]   Marie Floyd Northrop, letter of September 13, 1909 to L. W. Payne Jr. (New York Public Library: Walter Fleming Papers, box 6, f. 65).

[3]   Anonymous recollection published in *The Pittsburgh Dispatch,* December 19, 1889 (a few days after Davis's death). Davis was never "captain of the corps of cadets", but there seems no reason to doubt the accuracy of the rest. All early writers assume a beginning acquaintance at West Point, and the actions are thoroughly typical of the two men as their characters emerged in later life.

8

FORT GIBSON

A MODERN PHOTOGRAPH OF THE RECONSTRUCTION.

A few months after Northrop's arrival, a visitor described the place: "...The barracks were erected in a square form 700 by 800 feet... The buildings upon inspection appear to be fast going to decay, having been erected several years... the sides of the buildings are hewed logs, plastered with mud in the interstices—the roofs are covered with oak staves—the inside of the best houses are the square sides of the timber, sometimes white washed. Small windows admit sufficient light to see the way through the rooms, which have neither presses nor closets—nails drove into white washed walls contain our wardrobe...".[4]

Outside the stockade were the officers' quarters, kitchen, mess house, vegetable gardens, stables, commissary and other store houses, and the hospital. This last was much in use because the whole district was unhealthy, producing so much malaria and typhoid fever that Gibson was known as "the charnel house of the Army".[5] About five hundred soldiers of various types were stationed there.

Beyond the Fort stretched the prairies. The famous writer Washington Irving came out in October 1832 (ten months after Northrop's arrival) to tour the prairies from Fort Gibson. He found

> ... a vast tract of uninhabited country, where there is neither to be seen the log house of the white man nor the wigwam of the Indian. It consists of great grassy plains, interspersed with forests and groves... Over these fertile and verdant wastes still roam the elk, the buffalo, and the wild horse, in all their native freedom.
>
> These, in fact, are the hunting grounds of the various tribes of the Far West. Hither repair the Osage, the Creek, the Delaware and other tribes that have linked themselves with civilization, and live within the vicinity of the white settlements. Here resort also the Pawnees, the Comanches, and other fierce and as yet independent tribes, the nomades of the prairies or the inhabitants of the skirts of the Rocky Mountains.
>
> The regions ... form a debatable ground of these warring and vindictive tribes; none of them presume to erect a permanent habitation within its borders. Their hunters and "braves" repair thither ... commit sad havoc among the innumerable herds that graze the prairies, and having loaded themselves with venison and buffalo meat, warily retire from the neighborhood. ...
>
> Mouldering skulls and skeletons, bleaching in some dark ravine, or near the traces of a hunting camp, occasionally mark the scene of a foregone act of blood, and let the wanderer know the dangerous nature of the region he is traversing.[6]

The position of Fort Gibson had been chosen entirely for strategy. Its object was to control Indian migrations, which had been largely fomented by the white man. Since the time of Jefferson's Presidency and the Louisiana

---

[4] Henry Leavitt Ellsworth, *Washington Irving on the Prairie, or a Narrative of a Tour of the Southwest in the Year 1832*, ed. S. T. Williams and B. D. Simison (American Book Co., 1937), 2,4.

[5] Brad Agnew, *Fort Gibson: Terminal on the Trail of Tears* (Univ. of Oklahoma, 1980), 122, 163. Many facts in the discussion that follows are taken from this excellent book.

[6] Washington Irving, *A Tour on the Prairies*, ed. J. F. McDermott (Univ. of Oklahoma, 1985), 10-11.

Purchase, it had been United States policy to encourage Indians living in the eastern states to move west—out of the way (so it was thought then) of white settlement. During the Presidency of Andrew Jackson, encouragement turned to coercion, culminating in the Indian Removal Act of 1830.

The dispossessed eastern Indians were given minimal assistance to trek a thousand miles westward to an entirely new geography and climate. There they encountered other Indians already settled—tribes of different traditions and languages who often bitterly resented the intrusion of new-comers onto their lands. Feuds, massacres, and tribal wars followed; and the purpose of Fort Gibson (set strategically athwart the relocation areas) was to police the Indians, encourage or force conferences with each other—conferences moderated by representatives of the government which had caused all their trouble.

By 1830 a new element of disorder was appearing—in the shape of white pioneers invading even those designated Indian lands, demanding squatter rights and protection. Many were vicious characters. The commander at Gibson's sister Fort Towson (150 miles south near Red River) described the whites living in his area as "of the very worst kind—men who have fled from justice and who are now engaged in kidnapping negroes—horse rac-ing, gambling and selling whiskey to soldiers and Indians".[7] Among all those elements the soldiers of Gibson, Towson, and the other thinly strung forts were charged to keep peace and order.

Northrop had arrived at Fort Gibson before the end of 1831, six months after graduating from West Point.[8] As brevet second lieutenant, he would gradually be given assignments of responsibility in Company F. A compari-son of dates and places in his military record with the history of the Seventh Infantry at Gibson yields vivid glimpses of what this twenty-year-old en-countered in a rough place.

In March 1832 Northrop was sent as inferior officer in a forty-man detachment charged with making a military road from Fort Smith (an older fort to the south recently reactivated) southwest for a distance of 150 miles to Red River near Fort Towson. The road was to facilitate Choctaw immigra-tion. The road-making detachment had two wagons and $200 to last them all for ninety days—as everything at Gibson and the other Territory forts was chronically under-funded. Each mile they cleared for the new road was turned to quagmire by torrential spring rains. Fully a quarter of the force had to guard the wagons shuttling supplies to the work crews. As the road lengthened, more and more military guard was needed, and the road being hacked out by the rest of them grew rougher and rougher.

As they neared Fort Towson, they ran out of food. Towson supplied them rations for six days, but could spare no more as Fort Towson itself was nearly out of food until spring shipments came up the rivers. The road

[7]   Quoted in Agnew, *Fort Gibson*, 104.

[8]   NA, RG 109 (War Department Collection of Confederate Records), Generals and Staff Officers Files, Northrop, L. B. [hereinafter cited as NA, RG 109, Officers; Northrop is understood unless otherwise indicated].

builders had to go on half-rations, working frantically to complete the road ahead of starvation. In the end they bought a few head of cattle locally, to keep the wolf at bay—literally, since the whole territory swarmed with them—just long enough to complete the track and then stagger back over the 147-mile length they had opened in three months of back-breaking work on short rations.[9] As an officer, Northrop would probably have been spared the worst of the labor. But it was an unforgettable introduction to what soldiers could accomplish on very little food.

Northrop was again on "detached service" at Clark Springs, near Fort Towson, for most of the summer of 1832; there he found extremes of heat unknown even to a South Carolinian. By October he was back at Fort Gibson when Washington Irving and his party came to explore the prairies westward. In January and February 1833 Northrop was again at Fort Towson.

Then came a different kind of mission—escort duty to United States commissioners treating with the Osage Nation. Those Indians were native to the western plains. But the Great White Father in Washington had been sending hordes of dispossessed eastern Cherokee and Seminole into Osage lands, with titles and maps whose boundaries were often so carelessly drawn as to overlap each other.[10] The Osage wanted their native plains back in their own hands.

The Osage were described by Washington Irving as "stately fellows, stern and simple in garb and aspect. ... They had fine Roman countenances and broad deep chests; and, as they generally wore their blankets wrapped around their loins, so as to leave the bust and arms bare, they looked like so many noble bronze figures. The Osage are the finest looking Indians I have ever seen in the West. ... Their poverty prevents their indulging in much luxury of apparel."[11] They made an enormous impression on young Northrop, who would write nearly half a century later: "Fortunately my education was polished off by the indians, Osages especially teaching me to make few things answer many ends, and to be content with little."[12]

The commission to the Osage which Northrop accompanied in February and March 1833 was led by Montfort Stokes, a former Governor of North Carolina and old political crony of President Andrew Jackson. The second commissioner was a Hartford, Connecticut businessman, Henry Ellsworth, who had toured the prairies in the autumn with Irving. The third was a Utica, New York clergyman, the Rev. John F. Schermerhorn, who had repeatedly begged for government appointments. The fourth and last commissioner was the only one with any real experience to bring to the problem. He was Colonel Auguste Pierre Chouteau, and he quickly attracted Northrop's interest.

---

[9]   Agnew, *Fort Gibson*, 94-95.

[10]   The presence of Seminole in the Oklahoma Territory has led several writers to think that part of Northrop's service was in Florida. In fact he never went to Florida except very occasionally as a visitor in the 1840's and 1850's.

[11]   *A Tour of the Prairies*, 21-22.

[12]   May 9, 1878 to Davis (Rowland, VII, 269, where the year was mistakenly read as "1870") .

Chouteau had graduated from West Point in 1806. Since 1807 he had lived in the Territories with his Indian wife. He had two trading posts, the one near Fort Gibson familiar to Northrop almost on a daily basis. Irving (whom Chouteau had entertained there) saw it thus:

> It consisted of a few log houses on the banks of the river, and presented a motley frontier scene. Here was our escort awaiting our arrival; some were on horseback, some on foot, some seated on the trunks of fallen trees, some shooting at a mark. They were a heterogeneous crew; some in frock-coats made of green blankets; others in leathern hunting-shirts, but the most part in marvelously ill-cut garments, much the worse for wear, and evidently put on for rugged service.

Osage and Creek Indians frequented the trading posts:

> Besides these, there was a sprinkling of trappers, hunters, half-breeds, creoles, negroes of every hue; and all that other rabble rout of nondescript beings that keep about the frontiers...
>
> The little hamlet of the Agency was in a çomplete bustle; the blacksmith's shed, in particular, was a scene of preparation; a strapping negro was shoeing a horse; two half-breeds were fabricating iron spoons in which to melt lead for bullets. An older trapper, in leathern hunting frock and moccasins, had placed his rifle against a work-bench, while he superintended the operation, and gossiped about his hunting exploits; several large dogs were lounging in and out of the shop, or sleeping in the sunshine...[13]

Chouteau's other trading post, together with his homestead, lay forty miles north at the Grand Saline. He was the trusted friend of both Indian and white man. He commanded Northrop's total respect.

At the Osage conference the commissioners disagreed among themselves. Chouteau recommended the Indians to hold onto their lands and resist relocation, and he persuaded Stokes to this view. The other two favored relocation to "reservations" in still more out-of-the-way places. After a month of fruitless discussion, the Osage took themselves off to their spring buffalo hunts.[14] Young Northrop could see for himself the fallibility of officialdom. It laid the foundations of a deep-seated contempt for politicking that was to serve him both well and ill for the rest of his life.

Soon after the abortive Osage conference came different duty. During the winter just ended, a band of Kiowa in Mexican territory south of Red River had attacked some white traders returning from Santa Fe. White lives were lost, as well as $10,000 in silver. The commander at Fort Gibson received orders to make a show of U.S. Army strength southwest of the Mexican border. He sent out two companies, one commanded by Nathan Boone of Missouri, a son of the famous Daniel Boone. Among the officers was Second Lieutenant Northrop.

---

[13]   *A Tour of the Prairies*, 21-22.
[14]   Agnew, *Fort Gibson*, 107-8.

They left Gibson on May 6, 1833 and rode southwest for three weeks. Then suddenly a band of unidentified mounted Indians captured a private from Boone's company, and the young man was never seen again. The soldiers pursued the Indians as far as the eastern slopes of the Wichita Mountains. By then they were short of food and fatigued, and many were ill. So the infantry had to turn back in failure. They reached Fort Gibson on June 30 in no very good condition.[15]

* * *

As more and more displaced eastern Indians were forced west, the army troops policing the Territories needed reinforcements—in particular mounted soldiers. Congress responded in March 1833 by authorizing the creation of the First Dragoons. It was to be an elite regiment, comprised partly of experienced backwoods militia officers and partly of the best West Pointers—"young men of respectable families, who would act ... with feelings of pride and honour":[16] in other words, military diplomats. Lucius Northrop seemed an ideal candidate, and in August 1833 he was assigned to the Dragoons at their place of organization far to the north—Jefferson Barracks near St. Louis, Missouri.

Northrop arrived at Jefferson Barracks in October 1833. The regiment was to be bear-skin hatted, but neither bear-skins nor uniforms had arrived. Their horses had just come, and training began immediately. The new regiment's colonel was a Westerner, Henry Dodge (later Governor of Wisconsin and United States Senator from the state). The lieutenant colonel was Stephen Kearny (later to command the Army of the West in the Mexican War). The major was Richard Barnes Mason, son of the Virginia patriot of the Revolution, George Mason. Among the company captains were three future Union generals in the Civil War—Philip St. George Cooke, Edwin Sumner, and David Hunter. The regimental adjutant was Second Lieutenant Jefferson Davis.

The two young second lieutenants, Davis and Northrop, despite a three or four year[17] difference in age, were enough alike to be quickly drawn together. Both were Southerners—one from the West (as they counted things then), the other from the East. Both were from upper middle-class families not far distant from wealth and national politics. Both were West Point. And both compensated for private insecurity by a certain rigidity. Davis said of Northrop in 1835: "I have always thought Lieutenant Northrop rather pertinacious than yielding in his opinions, and his strict adherence to veracity I have considered a marked trait of his character...".[18] Northrop at almost the

---

[15] Ibid., 105-6.

[16] George Catlin, *Letters and Notes on the Manners, Customs, and Condition of the North American Indians*, II, 37.

[17] For questions about the year of Davis's birth, see *The Papers of Jefferson Davis* (Baton Rouge: Louisiana State Univ., 1971 ff. [hereinafter cited as *Davis Papers*], I, lxx-lxvi, n. l).

[18] March 9, 1835 (quoted in *Davis Papers, I*, 394).

JEFFERSON DAVIS

THE EARLIEST KNOWN PORTRAIT, SHOWING HIM A FEW YEARS AFTER THE
BEGINNING OF HIS FRIENDSHIP WITH NORTHROP.

THE ENGRAVING WAS MADE FOR DAVIS'S *THE RISE AND FALL OF THE
CONFEDERATE GOVERNMENT* (1881). ON RECEIVING A COPY FROM DAVIS,
NORTHROP WROTE:

*"YOUR PORTRAITS ARE VERY PLEASANT TO CONTEMPLATE; THAT OF
32 IS ALL RIGHT BUT THE BROW, WHICH WAS MORE PERPENDICULAR
I THINK AT FORT GIBSON...".*

same moment characterized Davis as "strictly and rigidly military... and I have frequently remarked to him in conversations that I thought him too rigid in the minutiae of the Service."[19]

After a month of training, still without arms or uniforms, the Dragoons left St. Louis in late November 1833 for a grueling 500-mile march through wilderness lands back to their permanent post at Fort Gibson. The savage Plains winter was beginning, but their colonel wanted to get them to base as soon as possible. When they arrived on December 14, they found nothing prepared for them and no quarters. The stables at Gibson were full, and the Dragoons' horses had to be turned loose in 40 degrees of frost "to sustain a miserable existence on cane in an Arkansas bottom".[20]

The Dragoons had to pitch tents until they could construct their own barracks a mile west of Fort Gibson. They called it "Camp Jackson" in honor of the President whose policies had created their regiment. It was nothing but a row of rough wooden barns, one to a company, which the men threw together as fast as they could to get out of their perishing tents. The barns, when they got into them, leaked frigid air, water, and ice; chimneys were the worst source of cold. Through it all, Colonel Dodge kept up their rigorous drilling, day in, day out. The atmosphere in the camp grew bad. In February 1834 Northrop protested to the Secretary of War against the regimental position assigned him.[21] In April Colonel Dodge felt that both Davis and Major Mason had taken a stand against him, and were his "inveterate enemies".[22]

In the spring of 1834 the Dragoons' first campaign was planned. It was to be a demonstration of army power southwest through Pawnee and Comanche country—to convince those Indians both to accept the arrival of more Indians from the east, and to leave in peace such white settlers as were already there. Difficulties of organization prevented the expedition from leaving until June 15. Thus the Dragoons encountered the full ferocity of a Plains summer—in their elaborate woollen uniforms and bear skins which had now arrived. Provisions of food, however, were seriously short. Both Davis and Northrop were included in the expedition, which also included the famous Indian artist George Catlin (1796-1872), who was to record any rare or unknown flora and fauna they might encounter.

A few days out they came into lands of little and bad water. Dysentery and malaria appeared, and soon spread to epidemic proportions. At several points, detachments of sick soldiers had to be left behind. By July 1 Catlin noted that nearly half the command were ill. Soon Catlin himself went down with fever and ague.[23] The remainder rode forward, subsisting largely by buffalo hunting. That involved headlong gallops over very rough ground—dangerous and debilitating to horses, though many Dragoons relished the

[19]　Ibid., February 14, 1835, 372.

[20]　Philip St. G. Cooke, *Scenes and Adventures in the Army,* (Philadelphia: Lindsay & Blakiston, 1859), 219-20.

[21]　Davis to Lewis Cass, January 29, 1834 (*Davis Papers,* I, 312-13).

[22]　Ibid., April 18, 1834 to George W. Jones, 317.

[23]　Agnew, *Fort Gibson,* 163-69.

sport. But Davis reported: "I do not recollect to have seen Lieut. Northrop chasing buffalo when he was either sick or well, and I think from what I know of Lieut. Northrop's attention to his horses, that he seldom if he ever did join a buffalo chase."[24]

They passed through sinister miles of matted forest known as the Cross-timbers. At last they emerged on the plains beyond and approached the Pawnee villages. Their reception there was fortunately friendly; in fact the Indians provided the soldiers with their few meals of substance. The conferences near the end of July met with success, even among the fierce Kiowa.

The long return journey was a catalogue of horrors. The elderly expedition commander, General Henry Leavenworth, died of fever, as did more and more of the men. At every encampment in the August heat, carcasses of the buffalo they slaughtered for subsistence turned the air fetid. In the search for ever scarcer water, they found one green pool where frogs walked on the surface. Catlin (now recovered) thought these a new species until he realized they were merely supported by the thickness of slime.

The first group of expedition survivors regained Fort Gibson in mid-August, and little bands of sick Dragoons staggered in over the next fortnight. The fort hospital filled with them, many suffering from cholera by then. The death toll was a hundred and fifty of the original five hundred Dragoons, and uncounted horses.

Northrop returned to find himself promoted to full second lieutenant. But he too was ill with malaria, and he remained sick for months. It began a pattern of recurrent illness which was to dog the rest of his military career. In October 1834, to escape hospital-sickness, he went north to stay with Colonel Chouteau at the Grand Saline. There at last he began to recover. But authorities at Gibson thought he had been gone too long. One morning a Dragoon appeared with a peremptory order to return. Northrop dismissed the messenger, and delayed his departure to the following evening. Next morning on the road he saw Davis approaching with two armed Dragoons. Davis sent the two back, and then asked Northrop why he had not started more promptly. Northrop pleaded ill health. When they got back to Gibson, Major Mason sent for Northrop; again Northrop delayed obeying the order.[25] That attitude seemed casual, whatever the illness. Mason was a martinet, and he did not forget.

Early in December 1834 Northrop returned to full duty. On the 7th, when he was officer of the day, a corporal's horse broke loose and bolted. Both Northrop and Davis declared that it was an unavoidable accident. Major Mason paid no heed, but ordered the unfortunate corporal punished by

---

[24]   March 9, 1835 (*Davis Papers*, I, 395). For evidence of Northrop's life-long interest in horses, see his letters to Davis of September 12, 1878, January 29 and May 1879 (Rowland, VIII, 279, 341, 394-5), the last two quoted below, pp. 300, 302.

[25]   *Davis Papers*, I, 426-27.

the wooden horse—on which he was forced to sit astride with heavy weights tied to his feet unable to touch the ground. Davis adduced Paragraph 129 of the Army Regulations wherein it was stated that a non-commissioned officer could not be degraded except for incapacity or misconduct proven before a court. Mason insisted on the punishment. The matter rankled on all sides.[26]

In mid-December Mason ordered the three companies under his command (which included Northrop's and Davis's) to lay wooden floors in their poor barracks. The weather was frigid and work progressed slowly. Mason sent an order through his new adjutant that the men's work was to be supervised by their lieutenants in constant attendance. Northrop took along a book to fill the dull, cold, noisy hours. But the book did not serve, and soon he decided that "the work would not be affected by his absence".[27] He went over to Davis to propose that they go to the camp race track and see which of them could spot the quicker horses in advance. Davis took the precaution of installing a junior officer to take his place at supervisor. Northrop did not.

They had been at the track perhaps ten minutes when the adjutant came up and prepared to arrest them both on orders from Major Mason, who had noted their absences. Davis pointed to his subordinate on duty; so only Northrop was arrested, to be confined to quarters. Northrop went to the barracks to retrieve his book before obeying the order to go to his own quarters.[28] Technically it was a violation of his arrest. The confinement to quarters seemed loose enough that Northrop went over to Fort Gibson that evening as usual to eat his dinner.

Major Mason charged him with breach of arrest. Mason sent the adjutant to say, however, that if Northrop would confess his mistake, the major would withdraw his latest charge. But Northrop sent back "that he did not consider it a breach of arrest when he went to dinner, and that he considered Major Mason's requirement for a reiteration as exacting from him an act of self-humiliation ...". He told Davis "that he would answer Major Mason that he had fully given his reply, and that he had no other to give."[29] So for a point of aggrieved honor, Northrop snubbed his commanding officer in a way certain to become generally known. Mason's answer to was to order Northrop court-martialled. In the interval before his trial, the young lieutenant was to continue his duties.

Five days later it was Davis's turn. Northrop recalled attending the Reveille on that particularly cold and rainy Christmas Eve. Davis (whose health suffered cruelly in the Plains winter) was not with his company. On returning from Reveille, Northrop saw his friend coming out of Major Mason's quarters. Davis was smiling and calm as he described what happened. Mason had summoned him to account for his absence from Reveille. Davis cited a regulation that in rain the roll was to be called by a subordinate.

26 Ibid., 419-20.
27 Ibid., 421.
28 Ibid., 390-1.
29 Ibid., 391-2.

Mason rejoined: "You know it is my order that all the officers of this Command shall attend the Reveille roll-call of their respective Companies!" Davis turned on his heel. Mason ordered him back, stating that he was not in the habit of receiving such treatment from officers when speaking on points of duty, and that Davis would consider himself in arrest and go to his quarters. Mason's order about Reveille attendance had never been put in writing. Moreover, he was well aware that Davis had suffered from lung trouble throughout the previous winter and had wanted to leave Fort Gibson before the winter then upon them.

Davis appealed to the commander at Gibson, General Arbuckle. Arbuckle asked Mason to drop the charge if Davis would offer formal apology. But Davis, like his friend Northrop, would not apologize. So Mason requested his superior to order that Davis be court-martialled near the time of Northrop's trial in February 1835.[30]

At the end of December 1834 Northrop was ill again. On January 5, 1835 he was up and about, and was seen in the tent of a fellow-officer by the camp doctor, who recalled: "At that time I told him that he wanted no more attendance ... but that he had better take good care of himself...". Northrop continued on sick-leave for a fortnight afterwards. On January 24, Major Mason sent for the doctor and questioned him. The doctor had made no further examination, but expressed the view that Northrop could report for duty. Accordingly Mason ordered him for duty the following day, and made him officer of the day. Northrop declined to comply, and this charge was added to the court-martial summons.[31]

The court-martial of Davis came first, beginning February 12, 1835. The court heard evidence from several witnesses including Northrop. On the sixth day, the court found that what Major Mason had charged against Davis was more or less true, but that it did not constitute "conduct subversive of good order and military discipline". Davis was acquitted and reinstated.[32]

The court-martial of Northrop followed on February 19. The charges were:

1. Absenting himself from the work party at the barracks on Dec. 20.

2. Breach of arrest in leaving his quarters to retrieve the book, and again in going to dinner.

3. "Conduct unbecoming to an officer and a gentleman" by remaining on sick leave beyond his time in January.

4. Refusing to return to duty Jan. 25 when so ordered.[33]

---

[30] Ibid., 359-61, 425-26.
[31] Ibid., 387, 393.
[32] Ibid., 358.
[33] Ibid., 383-84.

Northrop admitted the last, and pleaded Not Guilty to the rest. One of the witnesses was Davis, testifying to his friend's character. On March 16 came the verdict: "The court finds Northrop guilty of neglect of duty, breach of arrest, and disobedience of orders, but not guilty of unbecoming conduct. He is sentenced to be cashiered, but the court recommends the sentences be remitted."[34] Instead, Mason kept him in arrest for four months until July.

In March 1835 Jefferson Davis resigned his commission and left Fort Gibson to return to civilian life and be married. His bride was a daughter of Colonel (later General and President) Zachary Taylor. Northrop did not see his friend again for several years.

In May 1835, still technically in arrest, Northrop was one of a large force detailed to ride southwest and make a show of strength in Comanche territory bordering the Red River. That move was to soften up the Indians for a conference to try to cool an explosive situation. Elements in Texas were agitating for independence from Mexico, and both sides were busily inciting the tribes. Colonel Chouteau attended the conference as interpreter, and at last peace was declared.

For the Dragoons, the summer brought a repetition of the discomforts experienced the previous year, but without the epidemic sickness. Northrop returned to Fort Gibson freed from his arrest, and placed in command of his company. Yet he was not well, and was given another sick leave in September 1835. He reported back in command at the end of October, but remained ill for much of the winter. In April 1836, he left Fort Gibson on furlough, long requested, to recuperate on the southwestern plains near Fort Towson. There he stayed, according to army reports, for much of the year.

His treatment at Gibson by Major Mason continued to rankle. Northrop sent for a transcript of his court-martial. On the basis of it, he took the extraordinary step of preferring charges against his superior officer. Those charges would lead to the major's court-martial in the following winter. Meanwhile, on leave, Northrop applied for one extension after another on the grounds that he was not fully recovered. When at last he returned to Gibson in October 1836, Mason placed him in detention again.

The inquiry and Mason's court-martial lasted from October 20, 1836 to February 1837. The major was more or less exonerated, though his order of the wooden horse for the hapless corporal was cited as reprehensible.[35] Northrop instantly lodged an appeal against those findings with Alexander Macomb, Commanding General of the United States Army.[36] It was apparently without effect.

Northrop applied for detached service away from Fort Gibson as often as he could get it. Thus he was absent in May and June 1837, and again from

---

[34]   Ibid., 399.

[35]   Ibid., 430.

[36]   Ibid., 431.

October—to begin a mission of ten months. That mission had its origin in a growing perception that something would have to be done to pacify the Comanche, whose complaints over treaty-violations by their neighbors were fast becoming so many excuses for violence. It was decided to send Chouteau again, with a military escort. His mission was to persuade all the tribes in the Canadian River region to attend another conference—from which a delegation could be chosen to go to Washington and lay their troubles before the Great White Father himself. The situation was complicated by the fact that Texas was in open rebellion against Mexico, with both sides vying for Indian loyalties. Chouteau found many tribes joining the war "for predatory purposes only".[37]

Chouteau's escort was the Dragoons' Company F—Northrop's company. They set out in October 1837. When Chouteau met with little initial success, he decided to remain in Camp Holmes, 150 miles west of Gibson, for the winter. The main force of Company F had to return to their base, leaving just a small detachment with Chouteau. Northrop seized the chance, and asked on December 15 to command the detachment. General Arbuckle thought it well to let him do this. It gave the young lieutenant an unparalleled chance to study the Indians at close quarters.

When the colonel injured his leg, Northrop accompanied Chouteau's nephew to persuade the Cheyenne, Arapaho, and Pawnee to keep their treaties. They succeeded in extracting promises that they would all hold their hands until they could learn the War Department's plans for peace. It gave a hint of where Northrop's best talents might lie—in semi-independent diplomacy with the "noble savages" who had lived for uncounted centuries amid the barren splendors of wilderness without ravaging its environment for private gain.

Northrop gathered other experience commanding his little detachment. There was no doctor with them, and their medical problems caught his interest. In his family background had been the old grandfather doctor in Connecticut. And in Charleston his brother-in-law and first cousin, John Bellinger, was then one of the most brilliant and magnetic doctors of South Carolina. Northrop was to recall of his Plains service: "...the little knowledge which observation afforded me, with the aid of a supply of medical stores, was of *frequent* use and saved one man who was severely wounded."[38] Medicine afforded further one-to-one relationships.

By the end of August 1838 the Chouteau mission at Camp Holmes was concluded. The elderly colonel's health had suffered badly. Northrop himself, when back at Fort Gibson, was ill most of the autumn. Chouteau died at Christmas that year, and Northrop was chosen to guard the Indians on their journey to Washington early in 1839 to try to settle their troubles. But in Washington every solution became a tactic of delay as the whites consolidated their own wants.

---

[37] Agnew, *Fort Gibson*, 171.
[38] December 6, 1843 to Roger Jones (NA, RG 94, Letters Received, 56-N-1860).

* * *

Returning from Washington in the spring of 1839, Northrop found Fort Gibson beset by a new Indian problem. The Cherokee had originally inhabited lands ranging from Ohio to Georgia. Then the mounting government pressure for their removal had split the tribe in two. One faction, under their chief, The Ridge (often known as Major Ridge) and his son John, had cooperated with the United States, moved West and established themselves on lands granted to them east of Fort Gibson. The other faction, under their chief John Ross, defied the whites and held their eastern homelands.

In late 1838, the Ross Cherokee had at last been forced to vacate their eastern homes. They were pitchforked into a terrible trek westward through the winter. So many of them died on the way that it became known as "The Trail of Tears". The surviving Ross Cherokee arrived in the new Territories between January and March 1839 with grief and black anger in their hearts. They felt that if their brothers had not sold out earlier, but joined them in a stand in Georgia and Tennessee, all the subsequent disaster and heartbreak might not have come.

At the end of their "Trail of Tears", the Ross survivors found their more prudent brothers, the Ridge Cherokee, well established and reasonably comfortable on their new lands. The Ridge, with their own government in place, had begun to prosper. They offered hospitality to the newcomers. To an outsider there appeared no problem: it was simply Cherokee settling down beside Cherokee. The reality, recognized by Dragoon officers at Fort Gibson, was a tinder box.

The Dragoons set up a new camp on the Illinois River to police Cherokee factions. Northrop and his company marched out there in April 1839. It proved the unhealthiest place of all. When many soldiers died there, including the camp commander, they had to start another new post up on the Arkansas border with Missouri, called Fort Wayne. But before the end of June, Northrop was back with his company at Fort Gibson.

Northrop had a family interest in the Cherokee, which centered on the Ridge. President Jefferson, commissioning the Lewis and Clark explorations of Louisiana Purchase territories, had included in his precepts for treating with the Indians: "If any of them should wish to have some of their young people brought up with us, and taught such arts as may be useful to them, we will receive, instruct, and take care of them." That led to the founding of a school at Cornwall, Connecticut.

The man who became steward of that school was Lucius Northrop's uncle John, Amos Northrop's elder brother. Indian pupils were sought and found. One was John Ridge (1803-1839), the son of the Cherokee chief, The Ridge or Major Ridge, who at that time had his fine house in the Cherokee homelands of northwest Georgia. Another pupil at Cornwall was John's cousin, who had named himself after the Christian missionary Elias Boudinot.

JOHN RIDGE (1803-1839)

THE PRIDE OF HIS PEOPLE, THE HOPE OF HIS TRIBE.

ENGRAVED FOR T. L. McKENNEY AFTER THE PAINTING BY
CHARLES BIRD KING,

WASHINGTON 1825.

John Ridge had come to Cornwall in the autumn of 1818, to remain at the school for several years. The New England climate was hard, and in his third winter he became so ill that Mr. and Mrs. Northrop took him into their house. There he was nursed by their daughter Sarah Bird Northrop (1806-1856). Sally (who was Lucius Northrop's first cousin) and John Ridge fell in love; and after much local outrage and many trials they were married in January 1824. Returning to the Ridge home in Georgia, the young couple were soon embroiled in the fierce Cherokee controversy over whether to vacate their lands. When the Ridge faction went west in 1836, John and Sally went with them.

In the new territory John had turned shopkeeper. His station and homestead were close to where Fort Wayne stood. John also acted from time to time as his Nation's ambassador in Washington. He translated standard works of white civilization into the Cherokee language and promoted their distribution. Lucius Northrop certainly knew all this, and probably visited the young Ridges and their seven children in early June 1839, before his return to Gibson.

In the early morning of June 22, 1839 the sleeping Ridge household was stealthily approached by twenty-five rough men of the Ross Cherokee on horseback. Three of them entered the house, pulled John from his bed, and murdered him in front of his horrified wife Sally and their children. Those moments marked their twelve-year-old eldest son for the rest of his life. A quarter century later each detail remained sharp as the murdering knives, as he wrote: "In a room prepared for the purpose lay pale in death the man whose voice had been listened to with awe and admiration in the councils of his Nation, and whose fame had passed to the remotest of the United States, the blood oozing through his winding sheet and falling drop by drop on the floor. By his side sat my mother, with hands clasped and in speechless agony—she who had given him her heart in the days of her youth and beauty, left the home of her parents and followed the husband of her choice to a wild and distant land."[39]

The same morning the other Ridge Cherokee chiefs, John's father Major Ridge, and his cousin Elias Boudinot, were also murdered. (Only Elias's brother, Stand Watie, barely escaped. Ultimately he became a Confederate general. While the Ridge faction sided with the Confederacy, predictably the Ross faction allied itself to the Union side.)

Some of the murderers were known. It was not clear whether John Ross himself had been party to the murders, but he did not hesitate to profit. Refusing all cooperation with the Dragoons' efforts to bring the murderers to book or even call a conference with the Ridge faction, Ross insisted that he was now the clear and only Cherokee chief. At Fort Gibson, General Arbuckle spent a fruitless summer trying to achieve any justice. The situation grew more and more explosive. Larger and larger grew the estimates of the force of Dragoons needed to take the murderers. By September 1839 no one knew what to do.

---

[39]   John Rollin Ridge, *Poems*: Preface, 7-8, quoted in Thurman Wilkins, *Cherokee Tragedy: The Ridge Family and the Decimation of a People* (2nd ed rev: Univ of Oklahoma, 1986), 335-36.

SARAH NORTHROP RIDGE (1806-1856)

DAGUERREOTYPE, CA. 1850

Northrop was ill again in September—perhaps by now his standard reaction to duty at Gibson. After nearly eight years spent on and off at this "charnel house of the Army", with malaria and probably cholera dating back to that first terrible winter and summer as a Dragoon, who could say that his recurrent illnesses were not physical?

However that might be, Northrop was summoned by General Arbuckle, who clearly knew of the family relationship as well as the young soldier's extensive experience with Indians in general. By then the October nights were dark and often bitter cold. Northrop recalled: "I suggested giving no notice even to the men—to rouse them after tattoo and travel right out [beyond the Cherokee encampments] half the night—taking the woods in the neighbourhood of settlements—then search *back*—while news would be sent *forward* [from one Indian camp to the next distant from Gibson] of a party [of Dragoons] being out."[40] General Arbuckle asked him to lead the expedition.

On the third night, October 6, 1839, and doubtless overtired, Northrop's pistol accidentally discharged—it could happen very easily with those crude guns lacking safeguards—and the bullet went into his knee. His own analysis, written with medical knowledge acquired later, runs as follows:

> The ball fractured the patella [knee-cap], entered the joint, and is *now* lodged in the articulating extremity of one of the two large bones which form the joint, and eminent surgeons whom I have collected in consultation reject all idea of searching for it, or hope of extracting it.
>
> The intense inflammation, which extended to all the tissues of the joint—even to the bones themselves, produced long and copious suppuration and abiding irritation. Adhesions of the parts were formed, and false bone generated... The partial flexion which now exists is audibly obstructed, giving rise to heat and grating soreness. ... The lower portion of my back and spine sympathise largely in this morbid local condition. Cold and changes of temperature always affect me painfully.[41]

At the time, and for some months after, it was hoped that the bullet might move so as to become extractable. In that hope Northrop went south again to old Fort Leavenworth to try the benefits of sun and warm weather. They did not help. At last in July 1840 the case was given up as hopeless: "I left Fort Gibson—the surgeons considering me irrecoverable,—and the Comdg officer sent a hospital attendant to take me home—as I could only move with crutches."[42]

---

[40]   June 20, 1860 (NA, RG 94, Adjutant General's Office, Letters Received, 56-N-1860).

[41]   Ibid., August 29, 1848. Northrop referred to a medical certificate from the assistant surgeon of Dragoons, John B. Porter. Searches in National Archives have failed to find it.

[42]   Ibid., June 28, 1860.

CHAPTER 3

THE INJURED MAN

"On my arrival in Charleston, the three first medical men in my country were gathered in consultation,—and their treatment fully carried out."[1] They considered and rejected the possibility of amputation, but held out little hope for improvement. Northrop was restless. As soon as he could get a shoe on, he went to Washington and asked the Adjutant General for any duty. "He wrote me that I was obviously unfit, and not to attempt it."[2] Yet the young man, not yet thirty, allowed himself to cherish the notion that he might still receive a staff appointment with light duties in a warm climate.

With this in mind, he wooed and married a young Maryland lady of exotic name, Maria Luisa Euphemia Joanna de Bernabeu.[3] The date of their wedding was probably May 28, 1841.[4] Despite her name, Maria was three-quarters old American stock. Her Spanish grandfather, Juan Baptista de Bernabeu (1772-1834), had come to the United States as a young man. He had married Bathsheba White, descended from Thomas White (1599-1674) of Weymouth, Mass., and Edward Howell (1599-16??), founder of Southampton, Long Island.[5] In later years Don Juan became Spanish consul

---

[1]   June 28, 1860 (NA, RG 94, Letters Received, 56-N-1860). The three doctors were John Bellinger, S. H. Dickson, and Eli Geddings. All were graduates of the University of Pennsylvania, and all had taken leading parts in founding the Medical College of South Carolina in Charleston. See J. I. Waring, *A History of Medicine in South Carolina, 1825-1900* (S.C. Medical Association, 1967), 205, 222, 224, 235-6.

[2]   Ibid.

[3]   There are two ideas about pronouncing "Bernabeu". Evelyn Bartow, in the *Bartow Genealogy* (privately printed by Innes, Baltimore, 1878), 144, recommends Bernăbō. Present-day descendants agree on Bernabiew (to rhyme with "view"). That is close to the correct Spanish pronunciation of "eu". Moreover Dr. R. S. Steuart, who married into the family, spelt it "Bernabue", suggesting that he also pronounced it so.

[4]   No record has been found. In a letter after Maria's death in May 1889, Lucius Northrop wrote: "We had been married 48 years before" (Rowland, X, 136). And by a lucky chance the day is remembered by a granddaughter of the Northrops' second son. Mary Northrop Hunt was brought up by her grandparents, and remembers the date because it was also her grandparents' wedding anniversary. They had chosen the date to coincide with the anniversary of his parents (Conversation with the writer, 1990).

[5]   G. R. Howell, *The Early History of Southampton, L.I.* (1887, rpr Yankee Pedlar, nd), passim; *Bartow Genealogy*, 144-5. (The Bernabeu descent has been wrongly copied in *The Northrup-Northrop Genealogy*, 268.)

27

in Baltimore and then in Philadelphia. He corresponded with American patriots from George Washington downwards. Yet he remained a passionate Spaniard, as a granddaughter recalled: "Grandfather de B. always had the Spanish flag run up over his (Consular) house when a baby came, so that his children could all claim Spanish nationality."[6]

The eldest of the consul's ten children was Maria's father, John Joseph de Bernabeu. He also married into old American stock, his bride being Ellen Moale (1793-1846) of Baltimore. Maria, their second child, was born May 6, 1816.[7] Unfortunately, around 1818 John Joseph de Bernabeu was lost at sea. The widow and her three young children remained close to her late husband's family—especially to his sister and her husband, Dr. and Mrs. Richard Sprigg Steuart.

Dr. Steuart (1797-1876) had an outstanding medical practice in Baltimore before inheriting his family's ancestral estate "Dodon" (or "Doden"). It lay fifteen miles south of Baltimore, ten miles east of Washington, but was entirely rural. Dodon extended to four farms covering 1600 acres worked by 150 slaves. From the time of his inheritance Dr. Steuart and his family spent most of their time at Dodon. The young Northrops counted the Steuarts among their closest friends. (Maria and her children sheltered with them for some time after the Civil War.)

After Maria's death in 1889, Lucius wrote to Jefferson Davis (who had characterized her as a "gentle little wife)": "...You, as nearly all others, missed the point of her character. *Innocence* and *fearlessness* made her 'charitable', *calm*, and absolutely invincible."[8] The description suggests an ideal complement to her husband's energy and insecurity. She emerges hardly at all in her husband's surviving letters until their last years.

Maria was Catholic, and close to the time of their marriage Lucius joined her in the faith.[9] In professing Catholicism, he was also following examples in his own family. His sister Mary and her husband John Bellinger had become Catholic in the 1830's. His mother had been received into the church in 1840. His brother Claudian was also interested, and would follow the rest in 1844. For Lucius the deductive, closely reasoned doctrines of Catholicism could offer a refuge from a world which had failed to give him a secure place, and which persecuted his friends, the Indians. To such a man, adherence to a minority religion might also make its own appeal.

After his marriage Lucius wrote to the army adjutant general: "I had married with the understanding of carrying my wife to a garrison, having sought staff duty before suing her. ...In September [1842] I returned to

---

[6] Family papers in possession of Mr. and Mrs. Geoffrey Fielding and Arthur B. Steuart, of Baltimore. The Steuart papers are extensive and have provided much of the family information that follows.

[7] Gravestone, Bonnie Brae Cemetery, Baltimore.

[8] September 15, 1889 (Rowland, X, 136).

[9] His son-in-law Eugene Didier wrote ("The Scape-Goat of the Confederacy", in *Spare Moments*, November 1907, 9) that Northrop had been received into the Catholic Church by the first Bishop of Charleston, John England. England was away from Charleston from May to December 1841, and he died April 11, 1842. The most probable time for Northrop's Catholic baptism was therefore shortly before his marriage in May 1841 or during the early weeks of 1842. The earliest baptismal records now extant at Charleston Cathedral begin a few years later.

MARIA DE BERNABEU NORTHROP (1816-1889)

THE ONLY KNOWN PHOTOGRAPH, CA. 1870.

(NORTHROP FAMILY ARCHIVES)

Washington and at length, some official duty occurring in the Commissary department, it was offered to me in October."[10]

This was no ordinary assignment. The revolt in Texas raised the real threat of war with Mexico. The United States Army therefore wanted a comprehensive survey of potential sources of subsistence over a wide area of southwest territories. The task called for skill in collecting information and making comparative judgments over thousands of square miles. Northrop knew the region and many of the Indians in it. He set out in October 1842, to be gone four months. He went far up Red River, and turned in a comprehensive report.[11]

The winter exposure produced more pain in his wounded knee, and on March 15, 1843 he was relieved of duty. He asked for commissary duty at a southern (and therefore warm) post, but there were no openings. On April 15, the Commissary General wrote to Northrop that he had discussed the case with the Commanding General of the Army, Winfield Scott: "...and at all events you will not be disturbed until some opportunity offers for putting you on such staff duty at the south as we are now asking for you... Unless you desire to see the capitol it is unnecessary for you to come on here immediately."[12]

The hint seemed clear enough. Lieutenant Northrop should now simply accept the status and emolument of a disabled officer, leaving any future arrangements to Washington. Yet Northrop still resisted the attempt to put him on the shelf. He solicited a quartermaster's appointment without success.[13]

In November 1843 the adjutant general wrote again. It seemed that the colonel of Dragoons back at Fort Gibson had noticed Northrop's name on the rolls of the Commissary Department for the previous winter, and wanted to know whether the lieutenant was then sufficiently recovered to rejoin his regiment. The adjutant general said Northrop should either rejoin the Dragoons or make monthly reports of his continuing disability to retain his pension.[14]

To make monthly reports on an injury that all sides acknowledged incurable seemed an insult to the injured man. Northrop summarized his feelings in a later letter to the adjutant general:

> This proceeding towards me—notwithstanding...the applications to the Quartermaster and Commissary Genls for duty, and the care I had taken to explain my situation—harassed me, and I felt so discouraged by the seeming want of respect for a misfortune under which I had suffered enough without such addition, that if able I would have resigned at once. ...

---

[10]   October 11 and December 6, 1847 (NA, RG 94, Adjt. General's Office, Letters Received, 56-N-1860). The Special Order was dated October 7, 1842.

[11]   Ibid., October 11, 1847 to the same. No trace of the final report can now be found in National Archives.

[12]   Ibid.

[13]   Ibid., December 6, 1843.

[14]   Ibid., November 27, 1843.

I resolved to make an effort at independence that might ultimately enable me to relieve the service of a burden which I seemed
to be, while unemployed except in making monthly repetitions of
the same mortifying report.[15]

His "effort at independence" was nothing less than an aim at a new
profession. He would qualify himself to practice medicine. Had that choice
been prompted by his own injury? He had the experience of amateur doctoring on long detachment from Fort Gibson. Yet the notion of practicing medicine in Charleston must have come in some degree from the example of his
brother-in-law John Bellinger. In later years Northrop wrote to Jefferson Davis:
"Of all men with whom I have ever had to deal, you and John Bellinger have
seemed to me to be the most faithful in friendship."[16] Faithful friendship, to
a man placed as Northrop found himself, was the pearl beyond price.

The question of qualification arose. The Medical College of South Carolina had a good reputation, but the thought of sitting amongst boys hardly
more than half his age, many from families he was bound to know, could
not appeal. There was another way. In those days before physicians were
licensed, a man could practice medicine with a certificate from a preceptor
(who should himself be a qualified doctor). It involved merely attending the
doctor's practice with him for a certain length of time, and two periods of
observation in hospital wards.

The obvious preceptor was John Bellinger. It may have been Bellinger
who made it a condition that the hospital to attend should be in Philadelphia, the prestige place to study medicine in the United States then, both at
the time of Bellinger's own study there and that of his father before him.[17]
However the decision was arrived at, Northrop agreed to go to Philadelphia
for a limited time.

The plan to study medicine brought opposition from his wife and her
family. Northrop recalled: "It was contrary to the wishes and remonstrances
of her and her family that I undertook my plan; at the risk of losing rank,
while I might fail in its accomplishment."[18] Dr. Steuart knew all too well the
stony path to professional success in medicine. He would have known
Northrop's temperament well enough to estimate the chances for such success among many classes of patients. Worst of all, any new study for professional qualification might upset the status of his military pension. If his

---

[15]   Ibid., October 11, 1847.

[16]   August 6, 1864 (Harvard Univ: Dearborn Collection).

[17]   Many sources, and early ones, say that Northrop studied at Jefferson Medical College in
Philadelphia. There is now no record of his matriculation or study there, at the University of Pennsylvania
Medical School, or even at the Pennsylvania Hospital in Philadelphia (at all of which the records of
students are tolerably complete). The likely explanation, according to Dr. Frederick Wagner (Osler
Professor Emeritus of Surgery, University Historian, and editor of a recent comprehensive history of
Thomas Jefferson Medical University, *Tradition and Heritage*, [Lea & Febiger, 1989]) is that Northrop
"attended the ward rounds, lectures, and conferences at the Pennsylvania Hospital". For such
attendance, if his preceptor was elsewhere, the hospital would have kept no records (Correspondence
with Dr. Wagner, 1989).

[18]   October 11, 1847 (NA, RG 94, Adjt. General's Office: Letters Received 56-N-1860).

status as a disabled officer was disturbed, the army could well find an excuse to remove him from its rolls—and so eliminate his only income. There was no guarantee that medicine would provide another.

Still Northrop would not play the supine part. So he went again to Washington with the object of interviewing General Scott. Three times he tried without success. He did see Adjutant General Jones, who asked him to put the proposal in writing. He did so—reluctantly—on December 6, 1843, enclosing another of the hated statements of disability and rehearsing the history of the case. Both medical advice and his own observation

> ...have forced on me the conviction that I shall never be a sound man... If it was in my power I would resign at once, but I am dependent on my profession and cannot abandon it until I get another.
>
> While in Charleston I consulted the first physician there, who told me that I could not be prepared for practise under three years, nor get a diploma without attending two courses of lectures, which would include next winter and the following one. When an officer cannot do the full duties of his position, it is for the interest of the service to get clear of him. Under these circumstances it does not seem unreasonable for me to ask to be allowed to undertake this plan.
>
> If I recover my efficiency and join my regiment, the knowledge obtained will be useful as an officer... On the other hand, if I do not regain my efficiency, no time is to be lost in preparing myself for a change of profession by availing myself of all the facilities practicable.[19]

Yet in this very letter he had expressed "the conviction that I shall never be a sound man". So if the army accepted the plan for studying medicine, the apparent alternatives just mentioned would reduce to the single option of swimming or sinking by success or failure in the anticipated medical practice. Maria and her family had been right: and Lucius himself had in effect offered to set a limit to the previously open-ended arrangement by which he drew pay as a disabled officer.

That was certainly how the army read his letter. The adjutant general endorsed it with a positive recommendation to General Scott, who ordered that Lieutenant Northrop be granted "the indulgence necessary".[20] (The arrangement forced him also to give up any prospect of promotion during the time it operated: even in disability, he had written that he hoped for a captaincy.)[21] The adjutant general wrote to Northrop on December 11, 1843, approving the plan "with a view of leaving the army, should not your hopes of restoration be realized within a reasonable time."[22] The implied agreement seemed clear enough. Only the extent of "reasonable time" was not specified. Yet even there the implication was present: the three years which Northrop had requested for his new study.

---

[19]   Ibid.

[20]   The Adjutant General's endorsement was dated December 8, and General Scott's the next day (Ibid.).

[21]   Ibid.

[22]   Ibid.

Northrop seems to have made no protest at the time, and began his study with John Bellinger in 1844. The autumn of that year found Northrop, at the age of thirty-three, journeying north to attend lectures side by side with students little more than half his age. The damage to his ego was predictable: "My object was honorable and sustained me in view of the humiliation and violated feelings sure to occur to a man of my age and habits among students at hospitals and lectures."[23] However, he returned to Philadelphia for another winter in 1845-46.

Did he himself anticipate something short of success? During those years he tried, as opportunity arose, to go back to his first profession:

When war with Great Britain was thought impending [in 1845, over the Oregon Territory border], I expressly in that contingency waived this understanding [of leave for medical study], and while reporting myself unfit for dragoon duty, declared myself in readiness to attempt any thing for the service. This was long before I had completed my studies.

When war with Mexico occurred [in May 1846] I did the same thing. Having so declared in the last of May or early June 46 while on my way to attend the hospital in Philadelphia and reported that I was going there, I proceeded on but was prepared at any moment to leave if my services were accepted [by the army]. I considered that I had by this unexpected event been caused to give up the understanding, more than 6 months before the expiration of the three years.[24]

When no place was found for him in the Mexican War, a major conflict near a territory he knew well, it was a bitter blow: "I drew the conclusion that there was nothing left for me, but by economy and perseverance to render myself able, without the certainty of want, to resign my commission." At what point might he cut himself loose from the army? "...I have long intended and frequently declared since obtaining my degree that the first year I could realize about one half of my present pay I would resign."[25]

At the end of his time in Philadelphia, Northrop returned to Charleston. He and his wife took a house at the corner of Bee and President Streets, across from the United States Army Arsenal:[26] "...and have since been studiously and sedulously engaged in endeavouring with the aid of my friends to establish myself as a practicing Physician."[27]

Alas for plans and hopes. Perhaps Charleston distrusted a medical man newly qualified but middle-aged as they counted things then, who had only taken up medicine because of an all-too-obvious injury which he himself could not cure. All his old friends in the city doubtless already had established doctors of their own—doctors of the accomplishments and

---

[23] Ibid.

[24] Ibid.

[25] Ibid.

[26] Letter of August 22-23, 1906, from Northrop's eldest daughter Louise Didier (1850-1915) to her daughter Nina Didier Rose (MS in possession of Mrs. Geoffrey Fielding).

[27] October 11, 1847 (NA, RG 94, Adjt. General's Office: Letters Received 56-N-1860).

manners of John Bellinger—whom they would not willingly abandon for a man whose former life and sufferings had given him an uncertain temper and perhaps a scorn of physical pain. And his popularity as a doctor would not have been enlarged by his conversion in these years to vegetarianism, which he followed for the rest of his life.[28]

However it was, Northrop came to practice in Charleston largely on charity patients or those from whom little recompense was to be looked for. He continued to submit the monthly medical reports which had become the condition of drawing his disabled officer's pay.[29] That pay—with scrupulous saving, careful investment, and perhaps some help from his mother and the Bernabeus—enabled him to settle in Charleston with a modicum of comfort.

His sister Mary was there with her husband John Bellinger and their five children, though Mary was dying of consumption. Their younger brother Claudian represented the Charleston Parish of St. Philip and St. Michael in the South Carolina Legislature. Claudian maintained his law practice in Charleston, as well as a fashionable residence at 67 Meeting Street with his wife and growing family. Yet he asked for financial help, and at various times from about 1842 onward Lucius lent him sums amounting in the end to thousands of dollars—a measure of Lucius's financial position even in these years. Claudian repaid the money only in part, and slowly.

Claudian too had become a Catholic, and he was soon the lawyer for the Diocese of Charleston. He earned and spent freely, and liked to be a patron of art. Taste and charity came together in March 1846 when Claudian heard of an Italian exile in Charleston living with his family in penury, though he was a painter of fine pictures. European immigrants were not welcomed in the South as readily as in the North, but conservative Charleston kept a special regard for victims of the republican violence of Garibaldi. Claudian sought out the painter, who called himself "Pietro Martini". The poverty of his surroundings contrasted with exquisite manners and talent, but the man would not reveal his true identify for fear of his life.

Claudian rented a decent studio and accommodation for the painter and his family. He interested Lucius and John Bellinger in the case. At last, in dreadful secrecy, "Martini" told the Northrops his real identity—a secret they never revealed. They became devoted to him, and in the case of Lucius it amounted to something more than that: "So much impressed did I become with his fortitude, gentleness and resignation (so contrasted in a man of his evident passion and spirit) that I told him to consider me a brother— that I was ready to respond to any call, and that if an angel assailed him I would say it was a mistake and defend him... So that while knowing him

---

[28]　General Bradley Johnson, quoted in Northrop's obituary in *The Baltimore Sun*, February 10, 1894.

[29]　Northrop's obituary in *The Baltimore Sun* stated that he was on half-pay. His son-in-law Eugene Didier (in whose house Northrop spent most of his last years)stated that it was full pay. The "Scape-Goat of the Confederacy"; I, in *Spare Moments*, October 1907, 7.

only as Pietro Martini a friendless stranger, being Catholic I have as my most intimate friend got him ... to be the godfather of my only child."[30]

The first surviving child of Lucius and Maria was born January 27, 1847. They named him Juan Baptista de Bernabeu Northrop after the old consul, Maria's grandfather. At the baptism of "Juanito" on February 26, Pietro Martini stood god-parent side by side with Lucius's fifty-nine year old mother, Claudia Margaret Northrop.[31]

Just when life appeared to be settling at last into a comfortable pattern, Lucius received a letter from the adjutant general:

> Washington,
> September 21 1847
> Sir:
>
> Nearly ten months having expired beyond the period requested in your letter of December 7 1843, when a three year leave was granted you to study the medical profession, with the understanding that should you at the end of that time be still disqualified from performing duty, you would resign, it now devolves on me to call your attention to the subject, and to enquire whether you contemplate joining your company at once, or adopting the alternative presented in your letter above referred to, and upon which was grounded the usual indulgence of three years then accorded you—?
> I am, Sir,
>
> > Very Respectfully
> > Yr. Ob. Servt.
> > R. Jones
> > Adjt Genl.[32]

Northrop requested copies of the letter and document he had reluctantly written requesting the leave. Then he settled down on October 11 to a three thousand word reply. Extended review of circumstance, minute scrutiny of verbiage, repeated protestation of honor—all led to a denial that he had ever agreed to quit his rank and emolument as a disabled officer. The center of his argument was this: "I asked 'to be allowed to *undertake* this plan', I did not *pledge* myself to perfect it at all, or within any given time." Forcing him to choose between rejoining his regiment and resigning, he said, impugned his honor: "I am told of an unfulfilled engagement, by which whether I join my company or resign, in *either case* I must submit to reproach." He could not choose between such alternatives, he said. If such a choice must be made, the army would have to do it.[33]

---

[30]   Undated statement witnessed by John Bellinger and filed with a parallel statement by Claudian Northrop dated February 26, 1847 (Charleston Catholic Diocesan Archives [hereinafter designated CDA] 11 C 3). The Northrops' great-granddaughter Mary Hunt recalls family talk of earlier children not surviving (Conversation, 1991).

[31]   Baptismal Register of the Cathedral of Charleston.

[32]   NA, RG 94, Adjt. General's Office: Letters Received, 56-N-1860.

[33]   Ibid., ff 332, 337-8.

Adjutant General Jones passed the case to the Secretary of War, William Marcy. He enclosed the whole correspondence, including Northrop's latest long letter. The Secretary of War naturally took the opportunity to relieve the army of so exceptional and verbose an appendage. On January 8, 1848 he caused a letter to be sent from President James Knox Polk, dropping Northrop from the rolls of the United States Army.

Northrop appealed to his old comrade Jefferson Davis, recently returned from distinguished military service in the Mexican War to become a United States Senator from Mississippi. Davis quickly lodged protests with the adjutant general by letter, and he called on the Secretary of War.[34] When no progress appeared, Davis wrote the Secretary a letter marshalling legal arguments respecting Northrop's three-year leave: "...This the Adjt. Genl. has most strangely construed into a contract by which Lieut. Northrop was to surrender his commission at a fixed time. You sir will not fail to perceive that the position of the Adjt. Genl. could only be correct where an officer's commission could be bargained away for an indulgence...".[35]

When the Secretary of War sided with his adjutant general, Davis wrote to President Polk:

> I deny that Lt. Northrop's application warrants the idea of a contract or obligation to resign. I deny that an officer's commission can be made the subject of such sale or purchase. I deny that Lt. Northrop received any peculiar indulgence or advantage over other officers in like situation...
>
> The case was presented, that the errors of the Adjt. Genl. might be corrected; and the order rescinded by which a gallant and crippled officer has been stricken from the rolls of the army, because he avowed intentions creditable to him as a gentleman and a soldier. He has been disappointed, his wound has not healed, and his general health has become worse: he is therefore unable to support himself as he had hoped, and unless restored to his commission is debarred from any provision which may be made for a retired list of disabled officers.[36]

A fortnight later Davis wrote a further short appeal to the President, for the signatures of the Senators from South Carolina, Andrew P. Butler and his mentor, the aged Calhoun: "...We hope no invidious distinction will be made against this gallant, honorable, and unfortunate officer."[37]

At last on July 26, 1848 Davis was able to assure Northrop that he would be restored to the army rolls. Not satisfied with that, he guided through Congress a promotion for Northrop to captain's rank.[38] On August 12 Congress enacted both the reinstatement and the promotion to captain from July 21. Lucius Northrop's future seemed at last secure: he would only have to go on sending the hated reports of his disability.[39]

---

[34]   *Davis Papers*, III, 317; 424-25.
[35]   Ibid., May 5, 1848, 316-17.
[36]   June 23, 1848 (Rowland, I, 205-6).
[37]   July 6, 1848 (*Davis Papers*, III, 332).
[38]   Ibid., 446-47; V, 476.
[39]   Several such reports from Northrop survive in the Samuel Cooper Papers (#2482) at the University of North Carolina. The dates range from January 1853 to October 1854.

* * *

His family increased. His first son, born in 1847, was joined by another son and four daughters. All the daughters would bear their mother's
primary Christian name of Maria or Mary. First came Mary Louisa (Maria
Luisa de la Innocentia), born January 4, 1850. Two and a half years later
there was Maria Isabel, born June 2, 1852. Then on October 30, 1854 came
Edmundo Francisco Ximenes (named for an old Spanish monk and Inquisi-
tor General at the turn of the sixteenth century): his father called him Ximenes,
but he was later known as Frank. The family was completed with two more
daughters: Mary Claudia Margaret Bellinger, born June 7, 1856, and Clara
Maria Josepha, born May 27, 1858.[40]

By 1855 the family had moved to a larger house at the corner of Spring
and Ashley Streets, still far from the fashionable neighborhoods.[41] Northrop's
house was nonetheless his castle. He had made his slaves Catholic; and
(recalling his own childhood at the beloved Ashepoo Plantation) chose the
slaves' children as playmates for his elder son Bernabeu: "In raising my
child I chose that he should play with the sons of his nurse, of whose religion and training I had been careful, and her character was a guarantee that
this association was *safer* than with the children of my protestant neighbors; and I taught him that as he played with my slaves, he must expect
liberties and effusions of temper; this same justice which he *had* to exhibit
to his negroes, he would naturally expect from the Prefects" later at
Georgetown College.[42]

Long before his son's attendance at Georgetown, Lucius Northrop had
a ward there. That was Joseph Bellinger (1839-1900). His father, Edmund
Cussings Bellinger (1813-1848), was Northrop's second cousin, who had
inherited the old Landgrave's title, and lived most of his short life at the
Barnwell Plantation "Aeolian Lawn".[43] Before he died in December 1848, he
made Lucius Northrop his executor, and his only son Joseph became
Northrop's ward. When Joseph was twelve in 1851, it was time to send him
to boarding school. As one of John Bellinger's sons had recently been sent to
the Jesuit College at Georgetown (next to Washington, D.C.), this became the
choice for Joseph as well.

During the next five years, Northrop's letters to the president and staff
at Georgetown showed careful administration of his charge—paying the bills
and seeking receipts to enable him to make returns to the court supervisors
of the wardship. One letter of July 1852 exchanges botanical information
with the president, supplementing a gift of Carolina plants from Northrop.
When questionable influences threatened, the guardian was prompt to act.
In March 1853 Northrop wrote that Joe's mother had been persuaded by

---

[40]   Names and birthdates from the Baptismal Register (CDA).
[41]   Louise Didier to her daughter Nina, August 22-23, 1906. A Charleston City Census of 1855 (S.C.
Historical Society) shows the Northrops at this address.
[42]   August 11, 1867 to the Rev. B. A. Maguire, S.J. (Georgetown College archives).
[43]   Patterson et al., *Builders of Freedom*, 96-98.

Protestant relations to yield to her son's wish to leave college. Northrop "explained to her its impropriety, especially as I had received so polite a response to the representations made by me to the President at her request, in reference to modifying Joe's studies with regard to his capacity...". Then he set about reconciling Joe to going on with his education, "which I hope will continue until he reaps the benefits which I believe none are so competent to impart as the Colleges of the Society" of Jesus.[44] Northrop sent for his ward to visit him again in Charleston that summer; and the boy remained to complete his studies and graduate in 1856.

Lucius Northrop's relations with his brother Claudian were less happy. A leading cause was their involvement together in a scheme to establish a colony of Irish Catholics in southwest Georgia. That scheme was the brainchild of another Catholic convert from Charleston, Abbot Hall Brisbane (1804-1861). Brisbane was a soldier, a West Point graduate (1825) who, as colonel of the South Carolina Irish Volunteers, had so distinguished himself in the Seminole Wars (Florida, 1835-36) as to be dubbed "the South Carolina Hotspur". He was a man of many talents—construction engineer for an artesian well to supply Charleston's water; supervising engineer for the Charleston-to-Cincinnati railroad project; sometime novelist and professor of history, belles letters, and ethics at the military academy of Charleston, The Citadel.[45]

Brisbane owned many thousands of acres in Irwin and adjoining counties in Georgia—hundreds of square miles with hardly a road of any description, few isolated houses, endless desolation of fallen trees and pools of lime. The priest assigned to the district visited it only three times in his career, always with apprehension: "It was too remote in the interior, thinly settled, and sickly...a wilderness where the sight of every man inspired dread...".[46]

There, in spite of everything, Brisbane had conceived the idea of placing a colony of Irish Catholic immigrants. He involved both Lucius and Claudian Northrop and John Bellinger by selling them all parcels of the land. Lucius was perceptive enough to foresee trouble, and soon extricated himself by selling his land back to Brisbane, but not before lending nearly $1,000 to Claudian as Claudian's share of the purchase.[47]

The others pressed forward. In January 1845 Claudian Northrop and John Bellinger each conveyed a portion of their lands for $1 to the current Bishop of Charleston, Ignatius Reynolds, to make him a partner. Within five years the proprietors had engaged an agent in Liverpool, England, to advertise and sell the lands lot by lot to poor Irish Catholics wanting to emigrate

[44]   March 21, 1853 to Rev. P. Duddy, S.J. (Georgetown archives).
[45]   E. Haviland Hillman, "The Brisbanes", in *South Carolina Historical and Genealogical Magazine*, XIV (1913), 179-80.
[46]   O'Connell, *Catholicity in the Carolinas and Georgia*, 577-78.
[47]   Deeds of February 28, 1844 (Irwin County, Georgia Deed Book 3, 336-39) show Brisbane conveying 15,000 acres to C. B. Northrop and over 10,000 to John Bellinger, each for $500.

CLAUDIAN BIRD NORTHROP (1812-1865)

THE ONLY KNOWN PHOTOGRAPH, CA. 1857.

(NORTHROP FAMILY ARCHIVES)

because of the potato famine. Quite a few sank their life savings in the scheme to pay for land and passage. The first arrivals, however, sent back disastrous reports of the place. The would-be settlers felt cheated, and charged the proprietors (including Bishop Reynolds) with gross misrepresentation.[48]

At that point Lucius discovered his own name still being advertised with the others, despite the fact that he had sold out. Honor was outraged; and when Bishop Reynolds tried to assert religious authority to calm him, rage turned to fury.[49] Lucius demanded a public apology from the proprietors so all-encompassing, with legal threats so general, that Claudian wrote to the bishop's vicar-general, Dr. Patrick Lynch: "Such a proposition from a stranger would appear too senseless to be considered at all. ...I have heard of innocent men confessing guilt under urgent apprehensions of the fatal consequences of protesting [against] their guiltiness. I do not pretend to disparage the degree of torture we may escape by such puerile submission."[50]

The Northrop brothers were further separated by the death of their mother on February 12, 1855. Three weeks earlier Claudia Margaret Northrop had signed a will leaving practically everything to Lucius, making him sole executor with no accountability to anyone else. It was no sudden decision, the will stated, for she had planned it so since 1840. Of her other children, Mary was dead. And "for my son Claudian's education and support, I spent more than for both my other children combined, and by which he is now earning many thousands for himself...".[51] As Mary had married at sixteen, and Lucius's West Point education had been at government expense, the cost of Claudian's university and legal training had indeed exceeded the others. But Claudian, whose wife had died in 1853, had seven children to educate, the youngest only three years old.

Lucius, at his mother's request, raised a marble obelisk to her memory in the cemetery of St. Patrick's Church in Charleston, and composed an inscription for it concluding:

> ...By the grace of God, in her fifty-third year, she found the only true church, that governed by the vicar of Christ, and she submitted to it. Supported in her last night by the Real Presence, she died without fear. Nata 28th Dec., 1787. Obiit 12th Feb., 1855. Christian, say an Ave Maria for her sake.[52]

Lucius himself was to say his mother's prayers for the rest of his life. Thirty years after her death he wrote to Jefferson Davis: "Age quells emotion and crowns reason, the fidelity of friendship grows, and the love of a faithful parent resumes its sway. I love my mother *now* more than wife or children, and her last words to me, as her child, are the jewels of my life, due to my conception of her elevation, integrity, and devotion to truth."[53]

---

[48] O'Connell, 119-122.
[49] CDA 6 T 1, 7 D 5.
[50] April 23, 1850 (CDA 6 T 4).
[51] Charleston Probate Office, Will Book L, 319 (Box 94 #9).
[52] Transcribed by John Gilmore Smith and printed in *The Charleston Sunday News*, August 15, 1920. The inscription itself is now hardly legible.
[53] March 9, 1885 (Rowland, IX, 351).

Her legacy almost certainly helped Lucius to acquire the substantial house at 16 Mazyck Street, Charleston, to which he moved his family after her death.[54] His eldest daughter Louise was to recall it as "in what I suppose was not a nice part of the town. ... I remember Mamma was not pleased when Papa bought the house, but he liked it because it was near the Cathedral, & the Sisters of Mercy where we went to school, and because the house was very strongly built [—] had walls a foot thick & had a large side lot and very deep. Papa never cared for appearances [—] not for fashion nor what people said or thought, so a thing was right & reasonable, that was all he cared about."[55] It was a comfortable home set beside an inlet of the Bay of Charleston from which, with his family and slaves, he might look to the future.

Still the matter of Claudian's unpaid debt to him continued to rankle, as it still tied Lucius to the notorious colonization scheme. The debt, which Claudian readily acknowledged, stood at more than $4,700 with accumulated interest. Lucius claimed $6,000, the extra money by way of "damages". Claudian promised to discharge the lower sum, but the payments he made did not cover the mounting interest. At last Lucius decided to sue. And so in 1856 the Dickensian overtones of "Northrop v Northrop" spread through Charleston.

Lucius's lawyer filed the suit, and a writ was issued on February 23.[56] Two days later Claudian (who was acting for himself) wrote to Lucius's lawyer William Whaley. Whaley had misspelt Claudian's name on the document, which could have been used to cause delay. But Claudian advised his adversary in a finely patronizing letter: "It will be well for you to have full instructions from your client, and know what are his claims in action, as the form of the pleadings may be affected by your information. You will then be able to determine whether your action should be for assumpsit or debt. When you are fully informed, and prepared to draw the declaration, I will be happy to facilitate your proceedings, with the same disregard of nice technicalities that I have herein now shewn."[57]

Claudian offered to settle out of court.[58] He could do this by selling his house (already heavily mortgaged) and all his possessions in Charleston. But again progress was slow. Lucius filed his suit on January 2, 1857. On Claudian's free admission of the debt of $4,734.36, summary judgment was rendered for that amount. Claudian sold his house and property, and took his nine-year-old youngest son to live in rooms above his office. On March 12, Lucius received his money. Next day Claudian wrote his brother a letter without salutation, but offering an olive branch over the extra sums Lucius had claimed:

---

[54] The U.S. Census of 1860 shows them at Mazyck Street. Street name and numbers have been changed, but the house survives at 122 Logan Street. Because of subsequent landfilling, it is no longer near water.

[55] Louise Didier to her daughter Nina, August 22-23, 1906.

[56] Charleston Court of Common Pleas, Judgment Rolls: Box 70, Roll 14 (S.C. Dept. of Archives and History, Columbia, S.C.).

[57] February 25, 1856 (CDA 9 P 1, no. 1).

[58] April 25, 1856 (CDA 9 P 1, no. 3).

We cannot, at our time of life, look too confidently into the future; and therefore I shall be truly obliged to you, if you will take the trouble to inform me of the particulars...

Under this hope I conclude with the assertion that it will always give me pleasure to serve you; and that I do not suppose anything will occur in the future, as nothing has in the past, which can affect the feelings of unfeigned kindness which I entertain towards you and your family.[59]

One would like to know how Lucius responded to this letter, which is the last communication between the brothers now known. After Claudian's death in 1865, there was some evidence of Lucius's regard for his brother's children.[60] But the judgment of 1857 began the ruination of Claudian and his law practice in Charleston. Thereafter Claudian maintained a single priority—the best education for his children. In that he succeeded well.[61]

---

[59]   March 13, 1857 (CDA 10 C 8).

[60]   E.g. December 7, 1877 to Claudian Northrop the younger (CDA 64 N 4).

[61]   Claudian Northrop was able to educate his children through trust funds established by his late wife's family in New York. Their eldest son, named for his uncle Lucius, was educated at Georgetown, Mount St. Mary's College at Emmitsburg, Md., and the University of South Carolina; he became a newspaper editor and Circuit Court Judge. The second son John attended Annapolis and Mount St. Mary's, but joined the Confederate Army and was blinded at Gaines' Mill. The third, fourth and fifth sons, as well as his two daughters, were educated also at Emmitsburg. The third and fourth sons completed their studies at the American College in Rome. One became priest of the mother church of the Charleston Diocese, St. Mary's, before his early death in 1882. The other became Bishop of Charleston in succession to Patrick Lynch: Bishop Northrop built the present Charleston Cathedral, and served his diocese for thirty-three years until his death in 1916.

CHAPTER 4

THE APPROACH OF WAR

During the 1850's the gathering clouds of sectionalism darkened the United States. Lucius Northrop, having survived the crippling wound which ended his first career, the virtual failure of his second career in medicine, the local notoriety of more or less public quarrels with his only brother and with the bishop of the church of his conversion, had succeeded only in fatherhood and husbanding his own affairs. He had, by his late forties, turned in on himself: "The fact is I abhorred publicity. ... I was no politician—never identified with any party or set of men...".[1]

Thus the matter of Southern secession held no theoretical interest for him at first. "I felt under no obligation to study the question of sovereignty. I grew up in the creed, and held the doctrine, that the State was the final sovereign—that the citizen must go with his State, that all he ever got or did with the Federal Government was through his State in that relation, and that all claims of the former reverted to the latter when hostile attitudes were assumed."[2] First and foremost he was a citizen of South Carolina.

The clearest duty, in Northrop's view, was toward his family. There a definite threat seemed to rise in October 1859, when the abolitionist John Brown raided a U.S. Government arsenal at Harpers Ferry, West Virginia, with the avowed aim of fomenting an armed revolt of slaves throughout the South. In South Carolina, the slave population had long outnumbered the whites. Northrop drew the conclusion that he must "sell out & quit a land over which I saw terrible convulsions impending". What was true for his family was also true for his slaves. He felt "that my negroes had been intrusted to me by God; I had made many of them Catholics, that probably their fate depended on me, and that I would not desert them...".[3]

---

[1] July 7 and August 10, 1865 to the Rev. J. J. Early (Georgetown archives).

[2] July 7, 1865 to Fr. Early.

[3] Ibid.

The decision to leave Charleston was strengthened in August 1860 by the death of his best and oldest friend there, John Bellinger. Dr. Bellinger, the widower of Lucius's sister Mary, was only fifty-five; he had been forced to retire from practice some years earlier because of pulmonary tuberculosis.

The notion of leaving for safety pointed towards the country. That meant pursuing some form of agriculture, in case his army pension should become forfeit. He fixed on cotton planting, the occupation of his mother's family at Barnwell and Ashepoo.[4] Anywhere in South Carolina was impossible because its lands were much exhausted by generations of intensive farming. "Land here is poor or too high for a man to buy who has to husband his resources."[5] His own resources, according to the United States Census of 1860, amounted to $45,000 in personal property and $20,000 in real estate. Adversity had made him prudent.

His choice for an agricultural refuge fell on Arkansas—well out of the way of any conflict, as it seemed then, but sympathetic to slavery and rich in virgin acreage. All this was familiar to him from his time with the Dragoons, though to his family not at all. He contacted a local agent, William Woodruff, and before the end of 1860 secured 320 acres of uncleared land twelve miles from Little Rock.[6] He was hoping for more land in that district, but further arrangements were overtaken by events traced in his letters to Woodruff. Northrop wrote on November 8, 1860: "We are in exciting times and 'great events are on the gale'. Our legislature have passed the bill for a convention which will decree secession." Five weeks later, on December 14:

> I sympathise with the regret that all men of right feeling should have when discord and uncertainty succeed peace and produce suffering & ruin to many; but when 40 years of experience has demonstrated that unity of sentiment has given way to Jealousy; when one part of a nation has systematically struggled to get the power of breaking up the social system of the other part, when hatred more bitter than a state of hostility reigns between them, when not simply a *violation* of rights but a declaration have literally *educated* their people into the belief that their confederates are man stealers—eaters of human flesh in living by outraging their brothers, it is time to separate...
>
> I am confident our country is exploded, and while I am indisposed to belong to a weak nation, I am clear to establish a confederacy of slave states only. I do not speak as a Carolinian. I feel that our quarrel is for all slave holders & likewise for our negroes' welfare. I will not desert mine, who have the right to my protection and care. Unless we act now Jamaica [where insurrections had both pre-

---

[4] Didier, "The Scape-Goat of the Confederacy", I, 7.

[5] January 2, 1861 to William Woodruff, in W. E. Wight, ed., "Some Letters of Lucius Bellinger Northrop", in *Virginia Magazine of History and Biography*, vol. 68, no. 4 (October 1960), 462.

[6] May 3, 1873 to Bishop Lynch of Charleston (CDA 55 B 1).

ceded and followed the freeing of slaves in 1834] a thousand times magnified is before us.[7]

(The last two sentences seem to contradict each other until one recalls the traditional Southern view of black inferiority and the consequent perceived need to protect blacks from themselves.) Then Northrop gave a reading of Northern sentiment and its causes which was in several places not so wide of the mark:

> ...The politicians have played with the best instincts of mankind, have made the people of the north—country people I mean—believe their pretended views of slavery & slave-holders true,—I cannot [otherwise] account for the sentiment of the rural populations at the north, and I know that it will not change, because it is based on good instincts of humanity which have been most atrociously played on by their political deluders; hence I am sorry for the suffering which the masses will endure.[8]

Claudian Northrop held similar sentiments, and he gave them public voice. Alone in his widower's rooms above the law office now doing mostly Diocesan business, Claudian filled his time writing poems and pamphlets to thunder the Southern cause. A series of "Political Remarks by N." had appeared in *The Charleston Courier* during 1860; but at last they became too much even for the editor and his readers, and Claudian published the last three numbers in a pamphlet on his own account.[9] In the spring of 1861 Claudian closed his Charleston law office and went to administer a Catholic plantation at Lancaster in the northern part of the state. From there he published a small collection of "Southern Odes, by The Outcast, a Gentleman of South Carolina".[10] The little collection was dedicated to old Miss Harriott Pinckney, last surviving child of South Carolina's Revolutionary War General Charles Cotesworth Pinckney, a distant cousin and family friend of the Northrops.

Lucius hated those public protestations. Then Claudian's eldest son followed in his father's footsteps, and made a speech advocating a Southern attack on the United States army garrison presently occupying Fort Moultrie

---

[7] Many of these sentiments are to be found in pro-slavery tracts circulating widely then. One of them gained a special currency in Charleston when it appeared in 1860. Its author was a well-known South Carolina planter and member of the State Legislature, John Ferrers Townsend (1799-1881). Its full title was "The South Alone Should Govern the South, and African Slavery Should Be Controlled By Those Only Who Are Friendly To It." It accused the North of violating Southern rights by using "irresponsible majorities", and of inciting slaves to rebellion. It described the horrors which had attended emancipation in the West Indies, and recounted lurid details of John Brown's raid. Abolition of slavery in the American South would mean "the end of all negro labor, a jubilee of idleness, and a reign of sloth; until famine shall drive them to robbery or scourge them with pestilence...a war of races, the subjugation of the one to the other, certain poverty to the whites; degradation, want, expatriation." (See Theodore Rosengarten, *Tombee: Portrait of a Cotton Planter* (New York: Morrow, 1986) 205-6, 531. For an independent account of West Indian emancipation horrors in the Confederacy, and the consequent fear of Northern agitation among the slaves, see William Watson, *Life in the Confederate Army* (New York: Scribner & Walford, 1888), 28-29, 38-44.

[8] Wight, 458-60.

[9] Charleston: Evans & Cogswell, 1861. The prefatory note is signed in full.

[10] Charleston: Harper & Calvo, 1861.

in Charleston Harbor. The young man was named for his Uncle Lucius, and the embarrassed uncle wrote: "I saw the notice in the papers, considered the effort foolish and hoped that no body would suspect me of it."[11] But of course they did. Abner Doubleday, one of the Federal garrison at Moultrie, wrote bitterly after the war of Northrop's clamor to attack, and he added that Northrop might have had the grace to resign his United States commission before saying such a thing in public. Doubleday was misinformed on both points. The elder Lucius resigned his commission on January 1, 1861, one of the earliest Southern officers to take the step. He did it because South Carolina had become the first state to secede from the Union on December 20, 1860.

On January 2, 1861, the day after resigning the commission he had fought so hard to preserve, Northrop wrote to the agent Woodruff in Arkansas:

> In fact this is not State business. It is a family question; every individual Southern man should feel that he is contending for his own land. If this southern confederacy is not formed, then the Devil has broke loose in our land...I have never troubled myself with party elections or been interested in them, but I feel on this subject. ...
>
> Our State is *one*, our boys are spirited & ready & have been training for 12 mos, but we have no leaders of much ability, the Gov[ernor, Francis Pickens,] is weak; I have ever been declaring that nothing succeeds without a leader, & that my old friend Jeff Davis was the man, the time & the occasion as leader of the South. A man of comprehensive mind, administrative ability, accurate memory & always right in details, while of the highest morale.[12]

The friendship had continued quietly in the dozen years since Davis had secured Northrop's restoration to the army rolls and his promotion to captain. Davis was seldom far from Washington in those years. From 1853 to 1857 he had served with distinction as Secretary of War under President Franklin Pierce. Northrop visited the Davises occasionally, and sometimes recommended an appointment to Davis.[13] In 1857 Davis had returned to the United States Senate. There his advocacy of Southern rights did not prevent him from trying to effect a compromise within the divided Democratic Party. Such a compromise might have averted the election of the "Black Republican" Lincoln in 1860 and so averted South Carolina's secession. When Davis's own state of Mississippi seceded on January 9, 1861, he instantly prepared to vacate his office in Washington and return home.

Davis knew of Northrop's resignation from the army. On January 20, 1861, the day before his farewell speech to the Senate in Washington, Davis addressed a letter to Governor Pickens in Charleston:

> You have in your city an old and esteemed comrade of mine, when he and I served together in the U.S. Dragoons, his name is Capt L. B.

---

[11] August 10, 1865 to the Rev. J. J. Early (Georgetown archives). The younger Lucius (1839-1918) was originally named for his uncle; after this time he was known as Lucius Claudian Northrop.

[12] Wight, 461.

[13] In December 1853, Northrop recommended Dr. Steuart's son, John (NA, RG 94, Applications for Appointment, Civilian: Maryland, No. 2); in March 1855 Northrop forwarded a letter from Mrs. Nowland, the widow of an old sutler at Fort Gibson—at the same time apologizing for troubling Davis (*Davis Papers*, V, 333).

Northrop. As a son of South Carolina, he has deemed it incumbent upon him to leave the service of the United States, and has no doubt before this made himself subject to your command.

An intimate acquaintance with him enables me to say that to a high degree of professional attainment, he adds fine native intellect; before his physical disability, he was full of energy and from the natural fearlessness of his character prone to hazardous adventure. I know not what may be the present state of his health, with that exception I would not hesitate to endorse him for anything which a soldier could be called upon to do.[14]

Pickens made enquiries, and appointed Northrop Paymaster to the State Militia.[15] A commission was offered. Northrop accepted, abandoned his plans for Arkansas, and took up his first military post in nearly twenty years.

* * *

Five states had joined South Carolina to form the new Confederacy—Mississippi, Florida, Alabama, Georgia, and Louisiana—with Texas soon to come in. Early in February 1861 the Confederate States sent delegates to a Provisional Congress at Montgomery, Alabama. They enacted a provisional Constitution and a provisional central government. On February 9 the delegates elected Jefferson Davis provisional President of the Confederate States. Davis, who had been given command of the Mississippi State Militia, had not sought the Presidency; but a majority of the State delegations had voted for him, including Mississippi and South Carolina.

On February 26, 1861 the new President signed a bill to create the general staff for a Confederate army, modeled on the structure of the Federal army. Under a Secretary of War there was to be an adjutant and inspector general's office, together with Bureaus of Ordnance, Quartermaster, Medicine, Subsistence, and so on. Each of the Bureau chiefs would have the rank of colonel, with six or eight assistants and clerks. On March 6 the Confederate army itself was brought into existence: officers' and soldiers' pay scales were established in a new Confederate currency, clothing and horse allowances set. Again the model was the United States army, in which most of the new Confederate field officers had served.

President Davis appointed his cabinet. He selected men not out of personal obligation (for as he wrote later, he had no political debts to repay) but one cabinet officer from each of the new Confederate States. The South Carolinian, Christopher G. Memminger, became Secretary of the Treasury. The Secretary of War was Leroy Pope Walker of Alabama.

On March 11 Secretary Walker (clearly on instruction from Davis, as he himself was unacquainted) telegraphed to Lucius Northrop in Charleston:

---

[14] Huntington Library, San Marino, California, Huntington MS 20908.

[15] *The War of the Rebellion: A Compilation of the Official Records of the Union and Confederate Armies* (Washington: Government Printing Office, 1880 ff. [hereinafter cited as *OR*), ser. I, vol. 53, 157.

"Is your health such as to justify you in accepting a position in the Commissary Department of the Army?"[16] What were Northrop's qualifications? Most visibly, his mission in the winter of 1842-43 to survey food-producing areas of the southwest for the army. There was the added knowledge arising from his study of medicine. A basic qualification, together with West Point education, was his extensive experience of actual infantry and dragoon service over a wide range of territory and climate. From that he knew what foods would serve a soldier's nutrition, which were most easily gathered, how and where to acquire those not available locally, how much could be left to the men in the field to find and prepare for themselves, what should be provided from a central source.

From Northrop's own viewpoint, it was ironic that he—an essentially private man long retired and only recently enrolled in the service of his state—should be approached by the new central government of the South. Yet he had to admit that its principles were after all his own:

> I felt forced to respond. I gave up my interests (which powerfully impelled me otherwise) and accepted the humble position [at Montgomery]—knowing that I must lose every thing by the failure of the South, and could gain nothing by her success [being no politician].
> When crippled for active duty in the U.S. Service I tried in vain to get stationary duty in the Commissary Dept, and only did exactly the same thing when applied to by the Confederate Govt—to which I conceived my State had transferred all the claims to patriotic duty previously due to the U S Govt.[17]

On March 12, 1861, the day after Secretary Walker's telegram, Northrop wired his willingness to accept.[18] Walker telegraphed back on the 13th: "You are appointed if you will accept Commissary with rank of captain. Will you accept? If so come at once. Answer."[19] Northrop responded the same day: "Now paying troops. Will end settle & join as soon as possible. If that suits I accept."[20] Three days later he replied to what seems to have been a chaser from Davis himself, for on March 16 Northrop telegraphed directly to the new Confederate President: "No delay shall spring from me. Will resign positively."[21]

Parting from his family in Charleston, Northrop left for Montgomery on March 20, 1861. His arrival at the Confederate capital was greeted by an unwelcome surprise: "...I was told that in all probability I would be Commis-

---

[16] NA, RG 109, Telegrams sent by Confederate Secretary of War, microfilm publication M-524 [complete on one reel: hereinafter cited as M-524], f 6.

[17] July 7, 1865 to the Rev. J. J. Early (Georgetown archives).

[18] The telegram survives (NA, RG 109, Telegrams Received by the Confederate Secretary of War, M-618 [hereinafter cited as M-618], reel 2, frame 54), but the message as written is garbled: "Yes, & would not, accepted or held if it could not be efficiently filled."

[19] M-524, f 7. There had been an initial hitch over rank, as Northrop had been offered only a lieutenancy—below his old U.S. Army rank of captain (OR, ser. 1, vol. 1, 275).

[20] M-618, r 2, f 64.

[21] Davis Papers, VII, 69.

sary General. I refused when proposed and suggested others; one was found but he backed out."[22] The new government had approached Richard Griffith, an old friend of Davis from the Mississippi regiment during the Mexican War; but Griffith wanted a field command. Northrop later recalled: "I resisted for many weeks the offer of the position of Commissary General, until *ordered* to organize the Commissariat."[23]

On March 27, 1861 Secretary Walker signed the order making Northrop Acting Commissary General of Subsistence.[24] His rank was to be lieutenant colonel with monthly salary of $185, plus $45 for his twenty-five years' service in the United States Army. The permanent post was offered on April 9 to Captain William Maynadier, commander of the Frankford Arsenal near Philadelphia. But Maynadier, as a Northerner, had to refuse.[25]

So Lucius Northrop, having twice declined, was settled as chief of one of the largest bureaus in the Confederate War Department. Almost the whole of his experience in military administration lay in his service with the Dragoons by then a quarter century in the past. Yet Davis must have felt that he knew no better man to fill this vital post in 1861. He wrote later to Northrop: "I knew then, as well as now, that trading was a very small part of the qualifications required in a Commissary General, and that a military training was essentially necessary. ... I remember that you did not want to be Commissary General, and I still think it was good for the country that you did not have your own way."[26]

A glimpse of the two of them at Montgomery was to be set down soon after the war. The pseudonymous writer described himself as an official of the Confederate Government and a Catholic. Some of the writing is fanciful, but what is striking is that Northrop was seen as a generation older than Davis. In fact, Davis was the senior by three or four years; but his life to this point, whatever its difficulties, had been less wearing than Northrop's. The observer first evoked the scene at Montgomery. Then:

> With Mr. Davis walks an old gentleman, who bears so striking a family resemblance to him that one would be likely to consider him the wealthy "Uncle Joe" to whom the nephew owed so much. [Joseph Davis was in fact Jefferson's brother, but his elder by more than twenty years.] He seems an eccentric old personage, and jogs along with a limping, lazy stride. ...
>   What marked features he has—as marked as those of Jeff.— only more cadaverous. Nature made the two men like enough to be counted kinsmen; art and taste made them prefer similar colors in costume and cut of beard. But there the similarity ends. The old man's coat hangs as loosely as if it were four sizes beyond his measure, and his pants are "shapeless misfits", while his hat—such a

---

[22] July 7, 1865 to Rev. J. J. Early (Georgetown archives).

[23] September 1865 (draft) to President Andrew Johnson (Georgetown archives).

[24] *OR*, ser. IV, vol. 1, 191.

[25] Ibid., 215, 221.

[26] August 3, 1880, February 1, 1881 (Rowland, VIII, 483, 587).

shocking bad one. The younger man is a stickler for all the dress proprieties, and as scrupulously neat as the other appears slattern.

Draw near and catch an idea of their conversation. At once you perceive that the old man is a deep thinker, clear reasoner and a refined talker. Jeff. says little, but that little well. He is plainly desirous of listening to the other. Actually, they are not talking politics! From a scientific theme they have lapsed into theology. There the old man is master of the situation. He is a "pronouned" Catholic, while Jeff. is casting about for "a faith" within the wide range of Christian isms. ...They are very intimate, and certain to say much which delicacy forbids an "invited guest" to dwell on.

Turn away and learn from the first person we meet if that indeed be "Uncle Joe". And it is not "Uncle Joe" at all—only Dr. Lucius Northrop of South Carolina. Only! Why, he is the man who has just been appointed Commissary General of the C.S.A. ...[27]

---

[27] "Col C. S. Armee", "Rummaging through Rebeldom", in *The New York Citizen*, April 20, 1867, 3. The writer has been identified by William C. Davis as Charles E. L. Stuart.

CHAPTER 5

COMMISSARY GENERAL

In the history of the Confederacy to which he devoted his declining years, Jefferson Davis wrote: "To direct the production, preservation, collection, and distribution of food for the army required a man of rare capacity and character...". Summarizing Northrop's military service and experience, Davis concluded: "...To the special and general knowledge thus acquired, [he] added strong practical sense and incorruptible integrity."[1]

That last was a vital point. Opportunity for corruption in such a post was everywhere. Eliminating corruption wherever he found it became one of Northrop's preoccupations throughout the war. Charges of corruption against Subsistence Bureau agents, and especially against commissaries in the field appointed by generals and thus difficult for the Commissary General to remove, were to be frequent. Some charges were proven. But Northrop himself was never accused of personal dishonesty, and was almost certainly never guilty of it. Private integrity was the very basis for "the consciousness of rectitude" (a telling phrase exchanged repeatedly in the later correspondence of Northrop and Davis).

In 1867 the earliest Davis biographer, Frank Alfriend, wrote: "Hundreds of the most respectable gentlemen in the South willingly testify to the unimpeachable patriotism and purity of Colonel Northrop."[2] Hostile writers equally admitted it. Beauregard's biographer (and ghostwriter) Alfred Roman had hard things to say of Northrop in office, but he went out of his way to stipulate that Northrop "was known to be a man of character and education ... whose honesty none doubted".[3] Honesty was to be the new Commissary General's first principle, the cornerstone of all his policy.

His second principle was economy. Economy held a ruling place in Northrop's experience of life. Rigid economy of all things was the hard lesson he had learned from the Osage Indians. Short rations and foul water on

---

[1] *The Rise and Fall of the Confederate Government*, 2 vols. (New York: Appleton, 1881), I, 303.

[2] *The Life of Jefferson Davis* (1868), 500.

[3] *The Military Operations of General Beauregard*, 2 vols. (New York: Harper, 1884), I, 127-28.

the Plains had given him a measure of what men could and could not stand. His own austerity and the shunning of personal comfort might have been sharpened by the pain he felt more or less constantly in his wounded knee. Again as a Catholic, he did not look for ease in this life.

Northrop's hardheadedness emerged at the beginning of the war when his opinion was asked, as a doctor, of Confederate estimates for medicines during the first year of fighting. Drugs of all kinds were likely to be in short supply in the South.[4] He answered:

> ...It is to be borne in mind that our men are young and robust; that the probable seat of war is a healthful region; that but few chronic cases, which are the consumers of medicine, are to be looked for, and a whole class of medicine may be excluded; that all have homes and such cases should be promptly discharged; that the diseases of young, hearty men under exposure are almost always inflammatory and terminate in speedy death or rapid recovery...
>
> It may be assumed that $5 per head, in addition to the [hospital] rations already estimated for, will include all expenses for medicines, hospital stores, dressing, instruments, and other articles. Now, for 100,000 men, at $5 per head, $500,000; one sixth off for ten months [remaining in the fiscal year] leaves $416,000. Then deduct 25 per cent., as perhaps not more than 75,000 will be the average force during that time, $312,000.[5]

Economy indeed, but reasoned, and exactly what the new government needed to hear.

Yet the estimate took no account of the effects of large and protracted battles. Of such, Northrop had no experience. It might be that the same lacuna existed in his subsistence planning. Yet who in the first half of 1861 could truly anticipate the effects of land battles that were soon to reach a size far beyond anything ever seen on the American continent? The last large-scale fighting in the United States had been half a century ago, during the War of 1812. The oldest soldiers then alive barely recalled it. The Mexican War, in which many of the current commanders had fought, involved comparatively small forces fighting far away.

Moreover, economy was virtually enjoined by Confederate finance. The new treasury, together with the currency it handled, had been invented along with the rest of the government in February. On March 11, before Northrop was appointed, the Provisional Congress made its first appropriation for the army they had created: they set aside $912,500 for one year's subsistence.[6] However vast that sum seemed at the time, it was only a fraction of what was soon to prove necessary for troops daily increasing by dozens and hundreds.[7] Every other bureau and department felt the need for

---

[4] Northrop's friend Dr. Steuart in Maryland was already risking everything to send secret parcels of quinine and other drugs south whenever he could; and he continued to do it throughout the War as opportunity offered (Steuart family papers).

[5] *OR*, ser. IV, vol. 1, 315.

[6] Ibid., 147.

[7] See Northrop to Sec. of War Walker, April 22, 1861; *OR*, ser. IV, vol. 1, 231.

similar increases. How much could any of them expect out of a Treasury with a new and fragile currency? Rigid economy was clearly going to be needed from the outset—at some cost no doubt to the quality of army food.

Northrop's first principle as Commissary General—honesty—was self-recommending. His second principle—economy—was self-recommending in an ideal world. It might be otherwise with his third and final principle: centralization of the collection and distribution of food for the army by erecting controls over every aspect of purchase and supply he could manage.

In centralizing food supplies from the outset, military precept came together with Northrop's own experience. His education at West Point had constituted an extended lesson in authority. His military service in the southwest, his visits to Washington, courtship in Maryland, hospital training in Philadelphia, and occasional visits south to Georgia and Florida had combined to show him more of America than most of his contemporaries had ever seen; and thus enabled him to think of large territories in terms of interrelationships rather than purely local interests.

Then the crippling wound had forced a redefining of all his goals. The private insecurity thus engendered created a need to take charge of his own life to a degree not pursued by many. Success there—so important that he did not stop at his brother's financial ruin—became the final confirmation of a drive to exert personal control over everything entrusted to him. Only such complete control, said the history of Northrop's experience, could hope to prevent reversal and disaster.

Accordingly he decided from almost his first day in office to pursue what he would later characterize as "the beauty of *uniform united* action": "My system was to establish uniform principles of buying at fixed rates, never deviated from, *thus* avoiding competition and getting possession of every thing, and distributing inside, while fixing up terra culae to dwell in from within."[8]

Powerful external reasons also encouraged centralization of army's food supply in early 1861. The Commissary General's office had by definition been created to achieve some centralization. Yet there were powerful opposing forces. The entire South was permeated by a persistent affection for local arrangements and local ideas. Southern localism manifested itself in militias expanding through every Confederate state. Each state governor appointed his own militia commanders. Each commander appointed his own commissary to operate in the area of his post. Such commissaries reported only to their field commanders. So they were all outside the control of the Commissary General, and would function as licensed competitors to his bureau operations in every market. Northrop would recall the militia commissaries as fomenting both "competition and private speculation".[9]

---

[8] April 21, 1878 to Davis (Rowland, VIII, 182).
[9] December 6, 1884 to Davis (Rowland, IX, 313).

Any commissary in the field naturally favored local suppliers when he could. Many close-working relationships quickly developed. Some might be closer than high scruples should dictate. Northrop's first principle was to eradicate venality. He felt that as he must break up hoarding and speculation among farmers, so he must destroy speculation among field commissaries if and as it came within his power to do so. There, too, his most powerful weapon was centralization. But it was not a policy likely to find much popularity on any local level.

At the other end of the supply chain, competition for food among the separate military commands must also be prevented. Generals are not grocers. In rich areas, they would waste. In barren areas, they would starve. Northrop knew quite enough of the military mind to anticipate the vicious games of beggar-my-neighbor that would result from generals feeding their own troops. That could be effectively prevented only by centralizing both the collection and the distribution of food, to ensure that equivalent goods should carry the same price tag—the lowest possible price tag—throughout the Confederacy. The private interests arrayed against every phase of such standardization were certain to be formidable.

A further argument for centralizing the army's food supply lay in the current state of Southern agriculture. For many years up to the war, the lands of the South had been given over less to raising food and more to the cash crop of cotton. Huge profits from cotton had been opened by the invention of the cotton gin in 1792. From that moment, cotton began to consume more and more of the South's land. It was simply more profitable than any other crop. A big plantation could always sell its cotton for double the cost of raising it.

From time to time voices had been raised against putting all the South's eggs in one agricultural basket. But money talked, and the dominion of cotton marched on and on. Most of the fertile lands of the Deep South, where the climate was right for cotton, were relatively flat, lending themselves to vast acreages. Those flat lands were penetrated by broad and slow-flowing rivers, affording easy transport from the plantation landing to anywhere in the world. The ease of river transport had been a big factor in retarding the growth of railroads in the South.

Cotton profits readily bought food from the north and west, and still left more money for the planters to spend, entertain, trip, gamble, and drink away than any subsistence crop could earn. Let the North labor at raising food, because it couldn't raise cotton. Let the North build unhealthy mills needed to spin the cotton: let them industrialize to the further detriment of Northern life—in the Southern view.

Southern cotton extended its dominion across the Atlantic to Europe. "England's green and pleasant land" (in the words of the poet Blake) had been replaced in large parts of Lancashire and Yorkshire by "dark satanic mills". A million mill workers there, one fifth of the population, depended for their livelihoods on cotton from the American South. That dependence had been celebrated by South Carolina's Senator James Henry Hammond in

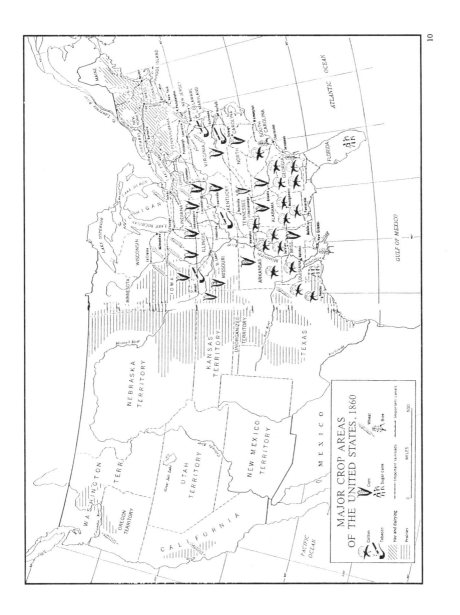

10   Paul W. Gates, *Agriculture and the Civil War* (New York: Knopf, 1965), 11-12.

a famous speech in 1858: "What would happen if no cotton were furnished for three years? I will not stop to depict what anyone can imagine, but this is certain: England would topple headlong and carry the whole civilized world with her save the South. No, you dare not make war on cotton. No power on earth dares to make war upon it. Cotton is King!"

Yet King Cotton also impoverished the South. The monoculture planting had exhausted the best lands of the Old South by 1850. (That was why Lucius Northrop could find no affordable land in South Carolina.) Cotton had then moved south and west into Alabama, Mississippi, Louisiana, Arkansas, Texas. More lands in cotton needed more slaves to work them. And thus cotton virtually revived an institution which had begun to grow moribund around 1800. The slave trade from Africa had long ago been stopped: so the price of slaves rose and rose. As the South's banking system was less and less able to cope with the large sums needed on credit for slave purchases, more and more planters borrowed from the North. Gradually the North had become a banking and even a shipping middle-man, siphoning off large volumes of cotton profits. Relations between the South and North deteriorated.[11]

Of food crops in the South, the biggest remaining in 1861 was corn. Corn was concentrated in the Confederacy's north and west—which would be just the places most vulnerable to Federal attack and plunder. Most of the rest of the South's food supply was purchased, for cotton, from the Upper Mississippi Valley: salt pork and bacon, beef, flour, hay, apples, butter, cheese. The Confederate Congress had recognized that fact in one of its earliest enactments. On February 18, 1861, in an act sealing Confederate borders against Northern goods, the Provisional Congress had specifically excepted from this prohibition all foodstuffs customarily imported from the Northwest. The food would still be admitted.[12] The question then became how long the North would allow those food staples to continue going South.

That raised the next question. Could the South's cotton economy be turned around? Could the South be made to feed itself? It was absolutely vital, in the coming conflict, that this should happen. So far as the army was concerned, Northrop meant to try. In the long run a centralizing policy for food offered the only way to a rational economy for the new Confederacy badly overmatched in both manpower and materiel.

Yet the South deeply wished not to centralize. The very name "Confederacy" suggested states less closely bound than the states of the North which remained "United". In the North, a powerful centralizing control over the citizenry had answered well to whatever remained of the Puritan heritage. Then the broadly mercantile, industrializing, middle-class interests there saw central government as providing solid advantages of tariff protection for burgeoning industries. The agrarian South wanted none of that, but only

---

[11] For an able discussion of the subject, see David L. Cohn, *The Life and Times of King Cotton* (Oxford University Press, 1956).

[12] Gates, *Agriculture and the Civil War*, 11-12.

free passage everywhere for her cotton. The South had no broadly mercantile middle class; political power there was in the hands of a privileged minority deeply concerned to preserve their position in and on their land.

Of course, the planters welcomed the new Confederate government at first. It offered a smaller, nearer, and perhaps weaker alternative to the distant power of Washington, D.C. But most Southern hearts did not really beat in time to any central government. For any central government must cut across too many entrenched private interests. Those interests would be certain to cry that the whole purpose of the war was to free the South from Yankee centralization.

The planters of 1861 did not recognize a painful paradox that faced them. The South had to sacrifice a large part of her beloved localism on the altar of centralization if she was to have any hope of vanquishing her powerfully centralized opponent. Only by centralizing, then, could the South hope to preserve much of her own private and particular local life.

War is a great educator. By 1864 many Southerners would see sense in Northrop's keystone principle of centralizing the army's food supply. But by then the best food-producing lands would be despoiled or lost; and Northrop himself would have grown exhausted and angry in a way to be understood fully perhaps only by those similarly gifted with insight but not with the diplomacy to convert others to it. The problem with centralizing Confederate army subsistence at the outbreak of the war was that it was three years ahead of public opinion in the South.

* * *

When Northrop opened the Subsistence Bureau at Montgomery in March 1861, he anticipated the appointment of a permanent Commissary General over him. Until the new man arrived, it was up to him to grasp any advantage that was offered. Northrop knew as well as anyone that the South was not feeding itself. Even the great staple of Southern diet, pork and bacon, would quickly fall short. He wrote: "The real evil is ahead. There are not hogs in the Confederacy sufficient for the Army and the larger force of plantation negroes."[13]

The South actually had more hogs *per capita* than the North, but Southern hogs were small and tough. One visitor from the North had seen them running wild through the woods of Virginia in the 1850's: "long, lank, bony, snake-headed, hairy, wild beasts". Georgia held the greatest number of hogs: "Long-legged, fleet-footed 'piney woods roosters' used to depending on Providence for food".[14] Farther west, hogs were better raised; but their population had been decimated by hog cholera in the late 1850's. Northern hogs were superior in every way, due to advances in animal husbandry there. Northern cattle were also superb. One visitor from the North dubbed Southern cows "pony cattle".[15]

---

[13] August 21, 1861 to Davis (Rowland, V, 127).

[14] Frederick Law Olmstead, *A Journey in the Seaboard Slave States* (*rpr* as *The Cotton Kingdom* (New York: Knopf, 1953), 52-53.

[15] Solon Robinson, *Facts for Farmers* (New York, 1870),14; quoted in Gates, 7.

It followed that the Confederate commissariat's first business was to purchase all the animals and meat it possibly could—especially from areas in and beyond the new nation's borderlands soon to be under enemy threat. Accordingly, as Northrop later recalled: "At Montgomery, I began to draw supplies from St. Louis, Cincinnati, and Louisville, contracted for deliveries of cattle from Kentucky. I arranged for buying and curing hogs in Tennessee and S.W. Virginia and Tidewater."[16] (Already the Atlantic coast was threatened by the United States Navy, ordered by Lincoln to begin blockading operations. The Confederacy had as yet virtually no navy of its own.)

Purchasing schemes were cobbled together—"by the action of State authorities in some cases, by the enterprise of private parties, and by [the Subsistence Bureau] through agencies of its own".[17] Out of something over three million Northern hogs made into bacon during the packing season just ended, the Confederacy acquired more than one million. That Northern bacon was to provide a basis for Confederate army subsistence during the rest of 1861 and for much of 1862.[18]

The ramshackle finances which achieved this miracle were described by a young observer (soon to join a company of volunteers in Mississippi) as "funds immediately furnished by private negotiation". Evidently the cash was borrowed on the personal surety of those making the arrangements. He continued: "...Merchants by the thousand quietly proceeded up the country and procured immense supplies of merchandise and wares, before the North had arrived at any distinct idea of our determination to be free, and of the certainty of warfare."[19]

Naturally it turned out that not all of the "merchants by the thousand" were moved by altruism. Many were speculators, and the young observer was quick to fix blame: "The Israelites, as usual, far surpassed the Gentiles in shrewdness at this auspicious moment, and laid in stocks (procured on credit) which, in almost every instance, were retailed at rates from five hundred to one thousand per cent above ordinary prices; cash being always exacted."[20] Speculation was then perceived as a Yankee and a mongrel trait. Future experience afforded Northrop ample evidence to explode any such notion of exclusivity.

---

[16] April 21, 1878 to Davis (Rowland, VIII, 181). One surviving letter illustrates operations in the spring of 1861. On May 1 Northrop wrote to Sec. of War Walker about an offer from Eli M. Bruce of Louisville to supply bacon at New Orleans and Montgomery. Northrop recommended the purchase of 2 million pounds, but only at Louisville (as cities farther south posed insuperable storage problems from climate), and only sides of bacon (as shoulders spoiled more quickly). (NA, RG 109, Letters Received by the Confederate Secretary of War, microfilm publication M-437 [hereinafter cited as M-437], r 1, ff 1262-63.)

[17] Report of January 1862 by Northrop's chief assistant, Frank Ruffin. (OR ser. IV, vol. 1, 873.)

[18] Ibid, 872-73.

[19] "An English Combatant" [identified by Robert Krick as Thomas E. Caffey], Battle Fields of the South (New York: Bradburn, 1864), 15.

[20] Ibid. The Southern dislike of Jews recently settled among them emerged in many writings of the period. There was a feeling that Jews set up near plantations as merchants in cheap liquor, clothes and trinkets were thereby encouraging slaves to steal from their masters in order to buy the new wares. Such trade also threatened the masters' control of their slaves in another way. A slave owner liked either to run his own shop or set up an arrangement with a friendly local merchant—either way controlling the purchases and dreams of his slaves. The arrival of the traders had opened alternatives which the blacks were not slow to embrace. See F. L. Olmstead, The Cotton Kingdom, 196-97.

The massive purchases of meat near and over Confederate borders used up much of the $912,500 voted by Congress for the whole year's subsistence. Yet the opportunities then offered would not come again, once the North woke up to the reality of war. Before the new session of Congress due to open on April 29, 1861, Northrop prepared a colossal estimate of army subsistence for the remaining ten months of the Confederate fiscal year: it totalled nearly five and one-half million dollars.[21]

Congress, when it convened, had other pressing business. All the War Department appropriations were put off to the last day of the session, May 21, 1861. Northrop fumed: "I wish Congress would vote an enormous money bill and then adjourn and let Jeff Davis call them when the money fails...".[22] He later recalled making the same kind of suggestion to the Secretary of the Treasury: "...In the beginning I urged Memminger to give me money without limit, that I might buy up every thing as fast as possible, but could not get it done by him."[23] Of course not. Yet before the war was half over, Northrop's wish would appear the wisest counsel in retrospect. At last on May 21, Congress voted the new subsistence request in full.

Instantly another problem reared its head. With congressional approval in hand, Northrop was still unable to extract much of the actual cash from the Treasury. Treasury Secretary C. G. Memminger was a close and careful man with a horror of inflation.[24] Attempting to head off pressures to print redundant money, he had floated a big government loan with the object of drawing privately held gold and silver into the Confederate treasury. Meanwhile, Memminger was retarding cash payments of funds actually voted by Congress in order to live within his income.

The Bureau chiefs complained loudly. Memminger proposed that they use government bonds he was just issuing to pay for present consumption. Evidently he anticipated a short war, because he urged the Secretary of War "to instruct your commissaries and quartermasters to make purchases on time and payable in bonds. Sellers constantly accept from the [individual] States, and from large factors, arrangements whereby they render in accounts once in six months, and then take time to pay in notes. Now, there is no reason that I am aware of why this cannot be done by our Government...". The Secretary of War passed these ideas to the Commissary and Quartermaster Generals "in the hope that you may be able to carry them out".[25]

Northrop tried to carry out Treasury policy, but he found farmers and suppliers everywhere reluctant to sell for bonds which would delay their actual payment for months or longer. When the Treasury would not give all the cash appropriated for army subsistence, the Commissary General had to limit his purchases. In order to guarantee continuous supplies of meat and

---

[21] April 27, 1861 (NA, RG 209, Officers).

[22] May 17, 1861 to Bishop Lynch (Wight, 463).

[23] April 21, 1878 to Davis (Rowland, VIII, 183).

[24] Burton J. Hendrick, *Statesmen of the Lost Cause* (New York: Literary Guild, 1939), 193.

[25] *OR*, ser. IV, vol. 1, 334-35.

bread, he often had to eliminate purchases of all sorts of other foods pre-scribed in Confederate Army Regulations (also copied from the United States) —fruits and vegetables, coffee, sugar, and so on—except when sellers would take bonds.

Thus it quickly came about that Subsistence Bureau rations provided on a regular basis to the Confederate armies came down to two staples. One was meat, fresh or smoked, purchased as economically as possible, and hence far from the quality well-bred young men were accustomed to at home. The other was wheat flour or corn meal with which to make bread. Northrop had decided that, in view of the quick spoilage of baked loaves in a hot climate, as well as the impossible volume such loaves would create in quan-tity shipments, the soldiers would have to become their own bakers. It proved to be one of his most controversial decisions.

Would a more experienced Commissary General have objected to such miserable constraints imposed from the outset and threatened resignation? The currency and the army were as new as the nation: all needed every possible support. Northrop himself was both trained and personally accus-tomed to expect privation in soldiering. And he was the old friend and com-rade of the new nation's President—whose honor was deeply committed to the success of the entire rickety venture.

The irony was that all this time the Confederacy had within easy reach a resource so powerful that the mere promise of it would have produced enormous sums of money straightaway. That was the cotton then growing in the fields of the South. Cotton could be promised to England and Europe, to be shipped when picked and ginned in the autumn at a time when the Lincoln blockade would still offer little hindrance. Perhaps even some of the old crop, though already committed for sale, might in the present emer-gency have been made available for immediate shipment.

One member of the Davis cabinet, Attorney General Judah Benjamin, suggested that the government purchase 100,000 bales and ship them to England. That would bring about $50 million in gold—a sum which must give the new Confederate currency greater stability than anything else, while affording broad purchases of war materiel including food. But Memminger decried it as "soup house legislation", and he convinced Davis and the rest of the cabinet against it. Instead, by withholding all cotton from England and Europe, they hoped to force those powers to intervene quickly on the Con-federate side in order to renew their supplies of cotton.

The Confederate cotton policy proved a failure. Within a year it was forcing planters to burn the South's most valuable asset wherever it came under enemy threat or trade it secretly to the enemy for whatever they wanted from the North; but not before the Commissary General had tried his hardest to get some of the cotton to barter for much-needed food. In that attempt he met nothing but obstruction for the first eighteen months of the war.

* * *

Beyond the problems of procuring food in the spring of 1861 lay the complementary problems of distributing it to the army. Many distribution problems arose directly out of the South's pattern of military organization, the state militias. Those embraced not only trained officers, but the large-spirited gentlemen raising companies and regiments for themselves to command. Each of the new regiments would have its own commissary, virtually independent of the Subsistence Bureau. The commissary in the field answered to his commanding officer, who was often in an indirect way also his employer. They all wanted to treat their new charges as well as possible. Many of the volunteers were from comfortable homes—young men with no experience of cooking or looking after themselves.

Large numbers of volunteers were being transported by railroad to training camps. Southern railroads were not too reliable, and there were many hitches and unforeseen delays. When delay came where there was no commissary arrangement in place, the new commanders improvised. Those improvisations could involve considerable cost. But when they learned of the new government Subsistence Bureau, they all sent in their bills for reimbursement. The Commissary General was to report: "A large class of accounts have been contracted by officers conducting troops from places of rendezvous and enrollment. Other commands, for which preparations of cold provisions had been made have, by delay on the [rail]roads, been provided on those occasions by special purchases absolutely necessary, generally economical. None otherwise have been observed."[26]

When an officer's bill was rejected by the Commissary General, the officer often had to pay it out of his own pocket. To a new commander, with no knowledge of the financial straight-jacket in which the Subsistence Bureau was operating, it must have seemed curmudgeonly. What a response to the flower of Southern youth gallantly springing to the defence of their beloved homelands! The Commissary General found his popularity suffering in several quarters. He wrote to Bishop Lynch in Charleston on May 17, 1861:

> I am making enemies as usual for I am refusing to pay many bills that ought never to have been contracted. Soldiers are provided with haversacks and canteens to carry cold provisions, and on forced marches to take enough for as many days as circumstances cut them off from the chance of cooking. Now because they are spared the fatigue of a march and go on [railroad] cars, their officers let them out at RR Stations 50/100 per meal.
>
> Before long War at that rate had better be settled by just seeing who has the most money, and the weakest purse submitting on a show of hands.

Yet in the main, two months into the responsibilities he had never wanted, Northrop was finding life tolerable, as he told the bishop: "I have you know great patience, so I jog along pretty well and have my own way. Mr. Walker [Secretary of War] understands me and is an upright straight forward man...".[27]

---

[26] OR, ser. IV, vol. 1, 872.

[27] Wight, 463-64.

In these early days of assembling the Confederate army, mechanisms for feeding troops in the field were primitive in the extreme. Many a new unit of volunteers found itself temporarily beyond the reach of any commissariat. It could happen even in such a city as Richmond, the capital of Virginia. There a company of eager youths had organized before their state actually seceded from the Union to join the Confederacy. Without waiting for any army arrangements, these young men had equipped themselves splendidly in Confederate grey frock-coats with fire-gilt buttons, gold braid, and calf-skin knapsacks especially imported from Paris.

They drilled every hour available, and lived at home. As soon as they were ordered to duty beyond the city, there was no commissariat to look after them. This was the recollection of twenty-one-year-old John Worsham when the company made their first march out of the city to Wilton, ten miles down the James River, on April 21, 1861: "We had nothing to eat, and did not know when or where we could get anything. One of our officers, however, had remained behind, and about eight or nine o'clock that night came up with a wagon loaded with cooked ham, bread, etc., and we had a jolly time over our supper, the first of the war." Presumably the officers or the men financed that supper themselves.

Three days later they were ordered to Fredericksburg by train. Again there was no food laid on for them: "Citizens invited us into their homes to supper." After a night encamped in the local courthouse, "we were supplied with breakfast by the citizens. We remained in the town, living in this manner several days." Then they went into camp with another company on the Fredericksburg fairgrounds, and for the first time Subsistence Bureau rations reached them. The volunteers found them crude and none too palatable:

> The men formed messes, each consisting of about ten men, each employing a negro man as cook, and we got on nicely, as we thought. The regular rations were issued to us, but in order to become accustomed by degrees to eating them, we sent the cook or some member of the mess into town, to get such articles as the market afforded.

The whole arrangement depended on well-stocked markets near at hand, and a well-to-do soldiery.

Three weeks later, in mid-May, Worsham's company was ordered away from Fredericksburg. Their extra comforts came to a sudden end:

> The cook of my mess would not leave Fredericksburg, and at Game Point we determined to cook for ourselves. I will never forget the first meal.
>
> We made a fire under the shade of a tree, made up our bread of meal (the government commenced to give it to us thus early), sliced our fat meat, and commenced to cook, and in about two minutes both meat and bread were burnt black on one side! We took them off the fire, cooled them, and tried again, and succeeded very well in burning the other side. We finally cooked everything we had and sat down on the ground to eat it.

The bread had no salt in it, no one had thought of that; the meat was so salt we could not eat it. We were disgusted, but the next day we had better success, and in a few days we got along all right.[28]

Worsham's company had been lucky to let themselves down slowly into the military mess-pot. The full shock of instant transition from civilian to military diet was experienced by nineteen-year-old Randolph McKim. He went after graduation from the University of Virginia to join General Joseph E. Johnston's camp in northwestern Virginia on July 11, 1861. That afternoon after drill, the men stacked arms and ran to the camp fires with enormous appetites, having had nothing since early breakfast. McKim was instructed by a slightly more experienced friend: "My host provided the 'dinner' by dipping a tin cup into a black camp kettle and procuring one iron spoon. He then invited me to a seat on a rock beside him and we took turns at the soup with the spoon, each also having a piece of hard-tack for his separate use. Alas! My dinner, so eagerly expected, was soon ended, for one or two spoonfuls of the greasy stuff that came out of the camp kettle completely turned my stomach...".

Reading any account of army subsistence in the field, the question must always be asked: how much prior experience had the writer of any military food? Before McKim had done a month's soldiering, he could write to his mother: "You have no idea how one gets accustomed to any sort of fare. I can now eat salt junk of the very fattest with great gusto, and drink coffee without milk, made in the company pot, and feel refreshed."[29]

In the West, veneers of civilization were thinner. Towns and markets were fewer and farther between, roads were rough and lonely, and in many places there were no railroads at all. Beyond the immediate confines of even the largest city stretched wilderness. William Watson, a young Scotsman, joined a regiment of New Orleans volunteers in April 1861. They made their first encampment on a race course outside the city, in pouring rain: "As no rations would be served out that night, a barrel of biscuits was sent...".

The New Orleans post commissary was Major Theodore Johnston. When he deigned to notice the new encampment, he opened for business on a strictly limited basis, as Watson observed:

The practice was this: An orderly sergeant made out a requisition for his company - say for 100 men for one day - flour, 100 lb.; beef, pork, or bacon, 75 lb.; coffee, 7 lb.; sugar, 14 lb., rice or pease, 6 lb.; candles, 6; soap, 2 lbs.; salt, pepper, vinegar, etc. This requisition was signed by the captain, and men were detailed to go to the commissary store to draw these rations.

The commissary takes the requisition and calls his assistant, and says to the men, "Well, you can get three-quarters ration of flour, half ration of pork, half ration of coffee, and half ration of sugar, and that is all."

The men would grumble and say, "We only got half rations yesterday."

[28] John H. Worsham, *One of Jackson's Foot Cavalry* (New York: Neale, 1912), 15-22.

[29] Randolph H. McKim, *A Soldier's Recollections* (New York: Longmans, Green, 1910), 27-28, 46.

"Can't help it, I am short of provisions, and there are other companies to serve as well as you, and all must get their share." He then sticks the requisition on the file...while he credits himself with full rations issued to 100 men as per requisition....I more than once nearly got into serious difficulty by insisting on marking on the requisition the actual quantity of provisions delivered.

Thus the commissary had a voucher for and was credited with supplying a full requisition when he had only supplied a small part of it, and he had the rest to sell for his own benefit. I have frequently known instances of a company, after giving the full requisition and being supplied with half rations on the ground that provisions were scarce, getting one of the army waggon drivers, and giving him money to go to the commissary store and purchase four or five pounds of coffee, or other necessaries, which had been kept off them, which he would obtain for money without the least trouble, and this sistem was carried on quite openly.[30]

Such abuses always became known, and almost invariably they were laid at the door of the Commissary General. But a field commissary like Major Johnston, appointed by a general, was not subject to Northrop's discipline unless he lost his position on the field. In Johnston's case that happened only after Vicksburg fell in July 1863. Then Northrop refused to reappoint him.[31]

---

[30] *Life in the Confederate Army*, 164-65.

[31] NA, RG 109, Letters Received by the Confederate Adjutant & Inspector General, microfilm publication M-474 [hereinafter cited as M-474], r 69, f 621.

CHAPTER 6

RICHMOND AND THE RAILROADS

At the time of Northrop's appointment as Acting Commissary General on March 27, 1861, the extent of Confederate territory had not yet been defined. At that moment the Confederacy consisted of just the seven states which had sent delegates to the constitutional convention a month earlier. Then Confederate troops under Beauregard captured Fort Sumter in Charleston harbor on April 14. That made a profound impression everywhere. Three days later the legislators of Virginia passed an Act of Secession to join the Confederacy. Arkansas followed on May 6, North Carolina on May 20. On that day Kentucky elected neutral status with partisans thundering on either side. Tennessee uneasily affiliated, but stopped short of seceding from the Union until late June.

Maryland, after internal dissension and fierce pressure from Washington, remained in the Union. (If she had not, the Federal capital would have been surrounded entirely by Confederate territory.) Then in the Virginia Alleghenies, small farmers were so unhappy at the secession of their state that they agitated—in the end successfully—to form a separate Union State of West Virginia. Until these loyalties were sorted out, the Confederate Government could not know the extent of what it proposed to govern.

The secession of Virginia to join the South on April 17 had deeply stirred both South and North. Within two days Federal forces impounded the river steamers belonging to the Richmond, Fredericksburg & Potomac Railroad. Those steamers had connected Washington to the company's northern railhead on the Virginia bank of the Potomac River. As soon as the Virginia Act of Secession was ratified by the state's citizens on May 23, Federal troops moved across the Potomac to occupy the town of Alexandria, Virginia opposite Washington. From that moment it was clear that Virginia, whose borders half surrounded the Federal capital, would be the immediate seat of the war.

Pressure grew to move the Confederate capital from faraway Montgomery to the Virginia state capital at Richmond—a hundred miles below Washington, and a strategic center from which to direct the South's struggle.

65

The city of Richmond extended a formal invitation, and the move was voted by the Confederate Congress. The task of transporting everything and everybody from Alabama commenced.

President Davis travelled to Richmond by rail. In his suite were his nephew Joseph Davis (soon to serve on his staff), the fire-eating Congressman Louis Wigfall, and Northrop. A few days earlier at Montgomery, Davis had foiled an attempt on his life. For that journey Northrop constituted himself bodyguard, as Davis was to recall long afterward: "...My friend and old army comrade ... was on the alert during the whole trip for the reappearance of the assassin."[1]

The Presidential party arrived safely on May 29, 1861. They were met at Richmond station by the mayor with a procession of carriages to take them all to the Spotswood Hotel (where Davis and several of his cabinet were to stay until suitable houses were prepared for them). Northrop shared his friend's carriage as cheering crowds lined the way.[2] Then they all settled down to business. On May 31 the commander of the Virginia Militia, Major General Robert E. Lee, ordered his state Commissary General and Quartermaster General each to turn over his office, staff, and files to the new national bureau chief who would succeed him.[3]

Northrop had now accepted the *fait accompli* of being permanent Commissary General. The President was to sign his promotion to the full colonelcy that went with the office on June 21 1861: then it would go to the Confederate Congress for confirmation in due course. Northrop's salary would now be $210 a month plus the extra sum for his years of U.S. Army service, a monthly allowance of forage for one horse, rent of a house and purchase of firewood.[4]

The problem was to find private accommodation in the suddenly overcrowded city, whose ordinary population of forty thousand had swollen three-fold.[5] A five-room house was made available to Northrop. It was at the corner of Grace and Fourth Streets, half a dozen blocks from the new government offices.[6] Northrop sent for his family to join him. Five rooms would be a squash for the eight of them plus servants after the comforts of their large house in Charleston. However, he kept possession of the Charleston house (and would retain it all his life, though he was never to live there again). His Charleston slaves he placed under the direction of Bishop Lynch.[7]

The War Department, along with the rest of the Confederate Government, began its Richmond life in the recently built United States Customs House, one of many Federal buildings appropriated by the Confederacy.

---

[1] Interview with J. Thomas Scharf, July 8, 1887, in *The Baltimore Sunday Herald*, July 10, 1887.

[2] *The Richmond Whig*, May 30, 1861.

[3] *OR* ser. I, vol. 51, pt. 2, 121-22.

[4] NA, RG 109, Officers: Northrop.

[5] Thomas Cooper DeLeon, *Four Years in Rebel Capitals* (Mobile: Gossip Printing Co., 1890), 86.

[6] *The Stranger's Guide and Official Directory for the City of Richmond* (Richmond: G. P. Evans, October 1863), 10.

[7] May 17, 1861 to Bishop Lynch (CDA 26 D 6).

There was never enough room, and soon the War and Navy Departments were hived off into the former Mechanics' Institute, facing on the Capital Square (in whose center stood the State Capitol, its legislative chambers now turned over to the Confederate Congress). But the Institute was still too crowded, and the Commissary General's office was moved again two doors along on Ninth Street. (By 1863 office and department had moved once more, just over a block south to 213 Main Street. Assistant Commissary offices and stores were a little southeast of that, convenient to the James River docks and to the only bridge taking troops and wagons across the river to the south.)[8]

From his new office, Northrop considered the position of things at the beginning of June 1861. Clearly the first large land engagements were going to be in northern Virginia. Federal troops were massing in Washington. Confederate troops to oppose them had been sent up to encampments in northeastern Virginia. Three Confederate strongholds had been established there.

The most important was the one closest to Washington, twenty-five miles to the southwest, at Manassas Junction. There the railroad coming out from Alexandria branched into two lines. One was the Manassas Gap line, running westward through the Bull Run and Blue Ridge Mountains, and then deep into the Shenandoah Valley. The other railroad from Manassas Junction was the Orange & Alexandria, running southwest. Sixty miles down from Manassas, there was a connection at Gordonsville to the Virginia Central, which itself ran east into Richmond and west to Tennessee.

Control of the entire rail network, which must become the backbone of Confederate transport now that the capital was at Richmond, depended on possession of Manassas Junction. Only a secure Confederate hold there stood between the Federal troops now occupying Alexandria and an easy train journey right into the Virginia heartland.

The other two Confederate strongholds in northern Virginia were also linked to railroads. One was at Aquia Creek, forty miles south of Washington on the Potomac. Aquia was the railhead of the Richmond, Fredericksburg & Potomac line. Confederate troops were posted between there and Fredericksburg to stop the Federals from boating down the Potomac and then climbing aboard the railroad to ride straight into Richmond.

The third Confederate stronghold in northern Virginia was at Harpers Ferry, up the Potomac from Washington sixty miles to the northwest. The Potomac forms Virginia's northern border with Maryland. Since Maryland remained in the Union, the Potomac marked the northern border of the Confederacy along its entire two-hundred mile length. Westward from Washington its Virginia banks ran round the top of the northern county of Loudoun, and on through gaps in the mountains nearly to the western end of Maryland.

[8]   *The Stranger's Guide*, 10; S. J. T. Moore, *Moore's Complete Civil War Guide to Richmond* (The author, 1973), 19, 38, 165; Richard M. Lee, *General Lee's City* (McLean, VA.: EPM Publications, 1987), 121-22, 126-28.

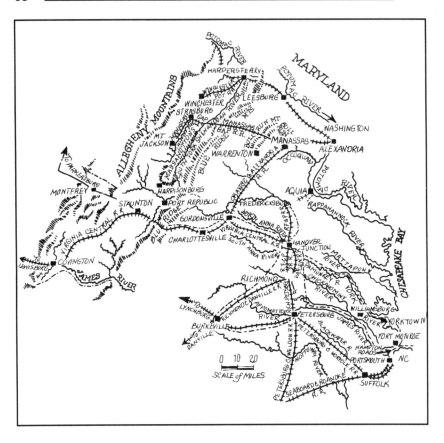

At Harpers Ferry, the Potomac receives the waters of the Shenandoah. This river, with its tributaries, stretches the length of the great valley that runs southwest between the Blue Ridge Mountains to the east and the Allegheny foothills to the west—the fertile corridor known as the Valley of Virginia. Since much of the Valley was not reached by any railroad, the Shenandoah was the highway to its interior. Whoever controlled the mouth of the Shenandoah at Harpers Ferry, therefore, might work his will in the best lands of the Valley.

Through the little town of Harpers Ferry, clinging to steep hillsides above the junction of rivers, ran the Baltimore and Ohio Railroad. Its tracks gave access eastward to Baltimore and Washington, and westward to Columbus, Cincinnati, Louisville and the northwest as then settled. Both of the B&O's extremities were Federal territory. But if the Federals gained control of that portion of the line running through Harpers Ferry, they would have access to a branch railroad running down to Winchester in the Valley of Virginia, and to the entire northern Shenandoah (called the Lower Valley).

Harpers Ferry had another importance: as an arsenal for the manufacture and distribution of guns to the United States Army. It was this arsenal that John Brown had raided in October 1859—and had been executed for his pains. Eighteen months later Harpers Ferry and its arsenal were raided again—this time by the Confederates, and with success. On April 18, the day after the Virginia Legislature vote of secession, a detachment of Virginia Militia had attacked and captured the Harpers Ferry arsenal.

The newly appointed commander of the Virginia Militia, General Robert E. Lee, had quickly sent Colonel Thomas J. Jackson (later known as "Stonewall") to hold Harpers Ferry and recruit forces in the district. Jackson had been superseded on May 23, 1861, by Joseph E. Johnston, recently resigned as Quartermaster General of the United States Army, and now a brigadier general of the Confederates. Johnston had field experience, but he was a cautious commander. He feared his Confederates could not hold Harpers Ferry. Lee pleaded with him not to move. If Harpers Ferry was lost, the South would lose control of the Upper Potomac and Lower Shenandoah Rivers, of both railroads there, and quite probably the whole northwestern Virginia. But Johnston insisted on evacuating Harpers Ferry in mid-June. He destroyed what he could of the B&O Railroad, and drew back up the Valley southwest to Winchester.

* * *

Everyone knew that railroads would be vital in the coming war. Wherever they had gone, rails and the engines and cars that ran over them had changed the face of transportation. A journey which had formerly consumed days—in tortuous navigation on rivers of unreliable currents and depths, or over roads where wheels could sink axle-deep in mire from sudden rains at any time of year—might be made on railroad cars in so many hours. By that token, the railroads would change the entire tactics and much of the strategy of war.

Yet none of the commanders or government officials on either side had any experience of railroads as instruments of war. Most railroad building had come in the years since the Mexican War, in which many of the present leaders had served; there had been no railroads in Mexico then. Both sides were going to have to learn how to use them.

The railroads of the South had been constructed largely during the 1850's in an atmosphere of feverish novelty, overnight building competition, and the hope of quick profits. The money to build them had been put together with every combination of private, local, and state finance. Lengths of individual Southern lines varied from a few miles to hundreds. The greatest concentration was near the Atlantic coast. Westward the lines thinned until they vanished in the swamps of Louisiana. A final scatter of short lines, separate from all the rest, ran around the Gulf coast in Texas.

Hasty construction had used the crudest engineering. Most lines had been built less for endurance than for quick profit. Embankments were usu-

SOUTHERN RAILROADS

TRESTLEWORK OF LIGHT WOOD DRIVEN DIRECTLY INTO SWAMPY GROUND.

ally of raw earth with little drainage. Ties were laid directly on the ground: the Southern climate was deleterious to exposed wood, whose life expectancy in such conditions might be about five years.

The wooden trestles over swamps were primitive, the spindly wooden bridges not much more, though often spanning across deep ravines at horrifying heights. General Johnston could not run the fine B&O engines captured at Harpers Ferry over his own lines because the heavier Northern locomotives "would crush the trestle-work of the Winchester road if brought upon it".[9] The trestles were also vulnerable to fire. Sparks from the woodburning engines universal in the South were such a hazard that permanent bridge-guards were employed to follow each train across the bridge with a bucket of water to put out any live cinders.

The wrought iron used for Southern rails was only about a third the weight used today in steel rails. Some Southern rails were so light as to be susceptible to breakage. All were likely to wear out after a decade's use. That meant that the earliest lines were due or overdue for total renewal at the

---

[9] Joseph E. Johnston, *Narrative of Military Operations* ... (New York: Appleton, 1874), 29. See also Jeffrey N. Lash, *Destroyer of the Iron Horse* (Kent State Univ., 1991), 11, 15. Johnston stupidly destroyed the B&O rolling stock instead of trying to reinforce his own lines to use it. He was one of the few commanders on either side with some inter-war experience of railroads, but seemed unable to apply it. Johnston's action over the B&O was the harbinger of worse to come.

THE ORANGE & ALEXANDRIA RAILROAD

NEAR MANASSAS; ONE OF THE LIFE LINES OF CONFEDERATE SUPPLY,
ALL SINGLE TRACK. A FEDERAL PHOTOGRAPH OF MARCH 1863.

time the war began—with materials which again had been imported largely from the North. The number of iron foundries in the South was tiny.

A few Southern railroads built their own engines, and some of the smaller lines had only one, and a few cars. Train speeds seldom exceeded 25 mph, and the maximum length was fifteen of the short cars of the time—especially when loaded with heavy freight. Most of the freight cars had been built basically to carry bales of cotton.

Competition made further difficulties. Teamster interests had seen to it that railroad lines did not connect directly to harbors (as at Charleston) or to each other (as at Richmond and Petersburg). Even when there was a union station physically linking two railroads, many trains could not run on one another's lines because of differing gauges. Gauge differences were defended in the South as jealously as the doctrine of States' Rights, and largely for the same reasons.

Very occasionally there was a union station joining two lines of identical gauge. When that happened, competition usually provided its own discontinuity, as Douglas Southall Freeman wrote:

> It was proverbial in Virginia that a railroad would make great effort to ascertain when a competitor's train would arrive at the junction—in order that it might be sure to have its own cars leave before that hour.
>
> As the railroads of Virginia were single-tracked, trains often had to wait on sidings for the passing of traffic from the opposite direction. In the entire State, these sidings and turnouts, including the main terminals, had a gross mileage of only sixty-eight. The R[ichmond,] F[redericksburg] & P[otomac] had no more than four and one-half miles of second track of all descriptions and locations, the Manassas Gap barely three and one-quarter, and the Orange & Alexandria a scant four miles. These three railroads, in case of invasion from the North, would be those subjected to the heaviest strain and the greatest congestion.[10]

In his excellent book, *The Railroads of the Confederacy*, Robert C. Black concludes: "The real explanation probably lies in the excessive Confederate faith in the doctrine of States Rights... No organization could appeal more logically to States Rights' doctrine than a Southern railroad company. Nearly every carrier represented a state, county, or municipal interest of the most vital sort, and it was all too easy for individualities and localities to regard any interference from Richmond as a plot in behalf of a competitor."[11]

A conference of executive officers of the various railroads had been called in late April. Secretary of War Walker asked their help in forming cooperative schemes for transporting army troops and materiel, including food. The railroad men answered that they would do their loyal best, and offer government transport at half their regular rates.[12] Instead many of them used the situation to maximize profits (in which they were supported by their backers, including everyone up to governors of states with interests to protect). At one conference after another, the rail men accomplished nothing but to raise all their rates.

A few Southern railroad men saw farther. One was the president of the Richmond, Fredericksburg & Potomac line, Peter V. Daniel, Jr. He came from a distinguished Virginia family. He was the son of a former Justice of the United States Supreme Court, and was himself an able lawyer. As soon as General Lee was appointed commander of the Virginia Militia in April 1861, Daniel had sent him a memorandum of rules for running an efficient train service in wartime. Among the recommendations were:

---

[10]   *Lee's Lieutenants*, 3 vols. (New York: Scribner, 1942), I, 683.

[11]   *The Railroads of the Confederacy* (University of North Carolina Press, 1952), 64.

[12]   April 25 and 30, 1861 (*OR* ser. IV, vol. 1, 238 and 269).

1.   Every engine and car should be removed at once from proximity to enemy lines.
2.   Every bridge must be guarded constantly, and the watchmen given tools for breaking up the track and approaches if ordered.
3.   Every railroad company should strengthen its existing flatcars for heavier loads, and should build as many new cars as possible—from the strongest materials, to the best designs.
4.   Train movements and speeds must be regulated by no one but the railroad engineers and conductors: authority divided with the military would be certain to result in collisions.[13]

All this won General Lee's endorsement. One of the suggestions was instantly carried out; before the Federal seizure of Alexandria, nearly all the cars of the Orange & Alexandria and Manassas Gap Railroads had been brought west to Manassas Junction. Several of Daniel's other suggestions called for extra manpower, money, and materials already in short supply in the South: they were implemented sporadically or not at all.

Daniel would not be discouraged. Two months later he was writing to President Davis and Secretary of War Walker about getting money and authority for laying track to connect the different railroads through the cities of Richmond and Petersburg.[14] Twice at least Daniel had interviews with Davis on the subject. Their conversations ranged from who should pay and who should borrow the sums needed all the way to how to placate the citizenry of Petersburg, who objected to the iron horse running through their fine settled neighborhoods. The most promising idea seemed to be a line construction so light that it could easily be torn out as soon as the war was over.[15]

By the time Northrop and the rest of the government arrived in Richmond at the end of May 1861, trains were already heavily involved in moving troops long distances. When troops were taken quickly over dozens and hundreds of miles, they could move overnight from a region where food was plentiful to where there might be none at all. So trains that moved soldiers often needed to move their food as well. The Subsistence Bureau would need the railroads as much as any part of the War Department.

Thus, the rails seemed to offer Northrop a powerful instrument to centralize both collection and distribution of food. Railroads might enable the Commissary General to range over much of the South, drawing from each section the best of what could be produced there. For foods produced over wide territories, railroad communication could also offer a means of controlling prices (and therefore speculation), and even perhaps of cornering entire markets to achieve the lowest costs. For foods not produced in sufficient quantities throughout the South, such as meat, a full use of the railroads might well make the difference between sustenance and starvation.

---

[13]   April 25, 1861 (*OR* ser. iv, vol. 1, 240-41).

[14]   Ibid., June 27 - July 17, 1861, 405-6, 417-18, 484-85. These plans had the strongest recommendations of Lee (Ibid., 394).

[15]   Ibid., 486.

That would certainly be the case in Virginia if Confederate troops should be heavily reinforced and then remain long in the northern counties. Those Virginia counties were rich in agriculture, especially Loudoun and Fauquier (just below it) where Manassas Junction lay. Yet a big army can soon eat the richest district bare. Then a large army, concentrated in the extreme northeast corner of the Confederacy, would be at the farthest end of every supply line. If and when that happened, sending food to them by the trains would become absolutely vital.

The question was whether the railroads could stand up to the extraordinary demands already being put on them. General Lee had written on May 31, 1861: "...The railroads are so constantly required for forwarding troops and munitions of war that the transit of other matter is necessarily delayed." [16] That the other matter being delayed could include food was clear to Northrop from the moment he looked at the position. He wasted no time in setting this view before the War Department: "From the time I came to Richmond I urged the opinion that the railroads would be found unequal to the demands that soon would be made on them, and that subsistence stores must sometimes fail to reach their destination. This terminated my duty, but not my apprehensions." [17]

Northrop was supported by Francis Gildart Ruffin (1816-1902), a Virginian who held the rank of captain in his state militia commissariat when Northrop took it over, and who was to become the Commissary General's chief assistant in Richmond. [18] Ruffin remembered:

> ...The deficiency of means of transportation ... engaged the attention of the [Subsistence] Bureau as soon as the Government was established in Richmond. This I know from having been consulted by the Commissary General on the transport problem a few days after his arrival.
>
> I at once took him to [Lewis Harvie, president of the Richmond & Danville Railroad running southwest from Richmond] who had given the subject much study, and who had projected a through freight schedule from New Orleans to Richmond. [19]

The subsistence advantage in such a plan was the access it promised to crops like sugar and molasses, grown in quantity only around the Gulf, as well as possible imports through the huge port of New Orleans.

Harvie's plan envisaged a run of five days and twenty hours over a thousand rail miles, involving ten railroad companies. To achieve it, he urged the creation of an intercompany freight car pool. That was just the sort of centralizing scheme to appeal to Northrop. Railroad interests would be certain to oppose it on many fronts, as threatening both their property and their profits.

---

[16]   *OR* ser. I, vol. 51, pt. 2, 122.

[17]   January 18, 1862 (*OR* ser. IV, vol. 1, 872).

[18]   *OR* ser. I, vol. 51, pt. 2, 40. It is wrongly claimed in G. G. Shackelford's *George Wythe Randolph and the Confederate Elite* (Univ. of Georgia, 1988, pp. 115, 123) that Ruffin was brought into Northrop's office by Randolph in 1862.

[19]   "A Chapter in Confederate History" in *The North American Review*, vol. 134 (1882), 109. See also Black, *The Railroads of the Confederacy*, 69.

Northrop took Harvie to see the Quartermaster General, in charge of army transport. That officer also opposed the plan. Quartermaster General Abraham C. Myers (1811-1894) was a professional soldier whose quartermastering methods remained those of his active service in the Mexican War. Now he gave his attention to the railroads when not preoccupied with demanding minutiae everywhere else. Moreover he was of the Southern conservative stripe that distrusted central power. He feared that any attempt at government control would irritate the railroad executives, the shareholders and Congressmen (he was quite right about that), and would cost too much (probably right about that too). He also feared the setting up of a railroad czar at the expense of his own authority. So he urged "co-operation" as a basis, and set his face against anything more drastic.[20]

Northrop tried and continued to try to circumvent the railroads' self-interest and Myers's timidity. The Commissary General was to write a steady stream of letters, memoranda, endorsements, and reports to railroad executives, to the generals, to President Davis himself. Frank Ruffin recalled ruefully in 1865: "I have myself witnessed several conversations on this subject between the Commissary General and the Secretary of War, in which he pressed his point with a persistence which, on any other subject, I should have thought pertinacity; and I take it for granted he had others of a similar character when I was not present. I have also heard conversations between himself and various members of Congress on the same subject. He had reason for the interest thus manifested."[21]

---

[20] Black, 100.
[21] *The New York Herald*, July 21, 1865, 3.

CHAPTER 7

POLICIES FOR STAPLES IN VIRGINIA

Treasury restrictions and inefficient railroads had reduced army menus in Virginia to three essentials. One was fresh beef: that must always come, in those days before refrigeration, from herds close to the camps. The second was flour or meal for making bread: that could be stored and transported if kept dry and free of pests. Finally there was the great staple of the Southern diet, pork and bacon: properly cured and properly stored, bacon could survive almost indefinitely even in Southern climates.

The bacon then in store, purchased beyond Confederate borders, might last a year or eighteen months. Beyond that, the greatest concentration of hogs and packers within the Confederacy lay in Tennessee, uncertain of loyalty, perilously close to Federal territory north and west. Moreover, Tennessee had been ravaged by hog cholera and short crops in 1858-59-60. With only one-tenth the usual production there, competition among buyers was keen and prices were high.

Army Regulations specified letting government contracts by competitive bidding. To do that in such a market would invite the unsuccessful bidders to compete (or even collude) against the government. It would, as Frank Ruffin wrote, "have wrought the double effect of raising prices upon the Government and preventing its full supply." So Northrop made a daring proposal. He would give a contract to each and every packer whose plant lay close to the Virginia & Tennessee Railroad, which practically meant all of them. The government would contract to purchase about half the bacon product of all these packers. Each was to operate only within a carefully defined district, and each would be paid $500 a month. That was "a much less sum than could have been made by the same parties operating on private account ... and the main object was to secure a full supply—cost, however important, being secondary to that."

Despite its contravention of regulations, the plan was approved by the Secretary of War to begin in early July 1861. Thus they could make use of the entire autumn and winter packing season; and at the same time, meat would be drawn continually away from borderlands under threat. To supplement the bacon, Northrop issued contracts across Virginia and Tennessee for salt beef, which would tide them over until another summer brought renewed supplies of fresh beef. It was not, as Northrop acknowledged, an ideal plan in an ideal world; he felt a heavy responsibility in recommending it.[1]

Three of the contracted packers came forward with help far beyond their contracts. That was the sort of private loyalty Northrop would elicit repeatedly in the early years of the war. J. H. Craigmiles at Cleveland, down the Tennessee Railroad near the Georgia border, advanced thousands from his own pocket to clinch bargains for the Subsistence Bureau when Treasury funds were delayed. By the beginning of 1862, Craigmiles had lent the Bureau nearly $900,000.[2]

A second packer, who owned two of the biggest plants along the line, was R. T. Wilson. He was a multimillionaire New Yorker (his daughter married Cornelius Vanderbilt) who had come south to give his loyalties to the Confederacy.[3] Wilson had a further huge packing plant at Nashville, up on the Nashville & Chattanooga line in central Tennessee. A few months later Wilson would be appointed the Bureau's cattle agent for the whole area.

Another big packery in Nashville was owned by John F. Cummings. He also had an enormous establishment at Shelbyville between Nashville and Chattanooga. Cummings was as generously helpful as the others. Soon he was commissioned major, with large duties of meat collection in the West. Thus the whole of eastern and south central Tennessee was fairly covered by government arrangements with packers.

The other ingredient in salted meat is salt. Salt is a basic necessity in the diet of animals. And curing meat, in those days before refrigeration, used up salt in quantities beyond any application in modern experience. In southern climates meat could not be kept above a day or two unless salted. Accordingly, Northrop established a virtual monopoly over the biggest producer in the South, Stuart & Buchanan at Saltville in southwest Virginia. The contract he had them sign called for as many bushels as they could produce at 75 cents. When their production was not enough, Northrop specified 10,000 bushels a month at that price. Later still more would be needed; and somehow the South's mines were able more or less to cope with these extraordinary demands.[4]

With those resources, the Commissary General could look at the immediate future with some confidence in the item of cured meat. When it was suggested that the meat ration of 3/4 pound per man per day might be re-

---

[1] *OR* ser. IV, vol. 1, 873-75. Ibid., 756-57. See also November 27, 1861.

[2] Ibid., 874.

[3] Frank G. Rankin, "Eli Metcalfe Bruce" (TS), ca. 1980: copy in possession of the writer.

[4] The only full length study is Ella Lonn's *Salt as a Factor in the Confederacy* (New York: Neale, 1933). It brings together much information and is cited by every commentator who approaches the field; but its division into topics of the author's making, more or less in despite of chronology, creates a veritable salt-mine for the reader.

duced, Northrop wrote to the Secretary of War on June 20, 1861: "...Experience has proved that men will eat their three fourths of a pound, and though negroes do well on less, and the peasantry of Europe on greatly less, and the Ryots of India with none, our people *must* have enough or become discontented." He expected that there would be "a sufficiency" for the Confederate soldiery.[5]

In June 1861 that expectation might have seemed justified even with numbers of men increasing every week. A month later for instance, on the eve of the first great battle of the war, Secretary Walker informed Northrop of the recruitment of four hundred additional regiments. That translated into an added 337,600 mouths to feed.[6] Before many months had passed, circumstances would force the Commissary General to change his mind about reducing the meat ration.

The second staple was flour. When Northrop arrived in Richmond, he found a store of very fine flour previously purchased by the Virginia Militia commissariat. It had been ground from wheat of the poor harvest of 1860, and consequently its cost had ranged from $8.16 to $9.21 a barrel.[7] In the spring of 1861, by contrast, the fields of the South were bursting with grain. That had been noted by President Davis in his address to Congress at the end of April: "A bounteous Providence cheers us with the promise of abundant crops. The fields of grain which will within a few weeks be ready for the sickle give assurance of the amplest supply of food...".[8]

To the Commissary General, the bounty of Providence translated into lower flour prices as soon as the new crop came to milling. He wanted to move in and buy the entire crop, since no one could tell when the Confederacy might have another such harvest. Treasury cash was not there. So again Northrop looked for some centralizing plan to overcome the constraints.[9] The plan evolved was complex.

The price of flour in any district of Virginia was traditionally fixed by the market price in the nearest city—Richmond, Alexandria, Washington, and so on. At each city, market prices were established for the season by quantities available of each grade, and the demand. Any flour producer of the district could receive the going price by bringing his flour to the district market.

Thus flour prices in Virginia always included the cost of transport to the market. If someone went direct to a country mill, flour ought to be available at the district market price less the cost of shipping it from mill to market. And so it came about that the closer to a city market a mill lay, the more its flour would bring.

---

[5]   M-437, r 1, ff 1422-23.

[6]   Ibid., r 5, ff 793-4.

[7]   Northrop, "Memoranda in relation to the purchase of flour", August 21, 1861 (Huntington Library, Eldridge Coll. Box 43; in *Davis Papers, VII*, 300, with one inaccuracy).

[8]   Rowland, V, 84.

[9]   *OR* ser. IV, vol. 1, 876-77.

The millers of northeastern Virginia had been accustomed to take their flour to markets in Washington, Alexandria, and even Baltimore. All were now in enemy hands. Some of the local millers might still be tempted to ship to those places if prices were good, despite the fact that their flour would then be lost to the South. The Virginia Militia had been doing what it could to prevent such exporting.[10] When Northrop arrived in Richmond at the end of May, he quickly persuaded the Virginia authorities to put an embargo on private shipments of flour out of the state.

The Commissary General then sought advice about finding some means to control Virginia flour markets without the money to buy all of the new crop. He consulted James Crenshaw, a proprietor in the great Richmond flour mills of Haxall, Crenshaw & Co.[11] Crenshaw had in fact served as Acting Commissary General of the Virginia Militia from the state's secession until the post could be filled by a regular soldier.[12] He became Northrop's adviser for flour, and almost certainly helped to shape the plan that Northrop evolved.

Richmond itself functioned as the flour market for millers south of the Alexandria district. Richmond flour prices had always been lower than farther north. That became the linch-pin of the Northrop plan. It was to be described by an observer close to the scene:

> ...The Commissary General considered that, as the farmers of [northeastern Virginia] had been deprived of their usual market in Alexandria, Washington, and Baltimore and compelled to send their produce to Richmond, they were only entitled to receive for that produce, when sold to the army, the Richmond price less the cost of sending it to Richmond from the place of production. He argued, for instance, that as the miller in Loudoun, if he sent his flour to Richmond, would have to pay, say, one dollar per barrel for the carriage, he should be content to sell it at Manassas or Centerville [the nearest village to Manassas Junction] for the Richmond price, less that charge.
>
> The farmers, on the other hand, contended that they were entitled to some benefit for having supplies so near the army. They said that if they took a barrel of flour to Richmond and paid a dollar for carriage, the Commissary Department buying that flour in Richmond would have to pay the same price to get it back to Manassas,

---

[10] On May 10 the militia commander at Manassas, Philip St. George Cocke, had ordered the colonel at the town of Leesburg in Loudoun County, Eppa Hunton, to seize flour at a nearby mill on the Potomac, inform the commissary at Manassas, and stop all supplies from going down the river to Washington (*OR* ser. I, vol. 51, pt. 2, 79).

[11] Three Crenshaw brothers were partners in the mills: Lewis Dabney Crenshaw (1817-1875), William Graves Crenshaw (1824-1897), and James Richard Crenshaw (1830-1891). There has been some confusion over their Christian names and careers. It may have started when Freeman's proofreader misread "Jas." as "Jos." (*R. E. Lee*, I, 640). The book's index then created a "Maj. Joseph R. Crenshaw", attributing to this ghost the military career of William (Ibid., II, 148). The confusion was compounded by Edward Younger in editing *Inside the Confederate Government: The Diary of R. G. H. Kean* (OUP, 1957). He cites the mill owners as "W. I. and Joseph R. Crenshaw" (38 *n* 11). The correct name "James" is to be found in many references throughout the *Official Records*; the earliest is cited in the following footnote.

[12] *OR* ser. I, vol. 52, pt. 2, 22.

and that the Department would lose nothing if it paid at Manassas, for a barrel of flour delivered there by the neighboring producer, the full Richmond price, inasmuch as it would thereby save the cost of transportation from Richmond to Manassas.[13]

On the surface it seemed a reasonable argument. Yet if acceded to, it would instantly set a precedent of paying more for any food that happened to lie close to Confederate positions. Every military movement would then be accompanied by rising prices. Extortion and speculation would flourish, with a financial motive established for anyone who had knowledge of troop movements and strategy to betray them.

Northrop saw no reason to share those reflections with the farmers and millers of northeastern Virginia. As some of them worked hand-in-glove with Confederate army commissaries in the field, he could not discuss his reasons with the commissaries either—especially the one at Manassas, where troops were rapidly concentrating. Could Northrop have found some diplomatic way of placating them to secure their cooperation? His own character and West Point training would probably have strangled such a notion at birth. Yet farmers and millers are not soldiers to be ordered about at will; and the Virginia citizenry were not prepared for any such abridgement of their rights this early in the struggle for their independence.

So Northrop established three big flour contracts in different quarters of Virginia—"ruling contracts" he called them. One was with a firm at Lynchburg, a hundred miles west of Richmond by rail. Another was at Fredericksburg, sixty miles north of Richmond (and less than that from Alexandria). Each contract called for 20,000 barrels of new flour to come to the Subsistence Bureau in Richmond at $5.00 each. Both meant heavy use of railroads; that seemed a lesser evil than allowing rapacious locals to wrest away control of these crucial supplies at the beginning. Moreover, as both places might lie under enemy threat (Lynchburg via the Valley of Virginia), buying their flour withdrew it from danger.[14]

The third "ruling contract" was the keystone of the scheme. It was with Crenshaw's own firm, Haxall, Crenshaw & Co. The Crenshaws were leading millers of Richmond, solid citizens who also owned not only the Spotswood Hotel but the mansion being readied for President Davis and his family. Their contract called for 25,000 barrels at $5.25, the higher price reflecting the fact that the flour was already at its market city. The contract provided for a further 25,000 barrels, the price of which could rise by 50 cents a barrel with each rise of 10 cents a bushel of wheat.[15]

---

[13] Charles G. Marshall, reporting information given him later by Major Robert G. Cole, chief commissary at Manassas from December 1861: from the collection of Marshall's papers edited by Maj. Gen. Sir Frederick Maurice under the title *An Aide-de-Camp of Lee* (Boston: Little Brown, 1927), 45-46.

[14] Northrop to Davis, February 11, 1880 (Tulane Univ. New Orleans, Louisiana Historical Association: Jefferson Davis Papers [herein after cited as Tulane], r 22, ff 747-52).

[15] *OR* ser. IV, vol. 1, 877.

The Commissary General published these ruling contracts widely, hoping they would establish firm prices throughout the state and bring the farmers and millers near Manassas to heel. Pointing to the large Haxall, Crenshaw mills close to his office, Northrop was reported to say: "Here are my magazines; I will bring those gentlemen to terms."

The man who remembered those words was a future commissary at Manassas, Major Robert G. Cole. Cole was certain that Northrop's words made his own job more difficult, and he was to convey his sentiments some months later to a staff aide to General Lee, Charles Marshall. Marshall would describe Northrop as "a man of no experience in business, but of great self-consequence". (Northrop could strike people that way, especially when promulgating orders he knew were important but was less sure of their working.) Marshall also reflected some Richmond newspaper speculation that James Crenshaw stood to profit from his own advice to the Commissary General.[16] Other annoyed parties were flour producers who did not hold ruling contracts, and army commissaries in the field ordered suddenly not to buy flour from their customary suppliers close to them.

Northrop realized that the flour plan, like the plan for salted meat, was far from perfect. Its weakest link was likely to be the railroads: flour contracted at both Lynchburg and Fredericksburg must first be shipped to Richmond, and thence to wherever it was needed. But where was an alternative? Allow the commissaries of separate field commands to run up flour prices against themselves and each other—enfranchising speculation and extortion amongst their own suppliers, with abundant (and therefore cheap) wheat then in the fields about to be harvested? Confess the weakness of the new Confederate currency at the outset of the war before all the world? Assume that Southern railroads would fail from the beginning, and pass up the clearest chance to try to make them work together for the government? Nobody then or later was ever to propose any real alternative to the Northrop plan.

In June 1861 Northrop ordered field commissaries everywhere in Virginia to stop making local purchases of old flour at high rates. Until the new crop was available, the Bureau would ship out the old flour in store from the Virginia Militia purchase. And one other anticipated difficulty was provided for. When the abundant new wheat came in, prices were expected to fall to 68 or 70 cents a bushel. If that happened, farmers might be tempted to hoard their crops against the hope of a rise in price towards winter. So the Subsistence Bureau announced that it would pay $1.00 a bushel anywhere and everywhere, as Northrop wrote, "to induce thrashing: otherwise little would have been brought to the mills".[17] Despite all the difficulties, large stocks of flour began to pour into Bureau stores in Richmond.

---

[16] Marshall, *An Aide-de-Camp of Lee*, 46-47. See below pp. 124, 182-83.

[17] January 26, 1881 to Davis (Rowland, VIII, 585). See also Ruffin's report of January 1862 (*OR* ser. IV, vol. 1, 877). The complexities of arriving at the "market price" for different grades of flour when no free market any longer operated were set out at length in April 1863 by James Crenshaw (M-437, r 91, ff 461-78).

In the Confederate West there was hardly a market structure on which to build such a scheme. One letter shows Northrop seeking help where he could find it. An inquiry had come from Mississippi Colonel William T. Withers, at Clarksville, Tennessee near the border with Kentucky. Colonel Withers wanted to know how much of the big wheat crop anticipated there he ought to draw from the surrounding country, how much to pay, and where to send the milled flour for storage. The political situation there was volatile, with loyalties everywhere fiercely divided.

Northrop's answer on July 30, 1861 sketched his earliest known flour plan outside of Virginia. Each region should supply the Confederate troops stationed in it, at prices controlled by the market in Nashville: "then if the sellers will not come down to the prices at which it can be manufactured and transported to points of deposit, gather in Kentucky." The Commissary General also sought Withers's help over bacon. He sounded as if he were suggesting trade over Confederate borders without quite saying so: "Now my dear General [sic] I address you on a subject of interest—Bacon for use till curing time. Can you not correspond and have quantities brought and deposited at Nashville? Reply at once and tell me what funds can do. I could if driven to it get starting exchange-arrange with [John T.] Shaaff", the commissary at Nashville.[18]

The third staple was fresh beef. The supply of cattle depended on arrangements made from day to day in the field, and it was difficult to exert any tight control. All the Bureau could do was to keep an eye on the numbers of cattle accumulated by each command. Ruffin was to report of those early months: "Whenever it has been practicable, the commanders of the different forces have not been interfered with in obtaining fresh beef in their several bounds. As a general rule, local officers can make such purchases as well as this department and with more satisfaction to the generals."[19] Those words seemed already to hold a world of weary experience. But before long the actions of the general at Manassas would force a tightening of this control as well.

Beyond the staples of beef, flour, and pork, Northrop had to order commissaries in the field not to buy other items in the ration unless for bonds—vegetables, fruits, lard, rice, sugar, molasses, coffee, vinegar, etc. The commissaries and their troops, he said, must "graze on want in respect of rice and sugar which were not essential, because parties would not receive Treasury bonds...".[20] Complaints were immediate and vociferous. Never in the history of army procurement, it was claimed, had commissaries been prohibited from buying rations that were for sale right in front of them as many items were, in the districts around Manassas. Why must they accept such prohibition from this new Commissary General? It must be mere red tape.

---

[18] NA, RG 109, Officers. Surviving records I have seen contain nothing further about these plans. Undoubtedly there would have been something in the Bureau files burnt at Richmond in 1865.

[19] OR ser. IV, vol. 1, 875-76.

[20] January 25, 1881 to Davis (Rowland, VIII, 585). In this letter Northrop recalled writing to Manassas in July 1861: Ibid., 457, in a letter of May 23, 1880, he recalled the date of writing as June 1861.

* * *

Government bonds were being refused by potential suppliers all over the South. Sometimes the Treasury sent bonds even when cash had been specified for staples by the Bureau. Widespread reports of troubles in making vital food purchases were soon coming in from the storehouses and distribution facilities Northrop was setting up at key points throughout the country. By August 19, 1861 he would write to Secretary Walker:

> The efforts of this Department, hitherto successful, will be abortive unless funds of a character such as will be received by dealers are furnished by the Treasury.
>
> The Agent of this Department in Atlanta, Mr. Shackelford, has industriously collected from the Counties around much salt meat and other articles, always and everywhere cash transactions. He has acted on the credit of this Government, and I made a requisition for $62,678.99 on the 13th of August in "Treasury Notes"—which are alone available for such articles; *bonds* have been sent to him, and he can make no further purchases.
>
> Capt. Shaaff, in charge of the Depot at Nashville, writes that only bankable funds are received for provisions, and that he has lost Coffee, already agreed upon, because he could not use bonds, which are not bankable. ...
>
> Capt. Palfrey, in New Orleans, states that the credit of the Government is suffering, and that he has been required by persons who have sold supplies [to him] to return in kind what remains unused, as part payment of their bills; for the present the requisition of $110,000, current funds alone, will suffice at that point, and is all important.
>
> The alleged reason for issue of bonds in lieu of Treasury notes is that there is some difficulty in the engraving.[21]

The Secretary of War sent that letter to the Treasury with his urgent endorsement. Secretary Memminger professed surprise: he had thought bonds "just the thing for Atlanta". Secretary Walker replied with a specific demand for $12 million cash on behalf of the Commissary General.[22] Then Memminger was forced to call the Commissary and Quartermaster Generals into his office and confess his difficulty. If paper money were issued too lavishly, it would fatally undermine the entire currency. Northrop tried his best to explain to those who depended on him without revealing too much: "... Money must not be called for too fast, but in small amounts, &c."[23]

Everything at the Treasury was being done to retard paying out both money and bonds. The delays in getting either into an agent's hands were described by Northrop in another letter to Secretary Walker five days later: "A requisition being made from this office for an officer [who had already lost time in communicating with Richmond]—it goes through the War &

---

[21] M-437, r 7, ff 411-12.

[22] *OR* ser. IV, vol. 1, 599.

[23] October 7, 1861 to Gen J. M. Withers (*OR* ser. I, vol. 52, pt. 2, 175). For Memminger's views on currency at this time, see his letter of October 15, 1861 to the Commissioners for the Confederate Produce Loan (*OR* ser. IV, vol. 1, 689-91).

Treasury Depts and a Warrant is sent to the officer: if he happens not to be where is an Asst. Treasurer, he has to endorse the warrant and send back to the Treasurer [in Richmond] before the notes are sent to him—or bonds."[24] There was no safety advantage in all this: funds could be lost in transit just as easily *after* the officer's endorsement was received in Richmond as before it was received. The sole visible advantage was Treasury delay. Apparently Memminger chose not to see that his actions were hobbling procurement in ways whose effects would be certain to accumulate.

Complaint brought no amelioration. Northrop wrote again to the Secretary of War in October: "The Secretary of Treasury declines giving precedence to this warrant [from Atlanta] unless authorized by a statement from yourself of its necessity... Maj. Shackelford's creditors are becoming clamorous and the credit of the Government is suffering."[25] The same protest was to be repeated many times over.[26]

Complaints from Manassas, where the number of troops was increasing rapidly, reached a crescendo. They focused on the lack of fresh vegetables in summer, when the vegetables lay in fields all around them. Northrop appointed a special agent to go there and try to make some arrangement consistent with Treasury restrictions.[27] Yet little of their government's currency troubles could be explained to the soldiers whose rations were short, or defective, or both, week after week. It began to be said that the Commissary General was a harsh man. Many started to question his competence. Northrop bore the complaints more or less in silence. His own character and his West Point training enjoined that.

---

[24] M-437, r 7, ff 1043-46.

[25] Ibid., 12, f 1017.

[26] See for instance Northrop's endorsement of April 23, 1862 on an application from the chief commissary of Tennessee to purchase much-needed bacon for cash (Ibid., r 74, ff 437-38).

[27] Northrop to Davis, August 21, 1861 (Huntington Library, Eldridge Coll., Box 43).

CHAPTER 8

MANASSAS

The concentration of Confederate troops at Manassas Junction had begun early in May 1861.[1] On May 22 Robert E. Lee, commander of the Virginia Militia, issued a guiding order to the sub-commander at Manassas: "...The policy of the State at present is strictly defensive. No attack, or provocation for attack will therefore be given, but every attack resisted to the extent of your means."[2] The policy of limiting Southern arms to defence had wide approval in 1861. Having asked only to depart in peace, the Southern states should pursue no aggression but only defend their own land. When the Davis government reached Richmond, that policy was continued and broadened.

The strategy of defence, and wide dispersion of troops to accomplish it, was duly conveyed to Brigadier General Pierre G. T. Beauregard when he was sent to Manassas at the beginning of June 1861. Beauregard's official biographer (who worked under his subject's eye) was to assert that these orders embarrassed the new commander: "To obey them implicitly was clearly an impossibility under the circumstances. They were calculated to destroy every vestige of discretion on the part of the commanding general...".[3]

Beauregard was forty-three, of Creole origin. His first language was French, which he had used at West Point to study the classics of Napoleonic strategy in their original texts. From an early age he worshipped Napoleon. Yet despite some distinguished service at lower ranks in the Mexican War, Beauregard had never yet commanded large forces on the field. He was (in the words of Douglas Southall Freeman) "an admirable actor in a martial role", displaying "great self-confidence on the basis of limited experience with troops".[4] His opening small victory of the war at Fort Sumter had caused

---

[1]   See Lee's orders and letters of May 6, 10, and 15 to Col. Philip St. G. Cocke, commanding the militia detachment at Culpeper, in *The Wartime Papers of R. E. Lee,* ed. Clifford Dowdey and Louis H. Manarin (New York: Bramhall House, 1961), 19-20, 23, 30.

[2]   *The Wartime Papers of R. E. Lee,* 33.

[3]   Roman, *The Military Operations of General Beauregard,* I, 67-68. It is generally accepted that Beauregard himself wrote much of the book.

[4]   *Lee's Lieutenants,* I, xxxii.

his popularity with the Southern public to soar. That was undoubtedly a factor in his selection (by President Davis, Adjutant General Samuel Cooper, and the President's military adviser General Robert E. Lee) to command at Manassas. Arriving there on June 1, 1861, Beauregard at once began to lick the amorphous groups of raw recruits into coherent military shape.

The new commander inherited a staff of officers at Manassas. The assistant adjutant general there was Thomas Jordan. Another West Pointer, he had served for years as a United States Army quartermaster until his resignation as recently as May 21. Appointed lieutenant colonel, the ambitious Jordan proceeded to attach himself to Beauregard with complete success.[5] The quartermaster at Manassas was Major William L. Cabell, also a graduate of West Point, and also recently resigned from the United States quartermasters. The commissary was Captain William H. Fowle, who had been at his post since the first Confederate concentration at Manassas.[6] He had established a useful network of suppliers in the district, from whom he easily drew adequate supplies for all the troops at Manassas including new arrivals.

The number of effective troops at Manassas, Beauregard reported on June 3, 1861, was about 6,000. To defend the place adequately, however, would require "not less than 10 to 15,000 men". Unless those could be provided promptly, he would have two alternatives: to retire toward Richmond on the approach of the enemy; "... or I must march to meet him at one of the said fords, to sell our lives as dearly as practicable."[7] That was the sort of Gallic rhetoric that made Beauregard a favorite with the press. It also suggested that the new general was thinking in terms of a large offensive, in spite of his basic orders.

If Beauregard could be heavily reinforced at Manassas, the way should be open to devise a grand offensive strategy in the Napoleonic mold. At Winchester, 60 miles away, sat Brigadier General Joseph E. Johnston with thousands of troops. If Johnston brought this whole force by rail to join Beauregard at Manassas, their combined strength could probably defeat the largest Federal army coming out of Washington. Then the way would be open for the combined Confederates to roll forward and retake Alexandria, overlooking Washington. He would propose it to the President.

Before that, the field at Manassas must be quietly prepared—quietly because the whole scheme contradicted the defensive strategy. Beauregard's first step "was to order the collection of wagons and twenty-five days' ra-

---

[5] Roman claimed (I, 66) that it was Jordan who had first drawn attention to the strategic importance of Manassas Junction for a Confederate stronghold. In view of the Virginia militia concentration begun there at least a fortnight before Jordan's resignation from the U.S. Army, the claim seems difficult to understand.

[6] Fowle is named as the commissary at Manassas in Cocke's letter of May 10, 1861 to Hunton (above, p. 79 n. 10). Long afterwards Frank Ruffin was to write: "...Joe Johnston & Beauregard both permitted themselves to be fooled by speculators like Fowle of Alexandria, who got himself appointed commissary" (November 5, 1891 to Gen. Bradley Johnson, in Francis Gildart Ruffin Papers, Virginia Historical Society, Richmond, Va.).

[7] Roman, I, 70.

tions for about twenty thousand men."[8] When Cabell could not get together enough wagons, Beauregard did not hesitate. Ignoring Quartermaster General Abraham C. Myers, he appointed a special colonel "... charged with the duty of procuring the necessary means of transportation for this command. ... He is further authorized to require of all officers and agents in the Quartermaster's Department, at any post in that department, efficient assistance in the prompt execution and accomplishment of these orders." What were other commanders or government agents supposed to do if Beauregard's colonel began commandeering their wagons? Or even their trains? It sounded as if Beauregard intended to do just that.

Meanwhile Commissary Fowle was directed to cooperate with the quartermasters in drawing "all their supplies of forage, grain, and provisions from the fertile country...".[9] What Beauregard's "25 days' rations for about 20,000 men" amounted to was the collection and constant storage of half a million daily rations. Although that was a staggering order to place with a field commissary, living was easy in summertime Virginia where cattle were abundant and flour available: Fowle ought to be able to do it.

In placing this grand order, however, Beauregard overlooked a vital point. If his field commissary succeeded in collecting such a pile of food, where could it be stored? There were no big storehouses anywhere within reach. Before the concentration of troops had begun a month before, Manassas had been nothing but a lonely fork of railroad tracks with a station. A new recruit to Beauregard's army, arriving one night, saw it thus:

> I could scarcely believe that this was a great military dépôt, there being nothing within my range of vision to indicate that such was the fact. The station itself was a low, one-storied building, about seventy-five feet in length, with bales and boxes scattered about; a house of refreshment close by was uninviting, and except one or two small cottages scattered here and there, naught was to be seen. ... A trooper or two would occasionally go jingling past in the direction of a cottage a few hundred yards in advance; and from the lights in windows, and groups seated around camp-fires in the orchard, I learned that the dwelling was General Beauregard's headquarters.[10]

Such an out-of-the-way place could not cope with vast accumulations of food. Dealing with such problems of collection and storage was a chief reason for the existence of the Subsistence Bureau in Richmond; but Beauregard had not communicated with them.

---

[8]   June 6, 1861 (Roman, I, 433-34).

[9]   Roman, I, 71-72. Roman in 1884 described the plan as aiming to drain the country of food between the Confederates and their enemies, adding that it was "most strenuously opposed by...Colonel Northrop". Collecting food in front of the enemy was in fact Northrop's policy; it has already been shown in foregoing pages, and on April 22, 1862 Northrop wrote: "My policy has always been to draw supplies from the front" (Endorsement on a letter from S.Schooler, M-437, r 70, f 886). When Beauregard first published his own claim in *The Century Magazine* in 1884, Davis wrote to Northrop: "I clearly remember your efforts to have the wants of the Army of Northern Virginia supplied from the country in front of it...and how you were obstructed by Beauregard and Johnston, but now with shameless disregard of the fact, Beauregard claims to have urged that course in vain upon you..." (Rowland, IX, 301).

[10]   [Caffey], *Battle-Fields of the South*, 19. Caffey dated his arrival at Manassas as May 1, 1861: that was probably a month in error, as Beauregard himself arrived only on June 1.

Northrop was later to write of Beauregard and Johnston before they went to Manassas: "I never had a difference with either of these men...".[11] Yet he had aired an unfavorable view of Beauregard already: "My estimate of the Hero of Sumter was announced in Montgomery on reading his report."[12] Northrop recalled making one attempt to approach Beauregard and his commissary at Manassas and take them into his confidence over the absence of rice: "I wrote to Fowle that the necessity of introducing the use of bonds, and reserving currency for essentials, required me to graze on want of the minor article *rice* until it could be thus bought... I made similar explanation to Bgd."[13] There is no record of any response.

Meanwhile, Beauregard had sent his grand strategy to the President. Looked at with hindsight, the basic idea of offence was good. An immediate combination might conceivably have offered the South a winning strategy at the beginning of the war. The South's power was every way inferior to her opponent's potential. Only at that moment the North was hardly organized; it had not yet occurred to most Northerners that armed conflict could reach their homes. The South by contrast was defending its own land. The best hope of a better-prepared inferior could well lie in the quickest knock-out blow before the slower superior gathered its force.

When Beauregard's plan was examined by Davis and his advisers in Richmond, however, they found it full of loopholes and question marks. How could the single-track railroad cope with moving Johnston's thousands to Manassas Junction almost overnight? And if it could, what then? Johnston out-ranked Beauregard as a general—though Beauregard's letter studiously ignored that point. If Johnston came to Manassas, would he not then command? Was Beauregard prepared for that? There was nothing in his letter to suggest it. Beyond all those questions lay what seemed to Davis a fatal flaw: removing Johnston from the Shenandoah Valley would uncover Beauregard's own rear. In that case, Davis answered Beauregard on June 13, 1861, "your possession [of Arlington Heights and Alexandria], if acquired, would be both brief and fruitless."[14]

Beauregard was not deterred. He looked southeast to the Confederate force guarding Aquia Creek under Brigadier General Theophilus Holmes. It seems likely that Beauregard then wrote directly to Holmes.[15] That was entirely irregular, because policy communications between separate command-

---

[11] January 26, 1881 to Davis (Rowland, VIII, 585).

[12] November 14, 1863 to Bishop Lynch (Wight, 467).

[13] March 8, 1880 to Davis (Tulane: Rowland's transcript in his VIII, 445 is defective).

[14] Roman, I, 77-78.

[15] On June 15, 1861 Holmes wrote to Adjutant General Cooper, suggesting that most of the Aquia and Fredericksburg force be sent to Manassas. As this letter appears only in Roman's *Beauregard* (I, 443), it seems that a copy of it was sent to Beauregard and remained with his papers. If so, the conclusion is nearly inescapable that Beauregard had done with Holmes what he did with Johnston a month later—instituted a secret and irregular correspondence (see below, p. 94). Holmes was never the general to launch such a proposal on his own.

ers were always to be made through government executive. Moreover, moving Holmes would uncover Beauregard's right, as well as opening a land and railroad route for the Federals to come down on Richmond. Again Beauregard's strategy met rejection. Again he went back to his drawing board.

*   *   *

By the beginning of July 1861 many of Northrop's policies limiting direct purchases of food on the field were being felt. Commanders and their commissaries saw these policies as intrusive and invasive. Fowle at Manassas continued to collect enormous numbers of beef cattle. To anyone not privy to Beauregard's food order, those numbers exceeded what was prudent to keep ahead at such an exposed place for the men actually there or expected in any normal way. Knowledge of that large collection reached Northrop in Richmond, but without any explanation. Northrop issued a special order directing Fowle to keep only enough cattle on hand to supply his visible needs. Fowle took no notice.

Then Northrop learned the details of a contract Fowle had made to butcher the meat at Manassas. The contract, with one Robert Beverley, specified that the butcher was to receive in payment the whole of the so-called "fifth quarter" from every animal—the products of hides and hooves. Those products were needed by the Quartermaster Bureau. Tallow made candles. Oil lubricated wheels and guns. Hides made saddles, bridles, and a whole range of leather goods. Accordingly Northrop wanted to stop paying away the "fifth quarter"—"worth $12 each in money value then, but invaluable to us as we were situated."[16]

He sought the advice of his Virginia assistant Frank Ruffin. Ruffin suggested that they consult with Burr Powell Noland (1818-1902), a leading gentleman farmer near Middleburg. That was in the center of the richest cattle country in Virginia, close to the border between Loudoun and Fauquier Counties, only twenty miles from Manassas. Noland was from an old Virginia family; he represented Loudoun in the Virginia House of Delegates; and he held the rank of captain in the State Militia. He knew all the influential families of the district and was related to several. He also knew a wide range of tradesmen—doubtless including butchers who might be persuaded to offer better bargains over the "fifth quarter". Northrop asked Ruffin to go up to Manassas, meet Noland there, and try to bring Fowle's cattle arrangements under some control.

Ruffin met Noland there on July 5.[17] Noland professed himself "ready to supply *any number* of beeves", and to secure economical butchering.[18] Ruffin put the better offer to Fowle. Fowle declined it. In a paper written at Northrop's request in 1864, Ruffin recalled:

---

[16] March 8, 1880 to Davis (Rowland, VIII, 445).

[17] The date of the visit is established in Northrop to Davis, April 27, 1864 (Didier, "The Scape-Goat of the Confederacy", II, 9).

[18] Northrop, "The Confederate Commissariat at Manassas", in *Battles and Leaders of the Civil War* (New York: Century Co., 1884-7), I, 261.

> ...When I told Capt:Fowle the purpose of my visit, he remonstrated against any change, asserting that he had made the very best arrangements that could be made, though he gave no reason for his opinion, notwithstanding I requested him to do so—.

The readiest explanation to anyone not privy to Beauregard's order might be that Fowle had some private interest with his chosen supplier. Ruffin continued:

> He went so far as to say that he could not consent to any change; and when I asked him if I was to understand him as refusing to obey an order of the Commissary General, he replied: "No: but he wished to be heard before any change was made." To this I replied that he should have the opportunity of a hearing, but he must avail himself of it in a reasonable time.[19]

No explanation came from Manassas even then.

Ruffin also discovered that Fowle had been buying flour above the Commissary General's prices. The very next day, July 6, Northrop sent out a directive: "Fowle was ordered not to make purchases at the rates he had been buying ($5.60 and $6.00) when [the new] wheat was worth 70 cents— to refer prices to me before he bought—to get corn meal to the utmost extent [as a delaying substitute before the new wheat crop was milled], and that when he could not supply enough flour in this way, to make requisitions on Richmond, where *was in store* much flour of the *old* crop bought before I got there and without my knowledge."[20]

Fowle began to buy corn meal, but he answered that the $6.00 flour had already been contracted and the bill would have to be paid. That raised Northrop's suspicions still further: "Virginia had prohibited the exportation of flour, many speculators had flour on hand, and wished to save themselves." Northrop himself then annulled the deal, whose price had been calculated "at Alexandria rates". "Such a precedent at the opening of the war had to be stopped."[21] It did not take Fowle long to report that he could not buy enough flour around Manassas at the Northrop rates.

So on July 12 Northrop began sending up the old flour from the Militia store in Richmond. It was invoiced at Manassas at its original high cost "according to Department rules".[22] That of course gave Fowle the chance to show that the price he was paying in his own district was less than the Commissary General charged to supply from Richmond. The sheer inadvisability of Northrop's passing on the high charge at such a moment suggests that he had not yet fathomed the depth of opposition at Manassas.

---

[19] MS at New York Public Library (Northrop Papers). In his paper, dated October 29, 1864, Ruffin mistakenly attributed the events to 1862.

[20] January 26, 1881 to Davis (Rowland, VIII, 581) and July 31, 1885 to Davis (Museum of the Confederacy, Richmond, Va.: Davis Collection). The latter makes clear that Northrop was quoting from a retained copy, one of many he had made before leaving his office in February 1865 (see below, p. 277).

[21] April 21, 1878 and January 26, 1881 to Davis (Rowland, VIII, 183 and 581).

[22] "Memoranda in relation to the purchase of flour", August 21, 1861 (Huntington Library, Eldridge Coll., Box 43).

The day after Northrop's order limiting Fowle's flour prices, Beauregard had issued Fowle a new order. Studiously ignoring the Commissary General and his Bureau, Beauregard demanded the constant maintenance of "ample provisions, including fat cattle, for 25,000 men for two weeks".[23] The number of men envisioned at Manassas had grown, though the time of holding their rations was sensibly reduced. It still amounted to 350,000 daily rations to be always on hand. Fowle's depot was entirely inadequate.[24]

Beauregard's order to Fowle (according to the general's report to Davis a month later) "drew from the Commissary General of the Army a letter so uncourteous to me that the want of time alone prevented me from inclosing it to you for your consideration."[25] Beauregard never produced the letter. The only other description of it appears in Roman's book: "In a letter, singularly ill-tempered and discourteous, that functionary arraigned General Beauregard for 'thwarting' his plans for maintaining the army, and went so far as to prohibit Captain Fowle from obeying the orders of his commanding general."[26]

As for Northrop's bureau, Beauregard acknowledged its existence in only a single demand made on July 8, the day after his latest order: the general wired for a new chief of Subsistence to serve at Manassas over Fowle. His choice fell on Richard Bland Lee (an elderly cousin of Robert E. Lee), who had resigned from a senior post in the United States Army commissariat on May 7 to take up a lieutenant colonelcy in the Virginia Militia commissariat.[27] Beauregard specified that the rank was to be retained on Lee's joining him: thus the new commissary at Manassas would rank every office of the Subsistence Bureau except Northrop himself. (Even so, R. B. Lee was dissatisfied with the rank: apparently he dreamt of commanding a brigade in the field.[28]) Northrop gave Lee no instructions except to investigate the arrangements of Fowle.

On July 14, 1861 (two days after Northrop began shipping the old flour up to Manassas) news came in that the first five hundred barrels of his new "ruling contract" flour were ready for shipment from Fredericksburg. But those barrels never started on their journey, because the first of the railroads involved in their shipment proved unable to handle them. As the

---

[23] Roman, I, 129.

[24] See above, p. 87, and below, pp. 92 and 108.

[25] August 10, 1861 (OR ser. I, vol. 51, pt. 2, 1071).

[26] Roman, I, 72.

[27] R. B. Lee was born about 1797. He graduated from West Point in 1817, served in the South and West, and from 1859 in Washington and Baltimore (George Washington Cullum, *Biographical Register of the Officers and Graduates of the U.S. Military Academy at West Point, N.Y., from its Establishment, in 1802, to 1890* [7 vols. in 8, Boston etc: publisher varies, 1891-1930], I, 165. See also the sketch in *Davis Papers*, VII, 299). Lee's Virginia appointment was made retroactive to date from March 16, 1861 (at which date his U.S. service still had seven weeks to run). NA, RG 109, Officers: Lee, R. B.

[28] NA, RG 109, Adjutant and Inspection General's Office: Letters Received, March to July 1861, ch. 1, vol. 45, pp. 186, 273.

line's president Peter Daniel was to inform President Davis on July 30: "Some eighteen heavy cannon lay on the cars of this company at Fredericksburg while they were urgently needed for the transportation of troops and supplies for the Government. A portion of them are still there with cannon on them which were carried there at least four weeks ago."[29]

The military had discovered that railroad cars offered a convenient and flexible form of warehousing, capacious and mobile at an instant's notice. The trouble lay in the limited number of cars owned by the railroads. Once a car was loaded with one thing, it was not available for anything else. It seemed a simple proposition. Yet none of the generals was quick to grasp it, unless it was Robert E. Lee.[30] But General Lee was only the Militia commander in Virginia then; he was in no position to issue plenary edicts.

On July 17—largely it would seem at Northrop's urging—the government appointed a special agent to take charge of rail transport for army necessities. William Sheppard Ashe, the able and progressive president of the Wilmington & Weldon (North Carolina) Railroad, was commissioned major and assistant quartermaster. But the terms of his appointment gave him no power to compel railroad cooperation; and Quartermaster General Myers remained suspicious.[31]

Other evidence of railroad misuse by the military emerged in Daniel's letter to President Davis written at the end of July. In it Daniel spelled out the obstacles currently preventing full use of the trains. "One of these is the use by the command or permission of army officers of railroad cars as stationary store-houses for baggage—much of it wholly useless to the troops and wholly unsuited to a campaign—and for provisions, munitions, and supplies for their troops." Just when railroad cars were needed to rush troops up to Manassas, Daniel wrote, 40 such cars stood empty near Strasburg out in the Shenandoah; 40 more stood obstructing the single-track Manassas Gap line at Manassas Junction itself, "loaded with useless trunks and baggage of the troops brought there long before", and 35 additional cars were on the single Orange & Alexandria line at Manassas—"also obstructing the track, and also brought there long before, and loaded with army provisions and supplies". Those 75 cars stood at Manassas thus immobilized, Daniel pointed out, "while timber and plank, suitable for erecting a store-house for the contents of these cars lay idle near at hand".[32]

Those were some early results of Beauregard's self-centered transport policy. Just as he commandeered wagons, so he had been commandeering trains at will—no matter what might be on the train or to whose relief it should be going. On the chance of getting Johnston's troops to join him at

---

[29] From a copy made for Northrop (Didier, "Scape-Goat", II, 9).

[30] OR ser. IV, vol. 1, 240-41.

[31] Black, The Railroads of the Confederacy, 65 ff. See the article on Ashe by James M. Clifton, in W. S. Powell, ed., Dictionary of North Carolina Biography (University of North Carolina, 1979), I, 56-57.

[32] Didier, "Scape-Goat", II, 9. Davis later commented on this letter: "I do not know how cars were obstructed from use as Mr. Daniel says, but have great confidence in any statement of his, in regard to such a matter" (April 9, 1879 to Northrop, in Rowland, VIII, 376).

Manassas, for instance, Beauregard had (as he said) "hastened to accumulate all possible means of railway transport at [Piedmont Station near Rectortown] on the Manassas Gap Railroad at the eastern foot of the Shenandoah".[33] Were the 40 empty cars at Strasburg, to the west, also waiting on the chance of Johnston?

The grossest display of Beauregard's misuse of railroads was the accumulation of 75 cars on the two lines converging at Manassas Junction. Many were full of soldiers' baggage. Why had the general permitted it? Why, simply because the splendid young men expected it, wrote Beauregard: "The Confederate army was filled with generous youths who had answered the first call to arms. For certain kinds of field duty they were not as yet adapted, many of them having at first come with their baggage and servants... Not to offend their susceptibilities, I then exacted the least work from them, apart from military drills, even to the prejudice of important field-works, when I could not get sufficient negro labor; they 'had come to fight, and not to handle the pick and shovel'...".[34]

In short the fine young men, who had come so heavily equipped, refused the demeaning labor of doing their own unpacking. And so their equipage was immobilized *sine die*. When General Johnston did come to Manassas, his eye met "such a quantity of baggage as no such army had ever before collected together. As the different regiments had been brought from their homes to Manassas Junction by railroad, the amount of their baggage had not been limited, consequently a trunk had come with each volunteer."[35] It was extraordinary, Northrop acidly observed, that Beauregard with his engineer's training should thus have "neglected his communications."[36] The general's transport policy would very shortly defeat every attempt to feed him from Richmond.

A quarrel thus began which was ultimately to blight the careers of both protagonists. Each was new in his responsibilities, untried at that level of command. Yet each was a proud Southern gentleman, graduate of West Point, owner of slaves, accustomed to have his orders obeyed. Surely the President and his Secretary of War should have compelled cooperation? In an established, ongoing government, such would have been demanded by the nation of its Executive. Yet the President and Secretary were practically as new in their posts as the antagonists themselves.

Both Northrop and Beauregard were centralizers. But beyond that lay a fundamental difference in outlook. In Beauregard's continuing idea of directing a smashing Confederate victory followed by a quick advance on Washington, the best thing was clearly to get in all the supplies offered. If victory came and the war was soon over, what did it matter how much they paid for their food?

[33] "The First Battle of Bull Run," in *Battles and Leaders*, I, 200.

[34] Ibid., 219. See also Roman, I, 71.

[35] *Narrative of Military Operations*, 98.

[36] "The Confederate Commissariat at Manassas", in *Battles and Leaders*, I, 261.

Northrop on the other hand was one of very few Southerners at that time who anticipated a long war. He also had an understanding that was rare then—of how insufficient Southern resources in both food and railroads would be to sustain a long war. The goal of all his planning, therefore, was to control the entire food supply over the million square miles of the Confederacy, the prices to pay and the transport to deliver it.

Yet though his strategy was diametrically opposed to Beauregard's, Northrop was in many ways a similar personality. He also was a planner, and when once he fixed his principle, he brooked no outside opposition—especially tactless, fiat-making opposition. Dissuading him from something he had thought through was sure to be hard task, a hopeless task for anyone trying to assume powers Northrop considered part of his own responsibility. Moreover, time was against them both: each felt that if he did not get his system established forthwith, it must fail. And each was probably right.

* * *

The resolute piling up of food at Manassas was a measure of Beauregard's determination to pursue the grand offensive. "Oh, that I had the genius of a Napoleon," he exclaimed in a letter written on July 8, 1861, as he worked at his newest variant strategy, designed to avoid Richmond's objections to the first two. Now he had (by his own count) some 18,000 men in his camp. But he was horrified by reports of a Federal force numbering anything up to 50,000 about to come towards him.[37] His letter complained bitterly of insufficient reinforcements.

Yet that letter was not written to the President. Instead, it was addressed to Congressman Louis T. Wigfall (who had attached himself to Beauregard at Fort Sumter in April).[38] Such a letter was at least of questionable etiquette, for it implied criticism of the chief executive. And Beauregard's back-door correspondence did not stop there. Five days later, on July 13, he sent his new strategy direct to General Joseph E. Johnston at Winchester.[39] Thus he hoped to enlist Johnston's support for the plan in advance of its submission to Richmond. Such a letter from one general to another, cutting out the President, was entirely irregular. Davis resented it.[40] Beauregard sent the plan to Richmond a day later.

In Beauregard's newest and grandest scheme, Johnston was still to come with his army on the train (leaving a skeleton force in northwest Virginia to make demonstrations), help Beauregard defeat the Federals at Manassas, then rush back on the railroad with his own force—together with 10,000 of Beauregard's men—to crush the enemy in the Shenandoah. Having done that, Johnston was to send a portion of his men to defeat Major

---

[37] July 11, 1861 to Davis (Roman, I, 82-83).

[38] Roman, I, 81-82.

[39] Ibid., I, 87.

[40] March 31, 1885 to Northrop (Rowland, VIII, 193-94, where it is undated). This letter answers two from Northrop, dated March 9 and March 27; on the latter Davis endorsed: 'ansd. March 31st '85' (Rowland, IX, 351-56). The present letter is answered by Northrop's of April 6, 1885. (Ibid., 364-65).

General George B. McClellan farther west in Virginia. And when all this had been accomplished, the triumphant Confederates should converge on Washington from three different directions and capture it in a pincer movement. Beauregard concluded: "I think this whole campaign could be completed brilliantly in from fifteen to twenty-five days."[41] That from a man who had never directed a major battle in his life.

The plan was as flawed as its predecessors. The Manassas Gap Railroad would never measure up to the complex, timed uses proposed; there were simply not enough cars and engines, and only the single track. The troops of both Beauregard and Johnston were mostly raw volunteers, entirely unfitted for such virtuoso professional military movements. Then Beauregard's numerical calculation showed that he was counting on Johnston for 20,000 men when, in fact, Johnston had barely half that number. (The mistake was ominous of the sort of detail Beauregard could overlook when pressure mounted.) Richmond rejected the scheme on July 16.[42] There would have been no reason to apprise the supply Bureau chiefs of it.

That night secret intelligence reached Beauregard that the huge Federal army was to move out from Washington at dawn. On the morning of the 17th he telegraphed to the President: "... Please inform Johnston of this, *via* Stanton, and also Holmes. Send forward any reinforcements, at the earliest possible instant, and by every possible means."[43] Davis wired back that more regiments were coming up from Richmond.

Then, late in the day, it seemed best to try to bring Johnston and Holmes to Manassas after all. Adjutant General Cooper telegraphed Johnston tactfully (as Johnston was Beauregard's military superior) that he should move his forces to Manassas "if practicable". The wire reached Johnston about 1 a.m. on the 18th.

It took time for the men around Winchester to gather up their camps and march the fifty-seven miles to the nearest station. Trains were slow; and the single track meant that after each train reached Manassas Junction, the entire line back to Piedmont Station had to be cleared before that train could return to bring more troops.[44] The first contingent of Johnston's men reached Manassas on the 20th less than twenty-four hours before the battle began.

Back in Richmond the Commissary General had what was clearly his first intimation that Beauregard was to be suddenly and heavily reinforced. Northrop wrote a month later: "... At midnight of the July 17, I received a telegram that General Johnston's command was coming to Manassas. By half after one o'clock, all the light bread and crackers that could be purchased in Richmond and all the hard bread in Commissary store had been forwarded [to the] Rail Road; and from that night the depot was crowded with supplies... Plenty of provisions were awaiting transportation at this end of the road, and plenty of cars at the other end detained, as is alleged,

[41] Roman, I, 87.

[42] Ibid., 85.

[43] Ibid., 90.

[44] There may also have been some deliberate interference amounting to treachery (Lash, *Destroyer of the Iron Horse*, 17).

for 'storing baggage'..."[45] All railroad cars from Richmond, however, were by then filled entirely with troops.

The battle began on the morning of July 21, 1861. Beauregard had been up most of the night before writing orders, as he had persuaded Johnston to let him take sole tactical command. When the day came, several of Beauregard's strategies miscarried: some of his orders were misunderstood, and some never reached their destinations due to faulty liaison. Yet all the while the new general was set on Napoleonic autonomy. At the height of the battle he actually asked Johnston to retire from the front and supervise troop movements to the rear. Johnston was incredulous, but when he understood that that was really Beauregard's desire, he took himself back.[46]

Throughout the day advantage see-sawed between the opposing armies. Then, well into the afternoon, a fresh column appeared on the Confederate left, the seat of fiercest fighting. Who were these new arrivals? Beauregard could not see at first, and feared defeat. Then doubt turned to joy. They were Jubal Early's forces and their sudden appearance appalled the wavering Federals. Beauregard ordered a general attack. The Federals turned and ran.[47]

They ran right into all the private carriages driven out from Washington that morning to see the Rebs get whipped. Federal soldiers and supply trains crashed through the fashionable spectators. Retreat turned to rout, and rout to panic as goods of every description were jettisoned. The Confederate troops were uncertain what to do, as many had no orders. Some began a pursuit. The most promising attempt was stopped in the gathering twilight by Major William C. Whiting on Johnston's staff—on nobody's authority but the major's own.[48] After that the Confederate soldiers, hungry from a whole day's fighting and marching without a pause, did not hesitate:

> Completely exhausted with our labors, the regiment counter-marched and bivouacked in one of the deserted camps, where barrels of excellent fresh crackers, hogsheads of hams and bacon, boxes of cheese, raisins, white sugar, coffee, tea, macaroni, well-fitted mess-chests, blankets, mattresses, and whiskey in abundance soon made us forgetful of our late privations. ...
>
> We found large numbers of beeves slaughtered and ready for butchering in their camps, but all the animals had been stolen from neighboring farms on their march. In fact the destruction of private property generally was so great that farmers were raving—they had been despoiled of almost everything, and nothing was paid for.[49]

Back in Richmond, Jefferson Davis had been unable to bear the suspense of waiting for the result of the first big battle. So he commanded a

---

[45] August 21, 1861 to Davis (Rowland, V, 127-28).

[46] T. Harry Williams, *P. G. T. Beauregard: Napoleon in Gray* (Louisiana State University Press, 1955), 80 ff.; Freeman, *Lee's Lieutenants*, I, 47-76. Johnston's own explanation, complex to obscurity, was published in *Battles and Leaders*, I, 248-50.

[47] Freeman, *Lee's Lieutenants*, I, 72.

[48] Ibid., 75, Johnston, *Narrative*, 472. Whiting was promoted to general after the battle by Davis.

[49] [Caffey], *Battle-Fields of the South*, 52-53.

special train—yes, it was possible for the President, and only required a single car—to take him to Manassas. He arrived on the battlefield in time to see the main Confederate force on their field of victory. He also saw the chance for a military pursuit of huge advantage, as he later recalled to Beauregard:

> In the evening of that day, being on the extreme left of our line of battle, I found a number of the troops who had recently arrived, and who therefore were in a fit condition for pursuit of the enemy; and as I thought, in a proper position from which to move for that purpose.
>
> There was a general complaint among them of hunger and want of provisions. I addressed several of the command, stating to them the importance of remaining where they were, and promised that when I reached the Head-quarters, I would have rations sent to them. Night closed in immediately thereafter, and I rode back in the dark to your Head-quarters.
>
> Upon inquiring for you, and hearing that you had not returned from the field, I directed an officer of your staff to have the promised rations sent out to the troops on the extreme left.[50]

The hungry troops that Davis had found were "recently arrived". Therefore they probably were Johnston's men. Those men had been provided with five days' rations before leaving the Valley at noon on the 18th to march to Piedmont Station. If they were without food now, Johnston wrote, "it must have been because they had thrown away their rations, then not unusual on a march."[51]

Davis ordered food sent out to those troops on the Confederate left, and a staff officer at Beauregard's headquarters said he would see it done.[52] Nowhere was there any suggestion that food was not easily available, ready to be sent. Johnston also recalled directing his own officers to send out food to troops encamped on the field.[53] The point should be carefully noted, in view of what was claimed later. There is nothing in either testimony to suggest any shortage then, and Northrop was later prepared to prove the same by reference to Fowle's reports covering July 21-27.[54]

Davis had not found Beauregard at his headquarters because Beauregard had been alarmed by a late rumor of further Federal movement on the Confederate right. So he had ridden out to remove those very troops that Davis had found promisingly placed on the left, and was busy sending them away to reinforce the right.[55] The rumor afterwards proved false.

---

[50] April 27, 1878 (Rowland, VIII, 185).

[51] *Narrative of Military Operations*, 59.

[52] Davis, *The Rise and Fall of the Confederate Government*, 2 vols. (New York: Appleton, 1881) I, 352.

[53] *Battles and Leaders*, I, 245.

[54] May 14, 1879 to Davis (Rowland, VIII, 389).

[55] Davis, *Rise and Fall*, I, 352.

Thus it was "a late hour of the night" before Davis could get both his generals at Manassas together for a conference. The President asked whether any troops had been sent to pursue the enemy. None had been. What troops were now in the best position to pursue? Probably General Bonham's. Well, then, should he not be given an order to pursue right now, even in darkness? Neither general answered.

Johnston was by nature a defensive fighter. He would certainly have had no stomach for a night pursuit towards a formidable enemy guarding its own capital. What about Beauregard? Had he yet returned from moving the troops from left to right?[56] In any case, command of the Confederate armies at Manassas would now formally pass to the senior Johnston. Was Beauregard in any position to oppose his superior?

In the embarrassing pause, Jordan recalled suggesting that Davis himself dictate an order for pursuit. The President began to dictate. Then someone said that the officer who had reported the Federal rout on the left was untrustworthy. (He was later proved on this occasion to have been entirely right.) The President was dissuaded, no order was issued, and no night pursuit undertaken. The reasons were all strategic, as Davis assured Northrop in later years: "There was nothing said to me after the battle about want of supplies or transportation as preventing pursuit. Then it was [Federal] fortifications with garrisons on the south side of the Potomac."[57] They were unmistakably the arguments of the defensive Johnston.

The following day dawned in heavy rain. It proved the beginning of months of almost continuous rain throughout Virginia. Soon the roads around Manassas were deep in mud. All that the Confederates attempted on the day after the battle was to gather up more Federals leavings in the vicinity.

---

[56] Davis's account of the battle night conference, quoting the recollection of Beauregard's AAG Jordan who was present, appeared in 1880. By that date, the Confederate failure to pursue on the night of First Manassas had long been seen as one of the great lost opportunities of the War, and both Johnston and Beauregard wriggled to get off the hook. In 1884 Johnston actually claimed not to have been present when the subject of pursuit came up between Davis and Beauregard: he said the subject had not been touched on after his arrival at Beauregard's headquarters at 11:30 pm (*Battles and Leaders*, I, 245). Beauregard, for his part, had Roman write that Johnston and Davis were both at his headquarters between 9.30 and 10. (Roman, I, 110; see also 114-15). Each general accused Davis of faulty memory. See also *Davis Papers*, VII, 393-94.

[57] May 20, 1879 (Rowland, VIII, 392). See also Davis, *Rise and Fall*, I, 356-61, and Davis to Northrop, March 3, 1885 (Rowland, IX, 348). Johnston spelled out the tactical reasons against pursuit in his *Narrative* (1874), 59-61.

CHAPTER 9

STARVING ON THE FIELD OF VICTORY?

What food was now at Manassas? There was whatever the Confederates had managed to capture from the fleeing Federals. There might be still some of the old flour sent up by the Subsistence Bureau in the days before July 18. And there were Commissary Fowle's collections, or what remained of them. It would have been difficult to add much to his stores in the days immediately after the battle: farms in front had been pillaged by the Federal army, and the district around Manassas had been drained by the increasing thousands of Confederate soldiers over the past seven weeks and more. If Fowle had managed to fill Beauregard's order for 350,000 daily rations before the battle, how much would now be left? Allowing 18,000 daily rations consumed by Beauregard's men on July 18 and 19, and an average of 30,000 a day (with the conjunction of Johnston's and Holmes's forces) after that, Fowle might still have had more than 200,000 rations on July 23. But he had no adequate storehouse.

And the weather was diabolical. On the day of the battle, July 21, the summer heat had been so fierce that dozens even of Southern soldiers and at least one regimental commander were overcome by sunstroke: heat like that would spoil fresh meat very quickly. Beginning that night, drenching rain had come to wet the inadequately protected flour stores and turn everything mouldy. Nothing was yet coming up from Richmond since the battle, as all the trains were dislocated.

The rainy morrow of the battle nevertheless began to reveal the extent of the Federal rout. Amounts of abandoned food were far greater than had been seen in the gathering dusk of the battle's end. Looking back at the previous night's conference of the generals with the President, Beauregard could kick himself if he liked: he had funked the unique chance to do exactly what he had dreamt of doing—with President Davis sitting right there urging him to do it.

99

Of course Johnston had dissuaded them. No one but Beauregard himself had called Johnston to Manassas. And now it emerged that Johnston would not be returning to Winchester; instead he was to remain in command at Manassas. Beauregard was also to remain at Manassas—under Johnston. Thus the Creole Napoleon would be condemned to watch his independent command being quietly digested by the defensive strategist who was his military opposite.

Johnston could be "a difficult and touchy subordinate" (in the words of Douglas Southall Freeman), but he was "a generous and kindly superior".[1] At Manassas he killed Beauregard with kindness. Only he would not let his junior take the initiatives any longer. Through protestations of warmest regard, Johnston gently turned down one offensive plan after another put forward by Beauregard over the next days and weeks.[2] So Beauregard would remain the hero of a single barren victory—a victory that looked like having no successor.

President Davis was also most kind. On the morning after the battle, with fulsome encomiums, he awarded Beauregard a promotion. That was, it turned out, on the suggestion of Johnston. The promotion still left Beauregard the junior general at Manassas. Was Davis's action then to be seen as a subtle punishment for Beauregard's irregular correspondences aimed at subverting government policy before the battle? Beauregard could think that too if he liked. His superiors had chained him up while they were fondly petting him.

Then who might be blamed for the defeat of all his fairest hopes? There sat Commissary General Northrop in Richmond. Northrop who had written him such a discourteous letter when he had only been trying to prepare the victory just consummated. Northrop, who had tried to negate Fowle's vital efforts with his own officious meddling. Northrop, whose fantastic pretension of controlling the whole Virginia flour market so as to pay less than anyone else had now left them without adequate bread because the trains would not run. Very well, let him suffer. Could he not be blamed for limitations on the military victory at Manassas?

The new chief commissary Richard B. Lee had arrived on July 19, just before the battle. He was soon shown which side of his bread had the butter. He supported Fowle's high prices and all his arrangements.[3] General Beauregard was duly grateful. He began to air the opinion that Richard Lee ought to be made Commissary General in preference to Northrop.[4] He encouraged Lee to feel "disparaged" on the grounds that his service with the United States commissariat had been longer than Northrop's own.[5] The suggestion was clear enough: Northrop owed his place to friendship with Jefferson Davis.

[1]   *Lee's Lieutenants*, I, xxxviii.

[2]   Roman, I, 131-37.

[3]   Northrop to Davis, August 30, 1880 and January 26, 1881 (Rowland, VIII, 491 and 582).

[4]   See e.g. Roman, I, 72.

[5]   Northrop to Davis, April 17, 1879 and August 22, 1885 (Rowland, VIII, 581, and IX, 390).

On July 23, 1861, two days after the battle, Beauregard had R. B. Lee write directly to Davis: "I am commanded by General Beauregard to inform your Excellency that the stock of provisions has become alarmingly reduced, in consequence of the non-fulfillment of requisitions of the Commissary General. The General directs me to say that unless immediate supplies are forwarded, in conformity with these requisitions, most serious consequences are inevitable."[6]

To read this, the entire fault lay with the Commissary General. Yet when had Beauregard or his commissaries sent requisitions for food to Richmond? Not until just before the battle at the earliest, it would seem; perhaps not until after it. And even then Beauregard was blocking information to the supply chiefs. That emerged in a protest sent to him on August 1 by Quartermaster General Myers. Myers had tried repeatedly to be helpful. Now he wrote to Beauregard: "The military operations and manoeuvres of your army are never divulged, and it is utterly impossible for me to know how to anticipate your wants."[7] If the friendly Myers was still kept in the dark, it was certain that Northrop must be sharing his fate.

The wording of R. B. Lee's complaint was too general to allow any specific conclusions to be drawn. Some indication of actual shortages could be read in a second telegram sent from Manassas next day. In it R. B. Lee regretted his inability to fill a requisition from nearby Fairfax Station, and stated: "With the exception of 3,000 rations intended to be sent to Louis Station, we are entirely without flour, bread, sugar, coffee, candles, and soap."[8] The small rations that had to be traded for bonds—plus flour, and therefore bread. Trains were still unable to bring the flour waiting at Fredericksburg; even the quantities of bread and crackers purchased by Northrop in Richmond during the night of July 17-18 were still awaiting transport from there.

As with many "private" messages emanating from Manassas, a copy of R. B. Lee's telegram to Fairfax Station "somehow" reached the government in Richmond. On the same day General Johnston telegraphed to Adjutant General Cooper: "I beg that supplies of provisions may be sent to us immediately. We are almost destitute, and in danger of absolute suffering."[9] In Richmond, the officer in charge of the Subsistence Bureau's depot, Major John Hayes Claiborne, reported that he had filled all requisitions from Manassas. The next day R. B. Lee changed his tune: "the supplies had not come owing to the Rrds being overtaxed."[10]

On July 29 Beauregard telegraphed to Davis: "Beg to suggest not to send any more troops here until provisions can be had. Some regiments are

6   Roman, I, 121.
7   Ibid., 125.
8   MS copy made for Northrop (Didier, *The New York Sun*, June 22, 1890).
9   Copy in Northrop Papers, NYPL.
10   Cited in Northrop to Davis, January 26, 1881 (Rowland, VIII, 582).

nearly starving." By then a fortnight had passed since any pre-battle ship-ments of food could have come from Richmond. If the Manassas commis-saries had not collected much since, the stores would indeed be approach-ing exhaustion even without the wasting spoilage caused by heat and rain. But there was an *addendum* to Beauregard's telegram, signed by R. B. Lee: "Hard bread and bacon most needed. Six hundred barrels of flour purchased—to be delivered tomorrow. Beef and cattle abundant. A regular supply of flour may be had on favorable terms from neighboring mills."[11] In other words, the price of feeding troops at Manassas was independence from Northrop's Subsistence Bureau.

That double message puzzled Davis: if abundance was available, why was the army starving? "I returned the telegram to Genl. Beauregard and called his attention to the inconsistency."[12] When Northrop was questioned, he not only confirmed the abundance of beef cattle still near Manassas, but was incredulous at their not being used: "If there had not been one pound of other victuals, the army could have carried on war with herds of beeves, doing their own transportation [on the hoof until killed and butchered], while subsisting the troops on healthy meat...".[13]

Northrop had had enough. He had already asked Adjutant General Cooper to remove R. B. Lee and Fowle from Manassas. When this informa-tion reached the President, he told Northrop to do it.[14] Their departure was to be delayed for three weeks until Northrop could get the man he wanted to run the Manassas commissariat. That was William B. Blair, who was winding up his current duties as Commissary General of the Virginia Militia.

Within a week after the Battle of Manassas, the failure to pursue the Federals on the night of their defeat was widely known. Speculation was rife about the advantages which might have accrued to the Confederacy by the capture of Washington—speculation to a great extent fueled by Beauregard's own widely advertised pre-battle schemes, hopes and rhetoric. Viewed in the aftermath, those schemes and hopes led to sharp criticism appearing in many Southern newspapers.

General Beauregard always kept a wary eye on the press. Now he did not like what he read. On July 29, eight days after the battle, he made a counter-move. He wrote another apparently private letter, filled with specu-lation on the unrealized possibilities of the late battle—and animadversion against the Subsistence and Quartermaster Bureaus in Richmond. It was an action highly irregular in a loyal soldier. And the privacy of the communica-tion was disingenuous, for it was addressed to William Porcher Miles and James Chesnut.

---

[11]   *OR* ser. I, vol. 51, pt. 2, 204.

[12]   August 1, 1861 to J. E. Johnston (Rowland, V, 119).

[13]   August 21, 1861 (Rowland, V, 128). See also September 11, 1885 to Davis (Rowland, IX, 391).

[14]   On the night of August 1, 1861. Date established from Northrop to Davis, August ?20, 1880: "You told me to do it, the night you moved into Crenshaw's house." That was the new Presidential mansion. (Rowland, VIII, 490). See Richmond *Whig*, August 3, 1861, and *Davis Papers*, VII, 205 *n.*

Miles had been one of Beauregard's commissioners who arranged the Federal handover of Fort Sumter in April. Then at Manassas in July both Miles and Chesnut were made "voluntary aides" to Beauregard. But the real point was that both were Confederate congressmen. Miles was chairman of the Congressional Committee on Military Affairs. Beauregard wrote to the congressmen:

> ...We have been out of subsistence for several days, some of my regiments not having had anything to eat for more than twenty-four hours. They have stood it, though, nobly; but, if it happens again, I shall join one of their camps and share their wants with them; for I will never allow them to suppose that I feast while they suffer. ... From all accounts, Washington could have been taken up to the 24th instant, by twenty thousand men! ... The want of food and transport has made us lose all the fruits of our victory. Only think of the brilliant results we have lost by the two causes referred to![15]

In view of what had taken place at Beauregard's conference with Johnston and Davis on the night of the battle, that was both *suppressio veri* and *suggestio falsi.* Yet Beauregard's letter found its mark. Miles read it out to the assembled Congress, who were duly shocked to hear that the heroes of Manassas seemed to be starving on the field of their victory—a victory which starvation had apparently made barren. On August 1 Chesnut introduced "A resolution respectfully requesting the President to inform Congress ... as to the condition of the Subsistence Department, and whether or not he has received any authentic information going to show a want of sufficient and regular supply of food for the Army of the Confederate States, or any portion of it, now in the field; which was agreed to."[16]

Instantly it went round the gossip mills of Richmond. Chesnut's wife savored piquant talk at her dinner table, and she retailed it into her diary:

> Now, if I were to pick out the best abused, where all catch it so bountifully, I should say Mr. Commissary General Northrop was the most cussed and vilified man in the Confederacy. He is held accountable for everything that goes wrong in the army. ...
> They say Beauregard writes that his army is upon the verge of starvation. Here every man, woman, and child is ready to hang to the very first lamppost anybody of whom that army complains. Every Manassas soldier is a hero dear to our patriotic heart. Put up with any neglect of the heroes of the 21st of July—never!
> And now they say we did not move on the right [sic] after the flying foe because we had no provisions—no wagons, no ammunition, &c &c. Rain, mud, and Northrop. Where were the enemy's supplies that we brag of bagging? Echo answers, where?

[15] *OR* ser. I, vol. 51, pt. 2, 176.
[16] *Journal of the Congress of the Confederate States of America* (7 vols.,Washington: Government Printing Office, 1904-5 [hereinafter cited as *Journal of Congress*]), I, 305.

Where there is a will, there is a way. No, we stopped to plunder that rich convoy, and somehow for a day or so everybody thought the war was over and stopped to rejoice. So it appeared here.[17]

Davis answered the congressional request for subsistence information on the day it was tendered, August 1, 1861. Those were still early days, and the Commissary General's plans long-sighted. The President cited overcrowded railroads. He also alluded to the apparent inconsistency of starvation reports with R. B. Lee's references to abundant beef and flour for easy purchase in the area. Finally, however, he assured Congress: "... Inquiries have been instituted as well to remedy irregularities as to prevent such occurrence in future."[18] The questions about subsistence at Manassas he sent to Northrop for his report.

Then Davis learned that the congressional inquiry had been set off by Beauregard's complaining letter to the two Congressmen. The President wrote temperately to Beauregard on August 4: "I think you are unjust to yourself in putting your failure to pursue the enemy to Washington to the account of short supplies of subsistence and transportation. ... Enough was done for glory, and the measure of duty was full. Let us rather show the untaught that their desires are unreasonable than, by dwelling on possibilities recently developed, give form and substance to criticisms always easy to those who judge after the event."[19]

Beauregard did not hasten to reply to this wise counsel. Once more he tried indirection. He sent again to Miles, calling for an entire reorganization of the Subsistence and Quartermaster Bureaus. Northrop should be sacked, and in his place they should have R. B. Lee—"the best man for Commissary General". Miles responded on August 6: "The President has not the remotest idea of removing Colonel Northrop. On the contrary, he is under the impression that he has done everything in his power in his department. You can readily see that there is, therefore, no possibility of the radical reform you suggest...".[20]

After digesting that, Beauregard wrote to Davis on August 10. It was a further exercise in disingenuousness:

I regretted exceedingly to hear that Colonel Miles had read my letter of the 29th ultimo in Congress. It was written only for the purpose of expediting matters, if possible... With regard to making timely requisitions on the quartermaster and commissary departments, not knowing what number of troops the War Department intended at any time to concentrate here, it was impossible to make said requisitions until after the arrival of said troops.

---

[17] *Mary Chesnut's Civil War*, ed. C. Vann Woodward (New Haven: Yale University Press, 1981), 124. Mrs. Chesnut did not take herself too seriously as political historian: "I write current rumor. I do not vouch for anything." (163)

[18] *OR* ser. IV, vol. 1, 512-13.

[19] *Davis Papers*, VII, 276; also printed in Roman, I, 122-23. The *OR* transcript (ser. I, vol. 2, 507-8) prints "drivelling on possibilities"; and that colorful error has been much quoted.

[20] Beauregard's original not found; quoted in Miles's reply (Roman I, 128).

So it was back to the government for not sending quickly enough the rein-forcements he had requested before the battle.

> I accuse no one, I state facts; but the facts referred to show a deficiency somewhere... My experience here teaches me that after issuing an order I have to inquire whether it has been carried into effect...

The faults, then, might lie equally with his own officers at Manassas.

> With regard to my remarks about marching on Washington, you must have misunderstood them, for I never stated that we could have pursued the enemy on the evening of the 21st, or even on the 22nd.

Then came quotations from his letter to the congressmen showing only that Beauregard's idea of Washington was meant to apply a day or two later. A postscript acknowledged that his soldiers were not after all starving:

> Some of the troops had only fresh beef; others not even that, for it was not always immediately available, and at this time of the year not to be kept over a few hours.[21]

That reflected only on Beauregard's own arrangements at his camp.

Northrop was shown this letter, and asked for his response. He wrote to Davis: "Troops should kill their own cattle, and should more than one day's supply turn out, if cooked, it will keep sweet for the next day."[22] Farming was widespread in the South, and such tasks presented no problems to many soldiers. In fact several commanders in the Valley of Virginia had begun to do it already.[23] But at Manassas Fowle's butcher still did his work and took his wages.

Beauregard's letter of August 10 to the President had also included another complaint: "Some of the brigades here have over 1,000 sick, due, the physicians say, partly to bad bread (for they cannot make it themselves) and to bad fresh beef, many of the troops eating at home only salt provisions and corn bread."[24] In other words, the fine young men were unaccustomed to rough army fare and cooking conditions. But even Beauregard's superior J. E. Johnston knew better than this: "Those who have seen large bodies of new troops know that they are sickly in all climates. Our Southern volunteers were particularly so, being attacked in the early part of their camp-life by measles and mumps... The former was often followed by pneumonia or typhoid fever. The ignorant attributed the prevalence of inevitable disease to extraordinary causes."[25]

---

[21]   *OR* ser. I, vol. 51, pt. 2, 1071-72.

[22]   August 21, 1861 (Huntington Library: Eldridge Collection, Box 43). Northrop recalled from his own days in the Oklahoma territory: "I have moved infantry 8 or 10 days on poor buffalo meat and they did well; detailed men could kill and supply every regiment every night, and it could be cooked by morning for 2 days." (February 25, 1885 to Davis, in Rowland, IX, 346).

[23]   John Worsham reported that when his regiment was transferred to the Staunton region on July 19, 1861, some soldiers shot the cows, others dressed the meat, "and in a short time we had our regular supper." (*One of Jackson's Foot Cavalry*, 39).

[24]   *OR* ser. I, vol. 51, pt. 2, 1072.

[25]   *Narrative of Military Operations*, 65-66.

Ill or not, the soldiers at Manassas were by this time undeniably hungry. The continued presence of 30,000 of them had begun to exhaust the whole district of food. When they tried to supplement their meagre rations by private purchases, extortion rose. One soldier was so delighted to learn that his regiment was leaving Manassas that he didn't care where their destination might be: "Any thing to get away from Manassas and Centerville, any place where we would have a change of scene, and find butter, eggs, and poultry procurable for money—all such articles having been consumed where we then were, or so few remaining that fabulous prices were asked for them." [26] It showed more clearly than anything yet seen that the Beauregard plan of local purchase and supply could not sustain the huge armies now in the field when immobilized more than a few days. The Northrop plan, with its dependence on railroads, was faring little better.

Another document from Manassas was also dated August 10, 1861. It was written almost certainly on Beauregard's order, to accompany his letter to the President. Its author was R. B. Lee, its purpose to compare prices of flour. On one side it set out prices asked by millers of the Manassas district—only a little higher than Richmond prices, and available on the spot. On the other side, it showed the extraordinarily high price the Commissary General was billing them for the old militia flour he was again sending up from Richmond, with transport charges added. The commissaries at Manassas did not discourage their friends among the farmers and millers from believing that the Commissary General was such a doctrinaire fool as to compel them to send their flour to Richmond to secure the lower price, and then send that same flour right back to Manassas, thus incurring double transport. To anyone who knew of Northrop's worry over railroad inadequacy from his earliest days in Richmond, the charge was ludicrous.

Nonetheless the anti-Davis press already flourishing in Richmond feasted on it.[27] It survived the War to reach the solemn pages of Joseph E. Johnston's *Narrative of Military Operations* (1874). Northrop specifically refuted Johnston's charge—though his explanation showed again the *legerdemain* of cost-accounting for the old flour that so maddened everybody at Manassas: "Johnston probably never saw this; knew nothing about the matter, and they concluded that I must have bought this flour, brought it to Richmond, and then reshipped it." [28]

A third paper also came from Manassas around this time. It was entitled: "Requests of the different Commanding Officers in regard to a change of diet, also stating what their commands have been used to...".[29] Northrop reported the requests as so varied that no system whatever could be applied

---

[26] [Caffey], *Battle-Fields of the South*, 71.

[27] See Northrop to Davis, January 26, 1881 (Rowland, VIII, 585).

[28] January 26, 1881 to Davis (Rowland, VIII, 582). See also Northrop to Davis, August 20, 1880 (Ibid., 490).

[29] In later years this paper disappeared, and it is unclear whether its author was Beauregard or Johnston. It is cited here from Northrop's answering paper of August 21, 1861 (Huntington Library, Eldridge Coll., Box 76). See also Northrop-Davis letters of April and May, 1879 (Rowland, VIII, 387-94).

to them "unless 'bacon', 'beans', and 'vegetables' were always at hand, and money ready to purchase them with. None of these conditions exist." He gave an illustration: "Some weeks ago I prepared to purchase Lard for the troops in case of necessity [i.e., a failure of meat supply], but could not effect this on bonds; delay in hot [railroad] cars will perhaps melt and injure it ... nor is it paid for yet."

For his part, Johnston organized a board of inquiry "to investigate and report on the condition of the transportation and commissariat of the Army at Manassas on the 21st of July [the day of the battle], and their daily condition for two weeks thereafter."[30] Johnston's board comprised the Manassas commissary and quartermaster, R. B. Lee and Cabell, together with one of Johnston's own men, Virginia Captain John Imboden. Their report has apparently not survived, and the only account of it now known was written by Imboden more than twenty years later:

> I have a distinct recollection that we found that on the morning of the battle there was not at Manassas one full day's rations for the combined armies of Johnston and Beauregard, and that on no single day for the succeeding two weeks was there as much as a three days' supply there. We found that there were not wagons or teams enough at any time to have transported three days' supplies for the troops if they had been put in motion away from the railroad.

Then the board went beyond its brief as Imboden remembered it, and proceeded to look at the time *before* the battle when Beauregard had sole military charge. That was before either Johnston or Imboden was on the scene, largely before R. B. Lee was there, and when Quartermaster Cabell had been overtaken by Beauregard's special colonel of transport. Undaunted by any of this, Imboden recalled their conclusions:

> We found that for weeks preceding the 21st of July General Beauregard had been urgent and almost importunate in his demands on the Quartermaster and Commissary Generals at Richmond for adequate supplies. We found that Colonel Northrop, the Commissary General, had not only failed to send forward adequate supplies for such an emergency as arose when General Johnston brought his army from the valley, but that he had interfered with and interdicted the efforts of officers of the department who were with General Beauregard to collect supplies from the rich and abundant region lying between the hostile armies.

Finally the board took itself into Beauregard's grand strategy:

> After reporting the facts, we unanimously concurred in the opinion that they proved the impossibility of a successful and rapid pursuit of the defeated enemy to Washington.

They duly sent it all to Richmond—only to have it returned by Judah Benjamin, Acting Secretary of War, after Walker resigned and left the office on September 16. Benjamin stated that "the Board had transcended its powers by expressing an opinion as to what the facts did or did not prove...".

---

[30] This and the following quotations are taken from Imboden's article of 1885 in *The Century Magazine*, reprinted in *Battles and Leaders*, I, 239.

The board made some grudging deletions and sent it back. Imboden concluded: "This was the last I ever heard of it. Who suppressed it I do not know."[31]

The report was never shown to Northrop. When he read Imboden's article in 1885, he rejoined in a letter to the editor who had published it: "General Imboden in effect charges Mr. Benjamin with suppressing, in order to shield my incapacity, an official report... General Beauregard was not 'urgent on the Commissary General for adequate supplies before the battle,' for there was no ground of complaint. It was *after the battle*, when the vision of capturing Washington had seduced him, that he tried to construct a ground of complaint anterior to the battle."[32] But Northrop would find himself compelled to point out again and again that he had never forbidden a field commissary from purchasing flour. Fowle himself had never asserted that.[33] "...No prohibition of a positive nature was ever made against his purchasing, but against his prices."[34]

On August 13 R. B. Lee telegraphed from Manassas that his supply of salt meat was so low he could issue it only twice a week to troops. He was out of sugar, coffee, candles and soap, but had purchased 2,000 barrels of flour. Next day, he reported that Beauregard and Johnston had themselves ordered further supplies from the neighborhood.[35] Yet not all of these shortages could be laid to exhaustion of the district or failures of transport. Even then Lee had no proper storehouse. Northrop wrote on August 21: "...Col. Lee reports that, during the recent heavy storms still prevailing, the perishable articles of supply had been unavoidably exposed and somewhat damaged, and he applied for fifteen tarpaulins, 20 feet by 30, which are now being made in Richmond. From this it would appear that he had even more than he could preserve."[36] No other hint seems ever to have come from Manassas about how much food had spoiled during the four weeks of almost solid rain since the battle, or about the failure to build any adequate storehouse during all those weeks of military inactivity.

The troubles at Manassas had caused Northrop to reconsider his *laissez-faire* policy of allowing field commanders to procure their own beef in every situation. He appointed five Bureau cattle agents for separate military dis-

---

[31]   It is not easy to fix the dates of the inquiry or report. Imboden recalled: "We organized early in August", and two weeks after the battle date would have brought them to August 4. But Benjamin did not become Acting Secretary until September 17. Six weeks seem a long time to spend if any urgency was felt. Moreover R. B. Lee left the Manassas commissariat on August 23. Either the report's first version had been rejected by Walker, or it lingered long in Richmond before meeting the disapproval of Benjamin.

[32]   "The Confederate Commissariat at Manassas", *Battles and Leaders*, I, 261. On August 22, 1885, Northrop wrote to Davis: "Genl. Imboden's article reveals for the *first time* to me that Johnston called a board of inquisition..." (Rowland, IX, 385).

[33]   Northrop to Davis, February 2, 1885 (Rowland, IX, 359).

[34]   Northrop to Davis, February 11, 1880 (Tulane, r 22, ff 747-52).

[35]   Originals not found; citations from Northrop to Davis, August 21, 1861 (Rowland, V, 124).

[36]   Ibid., August 21, 1861, 125.

tricts in Virginia, and R. T. Wilson as agent for all of Tennessee. Their duties would be "to collect cattle outside of our lines as well as within, to see to curing beef and pork, & to feed the army".[37] In Northern Virginia the agent appointed was Burr Noland: he quickly arranged "with a respectable man, Mr. Bonst, to butcher at 1/2 the 5th quarter, and to cure the Govt. 1/2, ... and to sell his half of the hides and tallow to the Govt. at prescribed rates."[38] Ruffin was soon able to report that all the cattle agents were achieving like results.[39]

The presence of the Subsistence Bureau cattle agents naturally irritated local suppliers, field commissaries accustomed to dealing with them, and by extension their generals. On August 16, 1861, Johnston himself wrote to Davis that "certain responsible business men are known to be ready to undertake to introduce a large stock of bacon into the Confederacy at a price far below that now paid in Virginia, the payment to be on delivery, and in Confederate States funds." Johnston asked for authority to make the arrangement.[40]

The notion of trading through an enemy's lines—with the enemy's potential suppliers, and thereby with the probability of the enemy's acquiescence—is apparently as old as the history of war itself. But the baseless cynicism of trading with the enemy revolted Jefferson Davis. His answer to Johnston did not respond by so much as a single word to the proposal. Davis concentrated instead on shortcomings attributable to the staff at Manassas: "Captains and colonels, instead of correcting evils by personal attention, seem to have been the sources of no small part of the impressions received and circulated."[41] Who were those captains and colonels but Fowle and R. B. Lee? Yet Davis did send Johnston's letter to Northrop.

On August 21, 1861 Northrop sent his answers to the accumulated questions and complaints. They were contained in a series of papers together with a letter to the President:

> General Johnston says that there should be always stores for twelve or fifteen days ahead to make an expedition. In this I fully concur, and think moreover that nothing can be as convenient as gentle cattle which carry the meat ration [on the hoof], rather than hogsheads of bacon.

Salt meats were nearly always subject to railroad transportation, and Northrop cited new evidence of trouble:

> ... Meats which were received from Nashville were delayed in coming here from twenty to thirty days, some of it spoiling in the closed cars—coming troops superseding all else...

---

37   Northrop to Davis, July 31, 1885 (Museum of the Confederacy, Davis Coll.).

38   Northrop to Davis, April 21, 1878 and January 26, 1881 (Rowland, VIII, 183 and 582). In later years Northrop thought the date he had appointed Noland cattle agent for Northern Virginia was July 25, 1861 (July 31, 1885 to Davis).

39   *OR* ser. IV, vol. 1, 876.

40   *OR* ser. I, vol. 5, 789.

41   August 20, 1861 (Rowland, V, 123-24).

He quite agreed that there were not enough hogs in the Confederacy to feed both the army and the people. As to the question of trading for them through enemy lines, he still hoped for more from Kentucky:

> ...but no plan for a large introduction has yet stood the test of examination. I am, therefore, rejoiced that one has presented itself to General Johnston, and hope the President will give the authority asked by him, and I will most cordially sustain his plan.

The President would do no such thing, and the records contain nothing much more about it. Northrop's letter concluded by calling Davis's attention once again to the parlous state of Treasury funding for Subsistence. By now there was evidence that bankers in New Orleans were refusing even Confederate notes. It was a terrible precedent.[42]

At least four papers accompanied Northrop's letter to the President. One was a report from Noland as cattle agent for Northern Virginia. Although that has disappeared, the three other papers have survived. One is devoted to railroad transport in relation to the Bureau supplying staples to Manassas. Another considers fresh provisions, both animal and vegetable. The third was entitled "Memoranda in relation to the purchase of flour."[43] The contents of all three have been presented in tracing the history of those matters through the foregoing pages.

Davis agreed with his Commissary General's basic conclusions, and he endorsed Northrop's letter: "The chief commissary with an army represents the Commissary Genl.; should concur in general principles of policy but of course never let want ensue, even if the generals neglect their communications and prevent the objects aimed at by his dept from being accomplished."[44]

Meanwhile the Confederate Congress had begun to act. On August 20, without waiting for Northrop's report to the President, Congress instructed their Committee on Military Affairs "to inquire and report forthwith what efficient legislation may be adopted to secure to our armies adequate supplies of wholesome bread and likewise of vegetables". The committee, chaired by Miles, did its work; and on the last day of its current session, August 31, Congress passed a resolution demanding "a daily ration of fresh vegetables ... whenever the same can be provided at reasonable cost..."; and "in lieu of the usual ration of flour, an equivalent of well-baked bread; and to this end [the Secretary of War] is authorized to establish bakeries in such numbers and at such points as may be necessary, or to make contracts for the supply of such bread."[45]

Both of these well-meant measures implied rebuke to the Commissary General, who in fact had already executed the first as well as funds would permit. It could indeed be charged that he had miscalculated the ability of volunteers to bake their own bread. But the provision of bakers and bakeries

---

[42] August 21, 1861 to Davis (*Davis Papers*, VII, 296-99; Rowland, V, 124-27).

[43] *Davis Papers*, VII, 300-301; (Rowland, V, 127-28).

[44] Rowland, V, 127.

[45] *Journal of Congress*, 375, 458.

would of course constitute another tax on the army's food, equivalent to the service of butchers for fresh beef. Moreover, fully baked bread would create major problems of storage and spoilage, as well as transport whenever military movements took significant numbers of soldiers away from their established base. But Congress having spoken, the Bureau would have to grasp this nettle.

A more contentious measure, introduced into Congress at the same time, called for a general inquiry into the administration of the Subsistence, Quartermaster, and Medical Bureaus.[46] An *ad hoc* committee was appointed for this, chaired again by Miles. By early September (after the close of the full Congress) it was beginning to collect information.[47]

A third bill, introduced on August 27, contained a long list of nominations of rank and promotion for army officers of the line and War Department Bureaus, sent in by the President for congressional approval. Near the top was the nomination of L. B. Northrop as full colonel and permanent Commissary General of the Army.[48] Congress took no action on this list before its session ended on August 31.

* * *

The man Northrop wanted as commissary at Manassas, William B. Blair, had come on duty on August 23, 1861. His impact was immediate. For the first time there was an economical arrangement for beef. Blair established a full working relationship with Noland as Bureau cattle agent. Now that the Manassas district was somewhat exhausted, Noland was collecting cattle and other supplies from counties north and west. Northrop was to refer to "Noland's report that he could not get my orders carried out until Blair relieved [R. B.] Lee—after which Hides were saved, Tallow also, and Oil boiled from the feet: value of 5th quarter saved $12 per head."[49]

Blair also achieved some reasonable working of at least a portion of Northrop's complex plan for buying flour. With Blair's support Northrop was able to place a special flour agent strategically at the northern end of the Valley of Virginia—"who bought all that people would sell at suitable prices, graded by wheat put at $1 less transportation to the usual market...".[50] The agent was James Ranson of Jefferson County.[51] It remained to be seen whether he and his assistants could repair (or even contain) the damage already done by Lee and Fowle among the millers near Manassas.

Blair was not a magician. Until railroads could be controlled and appropriated cash extracted from the Treasury, many items in the specified

---

46   Ibid., 374.
47   Secretary of War Walker to Miles et al., September 4, 1861 (*OR* ser. IV, vol. 1, 598-99).
48   *Journal of Congress*, I, 422.
49   February 11, 1880 to Davis (Tulane).
50   January 26, 1881 to Davis (Rowland, VIII, 582).
51   Ranson is specified in Ruffin's report of January 1862 as the only full-time flour agent for the Bureau until "very recently" (*OR* ser. IV, vol. 1, 877). Northrop's recollection in 1881 (Rowland, VIII, 582) that Ranson was of Clarke County may have been occasioned by the fact that by then Clarke was (and long had been) the northernmost country in Virginia: Jefferson County had been taken into West Virginia at the creation of that state in 1863.

ration must remain in short supply. To prevent inequities and squabbling among different commands, Northrop established a rule that sent to each command a "just proportion" of whatever could not be supplied in full. Blair managed it by making an order that all requisitions from the field (even if signed by a brigadier general) must be submitted to his office before they could be filled by the brigade commissaries from their stores. The brigade commissaries and one or two brigadiers complained loudly enough to be heard by the press.[52] Blair stuck stoutly to it. When the commissary of Hampton's South Carolina troops wrote of not receiving "fair proportion", Blair was able to report that "...they have been since August 28, 1861, the earliest day after I came upon duty (August 23, 1861) at which I could so systematise the affairs of the subsistence department here as to inaugurate such a system. I am not aware of any failure to receive such proportion by any part of the troops since that time."[53] And indeed no more such complaints from Manassas or elsewhere have survived.

On September 6 *The Charleston Daily Courier* printed a report from Richmond: "The Commissary General sent this morning nearly a hundred thousand pounds of sugar-cured hams, such as are used when our army is on the march, which avoids the necessity for any culinary artists—other stores are being rapidly shipped, so that no delay will be incurred. The commissary who held position last month [at Manassas], and whose inefficiency has been so extensively commented upon, has been deposed, and his substitute has received much encouragement by the satisfactory regards of his Chief."

Yet there was to be one more attempt to upset Northrop's arrangements for Northern Virginia. It reached the Secretary of War on September 7, 1861. The Secretary copied a portion of the letter to Northrop, specifying that it was written in reference to Manassas, and that it came "from a source entitling it to consideration". Those clues suggested the author as Johnston. The quoted passage objected to everything coming from Richmond, saying that food in the Valley of Virginia was plentiful and cheap; flour would be had at $1 less than in Richmond.[54]

Northrop's answer two days later repeated his "ruling markets" -less-transport argument. By that rule, the letter's proposal would set a price of $4.25 a barrel in the Valley. If that was the case,

> ...I will take it with pleasure, contracting with the party to furnish the whole Army of the Potomac. No such offer has been made to me from any source.
>
> Furthermore, I will contract to receive all the bacon he can deliver to Major Blair for two cents more than that I lately furnished to the Army of the Potomac from this city [Richmond].

---

52 *The Richmond Examiner*, October 2, 1861.
53 *OR* ser. I, vol. 5, 898.
54 Ibid., 833.

I add that Major Blair, who has authority to purchase flour to any extent on the principles of this department—which are admitted by the entire community and the millers to be correct (while objecting to the rule)—is now offering to the people of the Valley forty-two cents more per barrel than your reliable correspondent says they are willing to take.[55]

Nothing more of the "reliable correspondent's" offers appear in the records. But another offer to trade through enemy lines landed on the President's desk at the end of September. It came from Dr. Jeptha Fowlkes of Memphis, Tennessee—doctor, druggist, city alderman, bank president, newspaper editor. Fowlkes had a "messenger" in touch with Secretaries Simon Cameron and Salmon Chase of Lincoln's cabinet in Washington: through them "I can secure a large amt. of Bacon & Pork in coming season, & have *strong parties*, who will unite with me in a large contract for army. If desired, have me advised!" Davis endorsed this: "Commissary Genl, read and return."[56] Northrop (on the evidence of his later endeavors) would almost certainly have been in favor. Presumably Davis rejected it.

This secret phase of Confederate history was later conveyed by Assistant Secretary of War John A. Campbell to Robert Kean, the young Chief of the War Bureau. Kean wrote in his diary:

> I am told by Judge Campbell that in 1861 there were proposals from the contractors for the Federal Army to supply ours, one-half for cotton, the other for Confederate bonds; and it was believed the proposal had the acquiescence of the United States authorities; but it was rejected by ours, it seems to me most unwisely.
>
> The question is simply whether they suffer more for the comparatively small quantity of cotton, say 100,000 bales, or we for the indispensable articles of salt, meat, clothing, medicines. Besides it would have exerted a good influence to have had a few millions of our bonds in the hands of Northern capitalists.[57]

The railroads remained as hopeless as ever. On September 18, 1861 Commissary Blair at Manassas had begged Northrop to send 1,000 barrels of flour from Richmond, because shipments from Lynchburg and Fredericksburg (where the "ruling contracts" should have begun to work) had not arrived. The same day brought a complaint from the Virginia Central Railroad that their Richmond depot was so full of flour that if any more came they would have to leave it outdoors. The Central said that they had only two cars in Richmond; all the others had been commandeered by the military, and were marooned at Millborough (out in the Shenandoah Valley) or at Manassas.[58]

[55] *OR* ser. I, vol. 5, 836.

[56] Rowland, V, 138.

[57] *Inside the Confederate Government: The Diary of Robert Garlick Hill Kean*, ed. Edward Younger (New York: Oxford University Press, 1957), 32.

[58] *OR* ser. I, vol. 5, 857-58.

Northrop instantly appealed to Acting Secretary of War Benjamin. The matter quickly reached the President—who himself telegraphed to the quartermaster at Millborough and to General Johnston at Manassas. Benjamin wrote urgently to Johnston. The general turned to his own quartermaster Cabell, who then had some of the cars unloaded and sent down to Richmond. He denied ever using cars for storage, and added: "I cannot understand why the delays are always attributed to this place."[59] Cabell's denial soon turned out to be less than the truth.

Johnston sent Cabell's report to the President with a copy to Benjamin, accompanied by a covering note returning to his charge: "Flour could be bought at very moderate prices in the Valley of the Shenandoah, and brought to us, with certainty as to time, on the Manassas Gap Railroad."[60] Was it possible that Johnston himself had impounded the cars with the intent of encouraging his own subsistence scheme?

Benjamin meanwhile attacked Quartermaster General Myers, demanding to know who specifically was responsible for holding up the cars. Myers replied only that no cars were now at Manassas, though he had been told that one hundred had been there. Benjamin rejoined: "...This is only half the result required in my letter... I desire to know whose is the fault that the transportation on the road was so blocked up by the absence of cars from Richmond that the Commissary General was unable to get one thousand barrels of flour conveyed to the army in an emergency. ... Who was the delinquent? I must insist that the investigation be pursued until the question is satisfactorily answered."[61] Myers passed the buck to the government's railroad supervisor Major Ashe, and Ashe asked the superintendent of the Virginia Central. Then some of the truth emerged. There were still no adequate storehouses for supplies unloaded from trains either at Manassas or at Millborough.

Nobody in Richmond or at Manassas seemed able to construct warehouses or to make anybody else do it. Northrop asked no further pointed questions, nor did his men on the ground, nor did the field commissaries there. Not a line of correspondence on the subject can I find from any authority during the entire autumn of 1861. And the railroad cars continued to be held as storehouses at distant points.

What then of Cabell's claim to unload the Manassas cars quickly? Not a bit of it, said the Virginia Railroad superintendent when questioned by Major Ashe:

> It is not long since one of my employés, one who is considered a reliable man, saw thirteen trains at Manassas; eleven of these were loaded. Some of the trains probably came from Lynchburg. But as we have never sent more than two freight trains from Richmond to Manassas, you must see that there has been detention at one time, to say the least. I have no doubt there was good cause for it.

---

[59]   Ibid., 872-73.

[60]   Ibid., September 22, 1861, 873.

[61]   Ibid., 871.

I know that the cars have been detained at Millborough. There were probably fifty loaded cars there on Friday last. You have been obliged to issue orders to have them unloaded without a shelter for the goods.

This road was provided with barely [rolling] stock enough for the transportation of produce, &c., in ordinary times, and even then we had delays from want of cars at certain seasons. Now we have the armies of the West [of Virginia], the Northwest, and of the Potomac, the population of a considerable city, to supply. I think I am reasonable in saying that 75 per cent of the supplies for this army is taken over some portion of our road.

On top of everything else, the superintendent complained, government shipments were not regularized. A fortnight ago there had been nothing to send; now suddenly a thousand barrels of flour. Major Ashe added his own observation: "...It is almost impossible, without previous notice, to transport, on the moment, such a large amount as 1,000 barrels of provisions." The barrels had in fact gone off piecemeal over the past six days.

Yet the root cause of the problem remained the detention of cars as warehouses. Ashe dismissed Cabell's claim to quick unloading with a final plea to Quartermaster General Myers about "the absolute necessity of having cars loaded with freight discharged as soon as practicable. Every moment's delay is felt more than any person who is not acquainted with railroad schedules can conceive of."[62]

The Virginia Central superintendent was right about the breadth of his railroad's responsibility for supplying troops all over Virginia. But the Commissary General's problems were both more and less than they appeared from this. They were less in the Valley of Virginia, where rich farming districts could still easily support locally stationed troops where not too heavily concentrated. Thus with relatively few supplies from Richmond, John Worsham's regiment still found itself well off in "that great place for wheat, flour, and hogs, and democrats"—at least in summer and autumn.[63]

Beyond the Valley westward lay the Alleghenies and some of the wildest country in the eastern states. In these high, remote regions there were no railroads. Cart tracks (where they existed) were rough, paths few, farms often far between and poor. Extensive military operations over such terrain would almost inevitably demand more food than the country provided. Food could be sent by rail only as far as the nearest station—often sixty or a hundred miles away: from there it must be hauled by wagons over the roughest, steepest paths.

General Robert E. Lee had been out in the Alleghenies since late July 1861. He was trying to galvanize two quarrelling Confederate commanders, Henry Wise and John B. Floyd, into some offensive action against the gathering Federals before it was too late. Pitiless rain had drenched all of western

---

[62]   Ibid., September 23, 1861, 875-76.
[63]   *One of Jackson's Foot Cavalry*, 53, 55.

Virginia for weeks, miring every road in bottomless mud. When supplies failed to reach the separated Confederate camps through the rough mountain terrains, those failures were visited on the Commissary General. [64]

Food stocks were low enough for Lee to send an urgent request to Richmond on September 10. Northrop responded that food was "going forward with all the dispatch possible".[65] Then he learned that the field commissaries of the two quarrelling generals were bidding against each other, to the alternating profit and rage of local farmers.[66] Neither Northrop nor Lee himself was able to impose order on the quarreling commissaries or their generals, and in the end the President had to remove Wise.[67]

---

[64] Mary Chesnut's Civil War, 155.

[65] AAG George Deas to Lee, September 14, 1861 (OR ser. I, vol 5, 851).

[66] Benjamin to Northrop, October 16, 1861 (NA, RG 109, Letters sent by the Confederate Secretary of War, III, 183).

[67] Freeman, R. E. Lee, I, 541-604.

CHAPTER 10

SOLUTION AND DISSOLUTION IN NORTHERN VIRGINIA

The Federals did not remain idle forever. On October 15, 1861 the Confederate flour agent James Ranson wrote from Charlestown, Virginia to the President:

> The enemy crossed the Potomac at Harper's Ferry last week, and in considerable numbers—how many it is not easily ascertained, but sufficient to hold the place—and they have been arriving ever since, pillaging and ravaging as they advanced. The farmers below this place are being robbed of slaves, horses, and everything the enemy can use.
>
> Last night a lady swam the Shenandoah to let us know that the enemy were being re-inforced, and the first aim would be to destroy our woolen factories along the Shenandoah; also our large flouring mills. This will be done. The delay heretofore has been caused by the shipping of some 20,000 bushels of wheat seized at Harper's Ferry.[1]

It looked as if Ranson would not be able to continue his flour agency so far north much longer.

Yet by then the Subsistence Bureau was responding to the congressional directive to furnish Confederate troops with "well-baked bread". Hard bread was in strong request, for it stood up well in a knapsack during marches. Commercial bakeries found it difficult to manage, and even when apparently cool it would often turn musty when barrelled for shipment. So the Bureau bought its own bakery. By running round the clock, it could be made to turn out 280 barrels of hard bread a day. Ruffin reported: "This bread, made of superior flour, is cheaper by 12 1/2 per cent than it could have been bought from outside parties making a very inferior article." By January 1862 they would have respectable stocks of hard bread both at Manassas and in Richmond.[2]

---

[1]   *OR* ser. I, vol. 5, 898-99.

[2]   *OR* ser. IV, vol. 1, 878.

117

Soon after buying the bakery, Northrop hired a mill in Richmond, "and bought wheat instead of flour, and authorized similar operations elsewhere to stop speculations in flour; every sort of opposition and criticism by millers and the press followed. In a few localities where farmers would not sell, I sent flour from Richmond; this was effective...".[3] Both mill and bakery thus became further essays in centralizing the army's food supply. Neither made many civilian friends for the Subsistence Bureau.

Food prices were rising everywhere, especially in cities. One old lady in Richmond marvelled: "Coffee is now thirty cents per pound, and my grocer tells me I must buy at once, or very soon we shall have to pay double that price. Shameful!"[4] When it became absolutely impossible to buy coffee for the army within the Subsistence budget, Northrop placed his remaining stock in a special store for hospitals.[5]

Salt, needed at every level of housekeeping, rose more rapidly than coffee. In the spring of 1861 a bushel of salt had cost 50 cents almost everywhere. By August several newspapers were finding it necessary to insist that a bushel of salt ought not to cost more than $1. In October the market price in Richmond was $6 and then $8. Even granted that some shortages were appearing, it was clear that money was being made. By mid-November extortion was so blatant throughout Virginia that the governor seized the chance of an out-of-session convention of the state's lawmakers to draw emergency attention to it: "When the Legislature assembles much of the mischief will have been done, and hence my appeal to the convention to interfere."[6]

No one could find any remedy for a practice in which so many were at least potentially interested. Before the end of November 1861 Northrop would have to ask for another $13 1/2 million just to tide over to the end of the fiscal year in February next. All the other bureaus needed similar injections.[7] When Congress got round to enacting the extra appropriations, the sums requested were all cut down by a third.[8]

What if the army's meat supply should fail for want of salt or transport? To fill a temporary hiatus in the Confederate West, General Braxton Bragg had substituted molasses from New Orleans (where it was cheap and plentiful). The congressional appropriation would include, at Northrop's request, a special sum to purchase and store molasses.[9] Northrop also looked at further possibilities. In November 1861 he wrote to the commissaries at

---

[3]   January 26, 1881 to Davis (Rowland, VIII, 585).

[4]   [Brock], *Richmond During the War*, 79.

[5]   Northrop proposed to Secretary Benjamin to substitute for coffee a ration of whiskey, but that idea repelled Benjamin on account of the youth of many volunteers. Benjamin suggested a special ration of tobacco instead (October 28, 1861 to Northrop: NA, RG 109, Letters Sent by the Confederate Secretary of War, III, 239). In any case the production of Southern whiskey was soon stopped or rigidly limited by individual states, as it drew off so much grain. (See Ramsdell, *Behind the Lines*, 36-38)

[6]   *OR* ser. IV, vol. 1, 739.

[7]   Ibid., 764-65.

[8]   Ibid., 812.

[9]   *OR* ser. IV, vol. 1, 908-9.

Charleston, Savannah, and Fernandina in Florida: "... Let rice and molasses be used occasionally as a substitute for meat." He suggested actual amounts to make up a ration: "but all this must be tested by experiment. So of lard. Get some intelligent men to make the trial in camp and report conclusions."[10]

At Manassas, throughout the autumn of 1861, General Johnston kept his own and Beauregard's armies immobilized for months—eating and eating and eating. Even then their numbers were rapidly increasing; by November, Johnston himself would count 47,200 of them.[11] Would he not attempt some military offensive before simply making camp for the winter? The question began to be asked persistently. In Richmond Mrs. Chesnut reported the observation of her uncle, Alexander Hamilton Boykin, on the subject of Joe Johnston and his late brother Sidney:

> "Now", says Mr. Hamilton Boykin, "we all knew Sid Johnston, the General's brother. Never in his life could he make up his mind that everything was so exactly right that the time to act had come. There was always something to fit that would not fit.
> "Joe Johnston is that way too. Wade Hampton brought him here to hunt—he is Mrs. Hampton's cousin. He was a capital shot, better than Wade or I... But ... he was too fussy, too hard to please, too cautious, too much afraid to risk his fine reputation as a crack shot. ... The exactly right time and place never came. Unless his ways are changed, he'll never fight a battle—."[12]

Nobody seemed able to do anything about Manassas. Robert E. Lee was busy elsewhere. The President's attention was taken up by a continuing series of pettifogging protests from Johnston over his seniority among Confederate generals.[13] And Johnston, no doubt partly as a result of his own disaffection, communicated to Richmond almost nothing of his plans—if indeed he had any. For all the Commissary General knew, the Confederate armies at Manassas might remain immobilized there forever.

Winter was nearly upon them—a Virginia winter, harsher by far than most of the boys from the Deep South had ever known. Beef cattle could not be made available for slaughtering in great numbers at that season, if there was to be enough calving in the spring. So the main dependence in winter shifted to salt meat. How could sufficient salt meat be delivered to northern Virginia to feed the nearly fifty thousand soldiers at Manassas, plus any other commands not able to provide for themselves through the winter? Rail shipments of meat from Nashville were taking from one to three months.[14]

---

[10] November 22, 1861 (NA, RG 109, Officers: Guerin, H.C.). When no results emerged, Northrop caused a chaser to be sent to the three commissaries on January 27, 1862 (Ibid.); but the file contains nothing further.

[11] *Narrative of Military Operations*, 83.

[12] *Mary Chesnut's Civil War*, 268.

[13] *Narrative of Military Operations*, 82-83; *OR*, ser. I, vol. 5, 850-51; ser. IV, vol. 1, 605-8, 611; Rowland, V, 130-32.

[14] *OR* ser. IV, vol. 1, 872.

Northrop's continued pleas for government control of railroads were ignored. Private freight and passenger traffic always seemed to secure preference by paying the higher charges demanded of them by the lines, bribing the company agents, or both. The conclusion was inescapable: in the foreseeable weeks and months, meat for Manassas would have to come to a great extent from the district itself. The railroads had defeated Northrop's policy for meat, at least in the first round.

Could the Bureau cattle agent for the district, Burr Noland, somehow find enough meat to feed the huge camps at Manassas through the winter, despite inflation? Even if he could, there was every likelihood that severe weather would interrupt such a supply from time to time. Again the answer was to cure the meat: only thus could spasmodic supply be converted to regularized product.

No big meat packery existed within range of Manassas. Yet if one could be created near there, it would feed Johnston's army consistently. Such a packery close to Manassas would offer another advantage: that lay in using the perishable by-products of butchery which were not cured—heads, ribs, organs, and all those parts known collectively as offal. Offal was usually disposed of cheaply or discarded as it spoiled quickly. But if a meat packery was close enough to Manassas, the offal could be sent there to create thousands of fresh rations that would otherwise not exist. The cured meat could then be reserved at the packery against a rainy or snowy day when no animals came in. At the same time the accumulated stores of meat could be transported, if the packery were near a railroad, to any point if and when Johnston made up his mind to move from Manassas.

Where was the best site for such a plant near Manassas? Northrop consulted Noland, whose knowledge of the whole district was proved anew each day by the numbers of animals he still brought in. Noland suggested Thoroughfare Gap, the pass in the Blue Ridge mountains west of Manassas through which ran the Manassas Gap Railroad.[15] The site offered several large buildings quickly convertible, and the constant supply of fresh water needed to prepare the meat. Thoroughfare Gap lay hardly ten miles from Johnston's camp by rail, and the line ran westward deep into the Shenandoah Valley. From the Gap, therefore, meat could be shipped as easily east to Johnston as west to support Confederate forces defending the Valley.

Placing a packery so far north offered the added advantage of drawing animals from both sides of the mountains away from the enemy. There might be a disadvantage in the proximity of the enemy himself. Harpers Ferry lay only forty miles away: yet those forty miles ran along the chain of mountains. To the west, the northern Valley of Virginia would have to be defended by the Confederates to prevent the enemy from coming down and simply climbing aboard the Manassas Gap Railroad to ride right into Manassas Junction. To the east stood the Confederate outpost at Leesburg. (The Feder-

---

[15] Noland wrote around 1881: "The selection of Thoroughfare was doubtless made by me with the sanction of the Commissary General." (Evidence written at Northrop's request, quoted in Didier, "Scape-Goat", I, 7)

als made an attempt on Ball's Bluff, near Leesburg, on October 21 but were repulsed.) If the enemy overran Leesburg, the result again would be to make Manassas untenable. While Manassas was held, therefore, Thoroughfare Gap must remain safe.

Having consulted Noland over the plant's location, Northrop did not consult the general on either side of the mountains. In the east at Manassas was Johnston, silent as to plans, yet the source of many complaints. He could be expected to see, in such a heavy establishment so close to him, a brake on his military options. Especially should he decide to retreat from Manassas, the abandonment of such a facility could increase his public embarrassment.

West of the mountains, in the Valley, the commander was Thomas J. "Stonewall" Jackson, just promoted to major general but still under Johnston's command. Jackson was a very different character, and was rapidly to prove an imaginative, aggressive fighter. But he would be in no position to dissent from his chief over the location of a major plant to supply the Army of Northern Virginia (as it was soon to be known).[16]

So Northrop made up his mind. He was later to summarize his own thinking thus: "Thoroughfare was as safe, while Jackson held the lower [i.e., northern] part of the Valley, and J. Johnston covered the line from Occoquan [on the Potomac below Alexandria] to Leesburg. ... Thoroughfare was established in October [1861:] it was as safe as anywhere during the winter and opening of spring, and while we could confront the enemy; if we were unable to do that, where was a safe place? ...Under the same circumstances I would put it in the same place."[17]

When news of the packery at Thoroughfare Gap reached General Johnston at Manassas, he was predictably outraged. Not only had he not been consulted;[18] but also, in view of Northrop's well-known friendship with the President, it was at least possible that Davis himself had given personal approval for the plant. If that were the case, then this new packery could appear as an attempt at executive pre-emption of his own military options at Manassas.

Johnston made no secret of his views. His chief commissary that winter (after Blair retired in December on account of ill health) was Major Robert G. Cole. Cole soon conveyed what may have been the substance of Johnston's thinking to a friend on the staff, Charles Marshall. Thus instructed, Marshall was to describe the packery at Thoroughfare as "a remarkable illustration of the blind confidence of the Commissary Department in the ability of our Army to maintain its position... The suggestion that the depot was located at such an exposed place to suit the convenience of officers and agents of the

---

[16]   Freeman, *R.E. Lee*, II, 77-78 n6.

[17]   December 20, 1879 to Davis (Rowland, VIII, 436-37). See also Northrop to Randolph, April 1, 1862 (*OR* ser. IV, vol. 1, 1036).

[18]   According to Charles Marshall, Johnston later claimed to have been consulted, and to have remonstrated against the location (Marshall, *An Aide-de-Camp of Lee*, 44). I have seen no evidence to support that claim, and Johnston himself wrote specifically in his *Narrative* that the plant was established "without my knowledge". (99)

Commissary Department residing in the vicinity, and desiring to remain at home while discharging their duties, reflects too strongly upon those officers and agents to be accepted without strong evidence."[19] Noland's big farm in Loudoun county was of course widely known. This near-libel characterized the ignorance of those who wrote and spoke as Marshall did, and Johnston saw to it that there were many.

The new packery at Thoroughfare Gap was in fact the Commissary General's answer to weeks and months of harassment from the generals at Manassas who had combined—or was it conspired?—to blame him for every failure of Confederate finance and transport. If there was any element of overkill in Northrop's placement of his plant so close to Johnston's camp, it was to make absolutely certain that there could be no more complaints from there.

The fact was that the packery did its job handsomely. Being a government plan, there was no paying away of the "fifth quarter" as a butchering fee, or even half of it. Frank Ruffin reported in January 1862: "Every product is saved to the Government, because it either finds ready sale or prompt and grateful consumption by the Army."[20] Were the troops really grateful for offal? In their minds that winter, the government plant at Thoroughfare Gap must have been identified with an unending avalanche of the stuff. But all the while, behind the plant's doors, an invaluable stock of cured meat was quietly building up. Noland wrote: "It...was managed with economy both in the purchase and the preservation of meat. The army was abundantly supplied, and the surplus slaughtered and packed; so that we had between 1,500,000 and 2,000,000 lbs. of the best beef and pork the world ever saw, on hand...".[21]

When Johnston now ordered a fifteen days' supply of meat to be accumulated and kept always ahead at Manassas, it was done without a murmur. Then he ordered a further ten days' supply to be kept behind his line, half way down the Virginia Central Railroad at Culpeper Court House. That was done as easily. But the accumulation at Culpeper was made, Johnston later wrote, as "a preparation for the contingency of our finding it necessary or expedient to fall back from Centerville [the village close by Manassas Junction] to the line of the Rappahannock".[22] So his thinking began at last to reveal itself.

* * *

A vigorous anti-administration press flourished in Richmond. It was fanned by Johnston's and Beauregard's malcontent politicking from Manassas. Beauregard had submitted his official report of the July battle there only after repeated prodding. It was months late, and laced with contentious allegations over the failure to advance on Washington. The President was deeply offended. A section of the press took it up.

[19] Marshall, *An Aide-de-Camp of Lee*, 44-45.

[20] *OR* ser. IV, vol. 1, 874.

[21] Didier, "Scape-Goat", I, 7.

[22] *Narrative of Military Operations*, 83.

The Commissary General's friendship with the President was well known. Some of the press hinted that it was Northrop's only qualification for his post. The editor of *The Richmond Examiner*, Edward A. Pollard, constituted himself the special gadfly of the Subsistence Bureau. The prose was colorful, the tone indignant:

> No department of our army is more important than the commissariat, and none in which more mismanagement, waste and recknessness are exhibited. ...
> Rice, of which our men are entirely deprived, is a Southern staple. The same may be said of sugar; and yet, with a country intersected with railroads penetrating the very heart of the army, thus furnishing the most ample transportation, with a Government abundantly supplied with means for their purchase, the soldiers who furnish the means and defend the country are day after day informed by the commissaries that there is neither sugar, rice, soap or candles to be had.[23]

The possibility that inefficient railroads were hobbling transport, that want of ready funds was indeed affecting government purchase, was never looked at.

Day after day, week after week, *The Examiner*—and other Richmond papers scenting sales—retailed half-truths and half-informed speculation for their readership, amongst whom were probably a majority of the Confederate Congress. Northrop never answered such slings. His notion of military duty would forbid revealing to the world the rickety currency and rackety railroads that had forced such complication on him. The attacks affected him privately. Near the end of the year a Catholic nun in Richmond reported to Bishop Lynch of Charleston: "I saw Col Northrop and his family, they are looking badly—he made very kind inquiries for you, he is just as usual—no change—save that he looks broken down, his situation I believe is a laborious one."[24]

The first national election in the Confederacy took place on November 6, 1861. Davis ran unopposed for President, and he was confirmed by the electorate. They voted also on a full slate of representatives and Senators for a bi-cameral Congress: the newly elected Congress would take office on the opening day of a new fiscal year, February 18, 1862. Meanwhile the old Provisional Congress met for a final session. It was their longest of all, running from November 18, 1861 for three months.

One matter hanging over from August was the investigation of War Department supply bureaus. On January 11, 1862 a young congressman from Clarksville, Tennessee introduced a new resolution for a special committee to expose "abuses".[25] Northrop responded with a written statement covering a series of subsistence reports by Frank Ruffin.

---

[23] October 2, 1861.

[24] Mother Teresa, December 23, 1861 (CDA 26 S 7).

[25] *Journal of Congress*, I, 653-54, 676. The Tennesseean's original resolution covered only subsistence; Congress widened the scope to cover other bureaus as well.

Under "Salt Meats", Ruffin showed that about a quarter of the Northern bacon secured in early 1861 had been consumed; three-quarters of that unique stock was still left. He explained the reasoning behind the network of contracts with all the big packers along the Tennessee railroad, summarized results, and reported outstanding help given by leading packers who had "strained their credit to its utmost tension to ease the strain upon the Treasury". The rise in meat prices since the opening of the war was not more than price rises of other essentials: "They could not have been kept lower except by a military order prohibiting exportation. Such an order was applied for, but refused, to the great enhancement of prices." He characterized accusations of fraud in pork prices as "slander".

For salt beef, Ruffin described the parallel network of contracts. Beef was also packed in the government plant at Thoroughfare Gap, as well as in a new one at Richmond. As to fresh beef, he showed how commissaries in the field had been left to collect their own cattle where possible. But where the region was adverse or troop concentrations too heavy, the Bureau had appointed cattle agents. The men were listed with their districts, and economies resulting from their management detailed.

Turning to flour, he explained how the want of money to control Virginia flour markets in a bumper year had engendered the complex Northrop plan worked out with James Crenshaw. Then he confronted the accusations of self-interest leveled at James Crenshaw, especially since the price of flour had risen sharply (as Northrop had forecast it would). Ruffin showed that so far from profiteering, the Haxall, Crenshaw firm had actually returned part of their profit to the government: "... where they had an admitted right to a compensation of $6.76 per barrel [in view of the contract's sliding scale contemplating price rises in flour] they voluntarily remitted 26 cents per barrel, or $6,500 of their claim."

Ruffin added observations on minor items in the ration. Sugar and molasses were already purchased, and only awaited rail transport. Rice would be bought by contracts then being prepared, calling for bonds only in payment. As for salt, the Stuart, Buchanan contract promised "an ample quantity" for both the army and the contracted packers; contract terms were recited. Nothing was said about fresh vegetables as it was winter—or about coffee, now unavailable on terms within the Subsistence budget.

The whole file of reports and documents went on January 18, 1862 to the Secretary of War. Secretary Benjamin sent it on to the President with his own conclusion: the Subsistence reports "demonstrate the gratifying fact that the supplies have been provided with such foresight, energy, and prudence as to have cost the Government far less than could reasonably have been expected, and far less than they would now cost if the contracts had not been made."[26] Gratifying or not, that observation constituted a grim forecast of what would happen when the present contracts should either run out or be overtaken by such runaway inflation as to nullify them. The first instance of that lay only a few months in the future.

---

[26] *OR* ser. IV, vol. 1, 870-79.

Davis forwarded the Subsistence report to Congress. The committee decided to make further inquiries of the Commissary General. They got more than they bargained for. Northrop wrote a few days later to Bishop Lynch: "... I have had more hard work and more annoyance than is a due share for a life time during the past 6 months. ... I have had one sort of compensation & that was to tell the Congressmen that I cared not a snap of a finger for them or their commission. I told the Military Committee so repeatedly and this has been the burden of my intercourse with them."[27]

The committee nonetheless made a fair report to Congress on January 29, 1862. They realized that collecting such a vast army suddenly must bring teething troubles. Under suggestions to the Surgeon General, the committee excoriated bad cooking in camp, finding it largely responsible for the camp epidemics so widely reported. Under the quartermaster section, they recognized shortcomings of rail transport. At one point they verged on suggesting that the cars of all lines be pooled, but they recommended no legislation.

In the Subsistence section, the committee began by affirming the need to provide adequate food above every consideration of price or economy. They had clearly had an eye-opener as to the sheer complexity of Subsistence problems and operations. In fact their new knowledge led the committee men into contradicting themselves. On the one hand, they wrote: "Without system in the administration of this department, the most fertile genius would prove powerless, and the most abundant resources insufficient...". On the other hand, they found the circumstances so varied that "far more reliance must be placed upon the intelligence, the ability, and the zeal of the commissary than upon any system established for general guidance." In the end the committee were unable to say which of those factors had brought success. Subsistence success they reported in a single colossal sentence:

> The returns of this department show that although its chief supply has been obtained within the Confederacy, heretofore considered insufficient to support its population, with an untiring, vigilant, and remorseless enemy surrounding and endeavoring by every means to starve as well as subjugate, we have had our Army well fed, and with an amount on hand so large as to place us beyond the reach of want for the ensuing campaign [i.e., the year 1862], and trusting to a kind Providence for our usual seasons and the preparations that are being made throughout the Confederacy for the next crop, we need fear no coming want.[28]

The report was accepted by Congress *in toto*. The following day, January 30, 1862, the committee chairman called at the Commissary General's office to convey the favorable substance of their report. But praise from that source was unwelcome, as Northrop wrote to Bishop Lynch: "This morning the chairman was here and informed me of the nature of their report. I told him to remember distinctly that I have never tried to conciliate one of them;

---

[27]   Wight, 465.

[28]   *OR* ser. IV, vol. 1, 883-91.

LEROY POPE WALKER
(1817-1884):
SECRETARY
FEBRUARY TO SEPTEMBER 1861.

GENERALS IN GRAY

THE FIRST
CONFEDERATE SECRETARIES OF WAR

JUDAH P. BENJAMIN
(1811-1884):
SECRETARY
SEPTEMBER 1861
TO MARCH 1862.

he said that was well understood. They have in Congress charged me with rudeness to them. I consider rudeness a crime but am glad that they do understand that if I am confirmed [as Commissary General] it is because they want me."[29] He was confirmed by Congress at last, on February 12, as permanent Commissary General and full colonel. The vote was 44 to 3.

Northrop might have been better pleased by the praise of his own chief, Secretary Benjamin, included in his report to the President in late February: "The foresight and sagacity, the energy and integrity with which the business of furnishing food to such large numbers of troops over so extensive a country has been conducted are eminently creditable to the chief of the commissariat."[30]

* * *

In northern Virginia meanwhile disaster unfolded in slow motion. For months Joseph E. Johnston had been secretly wanting to retreat from Manassas. Two separate enemy threats worried him. First, Lincoln and his cabinet were so nervous about the continuing large Confederate camp thirty miles from Washington that the Federals could well move out an overwhelming army against Manassas as soon as roads dried at the end of winter. Then Johnston learned of a second strategy designed by the new Federal commander George B. McClellan: instead of moving on Manassas, McClellan proposed sending his forces down the coast in ships to the Virginia Peninsula, where the two rivers York and James would afford them broad highways right up to the gates of Richmond. Whichever plan was used, Johnston felt, he ought to withdraw his army and set it to guard Richmond. His thinking typified the defensive strategist.

What then of the enormous accumulation of personal baggage, ordnance, quartermaster and commissary stores at Manassas? What of the meat packery at Thoroughfare Gap? All must be abandoned—destroyed—as soon as possible. A Federal writer saw this: "... The rebel generals strip their armies for a march as a man strips to run a race. Their men are 'destitute' when they reach our [Federal] lines, because they cannot cumber themselves with supplies. They come to fight—not to eat."[31] The greatest genius of subsistence planning must fail in the face of military thinking like that.

Johnston had not communicated much of his thinking to Richmond. Instead, on January 4, 1862, he merely ordered his new commissary, Major Robert G. Cole, to telegraph the Subsistence Bureau to send further shipments from Richmond only as far as Culpeper Court House, down the line south of Manassas.[32] Apparently Cole telegraphed without result. Twelve days later, Cole telegraphed again, asking Richmond to stop shipments to Manassas altogether. He was to write: "On the 29th I repeated the request, indicating that the amount at Manassas was nearly double that required."[33]

29   Wight, 465.
30   *OR* ser. IV, vol. 1, 960.
31   Quoted in *Jefferson Davis: A Memoir by His Wife* (New York: Belford, 1890), II, 361-62 footnote.
32   Johnston, *Narrative*, 98 ff.; Northrop to Davis, August 22, 1885 (Rowland, IX, 385).
33   Quoted in Johnston, *Narrative*, 98*n*.

Cole's telegrams would have been addressed not to the Commissary General but to the Bureau storehouse in Richmond. As Northrop wrote: "Cole was in the habit of visiting Richmond on business with Depot Commissary [Claiborne] and returning without seeing me. He understood the proper place to do his business at."[34] In later years Northrop emphatically denied "ever having received such [telegrams], nor can I find any one who remembers them, but fortunately I have two letters from Cole in January—one before the 16th the other after and before the 29th, neither making the smallest allusion to excess, but expressing his satisfaction that the army was well supplied and satisfied...".[35]

At last the message of excess at Manassas reached Northrop: "When I was informed, I did what [Cole] should have done—telegraphed the shippers to stop."[36] That was just what Cole thought he had done. Johnston was later to claim that the Bureau had disregarded his instructions.[37] Yet during all these weeks nobody even up to the President himself seems to have had any inkling of Johnston's plans.

Not until February 20, 1862 did Johnston confer with Davis and his cabinet about withdrawal from Manassas. The mood in Richmond was gloomy, with news of disasters in Tennessee coming in every hour (see next chapter); and Johnston's personal relations with Davis remained distant. After much discussion, it was agreed that Johnston could withdraw from Manassas—where was not specified—but that he must take every precaution to bring off all the Manassas stores.

That day or the next, recalled Burr Noland (in charge of the packery at Thoroughfare):

> ... I had an interview with the Secretary of War and the Commissary General, in which I was told, as a state secret, that Manassas was to be abandoned, and that I was to proceed with all secrecy and dispatch to remove the meat from Thoroughfare.
>
> I went the next day to Manassas with General Johnston, who talked pleasantly though gravely about the matter, cautioned me to keep the information to myself, and to use the utmost dispatch. He said I could have the transportation necessary, and he thought about two weeks would be required to remove the stores. I told him that, with one train of ten or twelve cars [devoted exclusively to the purpose and available for constant, returning use], everything could be sent from Thoroughfare to Culpepper [sic] Court House in that time.
>
> I went at once to Thoroughfare, stopped all slaughtering, told the officers and hands in charge that the meat was needed at Culpepper; had platforms erected to correspond with the doors of the twelve cars, and on the [platforms] placed about 20,000 lbs of meat each.[38]

[34] January 26, 1881 to Davis (Rowland, VIII, 583).

[35] Ibid. In a letter to Davis of March 26, 1879, Northrop cited the dates of Cole's letters as January 24 and 30, 1862 (Tulane r 22, f 501-505).

[36] *Battles and Leaders*, I, 261.

[37] *Narrative*, 98-99.

[38] Quoted in Didier, "Scape-Goat", I, 7, where the date is given as February 20. Noland's official report of March 27, 1862 gives February 21 (*OR* ser. IV, vol. 1, 1039).

Besides Culpeper, some of the meat was to go south on the railroad to Orange, and some to the western end of the Manassas Gap Railroad at Mount Jackson. Arrangements to house it were made at both places, and staff engaged.

Almost nothing happened. The promised railroad cars never came, and the reason given was that "Johnston's command had taken control of the transportation"! Noland sought help from Johnston's chief commissary and quartermaster: the only result was a single use of 45 cars, which Noland promptly loaded and sent off to Mount Jackson.[39]

A look into Johnston's correspondence with Davis during these days produces an impression of less than full effort by the general himself. On February 25 Johnston wrote: "The accumulation of subsistence stores at Manassas is now a great evil. ... A very extensive meat-packing establishment at Thoroughfare is also a great encumbrance. The great quantities of personal property in our camps is a still greater one. Much of both kinds of property must be sacrificed in the contemplated movement." Three days later: "I regret to be unable to make a favorable report of the progress of our preparations to execute your [sic] plans. The want of an efficient staff and the wretched mismanagement of the railroad are the causes—and our endeavoring to save as much as possible of the great amount of public property collected here. [In other words, the endeavor to save that property was a mistake.] As I remarked to you orally, the measure must be attended with great sacrifice of property, and perhaps much suffering."

That day Davis wrote back uncompromisingly: "The subsistence stores should, when removed, be placed in position to answer your future wants; those cannot be determined until you have furnished definite information as to your plans, especially the line to which you would remove in the contingency of retiring." Davis disliked the whole plan of retreat, and told Johnston that if his effective army could be raised to a hundred thousand men he ought to be able to stay where he was and be poised to take the offensive. Johnston ignored that, and merely repeated that he could not get cars for subsistence removal. Davis attacked Quartermaster General Myers, who replied with an unhelpful recital.[40]

At Thoroughfare, Noland confronted complete frustration. The meat lay exposed on his platforms day after day. Trains passed and repassed, many of them empty; yet none stopped.

> On the 8th [March 1862] I received an order from Major Cole, commissary of subsistence, to destroy all the meat which was not removed by the 10th...; but on consultation with General Johnston and himself on the following day at Manassas, I was authorized to use my discretion and save from destruction as much as possible by hauling it to Warrenton [a few miles below Thoroughfare, and the railhead of a little spur running southeast into the main line below Manassas] by wagons and [by] giving it away.

---

[39] March 27, 1862 (*OR* ser. IV, vol. 1, 1038).

[40] *OR* ser. I, vol. 5, 1081, 1083-84, 1093.

I caused combustibles to be placed under every pile of meat for its immediate destruction when necessary. Guards were placed on all the roads leading to Thoroughfare to give notice of the approach of the enemy, and the people for many miles around notified to send in their teams [to haul the meat to Warrenton]. A liberal price in money and a load of meat was offered to each person who would send a wagon. The response to the call was prompt and gratifying, and on Monday the 10th we had about thirty wagons, and others promised for the next day.

That night the Confederate cavalry arrived with orders to destroy everything. Their leader, Colonel Thomas Munford, saw what Noland was doing, held his hand for precious hours, and actually impressed some further wagons overnight. Thus they got away fifty wagon loads more before Johnston's "peremptory" order was carried out to destroy everything. They burnt nearly 370,000 pounds of meat, 500 hides, much tallow, and most of the buildings at Thoroughfare.[41]

At Manassas itself, under Johnston's direct control, nothing whatever of subsistence stores was saved.[42] In the book he published in 1874, Johnston was to write sarcastically of the fifteen days during which Noland and Cole were moving heaven and earth to get the meat away as "quite long enough to subordinate the operations of an army to the protection of commissary stores exposed against the wishes and remonstrances of the general. ... It would not have been proper to bestow more time upon the preservation of commissary stores."[43] When these words met Northrop's eye in later years, he wrote bitterly: "I believe [Johnston] *wanted* the public property to be destroyed both at Manassas and Thoroughfare."[44]

At the time, in 1862, Northrop's official report merely drew the contrast of Stonewall Jackson's commissary management: "... In the falling back of the Confederate Army of the Potomac, no stores whatever were lost.[45] At Winchester, young John Worsham had seen that for himself. "Jackson's way", he wrote, "was to save everything already on hand and never destroy if there was a chance to save. It was a saying in the command that he would carry off a wheelbarrow load rather than let it fall into the hands of the enemy. While we were camped around Winchester, he was diligently at work getting everything out of reach of the enemy...".[46]

Johnston's motives for the wholesale destruction at Manassas and Thoroughfare may not have been wholly vindictive. He lived there in daily fear of a massive Federal attack. Such an attack had in fact been planned; it

---

[41]   Noland's report to Northrop, March 27, 1862 (*OR* ser. IV, vol. 1, 1038-40).

[42]   Ibid., 1040.

[43]   *Narrative*, 104, 446.

[44]   March 8, 1885 to Davis (Rowland, IX, 352). Note should be taken of a letter written by Jubal Early in 1877 to Davis: "I know that General Johnston sent General [Isaac] Trimble, an old rail-road man, to Manassas Junction to superintend the transportation of the stores &c to the rear, and there was some complaint that he took care to send all the baggage of his own brigade to the rear, while valuable public stores were lost." (Rowland, VIII, 3)

[45]   *OR* ser. I, vol. 52, pt. 2, 534.

[46]   *One of Jackson's Foot Cavalry*, 65.

was abandoned on March 8 for reasons unconnected with the Confederate withdrawal then about to begin.[47] McClellan seems to have known nothing of Johnston's retreat until he saw smoke from the destroying fires on March 11, and made a personal reconnaissance round Manassas to find "many wagons, some caissons, clothing, ammunition, personal baggage, etc. ... the country entirely stripped of forage and provisions."[48]

Try as he did to defend it afterwards, Johnston's destruction at Manassas laid the heaviest hand on the Confederate Army of Northern Virginia for the rest of the war. One of his officers, Lieutenant General Jubal Early, wrote afterwards: "The loss of stores ... at [Thoroughfare Gap], where a large amount of meat had been salted and stored, was a very serious one for us, and embarrassed us for the rest of the war, as it put us at once on a running stock."[49]

The meat network in Tennessee, which might otherwise have supplied Virginia, was partly overrun at almost the same moment. From then on the army in Virginia would have to be supplied largely through Richmond and the Deep South—with provisions purchased at distances for more and more money when the Treasury would supply cash, and delivered on railroads if they could find cars, engines, and an unencumbered and undestroyed run of track. If they could not, then the Confederate Army in depleted eastern Virginia might face starvation. That was the subsistence cost of Johnston's carefully planned retreat from Manassas.

---

[47]   Freeman, *Lee's Lieutenants*, I, 133 ff.
[48]   Quoted in Davis, *Rise and Fall*, II, 82.
[49]   Ibid., I, 468; Rowland, VIII, 7.

CHAPTER 11

FAILURES AND HOPES IN THE WEST

Beyond the Mississippi River lay Missouri, where the governor and many citizens supported the Southern cause. In 1861 they had placed state troops at the service of the Confederacy under former Governor Sterling Price. Federal forces opposing him were well organized, however, and in March 1862 after fierce fighting the Federals took the state. From then on the entire Upper Mississippi Valley was under Federal control.

East of the Mississippi, popular sympathies were deeply divided. In Tennessee the governor had transferred to the Confederacy his state militia with all its supplies. He recommended that the militia's Commissary General, Captain John T. Shaaff, be continued in service, and that Shaaff's post at Nashville be made a general supply base for western subsistence.[1] Northrop had accepted both recommendations.

Kentucky, just to the north, had tried to remain neutral in the war. But opinions there were so combative that its state militia broke into two rival factions, both recruiting furiously. Then on September 3, 1861 Confederate Major General Leonidas Polk had marched his forces into the state to seize Hickman and Columbus on the Mississippi River. The young Union Brigadier General Ulysses S. Grant retaliated by seizing Paducah—only thirty-five miles north on the Ohio River, not far from its junction with the Mississippi. The neutrality of Kentucky was shattered. That brought the entire northwestern section of the Confederacy under immediate threat.

Richmond quickly appointed a commander of Confederate forces west of the Alleghenies. He was General Albert Sidney Johnston (no relation to Joseph E. Johnston), a soldier of great reputation and an old friend of President Davis. Sidney Johnston arrived to take over the reins from Polk on September 15, 1861, but his responsibilities were far wider. His enormous new command stretched from the western borders of Virginia to Indian territories beyond the Mississippi.

Sidney Johnston drew his line of defence running through southern Kentucky from its eastern border with Virginia west to the Mississippi River at Columbus, which he fortified. That line, extending more than three hun-

---

[1]   *OR* ser, IV, vol. 1, 527.

dred miles, virtually defined the northern border of the Confederacy in the midwest. Yet Johnston had nothing like enough men to police its length. Along that line a Federal attack might come almost anywhere. The only certainty was that it would come. Federal gunboats were already beginning to enter the Mississippi River delta below New Orleans.

Eastern portions of Sidney Johnston's line could be served to some extent by Northrop's network of contracted meat packers along the Virginia-Tennessee railroad. But the railroad, like everything else in the region, ran between mountains that ranged northeast and southwest. As the railroad moved west, therefore, it also moved south—more and more increasing its distance from the Kentucky line the Confederates hoped to hold.

From Chattanooga, at the end of the line from Virginia, a different railroad ran northwest through Shelbyville (almost in the geographic center of Tennessee, and with Craigmiles's huge packery there) and on up to Nashville. Nashville contained the farthest north of the major packing houses in the Confederacy, and the biggest—those of Craigmiles and R. T. Wilson. Altogether two-thirds of the hogs for the army came from Tennessee; and two-thirds of those had been slaughtered and packed at Nashville.[2]

After some hesitation on account of Nashville's proximity to enemy lines, Northrop recognized that Nashville had to be the seat of government meat packing in the west. The facilities and organizations were there, together with the right climate. (Farther south packing was discouraged by heat and humidity; the Bureau did set up one plant in Louisiana, but the climate caused endless problems and expense.)[3] Once again Northrop did not consult the commanding general: he knew Sidney Johnston would not admit to any military uncertainty over Nashville in the autumn of 1861.[4] Northrop later summarized his own thinking thus: "When I was considering the chances, to determine on using the great packeries at Nashville, Shelbyville, and the current stock of those places, or of driving the stock south with no suitable buildings for large operations, I believed that Johnston would have to retreat and Nashville be possibly lost, but if beaten I knew not where there would be safety, so acted accordingly."[5]

Yet Nashville presented its own difficulties. One was an inadequate supply of local salt for curing so much meat. The several railroads found it impossible to bring sufficient quantities from the mines at Saltville, Virginia (where the government contract price was 75 cents a bushel). So the Bureau had to pay no less than $3 each for 40,000 bushels at Nashville.[6] That news was bound to make salt producers everywhere sit up.

Then the Tennessee packers ran out of barrels. The area did not contain enough coopers to keep up with the demand. The subsistence men

[2] Northrop's assistant Frank Ruffin reported on October 19, 1861 that 193,000 hogs had been slaughtered for the government in Tennessee. See Richard D. Goff, *Confederate Supply* (Duke Univ., 1969), 36-37.

[3] *OR* ser. IV, vol. 1, 875.

[4] July 31, 1885 to Davis (Museum of the Confederacy: Davis Coll.).

[5] December 20, 1879 to Davis (Rowland, VIII, 436).

[6] *OR* ser IV, vol. 1 878.

decided to try a half-measure. Packers close to Sidney Johnston's troops were told to brine and salt their beef and send it straight out to the soldiers. It all depended, as Frank Ruffin observed, on "timely transportation".[7]

With the possibility of Confederate retreat in his mind, Northrop had Sidney Johnston's cooperation in planning a series of large food depots ranging south from Nashville. They had two experts—Johnston's chief commissary at the pivotal Confederate point of Bowling Green, Kentucky, Major T. K. Jackson, and Northrop's man Colonel O. C. Boone—select sites to cover various lines of retreat. The first two were at Jackson, Tennessee and at Memphis, on the Mississippi River. A third was at Grand Junction, on Tennessee's border with the state of Mississippi. The two remaining depots were in Mississippi itself—west at Holly Springs, east at Corinth. The five depots were set up and equipped in October and November 1861.[8]

Once Sidney Johnston's line was at least sketched through Kentucky, Northrop was eager to extract more bacon out of that state of divided loyalties. He contacted an influential Kentuckian of known Southern patriotism[9], asking him to test the strength of Confederate sympathies among farmers in southern Kentucky, and then see about hiring a smaller packery as far north as seemed prudent. The man reported one available at Clarksville, sixty miles northwest of Nashville and just below the Kentucky border. The owners demanded $8,000 rent. Northrop wrote: "The alternative presented to me was to permit competition [against the Government] in an important position and lose results hoped for from Kentucky, or accept. The rent seemed extortionate, and I paused for information."[10]

The information Northrop wanted was assurance at the highest level that Sidney Johnston would be able to hold what he controlled in Kentucky. Frank Ruffin wrote later to his chief: "I remember how, before we packed at Clarksville, you ordered me to see Adjutant General Cooper and ascertain from him if General Albert Sidney Johnston meant to hold his lines in front of that point; how we were assured most positively that he did...".[11]

Then suddenly the whole responsibility of the Clarksville packery was taken off the Bureau's hands by their powerful ally R. T. Wilson. Wilson said he would go to Clarksville and hire the plant on his own account. The owners now demanded $10,000 rent. Wilson paid the money, took the plant, and began packing for the Confederate army almost in the enemy's teeth.[12]

The autumn of 1861 brought no advance of Sidney Johnston's forces, so there was no increase of Confederate influence in Kentucky. On Novem-

[7]　Ibid., 875.

[8]　See Northrop to Davis, March 27, 1885 (Rowland, IX, 355); July 31, 1885 (Museum of the Confederacy: Davis Coll.); and June 25, 1887 (Rowland, IX, 570).

[9]　The late Frank G. Rankin of Louisville, who had studied deeply the history of Kentucky in the War, suggested to me that the Kentuckian asked to tour the farms and advise the Bureau was Eli Metcalfe Bruce(1828-1866), owner of extensive packeries and a Confederate Congressman since 1861. (See above, p. 58 n. 16).

[10]　OR ser. IV, vol. 1, 871.

[11]　Quoted in Didier, "Scape-Goat", II, 9.

[12]　OR ser. IV, vol. 1, 871.

ber 27 Northrop wrote to Secretary of War Benjamin: "... As the hopes predicated on a more rapid advance of our forces have proved delusive, it has become necessary to draw from beyond our lines, where our currency will not answer." The Commissary General proposed to buy gold at 20 to 25 percent premium: that would violate Army Regulations, but he pointed out that the price of both pork and beef in Kentucky was a third less than in the Confederacy. He asked official sanction to buy the gold secretly. [13]

None of this would have been necessary if the Davis government had devised a coherent scheme for trading its greatest asset—cotton—beyond its borders and directly with the enemy if need be. There was no question that the enemy would accept cotton in payment for food or anything else: Confederate citizens along the borders were proving for themselves the power of that exchange every day of the week, whatever their government tried to do to stop them. Northrop had also had Fowlkes's offer to trade cotton for Kentucky bacon, but Davis would not allow it. [14]

Approval for the gold to purchase Kentucky meat, however, was given. In January 1861 Frank Ruffin could report: "The number secured is about 250,000 head of unusually large hogs, including some 20,000 which have been obtained from Kentucky within Federal lines at much risk and with occasional losses to those undertaking it." [15] It remained a risky trade, producing some derring-do and consuming a great deal of energy.

Yet Sidney Johnston remained sanguine. Around his advanced post at Bowling Green in central Kentucky, great concentrations of Confederate forces were building. One young officer, arriving there from the South, wrote: "On the 19th of December [1861] I reached Bowling Green, and found there a larger army than I had before seen,—65,000 men at least... Others were soon added, for on the 25th of December the Commissary General issued 96,000 rations, and by January 1, 1862 120,000 rations a day." [16]

The quick concentration of troops there created the same kind of commissariat difficulties as at Manassas six months earlier. Sidney Johnston, though more co-operative than the other Johnston, appointed extra commissaries who were unknown to the Commissary General. [17] They operated in a no-man's-land between the opposing lines; there they gave in to farmers' demands that they discount the Confederate currency when using it for payment—and often to farmers' demands for payment in gold. In early November 1861 Northrop remonstrated with Sidney Johnston to no avail. At last the Commissary General appealed to Secretary Benjamin, and Benjamin wrote to Johnston on December 26: "This is a war for national existence, and the Army must be fed, and it is impossible to pay for its food otherwise than in our national currency. ... Major Jackson, your chief commissary, informs the War Department that in some cases parties have succeeded in extorting

---

[13] Ibid., 757.

[14] See above, p. 113.

[15] *OR* ser IV, vol. 1, 874.

[16] William G. Stevenson, *Thirteen Months in the Rebel Army* (New York: Barnes, 1959), 73.

[17] Undated letter from Northrop to A. S. Johnston (NA, RG 109, Officers).

a discount of 40 per cent. You will at once perceive that a submission to such demands is equivalent to laying down our arms. ... Let the necessary supplies be impressed if not otherwise attainable...".[18] Yet no general wants to impress from an even potentially friendly populace; it is the surest way to alienate them.

What were the borderland commissary agents to do? As inflation rose and the value of Confederate currency slipped, nobody wanted to be paid in those notes—let alone Confederate bonds—when calculated at face value. The Federals were right around the corner. They might pay more, and even if they didn't, the United States currency was more likely to hold its value. Forty per cent off Confederate notes was probably a fair market discount in the late autumn of 1861.[19]

Then Sidney Johnston ordered a quantity of salt meat shipped from Clarksville—where Kentucky hogs made into bacon were supposed to be kept in store for the army as a whole—to his own troops at Bowling Green. And that, he said, was just an interim measure. What he demanded, as soon as possible, was an entirely new meat packing operation at Bowling Green itself, to create a forward base for his hoped-for offensive northwards. Northrop thought that entirely too risky, and took the extraordinary step of opposing Johnston's order.[20]

Johnston then went over Northrop's head and persuaded Secretary Benjamin to obtain a special appropriation for the Bowling Green packery. The money was paid through the Subsistence Bureau, and the man placed in charge was once again R. T. Wilson. Northrop tried to reassert control through a letter to Wilson, insisting that the new packery be used to create a reserve stock and not to furnish the daily knapsacks in Kentucky. He sent a copy to Commissary Jackson at Bowling Green, with instructions to interview Sidney Johnston and try to get his agreement. On January 11, 1862 Jackson reported what amounted to a polite refusal.[21] In fact Johnston's men consumed much of the meat packed at Bowling Green as soon as it was ready.

* * *

Just over a week later, on January 19, 1862, Federal troops attacked the eastern end of Sidney Johnston's defence line through Kentucky. In a sharp encounter at Mill Springs, ninety miles east of Bowling Green, Confederate General Felix Zollicoffer was killed along with many of his soldiers. The remainder fled back towards Knoxville, Tennessee, abandoning large commissary stores.

---

[18]   *OR* ser. I, vol. 7, 796.

[19]   Treasury Secretary Memminger was himself soon doing worse than that. A clerk in the War Department, John B. Jones, would confide to his diary on January 20, 1862: "Mr. Memminger advertises to pay interest on certain government bonds in *specie*. That won't last long. He is paying 50 per cent premium in treasury notes for the specie, and the bonds are given for treasury notes. What sort of financiering is this?" J. B. Jones, *A Rebel War Clerk's Diary* (2 vols, Philadelphia: Lippincott, 1866), I, 106.

[20]   December 20, 1879 to Davis (Rowland, VIII, 436).

[21]   *OR* ser. IV, vol. 1, 1036-7.

Within a fortnight parallel disasters occurred in western Kentucky. Union General Grant, at Paducah, controlled the mouths of two rivers, the Tennessee and the Cumberland. Both traced their courses south through Kentucky and deep into Tennessee (the Tennessee River in fact rose as far south as northern Mississippi). The Cumberland flowed past Wilson's new Confederate packery at Clarksville, and upstream flowed beside Nashville itself. Those two rivers offered Grant a double highway straight into the heart of the Confederate west. He soon took it.

Each river was guarded south of Paducah by a Confederate fort. That on the Tennessee was Fort Henry, so badly sited as to be partly under water in winter. Federal gunboats made short work there on February 6, 1862. A week later it was the turn of the guardian on the Cumberland, Fort Donelson. A three-day siege there culminated in Grant's famous note of February 16 to Brigadier General Simon B. Buckner: "No terms except unconditional and immediate surrender can be accepted." Grant had thus driven a double wedge right through Sidney Johnston's line. The Confederate western post at Columbus was half surrounded. So was Bowling Green in the center. Johnston had no choice but to pull back.

R. T. Wilson (in charge of meat packing at Nashville, Clarksville, and Bowling Green) had seen it coming. At the end of January 1862 he had made a special trip to Richmond to consult Northrop. Together they drew up a list of interior locations to which meat could be sent from exposed points, no matter what General Johnston said. Wilson returned and began to box up all the meat at Clarksville and Nashville that was sufficiently brined and salted to bear removal by rail. Then the fall of Fort Henry forced more drastic action, and he began rushing meat away south in almost any condition. In this he had vital help from his fellow-packer Craigmiles.[22]

Sidney Johnston started to evacuate Bowling Green on February 11, 1862. The news reached a stunned Nashville four days later. The day after that, Sunday, February 16, Nashville was stupefied to learn that Fort Donelson—less than a hundred miles west and the only defence on their river—had fallen. A Confederate officer recalled the city in turmoil, with well-heeled citizens trying to escape. The less affluent did better: "As the Confederate authorities could not remove all their commissary stores, the warehouses were thrown open, and the poor came and carried off thousands of dollars' worth. Some of these people subsequently set up boarding-houses and fed Union soldiers from the provisions thus obtained."[23]

Perhaps half the meat at Nashville was saved for the Confederate army, as Wilson reported to Northrop, but its condition was uncertain. At Shelbyville General Johnston himself directed the removal of stores, and most were got away.[24] Meanwhile the Federals occupied Bowling Green and Clarksville. Federal commissaries went through the Clarksville packery and storehouses, making inventories of their windfalls.

---

[22]   Ibid., 1035, 1038.

[23]   Stevenson, *Thirteen Months in the Rebel Army*, 87-88.

[24]   *OR* ser. IV, vol. 1, 1035.

It was not the end of Confederate meat supplies from southern and eastern Tennessee. But from then on, remaining portions of the state would be under constant threat. The investment of Subsistence property and endeavor in northwest Tennessee—placed there partly on insistence from the over-sanguine Sidney Johnston—was largely lost. Johnston had no plans for retreat—at least none to share with the Commissary General. Frank Ruffin was later to write: "... It is a fact, and has been a constant source of embarrassment to the [Subsistence] Bureau, that in only two cases has it ever been officially notified of contemplated movements of importance, and in none has it had an opportunity of working the Bureau to meet the necessities or contingencies of campaign."[25]

In regard to the Sidney Johnston fiasco, Ruffin wrote in later years to Northrop: "... The Department of Subsistence should have been put in possession of their plans, so as to provide supplies, or have been relieved of the responsibility by such orders as you often asked for and never received, as to the points at which you should place supplies and the quantity at each place; and you may remember that I advised you to resign your office in consequence of this failure to feed their armies themselves or let you feed them; and you declined on the ground of your personal relations with Mr. Davis."[26] An ambitious man would have done what Ruffin suggested without waiting for Ruffin to suggest it. Northrop was not ambitious, and had not wanted his post. Yet at this point he probably felt that no one else could do the job better, and that Davis needed him.

Northrop now lost faith in the Confederates' ability to hold any part of Tennessee. So he chose the great Tennessee meat packer John F. Cummings—whom he described as "a man of extraordinary efficiency ... most capable of estimating the resources of Tennessee"—nominated him major in the Confederate army, and charged him with a great task of removal. Cummings was "to collect supplies in Tennessee as a resource for general use". He was to leave enough on the ground for remaining Confederate troops, but send all the rest for safe-keeping to the huge Bureau warehouse in Atlanta, Georgia.[27] Atlanta lay half-way between Confederate frontiers east and west now, and as far north as was prudent. The Atlanta storehouse thus became the central point of Subsistence distribution, providing a large proportion of meat for Confederate soldiers east of the Mississippi during the next two years.

The rest of Sidney Johnston's story was soon told. In early February 1862 he had been joined by Beauregard, who had been virtually inactive since Manassas. Together the two generals decided that the only way to stop the relentless Federal advances in the west was to mount a gigantic pitched battle. The grand Napoleonic scheme showed the hand of Beauregard. He began collecting troops from all the surrounding commands, and soon had more than forty thousand.

[25] *The New York Herald*, July 21, 1865, p. 3.
[26] Quoted in Didier, "Scape-Goat", II, 9.
[27] Northrop to Sec. of War, January 12, 1863 (*OR* ser. IV, vol. 2, 351).

Once again the sudden concentration without warning to the commissariat created problems. On March 11, 1862 Beauregard announced that the local commissariat was out of funds and inefficient.[28] Before that he had insisted on a new chief commissary to outrank all subsistence officers in the west; once again he demanded R. B. Lee. The War Department acceded after some hesitation and with no blessing from Northrop. R. B. Lee had also been inactive since Manassas, suffering from effects of recent influenza, rheumatism, and general debilities of old age.[29] Lee arrived just in time for the Battle at Shiloh on April 6 and 7, 1862. It was a Confederate disaster, and Sidney Johnston was killed.

Beauregard pulled his troops back to Corinth (and later to Tupelo). Northrop at first ignored R. B. Lee's presence with them and continued to deal directly with the established officer, Major Moore. Beauregard complained to Richmond, with nasty animadversions on Northrop's skills and character.[30] On May 6, at Beauregard's insistence, R. B. Lee was announced as Chief of Subsistence in the Department of the West.[31] Northrop afterwards recalled: "I kept R. B. Lee well supplied with money after Shiloh."[32] But Lee proved no more able to feed 45,000 mouths in a poor country with no decent water than Major Moore had been. Illness began to spread through the camps. They were staying there, Beauregard insisted, to protect Confederate rail links after the fall of New Orleans to the Federals on April 25.

Shortages in Virginia among J. E. Johnston's troops, and the odious comparison of relative western plenty, decided Northrop to reduce the ration throughout the Confederate armies to match the ration of Northern Virginia. Beauregard promptly defied the Commissary General and issued his own ration orders; they included foods not part of the current Bureau ration at all. Beauregard cited outbreaks of scurvy among his men, and actually increased his troop's ration of sugar by 25 percent and rice by 50 percent beyond the amounts specified in Army Regulations. Moreover he invaded the special store of lard and molasses (neither a part of regular rations) which Northrop had laid in as a possible substitute for meat in case of emergency. Also Beauregard had coffee, and there Northrop pointed his boney finger at the new Secretary of War George Randolph: "... Contrary to the decision of the previous Secretary, you allowed coffee to be purchased for his army irrespective of price, while the rest of our forces were without

---

[28]   Roman, I, 540.

[29]   R. B. Lee had written to Northrop on December 1 and 15, 1861 to report himself fit for limited duty. Northrop declined to assign him. When Lee complained to Adjutant General Cooper on January 1, 1862, Northrop considered that Lee's age and ailments rendered him no longer fit for service (NA, RG 109, Officers: Lee, R. B.). It seems to have been an accurate assessment, in view of Lee's apparently voluntary retirement in weak health five months later.

[30]   April 16, 1862 (*OR* ser I, vol. 10 pt. 2, 422-23) and April 24, 1862 (Roman, I, 383).

[31]   NA, RG 109, Officers, Lee, R. B.

[32]   May 29, 1879 to Davis (Rowland, VIII, 394). See also, October 5, 1880, to Davis: "I have a mem. somewhere of the sums, and when he was relieved by [Major John J.] Walker, the latter had no occasion to apply for funds for over 7 months." (Ibid., 500).

it." Northrop finished his letter to the Secretary with a flat contradiction of Beauregard's claim that his plight was owing to "lack of foresight in the Commissary General", and a demand that Beauregard be required to furnish facts to prove it.[33]

Northrop followed that up with a visit to the Surgeon General's office, where he examined the health reports on Beauregard's troops. There was no mention of scurvy, and less illness at Corinth than elsewhere in the Confederate army.[34] Yet Beauregard's heavy ration remained in place—and R. B. Lee with it.

* * *

Sidney Johnston's over-optimism and Beauregard's selfishness had combined with disastrous Federal advances to wreck every rational plan for feeding the Army of the West. In view of the uncertain future, it seemed as vital as it was proving impossible to impose on that feeding some equality with Northern Virginia. What was needed was the right man out there to organize and oversee it all—a man of intelligence, diplomacy, familiar knowledge over the widest areas of the Confederate West, and above all energy and imagination. Just at this moment the right man walked into Northrop's office—probably sent to him by Jefferson Davis.

His name was William Broadwell. He was a young partner in the firm of New Orleans commission agents who had served the Davis family for many years, and the nephew of the firm's principal, Jacob U. Payne. In 1861 Davis had commissioned Broadwell a major and entrusted him with a special fund of one million dollars granted by Congress to equip and subsist the Confederate militia of Missouri. The task had given Broadwell experience over the whole spectrum of military supply, including correspondence with Northrop. He had done the job so well that when the Missouri militia was wound up in March 1862, there were hundreds of wagon loads of supplies, thousands of horses, and over $100,000 unexpended to turn back to the Confederacy. The Confederate commander in Missouri, Major General Sterling Price, had then sent Broadwell his special thanks "for the great energy, good sense and patriotic self-sacrifice which you have displayed in the execution of the responsible trust which the President, so fortunately for this State, confided to you."[35]

When Broadwell appeared in the Commissary General's office, Northrop asked him to become a general agent for Subsistence in the West, with wide powers of initiative and two specially detailed captains to assist him. Broadwell accepted. Northrop then identified two particular tasks, both necessitated by the fall of New Orleans. One was to collect a fleet of boats on the central portion of the Mississippi River remaining to the Confederacy, and "run up to points where the sugar & molasses can be transported" over the river to troops in the East. The other was to help the Bureau's cattle

---

[33]   May 31, 1862 (*OR* ser. I, vol. 10 pt. 2, 571-72).

[34]   June 22, 1879 to Davis (Rowland, VIII, 401).

[35]   Price's AAG T. L. French to Broadwell, March 23, 1862 (NA, RG 109, Officers: Broadwell, W.A.).

agent in Texas, George W. White, find the means and times to cross his cattle to the eastern banks of the river in the face of mounting Federal threats.[36] Beyond those specific tasks, Northrop directed Broadwell to "exercise your discretion in concentrating, at all points available to the troops, subsistence of every description". In the existing state of communications, "military necessities can only be judged on the spot".[37] Thus Northrop came close to making Broadwell a semi-independent Commissary General of the West (the power Beauregard had tried to get for R. B. Lee). It was a judgement of breathtaking speed and trust. Northrop wrote to Broadwell: "... You must exercise at all times any powers vested in you as a commissioner, and feel free to appeal to the patriotism of the people, and employ all other means in your power to meet the exigencies of the emergency—the design being to place you in the most confidential and agreeable relations with the Government...".[38]

On his way west, Broadwell stopped off in Atlanta and promptly sorted out a problem in the supply of cloth sacks for collecting grain in the West.[39] Arrived at his permanent post in Jackson, Mississippi, Broadwell instantly began to apply his special brand of intelligent help. He wrote to Northrop on June 4, 1862:

> Maj Lanier must if possible supply the troops in Lovell's Division from the Corn in this section and surplus Beef in the country: the consumption of both these articles can be materially reduced by a system of gleaning other things, which he has promised to adopt.
>
> Capt Dameron [Broadwell's chief assistant] expects to accomplish something in this way for the benefit of Beauregard's army. He has already dispatched agents to various points to gather up the surplus, and is making arrangements to ship 5 or 600 bushels of meal per day.

Then Broadwell found "considerable quantities of sugar & molasses at all the RR Stations exposed to the weather & suffering from pillage and waste". It was private property, waiting *sine die* on the inefficient railroads. Broadwell seized all he could find, delegating agents to repair damage, grade and weigh the goods, and give certificates "by which all claims can be ad-

---

[36] Northrop preferred using agents for two reasons. First, a single agent in charge of a district prevented the all-too-familiar phenomenon of one commissary bidding against another and raising prices (Northrop to Broadwell, August 5, 1862, in NA, RG 109, Officers: Broadwell); see also Frank Ruffin's endorsement on a complaint from J. S. Crump, May 18, 1863 (M-437, r 88, ff 426-27). And second, an agent could do his work without all the restrictions imposed on regular army officers—"and not be liable to diversion by military commanders". (Northrop to Broadwell, July 20, 1862, in NA, RG 109, Officers: Broadwell.)

Northrop defended G. W. White in the face of harsh criticism from Trans-Mississippi commanders like Albert Pike, who was outraged to see so much food being shipped away east when he felt a threat of shortage on his own ground (Pike to Randolph, June 26, 1862, in *OR* ser. I, vol. 13, 842). In April 1862 Northrop made White "general superintendent of purchases" for the whole of Texas. Next winter White asked for and was given powers of impressment, to prevent cattle being driven from Texas to Mexico—where they could be sold for gold instead of Confederate currency. Even after the loss of all the Mississippi River in 1863, White still managed to swim cattle across to supply the eastern Armies. See Northrop to Davis, January 26, 1881 (Rowland, VIII, 580).

[37] Northrop to Dameron, July 18, 1862 (NA, RG 109, Officers: Dameron, W.H.).

[38] Northrop to Broadwell, May 24, 1862 (NA, RG 109, Officers: Broadwell).

[39] Ibid., Broadwell to Northrop, May 29, 1862.

justed hereafter".[40] He did this under an order from the Secretary of War to impress any food held by speculators for resale, especially if it had been fraudulently labelled with government marks to secure its transportation. Yet Broadwell underestimated the sheer cussed ability of the proud Southern planter—or speculator, or both—to raise an almighty fuss when any government seized his rotting goods at the fairest valuation. Several planters complained so loudly that the Secretary of War decided all such owners must be given prior warning and chance for removal before any goods were impressed.[41]

Meanwhile Broadwell, on the night of his letter to Northrop, had set out for Beauregard's camp. He caught up with the general's retreat at Baldwin, Mississippi, and proved his diplomacy even on that stony ground. He reported to Northrop on June 7, 1862: "Genl Beauregard has been seriously embarrassed by incompetency in his Commissariat Department, and has most cordially seconded any suggestions offered him for improvement. The Chief Incumbent (R. B. Lee) is said to be a great invalid, and unequal to the emergency." Broadwell calmly ordered Lee's agents to stop paying the 12 1/2 to 15 cents a pound they had been giving for beef (while even at those rates collecting an insufficient supply). The new man showed how he could get all they wanted at 10 cents maximum, doubtless relying on White's importations from Texas. Old Lee was so outraged he accused Broadwell of impressment.[42]

Broadwell thought that both the barren soil of Beauregard's surroundings and his retreating troops' demoralization could be overcome. He submitted plans for getting temporary money for purchases from Southern bankers holding funds withdrawn from New Orleans before its fall. (One of the bankers was his own assistant Captain Dameron.) He appended a list of places where cash purchases could be made. And at the end, Broadwell found something for Northrop to chuckle over:

> Maj Lanier asked me why it was you had so little confidence in him. I told him that you were probably under the impression that he drove fast horses, gambled occasionally, kept a woman, and drank a quart of whiskey pr day—All of which he says is *true*, but nevertheless thinks himself capable of making a good officer & promises to do his duty.[43]

Three days after that letter was written, Beauregard requested the removal of R. B. Lee (apparently with Lee's consent). As for the general himself, he had been suffering from serious throat trouble ever since arriving in the West. With his gigantic army now at Tupelo out of the way of Federal attack, he decided to take himself off for rest and recuperation, and put Braxton Bragg temporarily in his place. Beauregard simply announced the change to Richmond, rather than seeking Richmond's permission. Davis, saturated with Beauregard's high-handedness, took the chance to remove him altogether and make Bragg permanent commander in the West.

---

[40] Ibid., William H. Dameron was another partner in the Payne firm of commission agents from New Orleans: he was now commissioned Captain. See biographical note in *Davis Papers*, VIII, 435.
[41] Broadwell to Northrop, June 19, 1862 (NA, RG 109, Officers: Broadwell); Ibid., Broadwell to Sec. Randolph, June 25, 1862. The original complaint is contained in M-437, r 39, ff 682-690.
[42] Broadwell to Northrop, August 8, 1862 (NA, RG 109, Officers: Broadwell).
[43] Broadwell to Northrop, June 7, 1862 (N.Y.P.L: Northrop Papers).

CHAPTER 12

SECOND HARVEST

To atone for reverses east and west, and for losses on the Atlantic coast, the Confederate Congress had demanded a scapegoat. It was Judah Benjamin, whose impatience with military protocol had made powerful enemies. In later years Northrop estimated him best of all the Secretaries of War under whom he served.[1] Benjamin loyally resigned rather than reveal to the nation and the world the facts and figures of short Confederate resources in the struggle. Davis had no intention of losing Benjamin's talents, and soon made him Secretary of State.

To the War Department, Davis appointed George Wythe Randolph, a Virginia aristocrat and the grandson of Thomas Jefferson.[2] One of Randolph's earliest actions was to persuade Congress to pass the first conscription bill ever enacted in America, and then persuade Davis to sign it. States' Rights governors made a great deal of trouble over it, and ultimately there had to be a matching Exemption Act, into which more and more essential workers were found to fit. Confederate conscription got off to a slow start.

It was also proposed that the central government should regulate agriculture in the same way. By early 1862 there had been widespread calls for farmers to plant cereals instead of cotton (whose cash markets the Davis government sought every way to reduce). "Plant corn and be free," advised Columbus, Georgia *Sun*, "or plant cotton and be whipped."[3] The old Provisional Congress had urged farmers to plant no cotton in 1862. The Commissary General advocated compulsion. The new Congress could not bring themselves to do it: intrusion into the sacred precincts of farmstead and plantation made politics too hot.[4] Yet with many of the best grain-growing areas either cut off by the Federals or trampled by rival armies, the outlook was growing bleak.

---

[1] April 21, 1878 to Davis (Rowland, VIII, 180).

[2] A recent biography, George Green Shackelford's *George Wythe Randolph and the Confederate Elite*, makes no real attempt to address subsistence or Randolph's relations with Northrop. The book's remarks about Frank Ruffin are in one respect seriously inaccurate (see above, p. 74 n. 18).

[3] Quoted in Gates, *Agriculture and the Civil War*, 16.

[4] *Journal of Congress*, II, 57, 80 (March 12 and 20, 1862).

143

A report came in about large stores of corn and other provisions in eastern North Carolina, close to Federal camps. The owners were reported willing to sell to the Confederates, but they had no transport.[5] Would the Quartermaster General compel the railroads to go and get what they could, and impose authority to stop Confederate generals along the line from seizing the trains for themselves? He would not, fearing to alienate the generals and the railroad barons.[6] In April 1862 a measure came before Congress to enjoin direct governmental control of railroads.[7] The railroad lobbies succeeded in having the bill gutted. Adjutant General Cooper then issued an order prohibiting military commanders "from interfering with the transportation of provisions on railroads" except in emergencies.[8] That was nothing but a license for them to interfere.

By the spring of 1862 inflation in the cities had raised prices by an average of two hundred percent. The citizens of Richmond were beginning to confront intractable problems. The prices of all the staples were being run up so viciously that the Provost Marshal, General John Winder, tried to impose price schedules throughout the city. The market men simply stopped supplies until Winder had to revoke his schedule. From then on Richmond was at the mercy of extortion. One lady recalled: "A fortunate speculator, having in store a vast quantity of salt when our troubles commenced, grew rich from the sale of this article alone, and was afterwards facetiously styled 'Lot's wife'."[9]

That was the market in which the Subsistence Bureau had now to buy food for the army. The old Provisional Congress, just before it disbanded in February 1862, had voted $4 1/2 million for Subsistence until April 1. To cover the following eight months to November 30, Northrop submitted an estimate of just under $40 million. It was scrutinized with the greatest care and cut down by the Secretary of War before sending to the new Congress. They in turn cut down all the Bureau estimates by a quarter again before granting the monies.

At the same time the Treasury proposed to tighten its restrictions on cash for all the bureaus, and to force the use of still more Confederate bonds. On April 7, 1862 Secretary Randolph forwarded to the President a letter of protest from Subsistence, written by Ruffin at Northrop's direction; on it Randolph added his own warning endorsement.[10] A fortnight later Congress simply shifted the problem when it empowered the Treasury Secretary himself to exchange Confederate bonds for articles in kind, and enjoined the Commissary and Quartermaster Generals to accept all such supplies at their rates of purchase in Treasury bonds. To make those purchases, the Secretary of the Treasury was to appoint agents of his own.[11] They would come into direct competition with commissaries and quartermasters trying to do their jobs.

5   *OR* ser. I, vol. 51, pt. 2, 515.
6   Black, *The Railroads of the Confederacy*, 100.
7   March 26, 1879 to Davis (Tulane r 22, ff 501-505).
8   April 29, 1862 (*OR* ser. IV, vol. 1, 1100).
9   [Brock], *Richmond During the War*, 113-14, 125.
10   *OR* ser. IV, vol. 1, 1049-50.
11   Ibid., 1079.

What could the Commissary General do to meet these problems? The new harvest was too immature to measure, and awash with rain. So Northrop had reduced the amount of the ration throughout the army. When that was done, there seemed to be only one other possibility: it was nothing less than a virtual abandonment of the comprehensive distribution from the center which he had fought so hard to set up. On April 27, two days after the fall of New Orleans, Northrop sent a circular letter (carrying the approval of Randolph) to the chief commissary of every separate command. It was phrased with the greatest care, touching only in the lightest way on the causes which had brought the Commissary General to such a pass. Then:

> In this aspect of affairs, proceed at once to make yourself fully acquainted with the resources of your district, with a view to support troops now and with reference to future crops, and especially ascertain the prospect of obtaining corn-meal [as a substitute for flour] in adequate, prompt, and continuous supply as soon as it may be needed, and the number and capacity of the mills for grinding it.
>
> In consequence of existing and probable scarcity of meat, arrangements have been made to distribute molasses as a substitute for part of the rations of meat throughout the army. The loss of New Orleans, likely to be followed by that of the few points on the Mississippi River from which sugar and molasses can be carried to the [eastern] interior, renders it necessary that you endeavor to limit the consumption of meat.
>
> Henceforth the rations will be a pound of beef or a half pound of bacon or pork, and the ration of flour or meal will not exceed a pound and a half of either.[12]

The abandonment of his major principle of supply shows that Northrop was not always blinkered and obstinate, as his enemies charged. The notion of each district supplying itself, however, would bring on all the difficulties he had foreseen, and perhaps some he had not. It would require more and more of the soldiers' time and energy to collect their own sustenance—with the gradual impoverishment of every district where soldiers stayed long enough to eat it bare. The practice would raise competition among the generals and thus encourage waste; and it would almost certainly increase the disparity of rations among their commands. Beauregard at Corinth had promptly demanded half the store of bacon Cummings was collecting in Atlanta as an ultimate reserve. Northrop protested to Davis, who had his military advisor Robert E. Lee answer Beauregard that each command must now take care of itself. Lee added a grim prediction: "This necessity ... may accelerate [military] movements which otherwise it might be deemed prudent to restrain."[13]

In fact commissaries of many commands, faced with persistent local shortages of flour and steeply rising prices, called heavily on the Commissary General's reserves. And corruption flourished; the Bureau chiefs tried

---

12   *OR* Ser. I, vol. 11, pt. 3, 553.
13   Roman, I, 580-81.

to appoint honest men, but the need for so many officers so quickly had made it impossible to vet them all from personal knowledge. Distance itself appeared to corrupt, and anywhere beyond a day's journey from Richmond seemed positively to invite vicious practice. Growing scarcities brought more and more reports of commissary impersonation by private citizens hungry for food or profit.[14]

Inexperience could also create shortage when a field commander appointed a supervising commissary without experience. In Virginia in the spring of 1862 Major General David R. Jones chose John Cheves Haskell for such a post. Haskell was from a distinguished South Carolina family, a grandson of Langdon Cheves. But he was only twenty-one, and had little military experience before being commissioned major to occupy his responsible post. Mature commissaries of the command had to report to him and get his approval for everything. In later years he told the story on himself:

> I had consequently to receipt to the Chief Commissary of the Army for the supplies of some 12,000 men. In a very short time I was charged with hundreds of thousands of dollars of provisions of all kinds, though I never saw any of them except perhaps when I met a drove of cattle or wagon-loads of flour and groceries. I was as ignorant of business as most boys who have had no experience, and had a clerk detailed to keep accounts and care for receipts, so that when I got well [from bronchial pneumonia] I found I was short hundreds of thousands of dollars.
>
> The brigade commissaries resented greatly having to ride several miles every day to get orders from me for their supplies, none so much as Major R. J. Moses... Moses was a most witty and amusing man, a great friend of mine after I ceased to be his superior officer. He it was who first found the lamentable state of my accounts, and at once set himself to work to straighten them out.[15]

The Commissary General in Richmond had little control over field appointments, but inevitably he took the rap for their blunders and shortages. *The Richmond Examiner* licked its lean chops at every rumored failure, and attacked Northrop's office as though it were vacant of humanity. It was all part of that paper's well-known campaign against the Davis government. Intelligent people recognized the mischief, and were as powerless as intelligent people usually are in the face of sensationalism suborning vulgarity. By July 1862 Mrs. Chesnut would write in her diary: "I do not see how the [New York] *Herald* or the *Tribune* could do us more injury than the *Examiner* of today. A bomb from the enemy's camp exploding in the *Examiner*'s office would not have hurt the Confederate cause."[16]

---

[14] Ramsdell, *Behind the Lines*, 21.

[15] John Cheves Haskell, *The Haskell Memoirs*, ed. G.E. Govan and J. W. Livingood (New York: Putnam, 1960), 29.

[16] *Mary Chesnut's Civil War*, 418. On October 18, 1862 *The Charleston Mercury* observed: "The devil does not hate holy water half so bad as the Government hates the *Examiner*."

When Robert E. Lee returned to Richmond in March 1862, Northrop asked him "for information respecting our ... prospects so as to guide my actions".[17] Together they made plans to remove Subsistence stores from the city if the Federals got too close. McClellan's forces were landing at the tip of the Peninsula, and soon they would try to move up. To oppose them, Joseph E. Johnston's troops gathered on the Peninsula below Richmond. On March 27 Lee told Northrop to find provisions for an extra ten thousand overnight.[18]

As Johnston's forces encamped down the Peninsula in cold, rainy weather, they sharply felt the lack of the supplies destroyed at Manassas and Thoroughfare Gap. The Peninsula was thinly served by railroads, its land had nothing like the fertility of Northern Virginia, there were no sizable herds of beef, and the spring weather was horrible. Jubal Early recalled: "... Our troops suffered greatly, as they were without tents or other shelter. Their duties were very severe and exhausting, ... their rations were limited, and consisted of the plainest and roughest food; coffee was out of the question, as were vegetables and fresh meat."[19]

Johnston fell back and back before Federal advances up the Peninsula toward Richmond. On Sunday, May 4 he abandoned Yorktown with a further heavy loss of Subsistence and other stores.[20] In later years Northrop encountered Captain William Berkeley of the 8th Virginia Regiment, who gave an account which Northrop conveyed to Davis: "... He says that when retiring from the lines established near Yorktown that [*sic*] Johnston ordered off all baggage trains positively, while men were ordered to prepare 3 days' rations without their cooking equipage, and then the move of the troops was delayed 24 hours—that the heads of barrels had to be knocked open [with the enemy's advance], water poured in and mixed with ashes and then more water and so on; that he saw a general destruction of provisions from a church [tower], rice molasses flour &c &c. all thrown together...".[21]

In Richmond the talk was all of enemy siege and citizen panic. Secretary Randolph ordered all the War Department Bureaus to pack their official papers against a need for instant removal. Davis told his wife she must get their children away to safety. Davis himself, having never until then followed any religion, was so apprehensive of the future that he took the step of being received into the Episcopal Church. That news, when it went round the departments, made the Catholic Northrop privately unhappy. He recalled afterwards to Davis: "My practice was to be cheerful in my office. One day several enquired, 'What was the matter? that I seemed gloomy.' At last one said to another, 'Oh I know. The President was confirmed yesterday and the Col. can't get over it.' It grieved me then, and still does, that the key which opens the mysteries of life is not in your possession, and that the veil of doubts which hang over every one outside the R. C. Church still invests you."[22]

17 *OR* ser. I, vol. 51, pt. 2, 743.
18 *OR* ser. I, vol. 11, pt. 3, 405.
19 Written in 1866-67 (Rowland, VIII, 13).
20 Evidence from Early (Rowland, VIII, 4, 16-17); and Davis to Northrop, February 1, 1881, (Ibid., 587).
21 Ibid., July 13, 1880, 479.

All this time Johnston divulged nothing of his plans for defending Richmond. He sent his quartermaster of transport, Major A. H. Cole (not to be confused with Johnston's chief commissary, Robert G. Cole) to the capital. A. H. Cole conferred with Northrop, Davis, and Robert E. Lee. He reported to Johnston that Northrop had a ten days' supply of food in Richmond for 70,000 men, but wanted to send away at least part of that in case Richmond fell. He had 10,000 cattle coming from the Valley of Virginia. Five million rations west at Lynchburg could be placed wherever Johnston wanted them. Northrop "says that there is no trouble about feeding your army for ninety days, if you will indicate where your line will be south and west of Richmond, in case we should be forced to give up the city. ... Colonel Northrop insists, if you can reoccupy Northern Virginia and the Potomac about Loudoun, that 100,000 men can be supplied from that country. This I doubt." (Had Northrop's planning discussion with Lee touched on the possibility of a new Confederate offensive returning to northern Virginia? It seems possible in the light of events later that summer, and some vigorous collecting of animals by Noland before that.[23]) Cole concluded his report: "I find Colonel Northrop very much disinclined to give information; he seems to consider it his patent article."[24]

In the light of Northrop's experience of Johnston so far, it was understandable that the Commissary General should be chary of giving too much information about extra commissary stores. Whenever Johnston got his hands on them, it seemed that wholesale destruction would follow as soon as the general wished to move.

Information was Johnston's patent article too. The more insistently Richmond demanded to know his plans, the more distrustful Johnston became. A fortnight passed with nothing but more Confederate retreating and more Federal advance towards the capital. By May 24 McClellan's forces had moved up to occupy Mechanicsville, almost in sight of Richmond. Davis sent out R. E. Lee to chivvy Johnston, and at last got a grudging half-promise that Johnston would attack the Federals on May 29. That information was much wanted by Northrop, who recalled: "The herds of cattle collected at Richmond were getting thin [as no more were being shipped there in case of evacuation] and might attract attention, so I went to Lee and was told of the day and the plan; I expressed my delight and confidence. His uncertain manner made me think it was not his."[25]

When May 29 came, nothing happened. For news had reached Johnston the night before that a big Federal force supposed to reinforce McClellan from the north had turned aside and stopped. So Johnston put off his attack. Under renewed Presidential pressure, he promised it two days later. But his orders to his generals were misunderstood by at least one of them, and the entire morning passed without much action.

---

[23] See below, pp. 150 ff.

[24] *OR* ser. I, vol. 11, pt. 3, 513.

[25] May 9, 1878 to Davis (Rowland, VIII, 271, where it is misdated 1870).

Davis, Lee, Randolph, Northrop, and as many others as had horses had ridden out to witness Johnston's battle to save Richmond. Looking over the Confederate dispositions brought back Northrop's old soldierly responses, as he recalled years afterwards: "I witnessed from the rear the opening on the Meadow Bridge road, and I think now a blunder at Mechanicsville. I rode from towards the front to where Lee was. He asked me where the batteries in front were. I replied I did not know but would find out for him—he declined. I had told Randolph some time before that I saw that we did not know how the Federals were disposed...".[26] What followed was a wretchedly muddled action, with no clear result for either side. Late in the day Johnston himself took a severe wound; it would keep him out of action for months.

* * *

To replace Johnston as commanding general in Virginia, Davis chose the man (little known to the public then) who was to become the most revered figure of the Confederacy, Robert E. Lee. From the moment Lee replaced Johnston, the Confederacy took the offensive and began to impose some will of its own on the shape and progress of the war. A fearful amount of territory and supplies in Virginia had already been lost through Johnston's hopeless defensiveness.

Lee took four weeks to gather his forces. On June 26, 1862 he pitched into the Federals. In a week of engagements later called the "Seven Days' Battles", moving clockwise south and east round the outskirts of Richmond, he drove the enemy off from the Confederate capital and sent them reeling down the Peninsula. The battles were costly to both sides and very bloody. One of Northrop's nephews, Claudian's son John, was blinded at Gaines's Mill on June 27.

After the battles, Confederate troops camped near Richmond were adequately fed, but the cooking continued bad. One of the 1st South Carolina Regiment (in which Claudian's eldest son Lucius was serving) recalled: "...Our rations were good and plentiful—three-fourths of a pound of bacon or one pound of beef, one and one-eighth of a pound of flour, with salt, and occasionally molasses, and even beans, at long intervals. But the bacon was almost invariably fried, and the bread was half cooked—two things which are certain to derange any stomach and bowels."[27]

On July 13, 1862 Lee began to move his forces north. His strategy was to draw the enemy away from Richmond and the Peninsula by moving his own army towards Washington—and it succeeded. But with forces every way inferior to the Federals, Lee's game could be only feint, manoeuvre, distraction. As he approached Manassas, he came into lands drained of supplies by the rival armies. The summer of 1862, following three months of drenching spring rains, was proving unrelievedly hot and dry; new crops were far below expectation.

[26]   Ibid.

[27]   J..F. J. Caldwell, *The History of a Brigade of South Carolinians...* (Philadelphia: King & Baird, 1866; *rpr* Morningside Press, 1984), 52.

On July 18 Major General John Pope moved Union forces into Virginia to shield Washington. He announced that his troops would "subsist upon the country in which their operations were being carried out". Pope's men began to impress food and supplies right and left in a deliberate policy of impoverishing Virginia citizens and stripping their lands. That would make Lee's northward progress much more difficult.

Before the end of July, flour supplies in Lee's army were dangerously low. Lee asked Northrop to get some flour that was inaccessibly placed in the country. Northrop could not obtain enough quartermaster's wagons for work in such remote and possibly exposed places, and asked Lee to detail wagons and men from his troops. Lee, in the midst of planning his further operations, replied on August 3 that he could not spare men or wagons.[28] Northrop must have looked ruefully back to the early summer of 1861— hardly more than a year ago—when with sums from the Treasury that now appeared pitifully small, he might have controlled flour markets throughout Virginia to obtain a large and comfortable reserve.

Lee's supplies became more and more dependent on wagons. With the Federal occupation of northern Virginia in late 1861, the railroad line between Manassas and Gordonsville had been repeatedly cut by both sides. Railroad bridges over both the Rapidan and Rappahannock Rivers were destroyed. Then on August 26 Stonewall Jackson's men, moving east to meet Lee, broke up the line at Bristoe Station between Warrenton and Manassas Junctions.[29] Without wagons, broken railroad lines meant that all Confederate troops moving north and west of the lowest break were virtually beyond the reach of Subsistence Bureau supply from Richmond.

Northrop had foreseen this—perhaps not in time to dissuade him from his first centralizing plan, but from the spring of 1862. His cattle agent Noland had men behind enemy lines in northern Virginia both east and west of the Blue Ridge Mountains. From their reports and his own knowledge, Noland said there was still much food there. But it would need military assistance to get it out. Noland had sought out Stonewall Jackson while in the Valley; Jackson promised help, but he had been suddenly pushed back in early June, so could do nothing. Noland reported to Northrop: "I then appointed agents, who at great personal risk penetrated the country & during the summer brought from within the enemy's lines many thousand cattle & sheep: in fact most of the meat consumed by the Army [of Northern Virginia] during the summer was thus obtained."[30]

It was all dangerous work. Noland's best cattle driver was arrested by Federal soldiers and paroled on condition he desist from further Confederate activities. In September Noland would invoke Northrop's influence to get the driver released from his parole under a new scheme of prisoner exchange recently agreed between the combatants after prolonged negotiation.[31]

---

[28]   OR ser. I, vol. 11, pt. 3, 662-3.
[29]   Lee, Wartime Papers, 265-66.
[30]   November 23, 1862 (New York Public Library: Northrop Papers).
[31]   OR ser. II, vol. 4, 879-80.

Having failed to get assistance from Jackson in time, Noland then also tried Lee. On August 23 he wrote on Northrop's orders to Lee's Assistant Adjutant General, Colonel Robert H. Chilton. Subsistence agents had reported as many as 10,000 head of cattle, 15,000 sheep, and large stores of bacon still held behind enemy lines by men loyal to the Confederate cause. Noland asked Lee for "the earliest notice possible when our Army crosses the Rappahannock that I may be on hand with my agents to procure this subsistence, which otherwise may be driven off or destroyed by the Yankee army as it falls back through that section." Back came a dusty answer: Chilton "wrote to me that Genl Lee was *sceptical* as to the amount of these supplies & hence, I suppose, I did not receive the aid asked for."[32]

Perhaps Lee had begun to think, in view of his northward offensive, that the animals of northern Virginia might best be left where they were. On August 24, 1862 (probably the day Noland's appeal came in to him) he wrote to Davis: "I think I can feed the whole army here if Colonel Northrop will give the necessary directions about collecting beef. If we can secure this country, the millers will give us flour. At first there will be difficulties, but they will be softened as we advance, and we shall relieve other parts of the country and employ what would be consumed and destroyed by the enemy. The theater of war will thus be changed, for a season at least, unless we are overpowered."[33]

There was a deep pessimism underlying Lee's offensive strategy. It is sometimes claimed that shortage of food was chiefly or solely responsible for that strategy. The evidence shows that scarcity of food in the war-torn areas Lee then approached was only one of many shortages that drove him to desperate action. (Had it been solely a question of food, Lee could after all have kept his forces close to Richmond where there was sufficient food.) Lee's pessimism and his offensive strategy both came from his understanding of how powerfully he was outnumbered and out-equipped in every department.

Thus events advanced toward a second major battle at Manassas. On the night of August 26-27, Stonewall Jackson stole up on Federal supply depots at Manassas in advance of Lee, repulsed a sharp counterattack, and then treated his men to a royal feed at Yankee expense. The contrast of Federal food made an unforgettable memory for John Worsham writing fifty years later: "It was hard to decide what to take, some filled their haversacks with cakes, some with candy, others oranges, lemons, canned goods, etc. I know one who took nothing but French mustard, filled his haversack and was so greedy that he put one more bottle in his pocket. This was his four days' rations, and it turned out to be the best thing taken, because he traded it for meat and bread, and it lasted him until we reached Frederick City [Maryland on September 6]".[34] Fear of renewed Federal attack had forced Jackson to burn all the rich remainder at Manassas before Lee could come up.

---

[32] November 23, 1862 to Northrop (NYPL: Northrop Papers). In later years it was suggested that Lee doubted Noland's competence (see Davis to Northrop, March 17 and April 9, 1879 in Rowland, VIII, 369 and 377). No evidence to support such a notion has come my way.

[33] *OR* ser. I, vol. 12, pt. 3, 942. See also *Battles and Leaders*, II, 511.

[34] *One of Jackson's Foot Cavalry*, 120-22.

Three days later, on August 30, 1862, Lee and his army faced the Federal forces close to the site of the first battle of Manassas thirteen months earlier. At this Second Battle of Manassas, the badly overmatched Lee won a victory by sheer skill. The field of victory then yielded a grisly contrast in the effects of Northern and Southern nutrition. One of Jackson's artillerymen noted two days after the battle: "Here we had a good opportunity of observing the marked and striking difference between the Federals and Confederates who remained unburied for twenty-four hours or more after being killed. While the Confederates underwent no perceptible change in color or otherwise, the Federals on the contrary became much swollen and discolored. This was of course attributable to the difference in their food and drink." [35]

Lee's Confederates marched away from Manassas north again because they could not hold their gains against the heavily superior enemy. Lee thought that an invasion of Maryland ought to provide the Confederates with ample food from lands never yet fought over. He hoped for other benefits too. The first might be a flood of new recruits from that state to the Southern cause. Farther afield, such an invasion might bring official recognition of the South at last from England and France: that in turn might bring the European powers themselves to insist that Lincoln lift his blockade of Southern coasts.

On September 4 and 5, 1862 Lee's forces crossed over the Potomac into Maryland. At Frederick they briefly encamped—a filthy, ragged, exhausted "ghost of an army" (in Freeman's description). Most were without good shoes, some without any. The boys of the South especially grew up barefoot in summer; some of them, moving along the soft dirt roads of Virginia, had thrown their shoes away. The stony roads of Maryland soon put paid to the tattered shoes remaining, and cut their feet to ribbons.

In fact, Lee had seriously miscalculated the exhaustion of his men. During the next fortnight straggling—rarely before a problem under Lee—reduced his army from 53,000 to 40,000.[36] And the people of Maryland gave Lee nothing like the welcome he had hoped for. Men did not flock to the Confederate banner. Women sold small amounts of food unwillingly at high prices. Nothing from Northrop's Subsistence Bureau could reach the Army of Northern Virginia beyond the Confederate borders.

A vital marching order of Lee's fell into Federal hands. That enabled McClellan to counter Lee's offensive with his large army. The two armies met over Antietam Creek in front of the little town of Sharpsburg. The battle there on September 17, 1862 was the bloodiest single day of the entire war. Lee, outnumbered more than two to one, was not dislodged. Yet at the end of that day both armies were on their knees. The Federals did not re-attack. But Lee was forced to collect his sick and wounded and retreat back across the Potomac into Virginia.

---

[35] Edward A. Moore, *The Story of a Cannoneer under Stonewall Jackson* (New York: Neale, 1907), 121-22.

[36] Freeman, *R. E. Lee*, II, 411.

In the West during those weeks, Beauregard's successor Braxton Bragg presided over a closely similar Confederate offensive and retreat. Again the quest for subsistence was one of several factors. On assuming control in the West in June 1862, Bragg had complained from Tupelo that he had not had enough fresh meat since the fall of New Orleans. The country immediately north of him had been stripped bare by the contesting armies, just as with Lee in northern Virginia. So Bragg aimed at enemy depots still farther north. The War Department coordinated Bragg's thrust northward into Tennessee and Kentucky with Lee's thrust northward into Maryland.

By mid-September Bragg was through Tennessee and into Kentucky. Like Lee in Virginia, Bragg overestimated the depth of Confederate support over northern borders. On September 17, however, he captured a big Federal supply depot at Munfordville, only 65 miles below Louisville. Militarily, Bragg seemed poised to drive his enemy beyond the Ohio River. He wavered, and allowed himself to be pushed back to Knoxville, Tennessee.

Unlike Lee and Jackson, however, Bragg brought off huge captured supplies. His wagon train was forty miles long, and it put him beyond want for months—even at the Beauregard ration still allowed by the War Department over Northrop's protest. Once again the Confederate West dined better than the Confederate East—and complained more loudly.

* * *

The harvest of 1862 throughout the Confederacy had been badly damaged by conscription, which drained away young and able-bodied men from farm and plantation. One Virginia lady wrote: "In many sections of our country, from which slaves had been driven or seduced to leave, the plowing and reaping, the hoeing and planting, were performed by men over the conscript age assisted by women, the delicate daughters of ease, whose faces the 'winds of heaven' had never been permitted to 'visit too roughly' ...".[37] In some places the remaining old men and the women could not keep order among the slaves. Many Confederate districts were deeply penetrated by Federal agitators encouraging blacks to disobedience and escape. Those remaining refused to work as they had worked a year earlier, to harvest what crops there were.

Nature herself seemed to conspire against the Confederacy in 1862. Three months of spring rains had produced rust that cut the wheat crop in Georgia to one sixth of normal. Western Virginia and eastern Tennessee were nearly as bad. Then had come three summer months of ferocious heat and drought, decimating much of the wheat that was left, as well as corn crops in many places. Flour prices in the country began to chase city inflation. Demand from the field threatened to strip bare the Bureau reserves of flour in Richmond. Speculation and extortion proliferated. Northrop went to the Secretary of War and had the embargo on flour exports from Virginia reimposed.[38] Yet requisitions from the field flowed relentlessly in, and the Bureau's flour reserves continued to drain away.

37 [Brock], *Richmond During the War*, 195.
38 *OR* ser. IV, vol. 2, 86; ser I, vol. 18, 777; Jones, *Diary*, I, 189.

When it was clear to everyone that the 1862 harvest was a disaster, Northrop was allowed to submit a special requisition to a new Congress. On September 15 he sent in his demand for an extra seven million dollars to purchase flour for the army for a year. He made the need crystal clear to Secretary Randolph, who approved it. Congress granted it in full in October.[39] Northrop instantly sent his agents to buy flour around Staunton in the Valley (since Staunton was once more precariously in Confederate hands). As Staunton was on the railroad, the Bureau men were directed to offer Richmond prices less transport thither. That was higher than Valley farmers had ever received. The high price was vital, Northrop said, to induce farmers to thresh their grain at once instead of waiting for prices to rise with winter—"and also in some instances because they do not wish to take Confederate money".[40]

Subsistence Bureau buying around Staunton was designed to leave Valley lands to the north free for Lee's commissaries to supply his army. There, in Rockingham County and towards Winchester, Lee's men had stimulated flour mills far from any railroad to unprecedented production. His commissaries paid less for their flour: the soldiers in many cases actually helped with production, and there was no transport trouble since consumption was virtually on the spot.[41] But farmers and millers up and down the Valley compared notes and soon discovered the price differentials. They caused their congressmen to complain to the Secretary of War, and Northrop had to defend his higher prices.[42] Yet despite further sharp inflation, the Commissary General's special flour fund would remain less than half expended. There was just not that much flour for sale then. The same was true of meat: stocks held in Richmond for Lee dwindled alarmingly.

Southern agriculture was also beginning to feel the effects of a heavy blow from the North. On September 22, 1862 Lincoln had issued his preliminary Emancipation Proclamation. The naked political intent emerged in the territory it covered: from January 1, 1863 all slaves were to be free—in the "rebellious" states only. Nothing was said about slavery still remaining in several Union states. (In fact both Delaware and Kansas were to retain slavery until after the close of the war.)

In the South of course Lincoln's Proclamation was only a piece of paper so long as the Confederacy had military power to prevent its enforcement. Yet the Emancipation Proclamation was a political masterstroke. First,

---

[39]   NA, RG 109, Messages to Congress: filed with Davis's Message of September 24, 1862; *OR* ser. IV, vol. 2, 113.

[40]   *OR* ser. I, vol. 19, pt. 2, 701.

[41]   Ibid., 700.

[42]   *OR* ser. IV, vol. 2, 153. Lee's men paid $10 to $12 a barrel (itself a measure of inflation since 1861, when Northrop had waited for the crop to come at $5 a barrel). The gossip mills of Richmond poured forth muddle and misinformation about the flour price differentials in the Valley. The War Department clerk Jones wrote in his diary on November 4: "The Government is impressing flour at $12 per barrel, when it is selling at $24" (*Diary*, I, 182). I can find no evidence that Lee was impressing flour at this date: it was a practice he always detested. And the Subsistence Bureau had no power to impress until 1863. As for Jones's "selling" price, Richmond—along with most capital cities—tended to regard its prices as universal.

it encouraged younger slaves to run away from Southern fields to the North, where they could be formed into black regiments to swell the Federal army. Second, news of the Proclamation sowed discontent and hope among slaves everywhere remaining in the South, making them more difficult to manage. Third, it created a new element of dissension in the Confederate body politic: where the War had begun for Southerners as a fight to save the people from invasion, the Emancipation Proclamation made it appear now more as a fight to save slave owners' property.[43]

Finally, the Lincoln Proclamation started the historical *canard* that the unique root cause of the war had been slavery. In the North at least, nobody until that moment seems ever to have thought so. Before then slavery had counted as one item in a long list of economic divisions. Now the Proclamation opened a way for the North to assume a high moral ground *ex post facto*. Lincoln himself never claimed that the war had been undertaken to free slaves. His object first and last, so he always said, was to preserve the Union: if that could be done without freeing a single slave (as he had said earlier in 1862) then he would not touch slavery.

The Confederate Congress, responding to pleas of women throughout the South who found themselves unable to control their slaves, passed legislation in October 1862 exempting from conscription one white man for every twenty blacks on a plantation, to keep slaves in order. But then poorer Southern farmers with fewer than twenty slaves, or with none, felt themselves discriminated against: "It's a rich man's war, but a poor man's fight," they charged. And so another division was driven into the South at a vital point—the production of food.[44]

---

[43]   Ramsdell, *Behind the Lines*, 45.

[44]   This exemption law raised so much discontent that the Confederate Congress repealed it in February 1864.

CHAPTER 13

PILLARS OF SALT

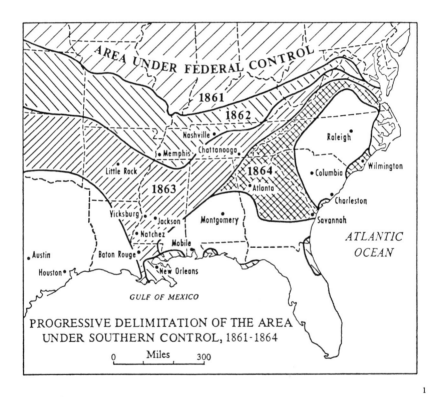

AREA UNDER FEDERAL CONTROL

1861
1862

Nashville
Raleigh
Memphis
Chattanooga
Little Rock
1864
Columbia
Wilmington
1863
Atlanta
Charleston
Vicksburg
Jackson
Montgomery
Savannah
Natchez
Mobile
ATLANTIC
OCEAN
Austin
Baton Rouge
Houston
New Orleans

GULF OF MEXICO

PROGRESSIVE DELIMITATION OF THE AREA
UNDER SOUTHERN CONTROL, 1861-1864

0   Miles   300

[1]

The Confederacy was steadily losing vital food-producing territory north
and west. Even before those areas began to be lost, the South had never been
accustomed to feed itself; it had always traded its cash crops of cotton and
tobacco for much of its food. When food importations in this way closed
after war began, Northrop and the state governors had actually made the

---

[1]   Gates, *Agriculture and the Civil War*, 126.

South feed itself. The menu was imperfect, but it was an historical first. Then circumstances conspired against them.

The Confederate commissariat faced a second winter of war with resources severely diminished. The bad harvest of 1862 and rising prices had fomented flour requisitions from the field so large and persistent as to decimate Bureau reserves. The crop failures also made for a thin population of scrawny animals and another outbreak of hog cholera. Both sharply reduced Virginia supplies for Lee.

Growing scarcities among the people, rising prices, and a depreciating Confederate currency produced a flourishing private trade along every border with the enemy. Davis loathed that trade, especially using cotton, which he and many others saw as the South's unique political resource. Its withdrawal, they still felt, might compel England and France to recognize the Confederate nation. Partly at Davis's behest, Congress had prohibited the transporting of Southern cotton, tobacco, sugar, rice, molasses, syrup, or naval stores to any enemy port or territory.[2] It left many planters without adequate markets for their crops.

The new law had been promulgated on April 18, 1862, as Federal gunboats began ascending the Mississippi towards the South's premier port, New Orleans. A week later New Orleans was in their hands. However, Union Major General Benjamin Butler, in charge of the city, saw no reason to stop Southern trade; he would be happy to sell "permits" to transship any goods through New Orleans. The goods might come from the city itself, from Federal stores, from Confederate lands west of the Mississippi, or via ships from the North or Europe. The consideration in almost every case was money or cotton.

Planters, private citizens, and merchants eagerly traded through New Orleans the cotton they had raised or owned (and could not otherwise sell) for necessities such as salt, growing scarcer every day around the Gulf Coast. On June 25, 1862 Jefferson Davis wrote to his wife: "How much better it would have been had the whole city been left a pile of ashes."[3] But Davis was a Xerxes trying to stem the tide. The army itself was irresistibly involved. General Richard Taylor wrote of the Lower Mississippi region:

> Out-post officers would violate the law, and trade. In vain they were removed; the temptation was too strong, and their successors did the same.
> The influence of the women was dreadful, and in many cases their appeals were heart-rending. Mothers with suffering children, whose husbands were in the war or already fallen, would beseech me for permits to take cotton through the lines. It was useless to explain that it was against law and orders, and that I was without authority to act. This did not give food and clothing to their children, and they departed believing me to be an unfeeling brute. In fact the instincts of humanity revolted against this folly.[4]

---

[2]   OR ser. IV, vol. 1, 1077.

[3]   Jefferson Davis: A Memoir by His Wife, II, 315.

[4]   Destruction and Reconstruction (New York: Appleton, 1879), 235.

All this was familiar to young William Broadwell, bending every effort from his rather mobile office at Jackson, Mississippi to raise supplies of food from the West. People on both sides of the Mississippi River—and on both sides of the war—soon came to know of the wide powers he held. And so it was that Broadwell could write to Northrop on June 27, 1862: "We have secured here over one thousand sacks of Salt recently smuggled out from N. Orls, and can contract for more at the price paid—$25 pr sk. One Party has offered to bring out 700 sks of Coffee at 45 cents pr lb. These men report that this business is managed by corrupting or bribing Yankee officials. I would be glad to learn your views as to what extent we shall encourage this smuggling."[5] Northrop telegraphed back: "Do as you think proper about getting further supplies from N. Orleans as stated in your letter 27th and your action will be approved."[6]

One party not so confident was the Confederate commander in the district, Major General Earl Van Dorn. As soon as he heard of it, Van Dorn issued a General Order that any attempt to trade with the enemy was punishable by death.[7] But Broadwell rode up to Vicksburg and "obtained the consent of the Comdg Genl to designate a number of schooners which can be allowed to pass our lines without molestation & bring out articles needed by the army." The general's "consent to designate a number of schooners" was Broadwell's euphemism for power to impress the boats.

In addition to food, it seemed they could acquire ordnance materials from New Orleans on the same basis. So the Chief of the Ordnance Bureau, Colonel Josiah Gorgas, was brought in. And Broadwell added a fascinating fact: his agents in New Orleans "negotiate with trading agents in partnership with Genl Butler's brother".[8] It was well known that the Butler family owned cotton mills in Massachusetts, and that all the New England mills were desperately short of raw cotton.

The Commissary General expressed his gratitude in a letter to Broadwell's assistant, Captain Dameron. Both of them had elected to serve without pay, and Northrop recognized the personal risks they were running to develop such a trade: "Mr. Broadwell & yourself, with a courage & moral self-sacrifice most rare, are endeavoring to serve our cause—and not merely by work, but by risking trouble and malignant interpretation... You must expect annoyance."[9]

That same day, July 18, 1862, Broadwell was writing to Northrop that he had permission (presumably from Van Dorn) to finance the trade by exporting cotton—"provided it does not reach our Enemies...".[10] It seemed there was a Frenchman, Jules Tardos, who claimed to be able to get cotton

5   NA, RG 109, Officers: Broadwell.
6   Ibid., July 6, 1862.
7   Ibid., July 4, 1862.
8   Ibid., July 12, 1862.
9   July 18, 1862 (NA, RG 109, Officers: Dameron).
10   NA, RG 109, Officers: Broadwell.

through the blockade for transport to Europe. Three weeks later, as if to illustrate the power of a cotton trade, Broadwell reported that one of his schooners loaded at New Orleans was being refused clearance by the Federals: "Capt Foster who manages this business thinks if he were allowed to send a little cotton to Genl Butler we could get everything we want."[11] Northrop was forced to answer: "The suggestions of Capt. F. will not be acted on by our *Govt* it would be decisive against the position taken on that point." Speaking for himself, Northrop made clear his own disagreement with the policy: "I would let them have as much cotton as would buy what we need...".[12]

On September 11 Broadwell wrote to Northrop:

> A reliable man from New Orleans just arrived, reports that Genl Butler has refused to issue any more permits for vessels to bring things in this direction, upon the ground that we offer nothing in exchange.
>
> As you have already been advised, he appears inclined to make money & is eager to do so by realizing some portion of the enormous profits to be made on the sale of Cotton exported from this Country—which, if permitted by us, he would exempt from capture so that it could pass the blockade.

At the same time Broadwell reported a renewed offer from the Frenchman Tardos to exchange 10,000 sacks of salt for the privilege of shipping 1,000 bales of cotton to France. Tardos "gets an exemption from seizure by paying Genl Butler & then getting the guarantee of the Consul that the Cotton will be sold in France." Making that arrangement with him would utilize cotton now wasting—exposed to weather and the risk of burning by Confederates or capture by advancing Federals. Broadwell added shrewdly:

> If the Govmt realize—as some persons—that the idea of forcing European nations to recognize us through the agency of Cotton *has exploded*, possibly they will instruct me to make similar arrangements to the one with Tardos to such an extent as will prevent suffering in the Army.[13]

There was no sign in Richmond that the Davis Government realized their cotton policy had failed.

A constant *obbligato* through Broadwell's reports was the plea for money, more money, and still more. He was being funded *pro tem* by Dameron. Thus on August 25, 1862: "I have borrowed some money, and may be able to spend a great deal if the trade with New Orleans continues as brisk as it has been." On September 4 Broadwell telegraphed: "One thousand sacks Salt arrived this day. Have arranged for purchase of large quantity of Sugar. Embarrassed for money." Northrop wired back that he had urgently

---

[11] Ibid., August 8, 1862.Butler's corruption was widely recognized South and North. His order allowing ladies of New Orleans who insulted Federal troops to be treated as women of the streets plying their profession earned him the sobriquet "Beast Butler". After the war, when his offers to the Southern commissariat became widely known in the North, *The New York World* retailed a quip that went the rounds: "Now this Butler was more Sutler than any other Beast in the field." (*The Diary of George Templeton Strong*, ed. Nevins and Thomas, *abr.* T. J. Pressly: Univ. of Washington, 1988, 367.)

[12] Ibid., August 19, 1862.

[13] Ibid., September 7, 27, and October 4, 1862.

requisitioned funds for Broadwell, and would requisition again. The Treasury was not doing its business. When money did come, Broadwell encountered rising difficulties and discounts in getting Confederate currency accepted at New Orleans. He had General Van Dorn's leave to trade back various non-controversial items like lumber and rosin, and that relieved some pressure.

*   *   *

One of the chief articles bought from the enemy at New Orleans was salt. Of all basic articles in short supply, salt was the one people could least do without. In Alabama the citizenry were threatened with a meatless diet from want of salt. On July 30, 1862 their Governor had written to Richmond proposing to trade cotton for salt, with a plan to avoid contravening the letter of the law: the Governor would trade the cotton with a Frenchman through a port actually in Confederate hands, Mobile.[14] President Davis gave a very grudging assent. Then the Governor of Mississippi, Alabama's neighbor to the west and equally embarrassed for salt, wanted to do the same.[15]

The Confederate armies, by contrast, were reasonably supplied. Salt was one consistent success of Northrop's Subsistence Bureau, and it was to remain so for most of the war.[16] From the outset he had pursued every possibility, encouraged every idea, found funds for every project.[17] The biggest deposits known in the South were near the southwestern corner of Virginia; the place was actually called Saltville. The location was dangerously open to Federal attack, and transport out relied on one lonely, circuitous railroad spur through the mountains.

Northrop had hesitated not an instant. At the beginning of the war he had contracted with the biggest producer at Saltville, Messrs. Stuart, Buchanan & Co., for all the salt they could produce at 75 cents a bushel. When their production proved insufficient, the Commissary General rewrote the contract to demand 10,000 bushels a month. He also contracted with the other producers at Saltville in such a way as to establish a near-monopoly there—just as he had done with the meat packers of Tennessee.

In April 1862 Northrop had made a new contract with Stuart, Buchanan. He kept the price at 75 cents, but now specified the production of 22,000 bushels a month.[18] That was well beyond army needs, but the growing weakness of Confederate currency in many places had made salt a regular medium of exchange. The Commissary General was laying in a supply for his

---

[14]   *OR* ser. IV, vol. 2, 21-22.

[15]   Rowland, V, 354, 365, 380.

[16]   For a modern evaluation (one of very few on any of Northrop's policies) see Herman Hattaway and Archer Jones, *How the North Won: A Military History of the Civil War* (Univ. of Chicago, 1983), 183-85.

[17]   One promising scheme was started with Northrop's blessing by a French geologist, M. J. Raymond Thomassy, who had made a thorough study of Southern lands. Thomassy directed the building of shallow vats and troughs along seacoasts to assist solar evaporation from sea water. It was expensive and vulnerable to the enemy. Thomassy died in 1863 before it could produce much salt. See Ella Lonn, *Salt as a Factor in the Confederacy*, 72-77; and Charles W. Ramsdell, *Behind the Lines*, 104.

[18]   Lonn, *Salt as a Factor in the Confederacy*, 68.

Bureau to supplement the short funds doled out by the Treasury. One reason the people of the South could not get enough salt was that the Subsistence Bureau had sewn up supplies so tightly.

The price of salt rocketed. Stuart, Buchanan asked Northrop to rewrite their contract to raise the government price. Northrop refused. In August 1862 the matter reached Secretary Randolph. He disagreed with Northrop (as he told the President) because the requested price-rise had been fomented entirely by inflation, and it seemed to him unwise to alienate and beggar the nation's biggest producer of salt.[19] So Davis allowed the increase. Northrop ground his teeth.[20]

Then the Confederacy had a windfall. The Governor of Mississippi had an agent looking for salt. In August 1862 the agent came to a salt mine belonging to Judge D. D. Avery, ten miles west of New Iberia, Louisiana and a hundred miles west of New Orleans. The mine was on a rather inaccessible island among the swamps and bayous honeycombing the Gulf coast west of the Mississippi Delta. The shallow waters did offer long zig-zag connections via Red River to the Mississippi River town of Port Hudson, still in Confederate hands.

By the first of September Broadwell knew of it. He already had his uncle Jacob Payne out at the Mississippi landing of Red River buying sugar and molasses for the army. Payne went to investigate the Avery mine and reported: the owner was sympathetic to the Confederate cause, but only one shaft was sunk and nobody knew the extent of the deposit. A week later Broadwell knew more: on September 8 he reported that the mine "promises to supply the Confederacy if properly managed". Northrop telegraphed back: "Press your salt operations to utmost extent you can for we want it all."[21]

The Commissary General's "we" this time embraced the Confederacy as a whole, army and people. Autumn was coming, and with it the time for hog-curing. The old Northern bacon laid in at the beginning of the war was just finishing. After the bad harvest and renewed hog cholera, hogs were thin and made less bacon. Without a good supply of salt, they would make none. In Richmond by mid-October Northrop's assistant Frank Ruffin was to report that the Bureau had only enough meat to feed Lee's army in Virginia for twenty-five days.[22]

At the remote Avery mine, both labor and transport were hard to find. On October 1, 1862 Broadwell drafted a circular asking planters of the area to furnish labor from their plantations to work the mine, in exchange for salt: it was approved by Northrop and Randolph.[23] Then he tried to get boats from the sugar trade to bring the Avery salt past Federal gunboats cruising

---

[19]   August 11, 1862 (NA, RG 109, Letters Sent by the Confederate Secretary of War to the President, I, 161).

[20]   February 1865 to J.C. Breckinridge (OR ser. I, vol. 46, pt. 2, 1221-22).

[21]   September 9, 1862 (NA, RG 109, Officers: Broadwell).

[22]   Testimony before Confederate Congress in January 1865 (Va. Hist. Soc.).

[23]   October 13, 1862 (NA, RG 109, Officers: Broadwell).

the waters to stop the crossing of Confederate sugar, molasses, and cattle.[24] Finding two steamboats under government contract but full of speculators' freight, Broadwell seized the boats and telegraphed for power to impress them. That too was forthcoming, and Broadwell wrote: "... I propose to organize a line of Steamers to run every day & do all the business."[25]

In practice it was not so easy. Conflicts blew up at Vicksburg over who could use the boats to carry what cargoes. Broadwell wrote on October 20: "... Everything we want is required by officers and Generals on the spot." In fact there were signs of rising jealousy of Broadwell's power and success. One sign of those troubles was his own request for promotion to a lieutenant colonelcy—and it was done.[26] Nonetheless he hoped "within 40 days to be sending a Steam Boat load [of salt] per day to Vicksburg".[27] He was at that moment on his way to see the Avery mine for himself. He had a new shaft sunk for exclusive use by the government, and by November 2 he reported "the mine getting out nearly 100,000 pounds of Salt per diem, with a prospect soon of largely increasing the production. The Salt is of the very best description...".

Yet the whole district around the mine lived in constant fear of Federal attack. Broadwell wrote: "The road is lined with planters moving to Texas with their negroes."[28] On Northrop's recommendation he visited the man in charge of the district, Major General Richard Taylor, to ask military protection for the mine. Taylor went to see it and promised to defend it "at all hazards," but his force of only 500 reliable soldiers would be inadequate.[29]

By the end of 1862 Broadwell had solved the labor problem at the mine: "Yesterday we got out 78,000 lbs—and this might be extended to almost any degree...". Yet there was still no transport adequate to convey the Avery salt to where it was needed desperately.[30] In Atlanta the keeper of the Subsistence Bureau storehouse, Major Cummings, had to impress salt on his own authority to prevent the loss of large numbers of hogs by starvation and disease.[31]

* * *

Broadwell's powers and actions seemed to overarch the entire Confederate Mississippi region. In early September 1862 he had sniffed out a family of currency counterfeiters named Paine or Payne, down from Kentucky

24   Ibid., September 6, 1862.

25   Ibid., October 6 and 7, 1862.

26   Ibid., Northrop to Broadwell, July 26 and August 6; Broadwell to Northrop, August 8 and September 13, 1862. Broadwell asked for the higher rank with its emoluments, as his own money was tied up in the fall of New Orleans, and he could no longer pay his board and lodging. Davis's approval was conveyed by Northrop on September 20, 1862.

27   Ibid., October 20, 1862.

28   Ibid.

29   Ibid., November 2, 1862.

30   Ibid., December 27, 1862 (on his third visit to the mine) to Northrop.

31   Telegram from a private owner of salt in Georgia, L. H. Johnson, December 22, 1862, with Northrop's endorsement of December 24 (M-618, r 13, ff 628-29). That impressment needed, and received ultimately, approval from the Secretary of War.

and dealing in cattle.[32] Investigation turned up more of the counterfeit. Broadwell arrested the lot of them, seized their counterfeit money and the cattle they had bought with it.[33]

At the same time Broadwell thought he had a plan to acquire for Northrop's Bureau "all the Sugar you want ... I have prohibited speculations [*copyist's mistake for 'speculators'?*] from coming in competition with the Government until a supply is obtained for the Army. If you think me right, please telegraph the Commanding General that you leave the Sugar business to my management."[34] There Northrop felt unable to give authority: "No power exists in this Bureau", he wrote back on September 20, "to interfere with the general business of the country—and as sugar is a luxury, it is not, in my judgement, a subject of impressment."[35]

In October 1862 the command of Mississippi forces passed from Van Dorn (increasingly unpopular with local people on account of alleged high-handedness) to Lieutenant General John C. Pemberton. Until Pemberton could arrive, the command was in the hands of Brigadier General Daniel Ruggles. He was an amiable old muddler, described by Broadwell as over-eager to accede to any suggestion made to him; the inevitable result was conflicting orders. On September 22 Broadwell told Northrop he had decided to let General Ruggles manage sugar purchases through New Orleans with his own men. That decision would turn out to be a costly precedent.

Then Pemberton arrived. He was less of an aggressive fighter than Van Dorn, and more of an organizing, systematizing general—who would be certain to distrust such semi-private, quasi-official work as Broadwell's.[36] Northrop anticipated trouble over the New Orleans trade, and warned Broadwell to explain the position with great care: "Call on Gen. Pemberton, & say that I requested you to give him in detail our plans—and ask his coöperation for what his own perception, I am sure, will approve of. I am now going to address him, requesting his attention to this." And Northrop virtually instructed Broadwell to resume control of trading with the enemy: "I believe your trade with N.O. must go on, & I approve of what you have done—and will stand up to the responsibility of going on."[37]

Soon two schooners sailed up from New Orleans without a murmur from the enemy, and their cargoes of salt and other necessities were re-

---

[32]   Not to be confused with Broadwell's uncle Jacob Payne (though anti-Davis press elements in Richmond would do so gleefully). Jacob Payne, following an interview with Northrop during the summer, had been all this time stationed at Red River landing to supervise the crossing of Confederate foods. See Broadwell to Northrop. August 31, September 6 and 13, October 7, 1862 (NA, RG 109, Officers: Broadwell).

[33]   NA, RG 109, Officers: Broadwell, September 12 and 16, 1862. For an account of the Paine or Payne family of counterfeiters, see Judith Ann Benner, *Fraudulent Finance: Counterfeiting and the Confederate States, 1861-1865* (Hill Junior College Monograph no. 3, 1970), 48-51.

[34]   September 16, 1862 (NA, RG 109, Officers: Broadwell).

[35]   Ibid., September 20 and 22, 1862.

[36]   Michael B. Ballard, *Pemberton: A Biography* (Univ. of Mississippi, 1991), 115-16.

[37]   October 13, 1862 (NA, RG 109, Officers: Broadwell). For an able summary of Northrop's reasons, see Ludwell H. Johnson, "Trading with the Union: the Evolution of Confederate Policy", in *Virginia Magazine of History and Biography*, vol. 78 (1970), 320.

leased by Broadwell. The ship merchant got his money, together with an understanding that he could use that money to buy Confederate cotton and ship it down the river, exactly as the salt had come up.

Somehow, probably through Pemberton, the news reached the ears of Frank Hatch, the former collector of customs at New Orleans when the port was in Confederate hands, and still district agent for the Confederate Treasury. The Treasury exercised a rigid control over cotton, and meant to maintain it. Hatch promptly impounded the vessels and wrote to Pemberton: "Without assuming to judge whether or not these clearly unlawful acts were justified by the exigencies of the case, it is quite clear that parties have assumed powers and authority which should only have been exercised by the commanding general, and I find this to be the cause of great complaint among our best citizens." Hatch cited confirming opinions from leading Mississippi lawyers.[38]

Almost before his ink was dry, more such ships were coming from New Orleans. Within two days Hatch had no fewer than thirty vessels in his custody.[39] Then, to his stupefaction, Pemberton ordered the release of the *Osceola*. Hatch complied, but vigorously protested to Pemberton:

> ... I have respectfully to submit that if military exigencies require the release (and of which exigency it is not my province in the slightest degree to question), that such requisition for release should be made upon this office...
>
> With your knowledge of the law it is hardly necessary to observe that even if trading with the enemy in extraordinary cases is assumed by military authority, the revenue laws are subjected alone to the authority of Congress, and I am sure you will agree with me in adding that entire harmony and co-operation between the War and Treasury Departments, so essential to the public service and interests, is most likely to be secured by a frank understanding of their respective rights and obligations.[40]

Pemberton then issued a prohibiting order. Of course it did nothing to stop *private* trading through the lines, which continued to increase. Within three months Hatch was writing to his chief Memminger that if they could not stop such trade, at least the Treasury ought to regulate and profit from it.[41] Pemberton's order, therefore, had only the effect of stopping up another of the shrinking channels of the Subsistence Bureau for feeding the army. That order also made so much noise that the Federals got wind of it, for they removed Butler from his command at New Orleans in December 1862.

---

[38] November 3, 1862 (*OR* ser. IV, vol. 2, 169).

[39] *OR* ser. IV, vol. 2, 173.

[40] November 7, 1862 (*OR* ser. IV, vol. 2, 172-73). Within a week the matter had reached the President's desk again. Two letters came from the Richmond agent of Barriére Brothers (New Orleans and Paris), offering to bring in through New Orleans salt, bacon, blankets, shoes, boots, and flannel— to be exchanged for cotton. On November 14 Davis rejected it, unless "in a last resort"—which he clearly did not think had arrived (*OR* ser. IV, vol. 2, 173-75).

[41] March 17 1863 (*OR* ser. IV, vol. 2, 459-60).

CHAPTER 14

FARTHER FETCHED MEAT

Another offer of supply through enemy lines had electrified the Commissary General's office in October 1862. It came once again from Dr. Jeptha Fowlkes (who a year earlier had offered such services to Davis). He wrote to Northrop that he could obtain "ten thousand hogsheads of bacon certainly, and probably twenty thousand more hogsheads".[1] He proposed to draw payment in cotton from an area near Memphis still in Confederate hands but under Federal threat: if the Federals came in, he said, the cotton planters would sell to the enemy rather than burn their crop.[2]

On October 30 Fowlkes himself walked into Northrop's office to renew his offer and press for action. Northrop was keen to accept, and that day wrote an urgent letter to Secretary Randolph: "If the Secretary of War does not think proper to authorize and sustain this plan, I request, in accordance with Regulations, p. 930, that he will designate where other purchases shall be made...".[3]

Instantly Randolph sent Fowlkes's letter with Northrop's warning to the President, together with Randolph's own legalistic justification for the trade: the law prevented *individuals* from trading with the enemy, but it did not appear to prevent the government itself from doing so. Randolph said he was fully aware of "licensing an objectionable trade... But the Commissary General, whose duty it is to study the question of subsistence and to inform himself of the sources of supply, and who has had the benefit of eighteen months' experience, having recorded his opinion that the Army

---

[1] Quoted in Ruffin, "A Chapter of Confederate History", 99.

[2] Ruffin's summary dated July 25, 1865 (Huntington Library: Eldridge Coll. Box 76). Fowlkes's original letter has not been found, but an unexecuted contract between Fowlkes and Northrop reciting terms, and proposing to exchange bacon for cotton pound for pound, is with Ruffin's papers in the Virginia Historical Society. Apparently before November 15 a second letter came from Fowlkes, expressing fear that the replacement of Butler at New Orleans would close the chance of trading cotton with the enemy. The only record of this second letter seems to be a summary of it in Jones's *War Clerk's Diary*: "He says it must be embraced now or never, or the enemy will soon make such dispositions as would prevent his getting supplies *through their lines*" (I, 196). Two further letters from Fowlkes dated December 17 and 18 renew the offer: Northrop's endorsement on them to the Secretary of War beg for action and deplore delay. No answer is with the correspondence (F.G. Ruffin Papers, Va. Hist. Soc.).

[3] *The New York Herald*, July 21, 1865, 2.

cannot be subsisted under the present arrangements, I must decline the responsibility of overruling him and entering upon an experiment which may result in ruin."[4]

Davis was incredulous. Food seemed plentiful enough in Richmond, if highly priced. The War Department clerk Jones had noted in his diary on October 18, 1862 (the very day Ruffin reported the approaching exhaustion of meat for Lee's army): "I traversed the markets this morning, and was gratified to find the greatest profusion of all kinds of meats, vegetables, fruits, poultry, butter, eggs, etc. But the prices are enormously high. If the army be kept away, it seems the supply must soon be greater than the demand."[5]

With all that food in Richmond markets, perhaps it was hard for the President himself to envision dearth and exhaustion elsewhere. Jones certainly found it so, and was "startled" when the Fowlkes-Northrop-Randolph letters came to his desk for copying or epitomizing: "I never supposed Mr. Randolph would suggest, nay *urge*, opening an illicit trade with 'Butler, the Beast'. This is the first really dark period of our struggle for independence." Jones concluded what any Southerner in the Confederate capital who knew the situation only in fragments might conclude: "I cannot believe it is a necessity, but a destitution of that virtue necessary to achieve independence." When Northrop's report of the wheat and flour difficulties for Lee's army came across his desk, Jones wrote flatly in his diary: "I don't believe it."[6] If Jones represented the man in the capital street, such opinions would be grist to the anti-Davis mills grinding busily in the Richmond press.

On October 31, 1862 the President returned the Fowlkes-Northrop papers with his endorsement. Davis was allowing himself to think that a want of Southern cotton in the North might even cause the Lincoln government to default on its own interest payments due at the beginning of 1863. So Randolph had to send the whole lot back to Northrop with this instruction: "Observe the President's endorsement, and report upon the practicality of delaying the proposed purchases until after the 1st of January next. It will be necessary to state, for the President's information, your estimate of the probable receipts under your present arrangements".[7]

Northrop asked Ruffin to assess the supply of meat for the next sixty days without trade through enemy lines. Two days later Ruffin sent in his estimate:

> ... General Lee's army is drawing very closely on the supplies of fresh beef, and at their present rate of consumption I do not think that there will be more than enough to last them until the first of January. The very severe drought in the past summer and early fall leaves the cattle so thin that the same number of bullocks does not

---

4 *OR* ser. IV, vol. 2, 151.

5 *Diary*, I, 172.

6 Ibid., 180 (November 1) and 183 (November 6, 1862).

7 Huntington Library, Brock Coll., Box 284. Printed in *The New York Herald*, July 21, 1865, 2. This text, and some of what follows, was later printed in E. A. Pollard, *The Lost Cause* (New York: E. B. Treat, 1867), 480-89. Pollard probably used Ruffin's long article in *The New York Herald* as his source.

go as far as it did last year, and the scarcity of supply is drawing much younger beasts to market than came last year.

Only a few cattle were coming over from the Northern Neck of Virginia tidewater, mostly driven in to escape enemy advances there. South of Virginia the situation was worse. Supplies in North Carolina were threatened by the enemy but could not be got away because there was no transport.[8] The same problem occurred in Georgia and Florida. In any case Florida was too far to drive cattle all the way to northern Virginia. The cattle from Texas being swum across the Mississippi were still farther removed; and whenever Broadwell started some east, they were always stopped by some intervening Confederate commander for his own use. Ruffin concluded:

> If to this estimate of short supply be added the waste committed by the soldiers, and permitted in some corps and perpetrated in others by the generals in command, I think it would be imprudent to estimate full supplies to January, and a fatal error to rely on full supplies after that time in any quarter.[9]

Northrop sent this report to Secretary Randolph on November 3 with a further warning: "Present efforts, even if successful, will not produce cured bacon by the 1st of January."[10]

And there the whole thing stopped. When nothing was heard after several days, Northrop told Ruffin to see Randolph again. Randolph advised him to prepare a statement comparing stocks of meat on hand now with those a year ago. Ruffin duly got up the comparative statement, which showed there were 100,000 fewer hogs than a year ago, and almost no beef for Lee. When all the material was sent to Davis, he sent back an ostrich-like delaying endorsement:

> The question submitted is one which a constitutional adviser would advantageously bring to a conference. The papers enclosed, particularly the statement of bacon on hand, does [sic] not sustain the conclusion presented. To solve the question a statement from the C.G.S. and a comparative view, based upon a return of the troops will be necessary. The resources of every portion of the Confederacy must be considered to reach a just estimate.[11]

---

[8]   The entire food gathering operation in coastal North Carolina was bedeviled by bad roads and a near dearth of rail lines. Subsistence Bureau correspondence with the North Carolina governor's office (November 2-12, 1862) is printed in OR ser. I, vol. 18, 764-66, 769, 771: at Northrop's request, Governor Vance offered his assistance in getting food away from eastern counties under immediate threat. (There was however gross and persistent hoarding and speculation throughout the State: see OR ser. IV, vol. 2, 181-82.) The military commander of the district, Brigadier General William H. C. Whiting, reported large quantities of rice which planters were willing to sell to the government: otherwise it would have to be destroyed to forestall enemy capture (November 14, 1862, Ibid., 773-74). Whiting's letter arrived in Richmond on the desk of Acting Secretary of War Gustavus W. Smith, who endorsed that the information had been sent to Lee: "When the pressure of the enemy on the north will permit, forces should, and I have no doubt will, be detached south of James River" (OR ser. I, vol. 18, 777). It was the same weary tale.

[9]   OR ser. IV, vol. 2, 158-60.

[10]   The New York Herald, July 21, 1865, 2.

[11]   Endorsement of November 13 on Randolph's letter dated October 30, 1862 (Huntington Library; Brock Coll. Box 284).

THE LATER
CONFEDERATE
SECRETARIES
OF WAR

GEORGE WYTHE RANDOLPH
(1818-1867)
SECRETARY MARCH TO NOVEMBER 1862.

GENERALS IN GRAY

JAMES A. SEDDON
(1815-1880)
SECRETARY NOVEMBER 1862 TO
JANUARY 1865.

STATESMEN OF THE LOST CAUSE

Ruffin exploded to the Chief of the War Bureau, Robert Kean, who wrote in his diary: "I am coming to Mr. Ruffin's opinion. He says he used to think Jefferson Davis a *mule*, but a *good mule*. He has come to think him a jackass."[12]

Secretary Randolph endorsed the latest executive delaying demand: "Commissary General—See the President's endorsement. He has forgot a conference on the subject at which General Lee was present."[13] Next day Randolph resigned his office. The precipitating cause was said to be the President's refusal to let Randolph make the military orders Randolph considered the duty of a Secretary of War.[14] But there can be little question that the President's persistent procrastination over the Commissary General's clear cries for help was a major element in Randolph's resignation.

Under the interim Secretaryship of Major General Gustavus W. Smith, Northrop had Ruffin revise his "comparative view" along the lines indicated. The document showed an actual increase in bacon stores of two million pounds—a monument to Northrop's determination to garner something for the future against steeply rising odds; but of course none of it was in Virginia. And there was an ominous shrinkage in the amount of bacon cured in 1862 as against 1861: even adding the increase of bacon stored, it left a "deficit" in 1862 of more than eight million pounds. The story of salt beef was the same: whereas last year they had packed 40,000 beeves, this year they had managed just 4,000. The situation of fresh beef was the most precarious of all: "The number of beeves from all sources available for General Lee's army, which consumes 1,000 head per week, does not this day exceed, so far as this Bureau knows, 8,500 head: and over 4,000 of them are about 250 miles removed from him at this time, and winter is at hand." Northrop himself concluded this disastrous report with a threatening new development. Cummings telegraphed that Bragg had just made an order to impound for himself all supplies being collected in Tennessee for shipment to Atlanta and Lee. Northrop had forbidden it.[15] But Northrop was far away from Tennessee, and Bragg commanded the ground.

On November 17, 1862 Lee wrote to the Acting Secretary of War. The general was preparing to move his troops eastward to defend Fredericksburg against another Federal advance. He too had contravened Northrop's order for reduced rations, and he wanted to increase the ration again: "It was stated that one great cause of straggling from the ranks was the insufficiency of the ration to appease the hunger of the men. ... The same condition of things now exists."[16]

The Acting Secretary sent this to Northrop. Northrop, in the midst of his own battle to achieve trade through enemy lines, made only the briefest endorsement: "Respectfully returned to the Secretary of War, with the re-

---

12 *Inside the Confederate Government*, 31.

13 November 14, 1862 (*The New York Herald*, July 21, 1865, 2).

14 *Inside the Confederate Government*, 28-31.

15 *OR* ser. IV, vol. 2, 192-93. See Cummings to Northrop, November 10 and December 5, 1862 (Va. Hist. Soc., Ruffin Papers): when 300 head of Cummings's cattle *en route* to Atlanta were kidnapped and taken back to middle Tennessee, Cummings threatened to resign. See below, pp. 207-09.

16 *OR* ser. I, vol. 21, 1016-17.

mark that the necessities represented merely add to the evidence previously furnished of the necessity of enlarging our sources of supply." It was a prime example of the sort of endorsement which, taken out of context, would suggest that the Commissary General was callous of all but his own infallibility. The reader of the foregoing pages will understand how little there was to add to all that had been submitted during the previous fortnight.

On November 21 the "Comparative View" came back from the President with another delaying endorsement. Davis demanded "an estimate ... of the amount of supplies that can be produced from sources within the Confederate States from which last year we could produce none, and state more fully the reasons for immediate action, and consider the relative advantages of procuring supplies from Memphis and from the vicinity of New Orleans."[17]

Northrop was not famed for docility or patience. In this case, however, when the result was vital, his response was impeccable:

> It will be observed that the President, through General Smith, calls for information on three points, and to that exclusively is the answer addressed.
> First. Every source within the Confederate lines from which supplies could have been obtained last year or this had been fully explored. All such have either been exhausted or found inadequate. If in any small portion of the Confederacy supplies have not been aimed at, it was because it was known that such portion would not afford enough for the current domestic supply of that particular area. ...
> Second. To state more fully the reasons for immediate action it is necessary to recapitulate.

He summarized the "Comparative Views": they showed a deficit in the food supply for the current year as opposed to last year of 43 percent; and not all of the year's counted supplies were yet safely delivered.

> The supplies now offered [by Fowlkes] are ample, and are tendered at lower rates in cotton, even at the extreme bid, than they can be bought at for Confederate currency in our own lines. If not availed of now they most probably never will be, for lack of power and opportunity. ...
> Third. As to the relative advantages of procuring supplies from Memphis and from the vicinity of New Orleans, the proposition to make such purchases is not a new idea.

Again he summarized the history. In view of the size the Confederate armies had attained, the reserve stocks of food held by the Bureau were by no means as large as they looked; and the best food lands near Lee were exhausted and overrun. Among the arguments for trading through enemy lines now, Northrop added two grim forecasts. The Avery salt mine in western Louisiana was under constant enemy threat (in fact it would fall to the Federals in April 1863). And there was already trouble over salt from a citizenry

---

[17]   *The New York Herald*, July 21, 1865, 2.

suffering "ruinous prices and great destitution". On November 10 at Greenville, Alabama twenty women attacked a railroad agent with cries of "Salt or Blood!". He had to open a large sack destined for the army and divide it among them.[18] It was the first instance of a new and horrifying phenomenon that would spread across the Confederacy in 1863—the food riot. Northrop rightly predicted others. He concluded his latest report to Davis:

> One responsible party in New Orleans offers to supply one hundred thousand sacks of salt, or more than is called for by the rapidly expiring contract at Saltville. Other articles such as coffee and flour are also offered from New Orleans. The supply of flour from that quarter will enable the soldiers from the Southwest to use that in part as a bread ration instead of corn meal, which must otherwise be their sole reliance for bread. The reserve of coffee for the sick is being rapidly consumed. No other prospect of getting more presents itself...
>
> ... The opportunity afforded by the venality of the enemy ought not to be lost. ... Its effect upon the *morale* of the enemy, and the political results of such a policy, however important in themselves, are questions which, as they have not entered into my calculations, I do not discuss.
>
> My action proceeds entirely from a sense of the absolute necessity of these supplies to feed the army and to subdue the want which has already manifested itself in General Lee's army and the Army of the West, under the privations to which they have been subjected.[19]

Nothing could be clearer; nothing more eloquent of the Commissary General's feeling for the soldier in the field. But the President answered never a word. The new permanent Secretary of War, James A. Seddon, told Ruffin that when the President went out to Mississippi in December 1862 to visit Bragg, Davis gave the general secret powers to trade with the enemy "should it become absolutely indispensable"—but added that he did not think it was so then. Further urgent applications in December 1862 and January 1863 went unanswered.[20] It proved to be, as Northrop had feared, his last chance to feed the Confederate army adequately in winter. Davis had thrown it away.

Why did Northrop not follow Secretary Randolph's example and resign? He was not getting the one thing he said he needed to feed the army. The President said it contravened the law: yet Davis had helped a Gulf governor around that law. Moreover, the President's delays to Northrop's pleas (where he could have rejected them out of hand) showed very clearly that he understood the position. Barely six weeks later Davis himself characterized the threatening shortage of food as "the greatest danger to a suc-

---

[18]   Gates. *Agriculture and the Civil War*, 38-39.

[19]   *The New York Herald*, July 21, 1865, 2. Part of the New Orleans merchant's letter is preserved with Ruffin's papers in Va. Hist. Soc.

[20]   Ibid. See Northrop's endorsement of January 2, 1863 on Jeptha Fowlkes's proposed contract dated December 17, 1862 (Va. Hist. Soc.: Ruffin Papers).

cessful prosecution of the war".[21] Yet in the end presidential principle had won out, leaving the Commissary General with a task he himself had defined as impossible.

To offset that fact, Northrop felt two counter-claims. One was his personal loyalty to Davis in a friendship stretching back thirty years. The other was his sense of duty. Northrop had never been a quitter, and pressure only made him stubborn. Any attempt to overpower or hound him would simply make him dig in his heels. If he could not feed the army adequately after all the efforts he had made, the schemes designed and executed, the reliable men placed at vital points, then it stood to reason (his own at least) that no one else could do better. In view of his nearly two years' experience at the head of the Subsistence Bureau, the presumption might be that no one else could do so well.[22]

* * *

There was only one remaining direction from which meat might be had: for salt meat, there could be a possibility of purchase in England. That would mean getting it across the Atlantic and then through the Federal blockade of Southern coasts—with all the problems of bulk and weight, containers and storage, and spoilage if shipments were held too long on the way. Equally it meant financial complication.

Ever since the opening of the war, the South had traded with Europe for arms. The trade had been organized by the Chief of the Ordnance Bureau, Josiah Gorgas. Knowing that Confederate lands and manufactories could not supply the ordnance needed for a successful war of independence, Gorgas had secured permission to send an agent to England to negotiate purchases of munitions. The agent was Caleb Huse, a graduate of West Point. In London, Huse set up a network of suppliers and shippers willing to aid the Confederacy.

Shipping arms to the South had grown more difficult as the Federal blockade tightened. Only the harbors at Wilmington (North Carolina), Charleston and a handful of Gulf ports were deep enough to receive ocean-going freighters; and those freighters were mostly too slow to outrun Northern blockaders. So a great transshipping business had grown up at offshore foreign ports—via Bermuda through Nassau, or occasionally through Trinidad, Havana, Florida, Matamoras (Mexico), or even St. John's (New Brunswick) and Halifax (Nova Scotia). British freighters would take cargoes destined for the Confederacy, but labelled otherwise, into those ports. There the goods were off-loaded and warehoused under the direction of Confederate agents (who themselves were often foreign nationals)—to await the chance of being run in ships of lighter draft and quicker speed into Southern har-

---

[21]   January 27, 1863 to Governor Joseph E. Brown of Georgia (OR ser. IV, vol. 2, 376).

[22]   For the similarity of Davis's own character, see Lynda Lasswell Crist, "A 'Duty Man': Jefferson Davis as Senator", *Journal of Mississippi History*, LI, (November 1989), 281-96.

bors. Success in getting through the blockade remained high; throughout the war the blockade-running success rate was over seventy-five percent.[23]

For the first eighteen months Huse had relied on commercial vessels. He used the Liverpool firm of S. Isaac, Campbell & Co. They had been convicted of shipping frauds in the Crimean War of 1854-56; but Huse thought he could control them, and they seemed eager to serve him. Back in Richmond, Gorgas was not so sure. The Ordnance Chief decided he wanted control of ships as well as shipments, and in the autumn of 1862 he secured $2 million worth of Confederate bonds to establish his own line of blockade-runners.[24] These light-drafted steamers would not be part of the Confederate navy (whose Secretary Stephen Mallory would have nothing to do with the fringe-operation). They were to be operated as a private fiefdom of the Ordnance Bureau. That was almost true of the entire Confederate blockade-running operation up to this time.

The Ordnance ships would bring in some medicines (which after all took little space) as an accommodation to the Surgeon General. But Huse declined to handle many of the large Quartermaster's goods: indeed he did his best to spoil the chances of a separate agent whom Quartermaster General Myers had sent to purchase supplies in England. As for Subsistence—bulky containers of cured meats unpleasant to handle, difficult to store, easily spoiled—Huse would not touch them.[25] Nor would his chief Gorgas have allowed him to do so. During the first year and more of the war, nobody had ever suggested shipping meat across the Atlantic: why should such an impractical plan be allowed to interfere with the flow of armaments now?

The Confederate navy meanwhile had European problems of its own. The navy needed to call on British shipbuilders to supply heavy vessels that could not be built in the South. But the British shipbuilders had shown no enthusiasm for Confederate money, either bonds or notes. In early 1862, therefore, Navy Secretary Mallory had worked hard to turn around the Davis Government's unwillingness to trade cotton. And he succeeded: by the middle of 1862 Mallory was shipping cotton to England to pay his shipbuilding debts there. Mallory's action gradually changed the outlook of Secretary Memminger at the Treasury, and government cotton was at last made available to the War Department and its bureaus for purchasing abroad.[26]

---

[23] Stephen R. Wise, *Lifeline of the Confederacy: Blockade Running During the Civil War* (Univ. of South Carolina, 1988), caption to Plate 22, between 212-213. The fascinating letters edited by Frank Vandiver in *Confederate Blockade Running Through Bermuda 1861-1865* (Univ. of Texas, 1947) contain disappointingly little about Subsistence. The "Cargo Manifests" printed at the end of the book do show increasing quantities fo food from April 1863 (see 111 ff.). Neither shippers nor receivers are identified: code-markings on the Manifests have not been printed because nobody knows what most of them mean. (No serious study of those Confederate codes has ever been undertaken.) Very large food shipments were probably intended for Northrop's Bureau: but again, only a detailed study of documents published and unpublished would have any chance of showing how much actually arrived.

[24] Wise, 95.

[25] See e.g. Huse to W. G. Crenshaw, April 10, 1863: "I do not think you should calculate upon receiving any money from me before June, and I cannot say that even then there will be any available for the Subsistence Department." (*OR* ser. IV, vol. 2, 539)

[26] See Seddon to James Crenshaw, May 23, 1863 (*OR* ser. IV, vol. 2, 565-66).

The news made merchant bankers in Europe prick up their ears. In October 1862 the Paris banking house of Erlanger offered the Confederacy a major "loan". It was in fact a high-risk speculation. Erlanger would manage a big Confederate bond-issue: the 20-year bonds, attracting $7^{1}/_{2}\%$ interest, would ultimately be convertible to cotton priced at quarter to a third of current European values. The Confederate Treasury undertook to redeem the bonds within six months of a peace treaty ratified with the North. As clearing house, Erlanger would pay £77 for every £100 bond. The ceiling was virtually unlimited, and Baron Frederick Emile von Erlanger made a special trip to Richmond to negotiate with the Confederate Treasury. Memminger decided on a limit of £3 million (just over $15 million at par), and Congress secretly approved the issue for the European market.[27]

Other Cabinet Secretaries and the War Department Bureau chiefs were apprised of it and promised pieces of the pie. In November 1862 Navy Secretary Mallory made plans to send an agent of his own to England with 1^{1}/_{2}$ million in the cotton bonds to pay for ships. The man selected was William G. Crenshaw (who had been serving as an artillery captain under Lee in Virginia). Before the war Crenshaw was a partner with his brothers Lewis and James in the family flour mills in Richmond, the firm which had made itself so useful to Northrop and the Subsistence Bureau.

William Crenshaw's mission presented Northrop with a golden opportunity. As the Ordnance agent Huse was absolutely uncooperative, Crenshaw's presence in England over a protracted period offered Northrop the chance of a knowledgeable man on the spot able and probably willing to serve the Subsistence Bureau also. The plan worked out with Secretary Seddon was described by Frank Ruffin as "an association of individual enterprise with government capital... Especially in a business as hazardous as blockade running would such an association be an advantage—as securing to the individuals the insurance of many ventures, and to the government the vigilance and intelligence of private parties."[28]

Crenshaw was to purchase or order in England a line of fast-running ships to bring goods through the blockade, and take cotton out again to pay the bills. Crenshaw's firm was to provide one fourth of the ships' costs, and the Confederate Government the rest. The shipping space in the vessels would be allocated one half to the War Department, a fourth to the Navy Department, and the remaining fourth to the Crenshaw firm. The Crenshaw goods were to come into the Confederacy duty-free, and all Crenshaw's purchases for the government and sales of government cotton were to earn him a $2^{1}/_{2}$ percent commission.

---

[27]   Schwab, 31ff.; Patricia L. Faust, "Erlanger Loan" in *Historical Times Illustrated Encyclopedia of the Civil War* (N.Y.: Harper & Row, 1986), 246; Richard C. Todd, *Confederate Finance* (Univ. of Georgia, 1954), 48-51, 182-83; Richard D. Goff, *Confederate Supply*, 119-21; Richard L. Lester, *Confederate Finance and Purchasing in Great Britain* (Univ. of Virginia, 1975), 23-24, 27ff. Douglas Ball's *Financial Failure and Confederate Defeat* (Univ. of Illinois, 1991) marshals facts and figures to criticize Memminger but shows no understanding of Subsistence problems and no knowledge of their solutions.

[28]   *The New York Herald*, July 21, 1865, 2.

Northrop's hopes were so high that he put in a huge Bureau estimate for 1863, based on "the possibility that the Bureau might be able to obtain, for issue to troops, all the articles prescribed by regulations as a part of ration".[29] They included a long list of things like coffee and soap, not regularly seen by the Confederate soldier since the first months of the war. Ordnance Chief Gorgas protested vigorously against this invasion of what had so far been his Bureau's monopoly; but Seddon held firm.

The Secretary of War wrote a letter to introduce William Crenshaw to James Mason, the Confederacy's diplomatic envoy in London. Crenshaw, he said, "has been one of the most intelligent, extensive, and successful merchants of our city; having besides other important enterprises almost inaugurated and established the coffee trade between Virginia and Brazil...". Crenshaw himself would explain the shipbuilding plans: these would require large advances: "I must rely on and invoke your authority and aid to facilitate to Mr. Crenshaw the command of adequate resources."[30]

Crenshaw arrived in London at the end of January 1863. By March he and Mason had signed an agreement with the shipping firm of Alexander Collie in Manchester. Collie had an irreproachable reputation, and had already been helpful to the Confederate Government in several ways. Through him, Crenshaw purchased one fine ship and commissioned the building of four others—all to be ready by late spring and early summer. To pay for them, Mason arranged for Crenshaw to have £55,000 from the Erlanger proceeds—apportioned among the Government Departments and Bureaus. The Subsistence Bureau made an extra contribution directly as Northrop was to report: "So anxious was this Bureau to aid that enterprise that it advanced $100,000 of its own funds in gold to the construction of steamers or purchase of provisions, as might be deemed best by Mr. Crenshaw, relying upon the cotton that should go forward to repay that expenditure and to make purchases of meat."[31]

All this time Huse had been in Paris working the Erlanger loan for his own funds. He returned to London in April 1863 to find the Crenshaw-Collie line building. Huse immediately sought to block Crenshaw's access to further funds. A full-scale quarrel blew up; in the course of it Crenshaw accused Huse of dealing with shippers of known corruption. Seddon asked the Confederacy's financial agent Colin McRae to investigate. McRae did find Isaac, Campbell & Co. guilty of sharp bookkeeping, though Huse was exonerated.

Seddon then separated the two agents. Huse would continue responsible for ordnance and medical shipments from Europe; Crenshaw would manage quartermaster and subsistence shipments. Thus emerged another of those sub-divisions of responsibility—especially financial responsibil-

29   OR ser. IV, vol. 2, 938.

30   December 18, 1862 (OR ser. IV, vol. 2, 244-45).

31   Ibid., November 20, 1863, 970. It is not clear whether this was the $100,000 Seddon told James Crenshaw he had to order Northrop to requisition in the Crenshaws' favor (OR ser. IV, vol. 2, 565). If so, it would have been only because Northrop was so short of cash for purchases at home. Northrop accompanied his remittance to Crenshaw with an order to purchase 5,000 tons of meat; that was later reduced to 1,500 tons in view of the hazards of transport. See below pp. 230, 234.

ity—so typical of the Confederacy. Writing to McRae in September 1863, Seddon laid this one squarely at the door of Huse.[32]

Whatever the rights or wrongs of private commissions as opposed to the monopoly urged by Gorgas and Huse, the net effect of the duplication may have been to raise Confederate capacity for blockade-running of vital supplies. Yet Huse's obstruction did cause delay and muddle. The first of Crenshaw's ships were not ready until late May 1863, and these brought over only a little meat. On June 4 Northrop wrote: "Importations from abroad were looked for by the 1st of May. A few mouthfuls have come."[33]

To try to expedite the meat shipments, much of it was consigned to larger vessels that were not blockade-runners, and landed at the Islands. There it waited and waited on the chance of smaller, faster vessels to run it through the blockade into a Southern port. But the smaller ships were always offered something easier to handle and more profitable. A lot of the Crenshaw meat from Europe was not to reach Confederate soldiers for nearly a year.[34]

---

[32] Ibid., 826.

[33] Ibid., 574.

[34] Ruffin in *The New York Herald*, July 21, 1865, 2.

CHAPTER 15

TROUBLEMAKERS

The winter of 1862-63 brought further troubles for Northrop and his Bureau in Richmond and elsewhere. First came Beauregard. Having recovered from his illness of the summer, he had been assigned in September 1862 to command the Department of South Carolina, Georgia, and East Florida. His headquarters were in Charleston—the place from which his Confederate service had started two years earlier—before Manassas, before Shiloh.

The Chief Commissary in Charleston was Henry Guerin—"of excellent character & ability," Northrop wrote, "known to me from boyhood."[1] Beauregard knew that Guerin was also Northrop's nephew-in-law. So perhaps, in the hurt pride of the Creole Napoleon having to return to the place of his Confederate beginnings, and considering the role in that circular promotion which he might attribute to the Commissary General if he liked, some attempt to abase Northrop's friend and relation was inevitable. Also at Charleston was Beauregard's toadying Assistant Adjutant General Thomas Jordan, only too eager to play upon the console of his general's *amour propre*.

Beauregard was reinforcing the forts in Charleston harbor against the real threat of Federal siege. He demanded a three-month's supply of cured meat to be laid into the harbor forts from Subsistence stores in Atlanta. He knew perfectly well that Northrop was straining every effort to keep that meat for Lee. So he began his campaign with a new letter to his friend Congressman Miles. On October 22, 1862 Miles had telegraphed back: "I am trying to get the three months' subsistence you have asked for. Commissary Northrop is unwilling to consent to so much, on ground that he has not enough at other points. Secretary [of War] is willing to give for a month or six weeks."[2]

---

[1] July 31, 1885 to Davis (Museum of the Confederacy: Davis Collection). Guerin (*b.* 1827) had married a daughter of Northrop's late sister Mary and her husband Dr. John Bellinger. When Dr. Bellinger died in 1860, Northrop and Guerin were both his executors. Guerin's young wife had died a few months after her father. When Northrop left Charleston for Montgomery and Richmond in 1861, he put his affairs in Guerin's hands (CDA 26 T 7, 35 B 1). It is not clear whether Northrop influenced Guerin's appointment as captain and associate commissary and quartermaster: if so it would have been a solitary case of nepotism in Northrop's career, so far as I know. See NA, RG 109, Officers: Guerin, H. C.

[2] Roman, II, 451.

When Beauregard again demanded meat from the Atlanta store, Northrop refused point blank. He did not believe that Beauregard's fortifications in Charleston harbor could withstand a Federal attack, and as a native of Charleston, Northrop could claim some knowledge on that point. Secretary Randolph told Northrop to do what he could for the Charleston forces. So Northrop directed Guerin to ask Beauregard how long he wanted the forts supplied, "and furnish *rice* and *corn* as an equivalent to the meat, which should not be risked...".[3] There was fair reason in this: withstanding a siege, however it might tax soldiers' energies from time to time, did not call for the continuous expenditure of energy needed for such marching and field manoeuvres as Lee was facing in Virginia.

When Guerin tried to carry out Northrop's instruction, Beauregard and Jordan accused him of disobedience. Apparently they abused him savagely and continually. Then Guerin reported to Northrop that one of Beauregard's regimental commissaries, Captain John S. Ryan, was corrupt. Guerin charged Ryan with embezzlement. Beauregard ignored the charge and merely transferred Ryan to duty at Sullivan's Island. There Ryan was charged again, and that gave Northrop his chance:

> I reported to the Sec of War that by law a Regimental Comsy separated from his Regt was out of commission. This was acted on, & Bgd telegraphed that he thus lost the service of one of his "most valued officers". I have the paper. This man feasted: Jordan & he told Guerin menacingly that he "had the ear of the Genl."
>
> Bgd. arrested Guerin & ordered him not to communicate directly with me. Guerin applied for charges, though his arrest did not suspend his duties; no charges were preferred, & Sec ordered his release.
>
> Bgd. dodged, & did not release him. At length I found it out & informed Guerin of his release.[4]

It brought up again the old issue of who actually controlled commissaries at posts—and who therefore could arrest and judge them. The Guerin case was watched closely by the War Department. Robert Kean wrote in his diary: "The fact is the General is wrong. He insists that all the officers of the staff departments in his military department shall correspond with their chiefs of Bureau through his headquarters. This pretension is not supported by the Army regulations, or by common sense."[5] Northrop joined Kean in attributing most of the trouble to Jordan.[6]

Instead of sending further charges against Guerin as promised, Beauregard wrote again to his friends in Congress. On February 9, 1863 he

---

³   September 21, 1865 to Rev. J. J. Early, S.J. (Georgetown archives).

⁴   July 31, 1885 to Davis (Museum of the Confederacy: Davis Collection). Northrop's summary, based on the old papers, is accurate with the exception that Beauregard did after much delay charge Guerin—and then altered the charges. See Seddon's summary in *OR* ser. I, vol. 14, 976-77.

⁵   *Inside the Confederate Government*, 39.

⁶   December 6, 1884 to Davis (Rowland, IX, 312). In July 1863 Northrop got his own back by exposing an irregularity in Jordan's promotion to Brigadier General (July 31, 1885 to Davis). Jordan would take his revenge at the end of the War by publishing a libellous article while Northrop and Davis were in Federal prisons and unable to defend themselves, as he thought. (See below, p. 290).

addressed his brother-in-law Charles Villeré, Congressman from Louisiana, abusing Congress for having "the sponge passed blandly over the absurdities and gross neglects of that poorest of all apologies for a chief commissary".[7] He meant Northrop, and the congressional confirmation of him in the wake of First Manassas.

Northrop had heard it all before. And so, while such a general made his accusations and the anti-Davis press thundered demands for new congressional investigations, the Commissary General went about his work. In the cold of winter, he found a way to extract a little grim fun from the situation. Mrs. Chesnut recalled:

> One day I saw Mr. Northrop at the President's. He is an eccentric creature. He said newspapers were not without some good uses. He wore several folded across his chest, under his shirt, in lieu of flannel. He said they kept out the cold effectually.
>
> Think of him with those peppery articles in the *Examiner* next his heart. There is abuse of Northrop in some of those papers that would warm up the spirit of the angel Gabriel—if he be the angel of peace.[8]

In the face of flagrant allegations against the commissariat in the press and complaints from generals, the Confederate Congress had for months felt pressure to investigate. (The previous investigation, conducted in the winter of 1861-62 and ending in approval of Northrop, had been done by the old Provisional Congress in its last days.) One later motion to investigate Subsistence had been set in train as long ago as August 18, 1862 by Congressman Lucius J. Gartrell of Georgia. He had demanded "some effective law requiring and compelling the Commissary Department to furnish more and better food for the Army".[9]

The scent of political blood twitched the nostrils of another Congressman, Henry S. Foote. Now nearing sixty, Foote looked back on a long career. He had been a United States Senator from Mississippi in the early 1850s, when Jefferson Davis first held the other seat from that state. Even then they were bitter enemies, as Davis recalled: "... After I had published [Foote], in 1851, as 'constitutionally a liar' (I having twice before that tried to bring him to a settlement with deadly weapons), his sayings and doings were never considered by me entitled to notice."[10] But Foote insisted upon notice. From his entry into the Confederate House (representing Tennessee) in February 1862, he had constituted himself before everything else the foe of Davis and all his works.

Foote was a burly little man with a bristling beard and a vicious temper which led him to fisticuffs on the floor of Congress. He was recalled by Sallie Brock of Richmond as

---

[7] *OR* ser. IV, vol. 2, 391.
[8] *Mary Chesnut's Civil War*, 438.
[9] August 18, 1862 (*Journal of Congress*, V, 296).
[10] April 25, 1879 to Northrop (Rowland, VIII, 384). See *Davis Papers*, II, 86.

... attacking at will any and every one connected with the Government, from the President to the lowest official, warring upon every department alike, with a hardihood and effrontery as admirable as astonishing. Battling with the Commissary General, the Secretary of the Navy, the Army and the Treasury, hurling his thunderbolts, red hot with righteous indignation against men who abused and lived upon government emoluments, bullying the members of Congress, provoking quarrels with whomsoever he chose, disturbing the peace of that body by his noisy invectives—he was unsparing in the manner as in the matter of his language, and he often threw in the teeth of his Congressional contemporaries the most violent and bitter denunciations. Possessed of no apparent amiability himself, he seemed altogether oblivious of such a quality in the breast of any other human being.[11]

A few days after Gartrell's motion, Foote proposed the establishment of a new permanent special committee to sit on commissary and quartermaster abuses. The committee was duly constituted, with Foote a vocal member—and Gartrell's motion handed to it. No visible result emerged. Given the supply and transport and cash conditions prevailing, it is not easy to see what could practically be done "to furnish more and better food".

In September 1862 bills had come from both Houses of Congress to promote to the rank of Brigadier General the Commissary General, the Quartermaster General, the Chiefs of the Engineering and Ordnance Bureaus—or some of them. House and Senate chewed it over for three weeks, and ended by rejecting all the promotions. Foote had taken a leading part in House opposition to Northrop's promotion—though he favored Quartermaster General Myers, a particular friend of his.

There was indeed corruption—probably a good deal of it—attributable to far-flung agents of the War Department Bureaus. With increasing scarcity of almost every useful thing, and real prices outstripping government salaries everywhere, it was more and more difficult for the handlers of government property to resist following their neighbors into peculation. The Georgia Legislature passed a particularly fierce resolution in December 1862 calling on the Secretary of War to investigate widely reported complaints of viciousness among Supply Bureau officers and agents moving horizontally through the populace.[12] Seddon sent it round to the Bureau chiefs. Northrop endorsed a single sentence: "Under existing circumstances and laws, the Commissary General of Subsistence has found it almost impracticable to obtain the removal of an officer when the facts obviously indicate it." He cited the case of Beauregard's Captain Ryan, not yet disposed of.[13]

---

[11]   *Richmond During the War*, 171-72.

[12]   *OR* ser. IV, vol. 2, 396-97.

[13]   Ibid., February 14 and 19, 1863, 398. The *OR* transcript also cites "the case of J. B. Magruder". This may have been a rare misreading by the *OR* editors. The general's brother was Allan B. Magruder, who had served as Whiting's commissary in North Carolina. A. B. Magruder complained that long-standing disputes with Northrop led to his resignation at the end of 1863 (NA, RG 109, Officers: Magruder, A. B.). Another case in which Northrop found it hard to remove an inefficient officer was that of the elderly, frail, and captious Major Theodore Lewis (M-437, r 149, ff 252-55).

MEETING CHAMBER OF THE CONFEDERATE HOUSE OF REPRESENTATIVES,
CAPITOL BUILDING, RICHMOND, VA.

VALENTINE MUSEUM, RICHMOND, VA.

HENRY STUART FOOTE
(1804-1880)
REPRESENTATIVE FOR
TENNESSEE
FEBRUARY 1862 TO
FEBRUARY 1865.

Congress then passed a law requiring the posting of a $50,000 to $100,000 personal bond by every commissary and quartermaster. Just those; not the disbursing officers of other bureaus. Commissaries and quartermasters were the most numerous of supply officers, and the ones who dealt most directly with the public. When anything did go wrong for any reason, they were almost always the ones there to be accused. Northrop protested against "invidious distinction".[14] In the face of all his efforts to keep a clean house, public perceptions of Subsistence men were more and more hostile.

In January 1863 Congressman Foote thought he had found a tender morsel. The Subsistence Bureau had entered into a new flour contract with Haxall, Crenshaw for half a million barrels to provide a foundation reserve for the Army of Northern Virginia. As the Haxall, Crenshaw mills were in Richmond, their flour offered the very minimum of transport troubles. Local gossip noted, however, that James Crenshaw functioned as the Commissary General's adviser on flour (the scope of William Crenshaw mission to England was still a secret); and was Northrop's assistant Frank Ruffin not a friend of the Crenshaw family? Then another flour producer for the government, Dunlop & Moncure, aggrieved at Haxall, Crenshaw's preferred place, renewed their complaint of favoritism.

So on January 13, 1863, the day after the House reconvened, Foote moved that the Haxall, Crenshaw contracts with the Subsistence Bureau "are of a nature to demand the promptest and most rigid scrutiny, with a view to the detection and punishment of fraudulent conduct on the part of certain official founctionaries and other individuals if such practices have actually occurred...".[15] Asked to name names, he named Ruffin.

Foote's motion drew instant response from Haxall, Crenshaw: they sent a letter (in those days known as a "card") to the press inviting the fullest investigation. Next day Ruffin inserted a longer "card", stating that he himself had no interest in Haxall, Crenshaw, and that at the time of the contract he had been laid up for more than three months with severe illness keeping him away from his office. He charged that Foote "has advertised himself as a conduit for calumny by inviting all, which of course includes malignants and malcontents, to make free use of his tongue as the medium of accusation". Ruffin challenged Foote to produce a single witness or shred of actual evidence.[16]

On the morning Ruffin's letter was published, the House was treated to an exhibition of Foote on highest horse. The press adored it:

> At the opening of the House Mr. Foote, of Tennessee, rose to a question of privilege. He said that his conduct in introducing a resolution of inquiry ... had called down upon him this morning in the columns of the Richmond *Enquirer* a denunciatory card, marked with the coarsest scurrility, breathing a spirit of defiance and menace, and containing several very gross misstatements of fact...

---

[14]   March 12, 1863 (M-437, r 105, ff 661-62).

[15]   January 13, 1863 (*Journal of Congress*, VI, 9).

[16]   Ruffin's letter of February 24, 1863, published that day in the *Enquirer*, sets forth his extensive summary of those events. Foote's answer in the next day's issue virtually admits that he had no evidence.

Mr. Foote said ... that the main particulars of the said flour contract had been supplied to him by persons of undoubted standing here, and been presented in the columns of newspapers published in the city of Richmond, and the character of the information given him left little doubt upon his mind ...

In other words, he had no real evidence at all. He portentously declined to identify any of his sources.[17]

A month later the committee reported that Ruffin had never been party to the Haxall, Crenshaw contract, and was not interested in it.[18] Foote then said he had "known nothing of it personally", but that the contract itself remained to be investigated. The committee proceeded to a scrutiny which appears to have exhausted all parties. They did not report back until April 21, 1863.

The committee then confirmed that Haxall, Crenshaw had afforded the very best terms that could be secured, enabling "the Government to obtain supplies of flour at a cheaper rate than could otherwise have been obtained". Moreover they reported that the rival flour producers, once they truly understood the contract (which had been kept largely secret from the public), "with one accord have pronounced the contract reasonable and just". Then the committee chairman, William P. Chilton of Alabama, issued what amounted to a rebuke to the politicking press and Congressman Foote: "It is greatly to be regretted that much injury has accrued to the Government already from these misapprehensions, and if this investigation shall satisfy the public (as it must when the proof is read) that the contractors are making sacrifices for the public good, in the matter of said contract ... the committee will be fully compensated for the arduous duties devolved upon them."[19]

Meanwhile a Congressman from Louisiana, Charles M. Conrad, had received complaints about the actions of Broadwell on and about the Mississippi. Envy of Broadwell's powers—apparently used independently, yet with Subsistence Bureau backing—had raised many enemies. There were government functionaries like the Treasury agent Hatch, jealous of his own prerogatives. There were owners of and speculators in the sugar Broadwell had seized.[20] There were owners and captains of boats Broadwell had impressed—some who got higher rates for transporting speculators' goods, others who loyally shipped government food and then found no money at Vicksburg to pay them while their expenses piled up. There were innocent victims of the

---

[17]   *Southern Historical Society Papers* (hereinafter cited as *SHSP*), vol. 47, 130-32. See also a long letter of January 8, 1863 from Haxall, Crenshaw to Northrop, making clear the sacrifices the firm were making to fulfil their contract, and Northrop's confirming endorsement (M-437, r 96, ff 498-503).

[18]   February 18, 1863 (*Journal of Congress*, VI, 114).

[19]   *SHSP*, vol. 47, 189-91.

[20]   One correspondence involving the Secretary of War in November 1862 pointed several accusatory fingers: yet as soon as the chief accuser, Wiley P. Harris, met Broadwell and Dameron and heard the truth from them, he voluntarily withdrew all of his own and his correspondents' charges. (NA, RG 109, Officers: Broadwell, November 9-24, 1862)

counterfeiting cattle dealers—victims whom Dameron especially had tried to help, and then had written ruefully to Northrop of finding "that the more one does to give assistance in such matters, the greater the abuse which is sure to follow".[21] There were the seemingly honest merchants whose prices Broadwell regularly beat down, and the speculators whose lives he made miserable.

On top of all, there was widespread outrage—some genuine, some disingenuous—at the indications emerging of Broadwell's trade with the enemy. As early as October 20, 1862 Broadwell himself had become aware of trouble brewing when he wrote to Northrop: "Genl Ruggles I learn is likely to be blamed in Richmond for the trade conducted by me—I think the responsibility more properly rests upon my shoulders. I am neither ashamed or afraid of any action in regard to this or any other business."[22]

In January 1863 Congressman Conrad introduced a motion calling on the President to give full information about the activities of "one Broadwell" in his state. Had Broadwell purchased goods through New Orleans? By what authority? Had the purchases come through enemy lines? Had Broadwell impressed steamboats and trains to transport his purchases? Was he an agent of the Subsistence Bureau? Or the Treasury? The Congressman demanded copies of correspondence between Broadwell and the Commissary General, copies of any other complaints made of him—and, in short, all the Broadwell papers held by anyone and everyone. The House resolved to ask for it all.[23]

Broadwell wrote directly to Congressman Conrad. He offered full cooperation and disclosure, adding that news of the investigation in Richmond had seriously hampered his own usefulness on the Mississippi, since a merchant's best capital was his own good name. He asked Conrad to investigate fully and then clear his name and Dameron's. He had to write a second time before Conrad returned a long, windy, self-serving, and deeply unpleasant reply in which he said that he could not be bothered with small fry like Broadwell and Dameron unless they were guilty; his real quarry was the Commissary General.[24]

Northrop had already sent to Congress (through the Secretary of War) a full statement of Broadwell's actions, with documents showing the authority for them.[25] Congress took no action either way. When their session came to an end in May 1863, they merely laid the matter on the table. It was the stupidest, most irresponsible thing they could have done, because it neither preferred charges nor settled rumors. Thus Congress virtually hamstrung the best agent Northrop ever had in the West.

In the summer of 1863 Broadwell was snapped up by Lieutenant General Edmund Kirby Smith, in charge of the entire Confederate Trans-Missis-

---

[21] Ibid., Dameron, W. H., November 28, 1862.
[22] Ibid., Broadwell.
[23] January 29, 1863 (*SHSP* vol. 48, 6-7).
[24] March 27, 1863 (NA, RG 109, Officers, Broadwell).
[25] Ibid., March 7, 1863.

sippi region after Federal control of the river cut the Confederacy in two. No longer able to communicate fully with Richmond, Kirby Smith had to initiate and shape many original policies for his far-flung command. One was the creation of a Cotton Bureau to manage and trade supplies of that vital article to get food and armaments for his soldiers. Broadwell made such a job of this that Kirby Smith, when he issued an order relieving Broadwell at the end of the war, added:

> The Commanding General cannot allow this meritorious officer to retire from his arduous and responsible position without an expression of his deep sense of obligation for the services he has rendered.
>
> Colonel Broadwell entered upon the duties of his office when the Trans-Mississippi Department was without credit abroad or supplies at home. By his integrity and ability he restored the one; by his energy and devotion he introduced the other.
>
> He is entitled to the thanks of his countrymen.[26]

So a kind of belated justice was done.

---

[26] Ibid., May 19, 1865, General Orders No. 50. Broadwell died in the burning of a steamboat on Caddo Lake, Louisiana in February 1869. (Columbia, *Missouri Statesman*, April 16, 1869).

CHAPTER 16

VIRGINIA WINTER
OF DISCONTENT

The sharpest problem facing the Confederate commissariat in the winter of 1862-63 continued to be the provisioning of Lee in Virginia. Lee remained throughout the winter to the north of Richmond, and that was where he needed to be. After the failure of the Federal campaign on the Peninsula below Richmond, McClellan had been replaced by Ambrose Burnside. Burnside's idea was apparently to batter his way south over land to take the Confederate capital. No one knew which route he would choose. Lee hovered about northern Virginia, trying to rest his troops—yet also keeping everything in instant readiness to move anywhere against Burnside.

The lands surrounding Lee appeared drained of food. The territory had been fought over and eaten over by both sides' armies for eighteen months. As the weather grew colder, both Federal and Confederate troops began stealing more and more farm fence rails for firewood. Without fences, every animal could run through any remaining crops—eating them, trampling and rooting in them. In Lee's camps ice formed every night. Little vegetable food could be dug, and roads were largely impassable. Supplies in the camps ran low, and there seemed nothing within reach. Once the food for today and tomorrow was gone, they appeared to be approaching starvation.

Yet all the while there was a general feeling—almost an understanding—that Lee's army was surrounded by food. Where was it? It was hidden by farmers and householders from their own army, because of the state of Confederate money. At the beginning of the war there had been perhaps one million dollars of Confederate notes in circulation, reasonably backed up by gold and silver. By March 1862, with no more reserves, so much money had been printed to pay the government's war bills that circulating notes had reached $100 million in paper value. By December 1862 it was $450 million.[1] The Treasury had to take on extra staff merely to sign the new notes

---

[1] J. C. Schwab, *The Confederate States of America: a Financial and Industrial History* (Yale, 1913), 165.

being printed, and it was reported that they could not keep up with the presses. Government bonds multiplied in the same way. On January 10, 1863 the Secretary of the Treasury would report to Congress that the issue of interest-bearing Confederate bonds had increased five-fold in five months; and more bonds were urgently needed just to raise money for the next round of war appropriations.[2]

The effect on values was inevitable. By August 1862 it had needed $1.50 in Confederate money to buy $1 in gold. A month later it needed $2—by the turn of the year $3, and rising.[3] With such runaway inflation, farmers were not bringing their food to markets, even assuming the impressments of army quartermasters had left them with any draught animals and wagons for the journey. Instead, the farmer was being forced into speculation, squirrelling away every ounce of preservable food against the twin specters of inflation and famine. If the farmer sold his food, the Confederate money he received would not hold its value a month—perhaps hardly a week.

Still there was trade of a kind. In many places near enemy lines, people began to show a distinct preference for Federal "greenback" notes over Confederate money. United States authorities were not slow to note that preference, and made sure the supply of greenbacks was profuse all along Confederate borders—ready to exchange secretly for cotton, tobacco, even food.

The complicated Virginia coastline east of Lee's camps was infested with Federal soldiers, or sympathizers, or people mainly interested in feeding themselves—or making money. At King and Queen Courthouse, between the York and Rappahannock Rivers (and less than fifty miles from Richmond) a Confederate conscription officer reported to the Secretary of War that food was actually being *exported* from the Confederacy: "The most illegal traffic is daily going on between this class of citizens and the enemy. Flour, pork, meal, and indeed almost every article, are being carried across the bay to the Eastern Shore, and across the Rappahannock to the Northern Neck of Virginia, and exchanged for Yankee goods which they now run through the lines to Richmond. This class of men are mostly conscripts and outrageous extortioners." Ought he to arrest the lot of them and confiscate their goods?[4] Secretary Seddon had to answer that while such trade was "demoralizing and illegal", the Confederate Government could not now afford to send any military force whatever into that region, so trade with the enemy was therefore probably inevitable among the citizens.[5]

In fact the entire Virginia Tidewater was honeycombed with private trade and blockade running—forward to Federal troops across the water in Maryland, and backward up the Virginia Peninsula rivers into Confederate Richmond. The runners drove a thriving trade.[6] Sometimes they brought in

---

[2] *OR* ser. IV, vol. 2, 309-34.
[3] Schwab, *Confederate States*, 167.
[4] January 7, 1863 (*OR* ser. IV, vol. 2, 302).
[5] Ibid., January 10, 1863, 334.
[6] A vivid description of this blockade-running can be found in [Brock], *Richmond During the War*, 203-7.

food, and some of that may even have ended up in Subsistence Bureau storehouses. But most of the smuggled imports were luxuries. And the net effect of all that trade—blockade running and hoarding and speculating—was to withdraw food from Confederate markets.

The results came last of all to Richmond. Shortages there had been noticed at the end of the previous winter (1861-62) and early spring, before the new crops came in. But it was when winter came again that shortages really began to bite. By January 1863 the War Department clerk Jones was wondering how to pay the rent of his house on his government salary, or buy food: "... None but the opulent, often those who have defrauded the Government, can obtain a sufficiency of food and raiment. ... Common tallow candles are $1.25 per pound; soap $1.00; hams $1.00; opossum $3.00; turkeys $4 to $11.00; sugar, brown, $1.00; molasses $8.00 per gallon; potatoes $6.00 per bushel, etc. These evils might be remedied by the Government, for there is no great scarcity of any of the substantials and necessities of life in the country, if they were only equally distributed." On January 30 Jones copied into his diary a Richmond newspaper's comparison of food prices showing a ten-fold increase in three years.[7]

Jones's impression of plenteous food in the country had been verified several weeks earlier by Northrop's cattle agent Burr Noland, trying to buy provisions for Lee's army in Virginia counties north and west. The food was there, but it was no longer really for sale: "... The Cattle were generally bought up by my agents during the summer, but there are several large lots there now held by speculators who refuse to sell them. The Hogs also in these Counties are in the hands of speculators and extortioners who hold them at such prices that I cannot buy them—& I would say here that unless the power to impress stock thus held for speculation is given to the officers of your Department the supplies for the Army [of Northern Virginia] will soon be exhausted."[8]

The traditional military answer to hoarding and speculation was impressment. If a commander saw real need, the rules of war allowed him or his officers to take possession of privately owned goods and dictate payment. Certain rules applied, at least in theory: friendly troops should not strip a farm or homestead of food for the family or for remaining animals; sufficient animals should be left to work the farm and also to breed another season. Congress had tinkered with the guidelines of impressment, but had so far lacked the grit to define sharply one of the most ancient military powers.

Slowly at first, and then with increasing momentum as harvests disappointed and prices rose and transport faltered, the generals and their brigade and regimental commissaries and quartermasters had impressed from every direction within reach. Suspicion rose that some field commissaries and quartermasters were getting as rich as the hardest-nosed speculators—feasting off the hunger of the army they were supposed to supply, and off

---

[7] *Diary*, I, 237, 240-41, 250.
[8] November 23, 1862 to Northrop (NYPL: Northrop Papers).

the people that army was supposed to protect. There were more and more reports of field-commissary and quartermaster impersonation by thieves, some of them wearing uniforms plundered from battlefield corpses. Protests from the citizenry rose to a sustained howl. Northrop took note of that howl.

Inevitably much of the accusation was directed at agents of the War Department Bureaus. Yet Bureau agents were in fact largely innocent of impressment, for the simplest reason. The Bureaus had never had the power of impressment conferred on them. Northrop had pressed and pressed for it from the beginning of the war, but Congress would not do it. So impressment remained virtually the perquisite of arms. Subsistence Bureau men could impress only on specific order by the Secretary of War. The Secretaries were all chary of giving such orders.

When his battle to trade through enemy lines was lost by the beginning of 1863, Northrop felt more and more strongly that he had to acquire the power of impressment. The potential rewards were enormous:

1. Hoards secreted in the country could feed Confederate armies in many places, especially in northern Virginia. Northrop's experts (often natives of the territories they worked) had much more extensive knowledge of local people and their secrets than most regimental commissaries.

2. Feeding troops from supplies close to positions minimized reliance on railroads.

3. The Subsistence Bureau would be enabled to do its job of feeding the army—and to be seen to do it—as never before.

4. Impressment by Bureau agents offered at least a chance of cleaning out an Augean stable, since impressments by the military almost always brought inequity, wastage, often spoilage from want of care, sometimes corruption. Having selected his own chief commissaries for honesty above all, Northrop had the right to hope that they could impose that character on their underlings. Honesty and straightforwardness should aid in making the draft of private goods everywhere impartial, systematic, and above all comprehensive.

5. Such a system, if comprehensive and perceived to be fairly run, would force the foul spirit of speculation out into full daylight exposure for all to see and condemn.

6. The exposure of speculation offered one of the very few practical means of applying a brake to ruinous inflation.

7. If good impressment worked, the Subsistence Bureau should afterwards have an easier time purchasing further supplies to rebuild its drained resources against an uncertain future.

So Northrop pursued the chance of Subsistence Bureau impressment with all his vigor. First he attacked his chief, the Secretary of War: Northrop asked Seddon to invoke a threat of universal impressment—"*in terrorum*" (as Frank Ruffin described it) "by publishing a general order that impressments *would be* made—which [it was] thought would cause holders to sell."[9]

9   In conversation with Robert Kean, March 27, 1863 (*Inside the Confederate Government*, 46).

If such an order raised still greater protests from the public, that might be no bad thing. For if only the outcry was loud enough, it would force the Congress to bring in a comprehensive impressment law; and any such legislation could now probably be made to include the War Department Bureaus. Seddon was intrigued and was inclined to try some half-measures. But he was dubious of his powers after only a few weeks in office.

Northrop then went down the only path left open. That was to encourage every Confederate commander to impress and impress and impress—to an extent that would force Congress to act. The Commissary General pursued that policy doggedly from late 1862 (as soon as he realized that the cause of trading through enemy lines was lost). If he was leading from weakness, it was because he had no choice. But he had a clear goal in view. He could not well write directly about that goal: so it can be reconstructed now only from hints dropped here and there.

The fullest demonstration of Northrop's purpose came in a series of disagreements with Lee extending right through the winter of 1862-63. Lee's side of the matter has been fully presented and long understood. Of all the Confederate generals, he was virtually the only one who refused to impress under almost any circumstances. Lee's kindliness (portrayed so well in the great biography by Freeman) revolted against the impressment of anything. He considered it fundamentally unfair and counterproductive. The people loved him for it, but it did not feed his army. Northrop's side of the dispute, by contrast, has never been looked at. Because the springs of his action have not been understood, he was condemned (even by Freeman) as either a callous monster or an ineffectual enigma. An understanding of Northrop's side in this matter is vital to comprehend what happened afterwards.

* * *

Lee now wanted Northrop to bring food for his army out of Subsistence Bureau reserves. What an irony it was. Distribution from the center had been Northrop's plan at the beginning of the war, and many of the generals had fought against it because there was plenty on the ground under their noses. Later, when shrinkage of food-producing lands and bad harvests and fighting and waste had reduced supplies, the Virginia general wanted Northrop's plan; and the breakdown of railroads forced Northrop to plead for collecting food on the ground.

Sending Lee's food from Subsistence Bureau stores in Richmond and Atlanta meant digging further into vanishing reserves. It meant using up food that might not be replaceable at any price unless inflation could be slowed. And it meant relying on railroads. Lee's was the closest of all the Confederate armies to Richmond, and a map of the territory between Richmond and Lee showed a coverage of railroad lines as good as anywhere in the Confederacy. But when one went out to look at the trains themselves and the tracks they ran on, a different picture emerged. The rail lines north of Richmond had sustained the heaviest use of any in the South since the war began. Rolling stock and rails were dangerously worn and bearing staggering loads. Wooden bridges carrying the lines over rivers and valleys were routinely burnt by one army and scrappily repaired by their enemy. When the Confederates made the repair, it was always out of worsening and vanishing materials.

As usual, Northrop had been hammering away at railroad inadequacy all the autumn. By November 1862 he was near despair, as he forwarded to the Secretary of War the latest sheaf of complaints. They concerned the key Virginia Central, over which all supplies for Lee from Richmond and the South must go. The harvest had been bad enough, Northrop wrote:

> Unless, therefore, something is done to afford transportation for all the wheat that can be procured, I do not see anything but failure and ruin to our Army. As much grain as is needed cannot be procured, it is feared, even if this transportation is afforded, and without that transportation is obtained in some way we must break down.
>
> I feel it my duty to urge this matter upon your attention. It cannot be considered too deeply, nor the remedy applied with too much promptness. The chances of procuring sufficient supplies are becoming every hour more and more doubtful, and the area of country drawn from smaller and smaller. I am powerless to remedy the evil, and can only lay before you the state of the case for your action.[10]

Northrop and others had already persuaded Davis—over the protests of Quartermaster General Myers—to create a new Bureau of Railroads with its own chief. Frank Ruffin recalled: "In September 1862, when it was determined to erect the railroad administration into a bureau, [Northrop] took to Mr. Davis, at his request, a gentleman he thought suitable to the task of mastering the question; and if he can be said to have intruded into anything, it is into that business."[11] The new railroad czar was not appointed until December 1862. He was William Wadley, an excellent and resourceful man, and he was given the army rank of lieutenant colonel. Even he could not bring the railroad companies to heel. When he called them to immediate conference and proposed government control, their answer was to reject the control and raise their rates again.

The bad condition of Southern railroads was not entirely due to corporate greed. On the last day of 1862, Wadley closed his report to Adjutant General Cooper with a plea over the worsening condition of all the lines' rolling stock and the dearth of experts to make repairs owing to conscription. Wadley begged the government to detail qualified men from army ranks or exempt them from conscription, and to furnish materials otherwise unobtainable to make repairs: "These difficulties must be remedied or the

---

[10] *OR* ser. IV, vol. 2, 158. The War Department clerk Jones reported in his diary for December 8 seeing a counter charge from the president of the Virginia Central—that the big flour contractor Haxall, Crenshaw were not unloading shipments of grain coming in to them quickly enough: they "are blocking up the [Virginia Central] depots, and fail to remove the grain. They keep whole trains waiting for days to be unloaded; and thus thousands of bushels, intended for other mills and the people, are delayed..." (*Diary*, I, 207). I have seen no other reference to this charge, but in view of strained capacities everywhere it seems likely enough. There had been an earlier complaint from Northrop to Seddon, dated November 7, 1862, that soldiers detailed from Richmond regiments to help in the Haxall, Crenshaw mills had not arrived. (M-474, r 25, ff 624-25).

[11] *The New York Herald*, July 21, 1865, 2.

roads will very soon be quite unable to meet the requirements of Government, and the election must now be made between letting them go down or rendering them the necessary assistance for successful operation."[12]

On the face of it, the choice seemed clear enough. But the South's few iron foundries and rolling mills were already pushed to their limits making armaments—without which the war would stop dead. As for exempting skilled mechanics, Lee himself set his face against that. His own manpower was too short. Also it would set a bad example, and thus redouble the difficulties of conscription everywhere.

As winter set in, Burnside advanced on Fredericksburg. There, on December 13, 1862, Lee stopped him. With inferior numbers ill equipped, Lee so out-generalled the magnificently caparisoned Burnside as to shut him up for the winter. The North was astounded. *The New York Herald* expostulated: "The finest and best appointed army the world ever saw, has been beaten by a batch of Southern ragamuffins!"[13] To ensure that Burnside remained shut up, however, Lee had to remain about Fredericksburg for the winter. He held his position in constant uneasiness.

The military situation around Fredericksburg had been so uncertain that Northrop felt forced to delay orders to Atlanta for Lee's meat until "it seemed settled that no farther advance of the enemy was to be expected".[14] When the meat was ordered from Atlanta, it did not come. Northrop telegraphed to Wadley and harassed Seddon. He sent agents to hunt up the train; it was found marooned on the wrong side of a burnt-out bridge in Georgia. When he tried to get another train from south of Richmond, he was met with reports of the old evil associated with Beauregard—"keeping cars unemployed to meet expected removal of troops". Lee himself did that repeatedly during the winter, because of uncertainty over Burnside. Northrop asked Lee's chief commissary, Robert G. Cole, to use his influence to get Lee to stop detaining cars, apparently without result.[15]

When a train of food did get through from Atlanta or points south, it was usually late and often significantly short of the quantities called for in the bill of lading. That happened despite Northrop's practice for some months past (at Wadley's request) of sending a "special messenger" with each train "in the hope that it would tend to obviate much of the delay consequent in transportation". It did not work. So Northrop asked Secretary Seddon to require each quartermaster along the route to check the bill of lading against the actual shipment and note any deficiency. He also backed up Wadley's request to have every shipping commissary notify each railroad involved of

---

[12] *OR* ser. IV, vol. 2, 272.

[13] Quoted in Jones, *Diary*, I, 320.

[14] Endorsement of February 16 on Lee to Seddon, February 11, 1863 (*OR* ser. I, vol. 25, pt. 2, 612-13). Northrop then said that he had placed the order for Lee's meat in Atlanta "on the 15th or 16th ultimo". The "ultimo", indicating January, was a slip of the pen. The order had in fact been placed on December 15 or 16, a day or two after the battle of Fredericksburg: Northrop later reported active pursuit of the missing meat from January 1, 1863 (*OR* ser. IV, vol. 2, 457).

[15] Northrop's endorsement of January 28 on Lee to Seddon, January 26, 1863 (*OR* ser. I, vol. 51, pt. 2, 675).

any shipment starting. Northrop himself doubted this would help: "The plan seems to be only a half measure, but Colonel Wadley requests me to do so, and I shall omit upon no occasion to do and to order to be done anything that I can to assist him in the discharge of his duties."[16]

Lee's letters through the winter of 1862-63 show that he did not really comprehend the railroad difficulties facing Northrop. On January 8 Lee answered Northrop's plea to use the surrounding country merely by observing that local resources were nearly exhausted, "... so that we are compelled to draw much more from our resources of subsistence in Richmond at the present time...".[17] On January 23 Lee wrote to Davis: "I do not know whether the difficulty arises from the want of provisions at Richmond or from delay in its transportation to this point... If the provisions are in Richmond, I think, by an energetic operation of the railroad, they can be readily transported. Great delay in the running of the freight trains ... could be avoided by zeal and energy on the part of the agents."[18] Such ignorance of the real state of affairs could have caused Wadley to weep. On January 26 Wadley appealed to Seddon for legislation to nationalize the railroads.[19] Neither Seddon nor the Congress would do it.

Lee sent R. G. Cole to Richmond to demand more food shipments. Then he learned some home truths, but apparently not all of them. Lee wrote to Secretary Seddon on February 11: "From the reports brought by Lieutenant Cole, chief commissary, I understand that the principal reliance for meat is based upon the present supplies at Atlanta and in Tennessee, and that the chief difficulty will be in its regular transportation by rail to Richmond. Will you allow me to suggest that energetic agents of the Quartermaster's Department be at once detailed, if it has not already been done, to attend to the transportation of this meat from Atlanta to Richmond?"[20] Either Lee had forgotten about Wadley and his Railroad Bureau altogether, or he was oblivious of Quartermaster General Myers's impotence which had led to the creation of Wadley's Bureau.

Trains of food were in fact coming up to Lee from the Subsistence Bureau all the time. Doubtless they did not bring all he needed for comfortable reserves. But a letter written to his wife shows that those trains were expected at short intervals: "No cars from Richmond yesterday," wrote Lee on February 23, "& I fear our short rations for men & horses will have to be curtailed."[21] A little later the War Department clerk Jones reported the Richmond depot always full, as 5,000 bushels of corn were sent to Lee every day.[22] On March 11 the Atlanta commissary Cummings reported supplying

[16] February 4, 1863 to Seddon (*OR* ser. IV, vol. 2, 384-85).

[17] *OR* ser. I, vol. 51, pt. 2, 667.

[18] *OR* ser. I, vol. 21, 1110.

[19] *OR* ser. IV, vol. 2, 373-74.

[20] *OR* ser. I, vol. 25, pt. 2, 612.

[21] *Wartime Papers*, 407.

[22] *Diary*, I, 334.

"the eastern armies with about 500,000 pounds [of salt meat] weekly."[23] But a lot of that was not getting through. On March 25 Seddon wrote to the railroad chief Wadley: "I learn with astonishment from the Commissary General that though since the 1st of January he has been urging the transportation of meat from his reserves at Atlanta to this city, he has not yet received in all more than 400,000 pounds."[24]

Northrop recruited his own "transportation agent" for the Subsistence Bureau, John M. Hottel (a man so able that he was soon headhunted away by Wadley). Hottel suggested reducing passenger traffic on the rails by one half; Northrop instantly urged it on Secretary Seddon. Reports had just come in that three different Subsistence depots in North Carolina were blocked up with food for shipment to Richmond and Lee, while the railroads were shipping private freight "which they say pays the best". Northrop adjured Seddon: "This condition requires instant remedy. ... [Lee's] army is living from hand to mouth as to meat and bread, due to a want of means to get both meat and wheat to market."[25]

Yet it was Lee himself—probably the only man with power enough to institute real change—who had refused to help. Whatever the pros and cons of his reasoning, the result was demoralizing in the last degree for those attempting to feed him. On April 1, 1863 Robert Kean wrote in his diary: "Wadley says he can do nothing unless he is allowed to have mechanics. General Lee has fought all winter *against* this, and now the evil, which much might have been done to remedy during the winter months, is nearly irremediable...".[26]

Lee's relations with the Commissary General in particular through the winter of 1862-63 revealed more and more clearly a chink in the great Confederate general's armor, a *lacuna* in his otherwise comprehensive preparation for his present responsibilities. His biographer Douglas Southall Freeman saw it: "Admirable as was the training of Lee it was not complete. ... Most of all was he lacking in any detailed knowledge of the service of supply. Belonging to the élite corps of the army [Engineers], he had never performed lengthy duty as quartermaster or as commissary... Nor had he and most of the other Confederate leaders been reared in a society that gave them a background for this homely but essential part of the work of a successful commanding general. ... In plantation life, while provision had to be made for clothing and feeding hundreds, this had been the task of overseers—and overseers were not apt to lead armies."[27]

---

[23] A. D. Banks to J. E. Johnston *(OR* ser. I, vol. 23, pt. 2, 680). Cummings's statement would have covered shipments not only to Lee but to other eastern commands such as Beauregard's at Charleston and perhaps Whiting's in North Carolina.

[24] *OR* ser. IV, vol. 2, 457. Seddon's further observations in this letter show that he was as ignorant as Lee of the true state of the railroads at any distance from Richmond.

[25] Endorsement of March 28, 1863 (*OR* ser. I, vol. 25, pt. 2, 687-88).

[26] *Inside the Confederate Government*, 47.

[27] Freeman, *R. E. Lee*, I, 458-59.

If Lee would not impress food immediately around him, and would not help repair the railroads to bring it from a distance, just one possibility remained to increase his food supply. That was to bring out the food still lying in remote quarters of western and northern Virginia. Some farmers there seemed willing to sell, but still had their food on hand because it was located at points far from any railroad. Its transport, Northrop estimated, would require at least two hundred wagons and teams. Only the army quartermasters could supply such a number. And since much of this outlying food was dangerously close to (sometimes within) enemy lines, the whole operation would also need the spying and protection of cavalry.

Northrop's cattle agent Noland had been begging for those things repeatedly over the last six months and more. During all that time Lee had found no way to accommodate him. Now it was winter: if roads were bad for wagons at least it was the season of military inactivity. Yet Burnside menaced, and Lee's ranks were thin. He felt he must still keep all his men in camp in readiness, and his wagons too. As for his cavalry, they were fully engaged in spying on Burnside.

One day around that time Lee himself called on Northrop in Richmond to press his concern about the very low stocks of food in his camps. Northrop in later years recalled the conversation thus:

> He came into my office... I renewed the subject [of getting food from outlying farms]. After a while he remarked:
> "Some morning you will be awakened by the enemy at Richmond."
> I replied: "I am glad, Genl. Lee, that you are at last awakened."
> He did not respond, but got up and went away.[28]

It may have been during this interview that Lee went so far as to say that responsibility for feeding troops did not rest with him. That remark so enraged Northrop that he was to tax Lee bitterly with it months later.[29]

Northrop felt a basic respect for Lee, as nearly everyone did.[30] Yet Lee was perfectly well aware of the food situation in outlying Virginia: he had written to Adjutant General Cooper as long ago as November 18, 1862 asking that prompt measures be taken to collect that food—only not with his men and wagon teams.[31] The plea had been sent to Northrop, and he had sent it on to Burr Noland. Noland responded with the history of his own attempts to reach that food and his failures since the summer to get Lee to provide help. Noland characterized the supplies remaining in outlying Virginia even now as "... enormous; fully sufficient I am sure to supply our

---

[28]   April 21, 1878 to Davis (Rowland, VIII, 180).

[29]   See below, p. 217.

[30]   Writing to Bishop Lynch on November 22, 1862, Northrop had contrasted Lee's leadership with Beauregard in Charleston: "I suppose the citizens had reason to be alarmed, having no leaders, but Genl Lee is a man of capacity." (CDA 28 D 6).

[31]   Lee wrote to Cooper probably because he had just learnt of Randolph's resignation as Secretary of War but did not know who was in his place. The letter to Cooper has not been found, but Northrop briefly described it in his endorsement addressed to Seddon on James Crenshaw's report (OR ser. I, vol. 21, 1091).

Army for 12 months; but with our utmost effort but little of it has been secured because the farmers had no transportation left them [after Army impressments of draft animals and wagons] & the Government was unable to furnish it. Nearly all that wheat is still in the producers' hands & generally in the stack."[32]

By the turn of the year food for Lee's army ran short. (The timing had been forecast quite precisely by Ruffin two months earlier, when arguing for trade through enemy lines: see above, pages 166-67.) Northrop had then advised Lee once again to use the surrounding country, and Lee had answered on January 8, 1863 that his men simply could not find enough there any longer. The next day Northrop summoned his flour adviser James Crenshaw, with the rank of lieutenant colonel, and sent him to Lee, armed with letters of introduction from himself and the Secretary of War. Crenshaw went up that day, January 9, returned, and reported to Northrop.

At Lee's headquarters Crenshaw had presented his letters to Assistant Adjutant General Chilton—only to be told, after being kept waiting two hours, that Lee refused to see him. The general sent word that Jeb Stuart had some cavalry in the Valley, and that they might possibly help. Crenshaw pointed out to Chilton that what was needed in addition to cavalry was a supply of draft animals and wagons, and that Lee's own superintendent of transport had already told him "the only difficulty in the way of supplying this Bureau with a sufficient number of wagons was an order which he had received from General Lee." Crenshaw's every argument was turned blandly away. Crenshaw then faced Chilton and told him

> ... that I did not see how, under such a state of things, our army could possibly be subsisted; and that the best remedy which this Bureau could devise (not having the direction or control of the transportation of the country) was the collection of large supplies of flour and other subsistence stores at many convenient points, ahead of immediate wants; and that the system of living from 'hand to mouth' must result in serious disaster, if not absolute ruin; and I ventured to express the opinion that unless all the departments of the Government and all the officers of the Government zealously cooperated in the collection of supplies, General Lee would see his army melt away for the want of subsistence; and that the questions which I had been directed by [the Commissary] General to submit to General Lee ... were of vastly more importance to the country than the entire and utter annihilation of Burnside's army, desirable as that would be.
>
> The result, however, of my whole interview with General Chilton was that, so far from any anxiety being displayed ... there was not, so far as I could see, even interest exhibited.

Chilton merely repeated that Crenshaw could see Lee's chief quartermaster and commissary on the subject. Crenshaw saw them both, as he told Northrop, "for I was determined to omit nothing on my part to carry out your wishes".

---

[32]   November 23, 1862 (NYPL: Northrop Papers).

But they both said, of course, that they could do nothing without an order from Lee.

Northrop was flabbergasted. He sent Crenshaw's report to Seddon with a long, sharp endorsement. Crenshaw had been sent to Lee, Northrop said, because "he was better fitted for the duty than any one known to me". The Commissary General summarized the history of Lee's own requests for this flour beginning in November, and of Noland's efforts to get Lee's help in securing it for months before that. Northrop concluded: "Had teams been procurable in any other way, General Lee would not have been applied to. This Bureau will continue its efforts, but will accomplish but little, it is feared. The Commissary General hereby absolves himself from all responsibility attending this deficiency."[33]

Lee's refusal to help acquire the outlying food could possibly have had one other explanation. Perhaps he had begun to plan his spring campaign northwards into Maryland and beyond. If so, the food in northern Virginia might then serve his army where it was, provided the Federals did not get it first. If any such ideas were in Lee's mind in January 1863, he seems to have shared no inkling of them with Northrop.

Evidently some high-level protest was addressed to Lee. On January 13 he told Seddon he could make cavalry available for the flour operation, but not wagons. The protest then went to the top. On the 19th Lee wrote to Davis that he had detached fifty wagons for the purpose—a quarter of the number Northrop wanted.[34] Lee had also to be compelled to collect wheat around Fredericksburg; he announced it done on February 11.[35] Robert Kean wrote in his diary: "A letter of General Lee's to the Secretary received February 14 shows that he has adopted what the Commissary General desired but that there is no concert of action."[36] Lee used the very minimum of his forces to collect bare necessities from day to day; he produced nothing of the surplus hoped for by Northrop.

When the meat from Atlanta did not come, Northrop ordered a new temporary reduction of the daily meat ration in Lee's army to one-quarter pound per man. To make up some of the deficiency, the Commissary General had given a special daily ration of one-fifth pound of sugar. That caused Lee to put forward a suggestion to Davis on January 19: why not offer to exchange the Bureau's sugar for meat?[37] Northrop was in no mood to dig into his small and dwindling sugar reserves for the man who had refused even to talk to Crenshaw. When Lee's suggestion arrived on his desk, Northrop endorsed: "It is not proposed by this Bureau to diminish its supplies or

---

[33]   January 12-13, 1863 (OR ser. I, vol. 21, 1088-91).
[34]   Wartime Papers, 392.
[35]   OR ser. I, vol. 25, pt. 2, 612.
[36]   Inside the Confederate Government, 39.
[37]   Wartime Papers, 392. Lee wrote about this idea on January 20 to Seddon, intimating that the exchange proposal had come from his commissary R. G. Cole (OR ser. I, vol. 21, 1100).

resources by barter; it is better to use the sugar, and to impress all the bacon that can be found, consistently with leaving a supply for the family; after that, barter would be beneficial."[38] In other words, Northrop doubted that all the meat being held in farms and households was "for the family". Military impressment was necessary to get the overage, whatever Lee's feelings on the subject—since the Commissary General's hands were still tied over impressment.

A week later Lee sent another suggestion to Seddon: "I think if the citizens of the whole county were appealed to, they would be willing to restrict themselves and furnish what they have to the army."[39] Such an appeal to the public would certainly be read as signifying that the Subsistence Bureau was incompetent. Northrop returned that proposal with a long endorsement rehearsing the history of his attempts to provision Lee over the last fifteen months, and of Lee's lack of cooperation culminating in the Crenshaw incident. He then dismissed-the specific proposal in a sentence: "General Lee's suggestion that an appeal be made to the citizens to forward supplies is noted by this Bureau, and is not approved."[40]

Somehow that correspondence reached the desk of J. B. Jones, formerly clerking in the War Department and then working for the Conscription Bureau. Jones concluded that Northrop's refusal was mere "red tape".[41] Next day Jones himself addressed the President, suggesting that if soldiers' "parents and sisters were appealed to and transportation be furnished, a sufficiency of food could be in this way obtained to prevent any suffering. From my experience when registering 'patriotic contributions' in the passport office, I fully concur in the opinion expressed by the soldiers, and I would be glad with the sanction of the Government to try the experiment again. I would use the press, but would not permit regular files of the papers to leave the Confederacy."[42] Jones was a former newspaper editor. How he proposed to stop his advertisements from reaching the enemy is a mystery.

The notion of calling on families to provide directly for their sons was a variant of Lee's proposal. In fact it offered an administrative nightmare, promising to produce miles of the "red tape" Jones himself deplored. And how was transportation to be furnished? When the Jones proposal reached Northrop, he endorsed: "The Commissary General has no experience as to this mode of raising supplies and does not think it a promising one, and respectfully refers it to the Secretary of War, if he wishes to direct it." Northrop knew Seddon would fight shy of such a cloud of gnats, and so he did. Seddon answered Jones: "... It is not deemed judicious, unless in the last extremity, to resort to the means of supply suggested. The patriotic motives that dictated the suggestion are, however, appreciated and acknowledged."[43]

---

[38] *OR* ser. I, vol. 21, 1101.

[39] January 26, 1863 (*OR* ser. I, vol. 25, pt. 2, 597).

[40] January 28, 1863 (*OR* ser. I, vol. 51, pt. 2, 674-75).

[41] February 18, 1863 (*Diary*, I, 261).

[42] February 19, 1863 (*OR* ser. IV, vol. 2, 405).

[43] Ibid., 412.

Lee had also begun sending subordinate commands to get food from the hinterlands. In late January he had sent out his cavalry Brigadier General William E. ("Grumble") Jones into western Virginia. Jones found only enough ready meat for himself and his men, together with large stocks of flour needing wagon transport.[44] In February Lee sent General James Longstreet with his men into southern Virginia and North Carolina. There, close to enemy lines, Longstreet could provision himself well enough, but he had no adequate transport for the rest—just as Northrop and Governor Vance had reported months ago when they tried vainly to remove it for the Confederate army.[45]

On March 4, 1863 Secretary Seddon, under great pressure, tried his own hand at impressment in Richmond to supply Lee. He directed Subsistence Bureau agents to seize all the local flour mills and warehouses, and ordered the enforced sale to the government at fixed prices of all the food brought into Richmond markets. The farmers were outraged and threatened to bring in no more. The Governor of Virginia and hundreds of citizens signed a petition condemning the Subsistence Bureau and all its works.[46] The furor did have one good effect: it seemed to make Lee realize something of what the Commissary General had been up against all that winter. Lee wrote to his wife on March 9: "The scarcity & high price of provisions are very distressing. We must eat less. We can live on very little."[47] It was what Northrop had been telling him for months.

With all the blood on the floor spilt over the question of provisioning Lee, it seems astonishing to realize that Lee's men had not starved at any time through the winter of 1862-63, nor were they starving now. The whole contest had been raised and driven by fear that they *might* starve, when stocks in camp dwindled toward a vanishing point and trains did not come. Yet many observers, from Lee himself downwards, noticed his troops' persistent good health throughout the winter. Lee had written to his wife on Christmas Day 1862: "Our army was never in such good health & condition since I have been attached to it & I believe they share with me my disappointment that the enemy did not renew the combat" at Fredericksburg.[48]

Part of the troops' good health then might be thought to have come from Lee's increase of their rations in November. Yet their good health continued after Northrop reduced the ration again in January 1863, in spite of their general's protests. On February 15 Robert Kean was to note: "The field officers are beginning to complain heavily of their troops' having insufficient food. It is a noteworthy fact that the health of the army is nearly perfect—doubly better than ever before, since the ration was reduced."[49] In

---

[44] *OR* ser. I, vol. 25, pt. 2, 598: and vol. 51, pt. 2, 676-77.

[45] See Steven A. Cormier, *The Siege of Suffolk* (Lynchburg, Va., 1989) passim.

[46] March 16, 1863, with Northrop's protesting endorsement dated four days later (M-437, r 100, ff 91-93).

[47] *Wartime Papers*, 413.

[48] Ibid., 380.

[49] *Inside the Confederate Government*, 39.

other words (as nutritionists never tire of telling us nowadays) appetite is not a reliable gauge of need. On April 9 Northrop requested that the Secretary of War order the same reduction for Longstreet's troops in southern Virginia and North Carolina,[50] and then wanted it for the entire Confederate army: his aim was always to save against a darkening future.

Northern Virginia still afforded chances for the soldiers themselves to purchase food—proving once again the contention of Northrop's Subsistence agents that food was there. Confederate troops had never been extensively served by the sutlers who followed Federal armies, but all sorts of local arrangements grew up. One was found in full operation by young Edward Moore, returning after recuperating from a wound to his artillery company's winter quarters near Guiney's Station below Fredericksburg in January 1863: "Once a week quite regularly an old negro man came to our camp with a wagon-load of fine oysters from Tappahannock. It was interesting to see some of the men from our mountains, who had never seen the bivalve before, trying to eat them, and hear their comments. Our custom was to buy anything to eat that came along, and so they had invested their Confederate notes in oysters. One of them gave some of my messmates an account of the time his mess had had with their purchases. When it was proposed that they sell their supply to us, he said, 'No, we are not afraid to tackle anything, and we've made up our minds to eat what we've got on hand, if it takes the hair off.' "[51]

More than a month later, with winter's end in sight, Langdon Cheves's grandson Alexander Haskell, serving in a South Carolina regiment encamped near Fredericksburg, wrote home to his parents on March 7, 1863: "The ration has been reduced to the amount which is supposed to be the very smallest upon which the average man of the Army could sustain health and strength in full vigour. The usual ration of flour 1 1/8 pounds is still given and will make in bread a good baker's loaf, in heavy biscuits a very small compass comprehends the weight: besides this is given but 1/4 pound of bacon (most of which is consumed in making the biscuits) with now and then a spoonful of sugar. I am happy to say that this does, so far, sustain the general health and strength of the Army unimpaired."[52]

All those witnesses would seem to agree that Northrop had calculated the soldiers' need finely, but not unrealistically for troops in camp. Yet the worry over starvation had gnawed them cruelly throughout that cold winter in northern Virginia. And returning spring would bring renewed manoeuvers, all demanding greater expense of energies.

* * *

The knowledge of Lee's situation at last galvanized the Congress to give Northrop the power of impressment. The need for some comprehen-

---

[50] M-437, r 103, f 371.

[51] *The Story of a Cannoneer under Stonewall Jackson*, 166-67.

[52] Louise Haskell Daly, *Alexander Cheves Haskell: the Portrait of a Man* (Norwood, Mass.: Plimpton Press, 1934; *rpr* Broadfoot, 1989), 93.

sive legislation had appeared graphically after Secretary Seddon had seized the Richmond flour mills and markets on March 4, 1863. A few nights later a government warehouse was burnt, apparently in protest. Outraged farmers and millers went to court and got a Virginia judge's injunction ordering the government to cease and desist from civil impressment.[53] That made it plain to everybody that a new law was needed.

Inflation was of course at the bottom of it. The discount rate of Confederate currency had gone from $3 in January 1863 to over $4 in March.[54] The Congress, alarmed at the level of Treasury expenditure, imposed a spending limit of $50 million per month. Treasury Secretary Memminger suggested to the War Department Bureaus that there could be enough for all if requisitions were made for the smallest amounts in the shortest terms. Often, he had noticed, a requisition had been passed and then not actually paid to the requisitioning officer for months. Northrop rejoined: "As often as otherwise, the amounts of Warrants issued remain unemployed because, though nominally to the credit of the officer, the money cannot be obtained."[55] In such cases, all that could feed troops where transport failed was impressment, which the Bureau had never been allowed.

Secretary Seddon began his summary of reasons for a new impressment law by observing that the "purchasing department" had now virtually no other way of obtaining supplies—partly because of speculation and profiteering, partly general mistrust of the government's ability "to redeem the large issues which such enhancements of price have rendered inevitable".[56]

After weeks of debate, Congress passed the new impressment law on March 26, 1863. The clearest statement of what it gave the Bureaus was spelt out by Adjutant General Cooper when he published it to the army: "The Quartermaster General, Commissary General, and Surgeon General may designate the officers and persons who shall be competent to make impressments to accumulate supplies at posts and depots."[57] To accumulate for the future: bureau impressments were strictly limited to that. Impressment for immediate consumption remained the perquisite of the military.

Northrop viewed his new powers thus: "The CGS feels too intensely the evils of wrong precedent not to carry out this part of his function with scrupulous adhesion to general principles. ... Conscription, taxation, impressments of labour, indeed all calls of the Govt for the defence of the country are nothing but impressments: and in view of the loss of territory, devastation, and destruction of stores by our Generals, none are more pressing or should be more willingly sustained than those for subsistence."[58]

---

[53]   Jones, *Diary*, I, 272, 279.

[54]   Schwab, *Confederate States*, 167. Gates's *Agriculture and the Civil War* (page 53) shows a steeper rise in those months, but the two authorities agree fairly well overall. By June 1863 Schwab shows a discount figure of $7 and Gates (June 15) $7.50.

[55]   April 18, 1863 (M-437, r 103, ff 24-28).

[56]   Report to the President, November 26, 1863 (*OR* ser. IV, vol. 2, 1008-9).

[57]   April 6, 1863 (*OR* ser. IV, vol. 2, 471).

[58]   Endorsement of September 28, 1863: "Explanations of Impressments & c." addressed to Secretary of War (M-437, r 105, ff 914-16).

Nobody could quarrel with feeding the army—unless that could no longer be made to square with feeding the populace.

Much of the new act and concomitant army orders were taken up with mechanisms for determining a fair price as between impressing buyer and reluctant seller. One mechanism—each side choosing referees for each transaction—was soon obviated as too cumbersome to be workable. An alternative was for permanent referees to be appointed by the central government on one hand and by the state governor on the other. Those permanent referees should agree a schedule of prices for all regularly impressed items, and publish the schedules in newspapers. Northrop had long advocated this.[59] It became the method widely used, despite nearly universal claims that the schedule-prices were far below the market.[60] That was an attempt to control inflation, the government said. Yet the rapid inflationary spiral would make it necessary to print revised price-schedules every month or two. It remained to be seen whether inflation would outstrip the bi-monthly revisions.

Anticipating the passage of the new impressment law, Northrop had already devised a comprehensive scheme to drain the country of excess food. That scheme, approved by Seddon, was set out in a circular letter of April 15, 1863 addressed to each man selected to be the chief commissary for his state. The state commissary would "divide his State into districts, say some four or five, with a chief purchasing commissary or agent selected for each district ... these districts to be subdivided and sub-commissaries or agents selected for each subdivision...". From every one of them, the immediate superior was to require "full reports of their present and contemplated operations, the prices they are paying, quantity and description of the supplies being obtained, and the promise for the future". Such reports were to be submitted every ten days. "... Therefore, wherever our armies move, all the supplies of our country will be tributary to their use. Then application will be made to prevent army commissaries from competing with this Bureau's commissaries or agents, and the chief commissary of each army directed to supply his wants by application to such Chief State Commissary of this Bureau as may be indicated by the Commissary General...".[61]

Of course it was a visionary scheme. Its chances for success in eliminating competition from army commissaries depended entirely on early

---

[59] See Northrop's endorsement of December 5, 1862 on a protest received from G. W.York of Warren County, Tenn. (M-437, r 79, f 739). Northrop was equally persuaded of the need for promptness in arbitrating disputed claims and in paying them (Ibid., r 105, ff 579-82). Yet here too Treasury obstruction entered the picture: the ultimate effect, as Northrop repeatedly pointed out to his superiors, was to reduce the army's supply of food.

[60] See the comparison in Jones's *Diary* of wholesale prices in Richmond with government price-schedules at the end of May 1863 (quoted below, p. 231).

[61] *OR* ser. I, vol. 24, pt. 3, 990-91; also printed in vol. 32, pt. 2, 524-25. The appointment of a single man in charge of each district, questioned by Davis, was defended by Frank Ruffin thus: "... The only way to give satisfaction to Govt & People is for 'one agent' to have charge of the whole department... Experience amply demonstrates the evils of dividing districts among independent agents, whether their responsibility be to the Commissary General, to their respective commanders, or partly to both. ... The whole plan is analogous to the division of the country into various military departments..." (May 27, 1863: M-437, r 88, ff 420-27).

and continuing results. Serious shortages or even inconsistencies of ration from one place to another could bring it down as a house of cards. Yet it could not have been started earlier, since neither Congress nor populace would have accepted it. Would they accept it now? If not now, it was unlikely they ever would—and would indeed allow their army to starve.

On April 4, 1863 Congress had passed a joint resolution urging people everywhere to stop planting cotton and tobacco, and to plant food instead. Then, at congressional request, President Davis published an address making the appeal more personal. There was enough meat in the country, Davis insisted; but transport and winter roads had been so bad, and speculation so rife, that the government had been "unable to gather full supplies". The people should voluntarily contribute their surplus, and thus withdraw it from the hands of speculation and greed.[62] It was close to the plan proposed by Lee in January. Nobody in Richmond believed it would work.

At that moment Congress was preparing a new tax bill to pull the carpet out from under contributor and speculator alike. It was passed on April 24, 1863, just a week before Congress was to break for the summer, not to reconvene until December. The new bill contained ten closely printed pages of swingeing impositions. There was to be a progressive income tax: it was another first for the American continent, and would not be followed in the United States for another fifty years. But the tax which was designed to aid army subsistence most directly was a new tithing tax-in-kind.

Every farmer and planter throughout the Confederacy was to reserve to his own family 50 bushels of sweet potatoes, Irish (*i.e.*, white) potatoes, and wheat; 100 bushels of corn; and 20 bushels of peas and beans combined. Then he was to deliver to the government in marketable condition one-tenth of all the rest of his produce. All would be brought to a government warehouse (to be designated or built within eight miles of the place of produce) under a penalty of 50 percent extra for late or non-delivery. Another section of the new act ordered each farmer and planter to provide to a government assessor an estimate of all the hogs he would slaughter up to March 1, 1864 and to deliver one tenth in bacon (figuring 60 pounds bacon to 100 pounds pork). There were also money taxes of one percent value on all cattle, horses, asses and mules not in agriculture. Beeves would be taxed as income.[63]

Very often, it turned out, the food to be taxed lay far from any transport, at farms too scattered to build depots. In such cases the act provided for the tithe-in-kind to be commuted to a money tax. Transport problems were so severe that it proved impractical in nearly half the counties of the Confederacy to collect some or all of the tithe-in-kind.[64] Thus the new act showed more clearly than anything yet the extent of the country's transport problems.

---

[62] April 10, 1863 (*OR* ser. IV, vol. 2, 477).

[63] *OR* ser. IV, vol. 2, 521-23.

[64] Gates, *Agriculture and the Civil War*, 64.

The whole operation was under the Quartermaster Bureau. They had to find all the expert assessors. (Many of them were able-bodied men, and as such being pursued through the bureaus by conscription officers having more and more difficulty meeting their rising quotas.) There was to be a chief quartermaster in each state. Under him, a new category of "post quartermaster" would supervise collections in each congressional district. They would also be responsible for the safe storage in the new depots and prompt transport of the food in good condition to wherever it was needed.[65]

Inequities real and imagined were soon thundering in the press. When corruption was rumored or brought to light, Southern rhetoric overflowed far beyond what today would be considered the limits of libel. Fewer reports were made, in the nature of things, on the system's good working and real help to local commissaries. One which has survived in the reminiscences of a North Carolina regiment may stand for many. Their commissary was Major Thomas McKoy: "He would always take charge of our cooking details, and often sit up all night to prevent delay in preparing the rations. At Liberty Mills [just north of Gordonsville, Virginia] he scoured the country, collected the tax in kind, stored his provisions in a log house built for that purpose, and thereby prevented a great deal of suffering that winter."[66]

During the time Congress was drafting the new tax law, Northrop had been on his way to Milledgeville, Georgia. There he was to confer with the Governors of North Carolina, Georgia, Alabama, and Mississippi on the subject of governmental regulation of farming. Passing through one of the best corn areas in Georgia, Northrop saw not one acre in five planted with corn or prepared for corn. Old legislation still on the books actually aided the clearing of new land for cotton planting, and in places it seemed the farmers were going back to it, perhaps because of all the food impressment and taxation.

Three schemes for government control of farming had been proposed by General Braxton Bragg. One was to prohibit the planting of cotton and tobacco throughout the Confederacy. The second was to require every planter to put a specified proportion of his land to grain. Bragg's third idea was the one that appealed to Northrop: it was that the state governments should operate all the plantations—next door to nationalization.[67] There was little prospect that either the President or Congress would agree to that. In any case Congress would not reconvene for another seven months and more. The first big receipts from the tax-in-kind were due in the autumn: breadstuffs and vegetables. The bacon tithe was not due until the end of the curing season in February 1864. The rest of 1863, therefore, would depend very much on what success could be made of Subsistence Bureau impressments.

---

[65]   The quartermasters would take advantage of their control to serve themselves first—sometimes at the cost of the Subsistence Bureau. See correspondence of the South Carolina Chief Commissary Henry Guerin with Northrop's assistant Seth Barton French, March 24-June 1, 1864 (NA, RG 109, Officers: Guerin).

[66]   *SHSP*, vol. 10, 428. The winter referred to was 1863-64.

[67]   Gates, *Agriculture and the Civil War*, 31-32.

CHAPTER 17

PIGGERY IN THE WEST, PENURY IN THE EAST

Lee's Army of Northern Virginia was the only Confederate force to face a real threat of insufficiency in the winter and spring of 1863. The armies of the West were far better supplied, yet their generals complained and complained: and the effect of those complaints sharply worsened the plight of Lee. At the head of Confederate armies in the West was Joseph E. Johnston, recovered from his wound of the previous May and arrived at his new post in December 1862. Three major figures were under him.

In Confederate territories west of the Mississippi there was, from March 1863, Edmund Kirby Smith. His command was so distant and so scattered that he soon began to run semi-independent collections and distributions of his own supplies.[1] There was still much to be had in those lands. When General Richard Taylor went west of the Mississippi, he recalled: "... I sent for the colonel of a mounted regiment from western Texas, a land of herdsmen, and asked him if he could furnish men to hunt and drive cattle. 'Why! bless you, sir, I have men who can find cattle where there *ain't any*,' was his reply."[2]

East of the Mississippi River, Bragg commanded the Army of Tennessee, and Pemberton the forces in Mississippi and East Louisiana. Pemberton's department centred on Vicksburg, a key defence to all the crossing points left to the Confederacy. After a visit from President Davis to these areas in December 1862, it was understood that Pemberton should defend Vicksburg to the last drop of Confederate blood in order to keep open both banks of the river.

Since his arrival Pemberton had been busy systematizing everything in his department.[3] Broadwell, as an illogical and perhaps uncontrollable

---

[1]   No study of Kirby Smith's commissariat has ever been made. Some hints of how things worked can be gathered from James L. Nichols, *The Confederate Quartermaster in the Trans-Mississippi* (University of Texas, 1964).

[2]   Richard Taylor, *Destruction and Reconstruction*, 54.

[3]   Ballard, *Pemberton*, 115-20.

entity, had to go. Pemberton appointed a commissary of his own, Major Theodore Johnston, who proceeded to negate all the remains of Broadwell's arrangements with New Orleans and other enemy places.[4] Yet considerable stocks accruing from those arrangements still lay under Pemberton's hand. His department had benefitted richly from cattle swum across the Mississippi and from all the sugar and molasses traded by Broadwell and his agents (and still awaiting transport eastwards).

Then Pemberton announced (apparently with the blessing of his chief General J. E. Johnston) that he would subsist his own army entirely from within his own territory. He obtained permission to exclude from his district all commissary and food-procuring agents not of his army.[5] And he embargoed the exporting of any food from his territory. Northrop immediately drew attention to Broadwell's sugar and molasses stored there. Pemberton replied that he would require all that. Northrop raised hell with the general, the Secretary of War, and the President; but he got very little of Broadwell's remaining sugar and molasses for Lee or anyone else.

Pemberton's embargo also affected his military neighbors. To the south, Brigadier General Simon Bolivar Buckner commanded the area around Mobile, Alabama. Even in peacetime, Mobile had always drawn its food from Vicksburg and the North. With their food thus cut off, the citizens of Mobile were threatened with starvation.[6] At last Buckner had to open his commissary stores to the people. And then of course there was insufficient to feed his own men. By April 1863 Buckner was trying to start independent blockade-runners to succor his troops.[7]

Pemberton meanwhile stockpiled food and materiel at Vicksburg to withstand a siege. Soon he had more than he could look after, as there were no adequate storehouses. Reports reached Northrop that 60,000 bushels of corn had spoiled at Port Hudson from exposure. It was Manassas all over again. Yet nothing was ever enough for the siege-minded general. In Richmond, Robert Kean wrote in his diary: "Pemberton, who sometime ago asked leave to be allowed to shift for himself in providing food, has starved his army and cries out lustily to the Commissary General for aid."[8]

North and east of Pemberton, the Army of Tennessee was commanded by the unpopular Braxton Bragg. Bragg had his talents, and the friendship of the President. But he was a bad diplomat, and had no personal magnetism for his troops. Retreating back on Murfreesboro after his ill-fated expedition into Kentucky, Bragg had brought with him a huge wagon train of captured

---

[4]   Major Thomas Reid to Seddon, May 7, 1863 (Ruffin Papers, Va. Hist. Soc.); Northrop to Seddon, September 28, 1863 (M-437, r 105, ff 914-16).

[5]   See the report of the Vicksburg agent W. H. Johnson to Northrop, August 10, 1863 (OR ser I, vol. 24, pt. 3, 1051-52).

[6]   Gates, *Agriculture and the Civil War*, 116-18.

[7]   OR ser. I, vol. 23, pt. 2, 786.

[8]   *Inside the Confederate Government* (entry dated March 28, 1863), 46-47. See Pemberton's telegram of February 22, 1863 complaining that his commissary is out of funds, and Northrop's laconic endorsement of the following day, stating that the C.G.S. made requisition for funds on the date requested: "This is all that this Bureau can do in the matter." (M-618, r 13, ff 1119-20).

Federal supplies. Yet he still insisted on heavy drafts of meat from Subsistence Bureau stocks, and J. E. Johnston gave his blessing.

Bragg's drafts on the Bureau were particularly damaging in view of where he was. Middle Tennessee was the last remaining major source for meat-with-transport in the entire Confederacy. The manager of Northrop's storehouse in Atlanta, Major Cummings, had been drawing most of his meat from middle Tennessee long before Bragg arrived to set up his camps there late in 1862. When Bragg did arrive, Cummings was careful to leave enough on the ground for him.[9]

Then at the turn of the year Bragg fought a bloody and disastrous battle. It ended in his retreat from Murfreesboro; and with it, the Confederate abandonment of middle Tennessee. Cummings continued to operate agents in the lands newly lost, as he would report: "The most of the subsistence that they are now collecting is being obtained from near or within the enemy's lines; indeed, some of my agents are operating in the rear of the Federal lines, and with much success. Their success, however, is to a great extent attributable to my having furnished them with [Federal] bank-notes, which were drawing supplies that could not be reached with Confederate Treasury notes...".[10] Cummings's greenbacks were provided by Northrop—either directly or by letting Cummings have some of the precious little reserve of gold he had managed to husband for the Bureau.

Bragg demanded all the food that Cummings bought—from lands Bragg himself had lost. He placed his own embargo on exports of meat from Tennessee to any other part of the Confederacy. And he commanded heavy drafts from Atlanta to fill in the corners. The other Southern armies might starve until he had supped his fill from his "own" lands.

On January 12, 1863 Northrop wrote to Seddon. He reminded the Secretary that meat reserves that winter were less than half of those for the previous winter—with vastly greater numbers of men in the field to feed and Lee in Virginia threatened with starvation: "I therefore earnestly recommend that General Bragg be instructed to subsist his army from the resources of the country he defends, and be forbidden to stop the passage of hogs to Major Cummings...". And again Northrop begged for authority to trade through enemy lines: ".. Without such an arrangement the armies cannot be fed."[11]

Northrop telegraphed to the commissary at Tullahoma, Major John J. Walker, for details of Bragg's current ration there. Walker answered on January 31 that his troops were getting "Bacon (8 ounces to the ration) 2 days a week, and fresh pork or beef (16 or 20 oz. respectively) the other five; Flour (16 oz.) 2 days a week, and corn meal (20 oz.) the other five; Rice, sugar, molasses, vinegar, soap, and salt more or less regularly." Northrop sent that to Seddon, asking him to compare it with the smaller ration orders for all Confederate armies approved by Secretary Randolph in April 1862, and posing a sarcastic question:

[9]   Cummings to Northrop, November 10 and December 5, 1862 (Va. Hist. Soc.: Ruffin Papers).
[10] April 4, 1863 to W. P. Johnston (OR ser. I, vol. 23, pt. 2, 771).
[11] OR ser. IV, vol. 2, 350-51.

Information is respectfully asked whether or not any authority was ever conferred on Gnl Beauregard or Gnl Bragg to set aside or disregard the Regulations for the Army of C.S. When circumstances render it impossible for all the component parts of the ration allowed by Regulations to be issued, is it for the Generals Comd'g, or the Sec of War to decide what changes shall be made?

It was vintage Northrop—not calculated to charm. Its date was February 12, 1863. Seddon did not answer until March 27. When he did, he wrote only:

No such authority has been given to either Genl Bragg or Genl Beauregard—Of course the power of changing the ration is retained by the Dept.[12]

Not a word about asserting the Department's authority to curb Bragg.

Following Bragg's defeat and retreat from Murfreesboro, pressure had grown for his removal. The obvious successor was Joseph E. Johnston, already on the ground as supreme commander in the West. Johnston was reluctant, but he began to take over some direct responsibilities for Bragg's army. On January 29, 1863 he wrote to Seddon about their subsistence: they had now fed off their ground "for seventy or eighty days", and he claimed the area was exhausted. He said nothing about Bragg's heavy drafts on Atlanta, but wanted more from there for himself.[13] Seddon asked for details. On February 4 Johnston telegraphed a complaint not about quantity but about variety: "This army is suffering from the use of fresh pork. It has no other meat. I respectfully recommend that it be permitted immediately to draw salt meat from Atlanta and fresh beef from Major Cummings, in North Georgia."[14]

Johnston wanted Cummings's men in his own territory to stop salting beef altogether and let the Army of Tennessee have it fresh—for he was contemplating military movements northward to join Pemberton at Vicksburg. Johnston argued: "Meat salted now cannot be saved. Our troops have not the means of boiling meat, and therefore throw away the greater part of this, except when pressed by hunger."[15] Even in the face of apparent privation, then, the trail of waste which had marked Johnston's path through Manassas and the Virginia Peninsula was to mark his path towards Vicksburg. It was observed by an English visitor, Lieutenant Colonel Arthur Fremantle, at Johnston's camp in May 1863: "The men are constantly in the habit of throwing away their knapsacks and blankets on a long march, if not carried for them...".[16]

Northrop endorsed Johnston's telegram: "The army in Virginia is in a critical condition for subsistence, and the supplies referred to at Atlanta and in Northern Georgia are needed for it, and are held for it, and it alone. ... Not

---

[12]   M-437, r 105, ff 720-23.

[13]   *OR* ser. I, vol. 23, pt. 2, 618-19.

[14]   Ibid., 625-26.

[15]   February 25, 1863 (*OR* ser. I, vol. 23, pt. 2, 647).

[16]   *Three Months in the Southern States* (Blackwood, 1863), 122.

a pound of the rations asked for by General Johnston can be spared for his army; and if he is permitted to take it, it will be that much abstracted from an army far more in need than his own."[17] Northrop in these days was observed by Robert Kean, who noted on February 17: "The Commissary General gets more and more gloomy and complains heavily of department commanders robbing the little stores he is able to scrape together for the future."[18]

Seddon delayed answering Johnston for nearly three weeks. Then he went so far as to suggest that Johnston subsist himself from behind enemy lines in Kentucky "by even irregular means". Northrop, he said, would lend the special expertise of Cummings, closely familiar with the district.[19] A week later Seddon added: "We are ransacking every portion of the Confederacy, and in addition I have authorized enterprises and contracts of even an extraordinary character to procure supplies from abroad, even from the United States."[20] So at last Seddon was beginning to do what Northrop had been asking to do virtually since the opening of the war. Kean noted in his diary that the Secretary had authorized the exchange in northwestern Virginia of tobacco for fat cattle. When the Davis Cabinet learned of it, they stopped it instantly.[21]

Meanwhile Johnston had grown impatient, and placed his requisition on Atlanta. On March 2 Northrop had an anguished telegram from Cummings: "Genl J. E. Johnston orders from me 165,000 pounds bacon or bulk pork to be shipped immedy. What shall I do? Answer me at Chattanooga immed."[22] Johnston had also persuaded Davis to appoint a new special commissary for his army—a former newspaper man named Arthur D. Banks. Northrop refused to recognize him, and continued to use his own men on the ground. Banks found fault with Northrop and all his works. When he went to Atlanta to see for himself, Banks had an eye-opener over Cummings's supply to Lee.[23] Yet Banks, in common with almost every other soldier of rank on the Confederate field then, showed no real comprehension of the disastrous shrinkage which had befallen the Southern food supply. He claimed to have injected energy into Cummings with regard to north Alabama, where a million pounds of salt meat were supposed to be available; he said nothing about cash to buy it or transport to bring it. Generally he made a lot of noise.[24]

[17]   February 5, 1863 (OR ser. I, vol. 23, pt. 2, 626).

[18]   Inside the Confederate Government, 40.

[19]   February 23, 1863 (OR ser. I, vol. 52, pt. 2, 426-27).

[20]   March 3, 1863 (OR ser. I, vol. 23, pt. 2, 657-58).

[21]   Inside the Confederate Government (entry for March 7), 41; (April 1), 48. Kean (a protegé of Seddon's predecessor Randolph) pointed his finger at Davis and his allies in the Cabinet. Yet as Kean noted on March 15, Davis himself was compelled to allow General Kirby Smith in the Trans-Mississippi to trade cotton to the enemy for meat (Ibid., 45).

[22]   M-618, r 13, f 1217. Northrop's endorsement (f 1216) shows again the Commissary General's powerlessness to protect his own stores from such a draft. See also Northrop to Seddon, March 2, 1863 (OR ser. IV, vol. 2, 414). Some commentators have mistakenly associated this with Lee's ration. In fact it shows Northrop's fear that Johnston was about to promulgate his own ration orders for the armies of the West.

[23]   March 13, 1863 to Bragg's Assistant Adjutant General Colonel B. S. Ewell (OR ser. I, vol. 23, pt. 2, 688-89). See also Banks to Johnston, Ibid., March 15, 695-96.

[24]   For Bragg's unfavorable opinion of Banks, see Bragg to B. S. Ewell, March 18, 1863 (OR ser. I, vol. 23, pt. 2, 707).

Bragg ordered 400,000 rations from Atlanta to subsist his troops until the end of March. Cummings sent 190,000 pounds, and refused any more without an order from the Secretary of War. He telegraphed privately to Northrop: "I hope the order will be given at once for reduction of rations in this army." Northrop sent the wire to Seddon with his own recommendation to reduce Johnston's army to a quarter pound of meat if it could be supplemented with sugar or molasses.[25]

When subsistence had gotten into a similar tangle through Beauregard's attempt to get his own ration in the West in the spring of 1862, Davis had sent out Albert Sidney Johnston's son, Colonel William Preston Johnston, to investigate. Now Davis sent Preston Johnston again. W. P. Johnston visited Atlanta, Montgomery, and J. E. Johnston's various camps. He reported: "There is a vast improvement in this army since I inspected it last at Tupelo... The army lacks no physical element of success." Yet he found future prospects for its subsistence very far from satisfactory: "It is recommended to allow the use of State money where necessary, and to send forward molasses, which can be advantageously exchanged, 1 gallon for 8 pounds of bacon, and which will bring to our lines, even from beyond the enemy's, a supply of bacon which neither force nor persuasion can otherwise obtain." He added that Generals Leonidas Polk and William J. Hardee had actually named an agent at Memphis (then in enemy hands) who "should be employed to exchange cotton for bacon".[26]

A sub-report from Cummings stated that his men were operating as well as possible behind enemy lines, using greenbacks or gold (the Davis Government had barred the use of greenbacks in Tennessee, but not in Kentucky). They were the only alternatives to trading cotton. Cummings finished by reporting that most of his Atlanta warehouses were without guards because of conscription. Quantities of supplies were being stolen.[27] Preston Johnston endorsed: "Whatever is resolved on in regard to subsistence must be done with promptness and decision. The question will not brook delay or indecision."

Yet delay and indecision were enthroned in Richmond. Davis had his principles: however many times he might be forced to give way in this case or that, he was always ready to return to them. And Secretary Seddon would not stand up to him as Randolph had done. Robert Kean wrote in his diary on April 1, 1863: "The truth is that the Secretary has been too deferential to the Army officers. They have thwarted whatever of policy then was in supply by their clamor against details, and Mr. Seddon has 'recommended to the favorable consideration of' where he might and should have given instant orders. ... The Commissary General is in low spirits and looks haggard."[28]

---

[25] M-618, r 14, ff 56-57.

[26] April 15, 1863 to Davis (*OR* ser. I, vol. 23, pt. 2, 759-60).

[27] Ibid., April 4, 1863 to W. P. Johnston, 770-72.

[28] *Inside the Confederate Government*, 47-48.

Seddon continued to urge Johnston to do what he himself had been forbidden to do. He wrote to Johnston on April 17: "... I would not recommend any relaxation of effort on your own part to obtain from within your own department or the well-stocked counties of Kentucky [behind enemy lines] all possible supplies. I am informed that you could probably obtain considerable supplies from Kentucky, if you felt authorized to trade cotton or sugar for meat. I have not hesitated to make contracts in relation to cotton in exchange for subsistence stores, and, so far as the Department can authorize, you are empowered to employ or sanction a similar exchange...".[29]

Johnston ordered his friend Banks to investigate the possibilities. Banks expressed no confidence in Northrop's recently announced system of districting, and of course suggested the establishment of rival supply depots.[30] Banks received his general's approval to buy sugar and molasses to exchange with the populace for meat—in direct opposition to War Department impressments then beginning. He urged Johnston to consult his own needs before permitting any sugar or molasses in the district to be shipped out to the Subsistence Bureau, even to aid Lee. At the same time Banks reported: "The commissary arrangements in this district look well. They have about 250,000 pounds of salt meat in depot, and about 2,200 head of cattle either herded or engaged. This meat has been secured chiefly by exchange for sugar and molasses...".[31] Northrop was bound to oppose such bartering away of what he had to regard as capital stock (as he had opposed Lee's proposal to barter sugar in January). Bureau impressment now might bring in meat without touching sugar and molasses. But Northrop was overruled, as Banks wrote: "The exchange of sugar for meat, stopped by order of Colonel Northrop, has been resumed, and will go on actively."[32] Thus Johnston declared independence from the Subsistence Bureau, even as Pemberton had done. Each was basically running a rogue operation off a rich district.

Johnston was nominally in command of Pemberton at Vicksburg. Yet Johnston did not think Vicksburg ought to be defended. To him it seemed more important for Pemberton's army of 32,000 to unite with his own force; that way they might face off the Federals wherever else they attacked—even at the cost of losing Vicksburg. In Johnston's defensive outlook and personality, the orders of the President were expendable; mobility was all.

Pemberton stuck to his siege guns. When Johnston ordered a junction of forces outside Vicksburg, Pemberton simply failed to comply. By mid-May the Federals under Grant had shut him up inside Vicksburg. Johnston then failed to come to Pemberton's aid; he marched north so slowly as to allow Grant to get between them.

29   OR ser. I, vol. 23, pt. 2, 775-76.
30   Ibid., April 23, 1863, 786.
31   Ibid., May 15, 1863, 816-17.
32   Ibid., May 18, 1863, 840.

Vicksburg fell on July 4, and soon the Union controlled the entire Mississippi River from top to bottom. The Confederacy was cut in two. No more supplies could come east on a regular basis from the Trans-Mississippi. At Vicksburg the Federals broke into Pemberton's storehouses. There they found more than 100,000 pounds of food—much of it collected by Broadwell for Northrop's Subsistence Bureau, stopped in transit to Richmond and Lee. Pemberton's commissary, Theodore Johnston, reported afterwards: "There was in Vicksburg when it surrendered half as much bacon as there was in the whole Department of Mississippi and Eastern Louisiana when I was assigned to duty."[33]

During that time J. E. Johnston's army lay one hundred and twenty miles east at Meridian, Mississippi. On July 28—with Lee's Army of Northern Virginia in desperate need of everything—Johnston's man Banks ordered another quarter million pounds of bacon from Atlanta.[34] Two days later the regular commissary at Meridian, John Shaaff, ordered half a million pounds. Northrop pointed out the duplication to Secretary Seddon; and that brought Banks's short career as supernumerary Johnstonian commissary to an end.[35]

* * *

Food had become scarce in markets throughout the South. In March 1863 there were food riots in North Carolina and then in Atlanta. In Richmond itself on April 2 a mob rampaged through the streets shouting "Bread or Blood!" They plundered stores of bacon, flour, shoes and other things. Full-scale looting threatened. A personal appeal from the Governor of Virginia was ignored. Only when President Davis himself appeared and made a heartfelt address, emptying his pockets and giving them all the money he had, did they disperse. Immediately afterwards there was similar rioting in Petersburg, Virginia. Smaller food riots broke out elsewhere. The Southern press was asked to keep silent about the riots, but news leaked out.

The press made up for their restraint by attacking the Commissary General. He had "criminally neglected his duties, or was incompetent to their performance," shouted *The Richmond Whig*: "Through his remissness, the Army is reduced to the point of starvation."[36] "The Commissary General and all his aides and advisers should be hung just as soon as a jury can be impanelled to convict." The authors of those sentiments seemed to learn nothing from the shortages in civilian markets all around them. When a reader asked if the accusations against the Commissary General were true, no answer was forthcoming in the papers.[37]

---

[33] Report dated from Mobile, Ala., August 6, 1863, to Northrop (*OR* ser. I, vol. 24, pt. 3, 1046-48). See also the report of the commissary agent at Vicksburg under Major Johnston's predecessors, Cuney and Broadwell (Ibid., 1051-52); and Johnston's report of stores on hand at Vicksburg, Port Hudson, etc., April 15, 1863 (Va. Hist. Soc.: Ruffin Papers). After the fall of Vicksburg, Northrop declined to reassign Major Johnston, recalling that the man had also served (or mis-served) Gen. McCullough in 1861-62 (Endorsement of October 31, 1863 to Adjutant General Cooper, M-474, r 69, f 621).

[34] *OR* ser. I, vol. 23, pt. 2, 934.

[35] Ibid., July 31, 1863, 934-35. See also Northrop to Davis, January 26, 1881 (Rowland, VIII, 584) and February 2, 1885 (Rowland, IX, 338).

[36] Quoted in Goff, *Confederate Supply*, 88.

[37] Thomas Robson Hay, "Lucius B. Northrop: Commissary General of the Confederacy", in *Civil War History*, vol. 9, no. 1 (March 1963), 9.

The truth was that nobody had ever offered any better comprehensive plans than Northrop's, or even (after the beginning of the war) any viable alternatives whatever. By the spring of 1863 there might or might not have been enough food left in the South—what remained of the South—to feed the citizens and the army, but equitable distribution could no longer be brought to bear.

For the spring of 1863 Lee planned a new campaign northward into enemy territory. On March 27 he reported to Seddon that his men were coming narrowly through the winter's privation; but what had barely sufficed for men at rest in winter camps would never support the demanding marches of Lee's planned offensive. He succeeded in getting his ration increased again beyond what Northrop thought prudent. Lee had told the Secretary of War that he understood every other Confederate army was better supplied than his own.[38]

Northrop made a tough endorsement on that. He wanted all the other Confederate armies reduced to Lee's old ration—"a measure quite appropriate to the present condition of the country".[39] Northrop forecast that Lee would soon be in want not only of meat, but once again of flour; he apologized to Seddon for bringing up the matter again, but reminded the Secretary of Lee's refusal to see Crenshaw on that very question. And he condemned the waste of time ever since. Lee had collected just enough food to feed his men but nothing over; and now again the general had other plans for his forces.[40]

Seddon begged Lee to assign the cavalry, as he moved north, to a food-collecting operation under Colonel Thomas Munford. Munford was requested by the entire commissariat in view of his intimate knowledge of the area.[41] Lee returned no answer about Munford. He said he was sending his nephew Brigadier General Fitzhugh Lee's brigade into Loudoun County because it happened to fit with tactical manoeuvres. Still he was doubtful: "As the enemy has a large force of cavalry in that region, I do not know how long I shall be able to keep this small brigade so far advanced...".[42] He said nothing about wagons.

All this time there were persistent failures in the shipments of meat from Atlanta. During April 1863 only a little actually reached the Army of Northern Virginia. When Northrop demanded an explanation, Cummings

---

[38] *OR* ser. I, vol. 25, pt. 2, 687.

[39] When General William Whiting in North Carolina ordered an increased ration, Northrop applied on April 9 for an order restricting his entire force, and Longstreet's, to one quarter pound of bacon. (M-437, r 103, f 371).

[40] *OR* ser. I, vol. 25, pt. 2, 688. In the light of all the correspondence it seems wrong to suppose with Freeman (*R. E. Lee*, III, 19) that a search for food was the unique guiding motive in Lee's plan for another campaign to the North. (Lee's aide Charles Marshall had thought the Maryland campaign of 1862 was primarily determined by a search for supplies, but not the campaign of 1863: see *An Aide-de-Camp of Lee*, 144-53, 157, 250-52.) Lee's hope for fresh fields of provisions was one item in a long list of possible advantages; the prospects remained very much as Lee himself had canvassed them in 1862. See above, p. 159; and Goff, *Confederate Supply*, 186.

[41] March 31, 1863 (*OR* ser. I, vol. 25, pt. 2, 693-94).

[42] Ibid., April 4, 1863, 703.

wrote from Atlanta (as Northrop summarized) "... that he was peremptorily ordered by General Johnston to stop everything else until he had supplied his army. He [Cummings] also furnishes a memorandum of the shipments made to that army in the month of April, as follows: 1,101,910 pounds of bacon, 102,055 pounds of cured beef, besides 923 head of beeves. This occurred while it was a critical question if General Lee's army could get provisions to hold its position." Then Northrop reported less than 17 million pounds of meat remaining in store for all the armies—nowhere near enough to last until next winter's bacon came in. The answer, repeated the Commissary General, must be to reduce the ration throughout the Confederate armies. In the winter just past, he added, one scarcity had worked to the commissariat's advantage: lack of salt for the populace had forced them to sell much fresh meat to the army. It would hardly happen again.[43]

In May 1863 Lee won a brilliant battle against superior Federal forces at Chancellorsville. In the bitterest irony at that moment of triumph, Stonewall Jackson was mortally wounded by the mistake of his own men. Lee grieved and was forced to reorganize his entire command structure as he pushed north. He gave occasional orders for his subordinates to assist the commissaries when military movements took them to appropriate areas.[44] Again they gathered only enough for immediate day-to-day needs.

While moving through Maryland towards Pennsylvania, Lee was out of reach of the Subsistence Bureau. On June 23 he wrote to Davis about his collections of food: "We use Confederate money for all payments. I shall continue to purchase all supplies that are furnished me north of the Potomac, impressing only when necessary."[45] Longstreet's forces had come up to join Lee's offensive, but it is not clear that they actually brought much from their North Carolina forages of the spring.[46]

With Longstreet came the English observer who had visited Johnston a month earlier, Colonel Fremantle. The Englishman described the attempts of Longstreet's commissary, Major Raphael Moses, to acquire a three days' supply of food at Chambersburg, Pennsylvania:

> Major Moses did not get back till very late, much depressed at the ill-success of his mission. He had searched all day most indefatigably, and had endured much contumely from the Union ladies, who called him "a thievish little rebel scoundrel", and other opprobrious epithets. But this did not annoy him so much as the manner in which everything he wanted had been sent away or hidden in private houses,

---

[43]   June 4, 1863 (*OR* ser. IV, vol. 2, 574-75). The Confederate Army as a whole continued well supplied with salt. The Avery mine in Louisiana had been lost to the Federals in April 1863, but the mines at Saltville, Virginia continued to produce prodigiously.

[44]   E.g. June 7, 1863 to Imboden and June 12 to Samuel Jones (*OR* ser. I, vol. 27, pt. 3, 865 and 885-86).

[45]   *Wartime Papers*, 530.

[46]   Too few papers appear to survive to make a judgment. See Raphael J. Moses, MS Autobiography (University of North Carolina) and Freeman, *Lee's Lieutenants*, II, 477-78. Cormier's *The Siege of Suffolk* claims success for Longstreet's food-gathering but admits that adequate documentation is lacking. My own feeling is that any appreciable success would have found some reflection in Lee's surviving papers.

which he was not allowed by General Lee's order to search. He had only managed to secure a quantity of molasses, sugar, and whiskey.

Poor Moses was thoroughly exhausted; but he endured the chaff of his brother officers with much good-humor, and they made him continually repeat the different names he had been called. He said that at first the women refused his Confederate "trash" [currency] with great scorn, but they ended in being very particular about the odd cents.[47]

On July 1 the Battle of Gettysburg began. After three days' fighting the Confederates could not continue because they were nearly out of ammunition. On July 4—the day Vicksburg surrendered in the West—Lee organized his retreat from Gettysburg. Dining next evening with Longstreet and his staff at a large tavern on the Hagerstown Road, Fremantle saw the proprietors' distress over the Southern commissaries' ruthless killing of their animals for food: "To all which expressions Longstreet replied, shaking his head in a melancholy manner—'Yes, madam, it's very sad—very sad; and this sort of thing has been going on in Virginia more than two years—very sad'."[48]

The long Confederate retreat through Maryland and the recently admitted Union state of West Virginia included Federal prisoners. The Federals' shock at their instant translation to the Southern commissariat was recalled by John Collins of the 8th Pennsylvania Cavalry: "We got about a pint of flour every other day, and with it now and then a piece of rusty flitch... While waiting for transportation to Richmond, we were amused to note the esteem in which the people held the Confederate money. Those who brought wares into our camp for sale at first refused to sell at all except for Federal money. When the officers threatened to expel from the camp any who did that, they would ask to see the money before naming the price, and if it was Federal, the pie was a quarter, but if Confederate, it would cost a dollar."[49]

Lee's own ranks had been thinned by desertion before Gettysburg. In the aftermath of retreat, desertion redoubled as another harvest-time approached. Virginia soldiers who knew that wives, mothers, children, and old men left on the farms and plantations would be hard pressed to get in enough crops to sustain even their own ragged families through another winter went to help them.

For those remaining in Lee's ranks, immediate sustenance was not a special problem. As they moved south through Virginia, Subsistence Bureau rations reached them again, and were supplemented by their own enterprise. Ned Moore remembered: "Soup was a favorite dish, requiring, as it did, but one vessel for all the courses, and the more ingredients it contained, the more it was relished. Merrick claimed to be an adept in the culinary art, and proposed to several of us that if we could 'club in' with him he would concoct a pot that would be food for the gods. He was to remain in camp, have the water boiling, and the meat [rations] sufficiently cooked by

[47]   *Three Months in the Southern States*, 249-50.
[48]   Ibid., 204.
[49]   "A Prisoner's March from Gettysburg to Staunton", in *Battles and Leaders*, III, 432-33.

the time the others returned from their various rounds in search of provender. In due time, one after another, the foragers showed up... As some fresh contribution, which he regarded as especially savory, was added, Merrick's countenance would brighten up... His handsome suit of clothes, donned at Hagerstown, was now in tatters, which made his appearance the more ludicrous as he cut the pigeon-wing around the seething cauldron."[50]

[51]

CONFEDERATE ARTILLERYMEN AT DINNER.

The food Lee's soldiers had then lingered in the memory of their Ordnance Chief, Colonel Edward P. Alexander, as "better rations than we ever got again".[52]

Behind the day-to-day feeding of Confederate armies in the field, and the hospitals, and the multiplying prisoners-of-war held in Richmond, Subsistence Bureau reserves continued to evaporate through the season of another harvest. Lee, his soldiers now resting, offered the Bureau no help in collecting any food beyond his own day-to-day needs. Northrop could not understand such lack of foresight, even if the men had been exhausted by fighting and marching, retreat and demoralization. The Commissary General's

---

[50]   Edward Moore, *The Story of a Cannoneer*, 187.

[51]   *Battles and Leaders*, III, 359.

[52]   Ibid., 745.

accumulated frustrations with Lee boiled over as he took his pen to the harshest sustained criticism he is known to have addressed by any Confederate commander.

> General:
> ... My last conversation with you respecting subsistence stores terminated by your stating substantially that the responsibility in that direction did not rest on you.
> There is, in my judgment, no isolating of responsibility in any of the machinery of war as a means of defense where loss of territory within which supplies alone can be got diminishes chances of supply and increases difficulties. While I do not feel troubled by any responsibility except that *in foro conscientiae*, I cannot satisfy myself therein without the above statement, and letting a man, whose views were so influential in preventing what I believed necessary, understand my present views of the situation of his army in respect to the chances of continued subsistence on the scale now existing.

He cited Bragg's huge uncontrolled drafts on the reserves in Atlanta. That left less than two million pounds of bacon there altogether. Only half a million pounds was available in Richmond.

> It is quite certain that want awaits both armies [Lee's and Johnston's], even on the supposition that our efforts to import from England are far more successful that heretofore. Not one of the contracts to import from the North [through enemy lines, still opposed by Davis] has been fruitful.
> A short time ago [before Gettysburg], failing to obtain from the Secretary of War authority to reduce the [meat] ration to one-quarter pound, I got his agreement to place the ration at one-third of a pound when not in actual movement, and one-half pound when at hard labor or on the march. I shall urge him now to make a further reduction of the one-third to one-fourth and the one-half to one-third.
> I write to inform you of the actual circumstances and those impending, and propose for your consideration the propriety of keeping your army on the most rigid construction of this rule.
> I am, general, very respectfully, your obedient servant,
> L.B. Northrop.
> Commissary General of Subsistence.[53]

A copy of this letter went to the Secretary of War. Six days later Northrop followed it up with a renewed demand on Lee for wagons to collect outlying stocks at harvest-time, all over Virginia. A total of four hundred wagons was needed, and the Commissary General detailed precisely how many were wanted for each district, where and why.[54]

A week later Lee replied to both letters. Clearly Northrop's expression of real anger had moved him. As he took up his pen, Lee's celebrated temperateness and self-control were never more in evidence. First he addressed the ration: "If the reduction is made, I think it ought to extend to all the armies, and not to this alone, as was the case last spring. ... I agree with you

---

[53]　July 23, 1863 (*OR* ser. I, vol. 51, pt. 2, 738).

[54]　*OR* ser. I, vol. 51, pt. 2, 742-44.

that every effort should be made to accumulate subsistence in Richmond. The necessities of this army and the uncertainty of depending upon our railroads render this apparent." Then came apparent an about-face over wagons: "Every assistance that I can give with the army transportation in collecting the grain and transporting it to the depots will be afforded, and immediately on the receipt of your letter, Colonel Corley was directed to furnish to the commissary agents you have named the number of wagons you require, or as many in proportion as could be spared for that purpose." There followed details of wagons and teams available: they were hardly a tithe of what Northrop had demanded. Even then Lee added a *caveat*: "As they form a part of the army transportation, and may be needed for its use at any time, there is an objection to turning them over to the commissary agents, but I desire they shall be used in the way you propose."[55]

In practice there were all sorts of difficulties with Lee's subordinate commanders.[56] It was not ill will—only shortage of supply in every useful article throughout the Confederate army. The wagons and teams actually made available to the Subsistence Bureau then, in the nick of time to gather the 1863 harvest, did undoubtedly make some increase of reserves for the Army of Northern Virginia and so staved off real want one more time. But not enough of anything was collected anywhere along the line to make any-one feel secure about the future.

Lee also supported Northrop's plea to limit passenger trains. On August 7, 1863 he wrote to urge Seddon "that when the freight trains cannot bring the usual supplies or sufficient supplies, that the passenger trains should be temporarily stopped, and the whole force of the road devoted to supplying the army."[57] But again nothing much was accomplished because Seddon would not even then risk such an exercise of dictatorial power in the face of en-trenched railroad interests, and Davis seemed always opposed to it.

Lee's earlier refusal to help repair the railroads came home to roost that autumn. The general himself would write to Secretary Seddon in November:

> The condition of the Virginia Central Railroad, on which we depend almost entirely for our supplies, seems to become worse every day. Col. Corley reports the frequent accidents of cars running off the track, and that the track in many places is very bad. I beg you to consult the President and Superintendent of the road as to what measures can be taken for its repair before the winter fairly sets in. ...
>
> If this cannot be done, the only alternative will be to fall back nearer to Richmond. This would leave not only the railroad, but the richest portion of the State of Virginia at the mercy of the enemy.[58]

It seemed to hint that Lee, having reversed himself over making wagons available, might also be willing to reverse also his refusal to detail expert men to repair the railroads. The hint would be taken up by Seddon a fort-night later.[59]

---

[55]   August 5, 1863 (*OR* ser. I, vol. 29, pt. 2, 625).
[56]   E.g., Arnold Elzey (*OR* ser. I, vol. 29, pt. 2, 655-59).
[57]   Ibid., 628.
[58]   November 12, 1863 (*Wartime Papers*, 622-23).
[59]   See below, 237.

Railroad affairs were in a parlous state. In the spring of 1863 the Confederate Congress, for reasons best known to itself, had refused to confirm Davis's appointment of William Wadley as Supervisor of Railroad Transportation.[60] A new man, Frederick William Sims, was put in his place. Sims was as good as Wadley, and equally ineffectual in persuading the government to take the measures needed. He was to insist, as Wadley had, that the only remedy for railroad dereliction was railroad repair.[61] Considering that no new rails had been rolled in the Confederacy since 1861, and that the government was now assenting to the dodge of removing rails from one point when they needed track somewhere else, Sims's objective was as remote from conquest in 1863 as the outer universe.

* * *

The farther west, the better the supply of food; it seemed an immutable law of Confederate production. After the fall of Vicksburg and the loss of the Confederate Mississippi River, General Edmund Kirby Smith had set up his own bureaus in his Trans-Mississippi territories. A hundred and twenty miles east of the river at Meridian, Mississippi, Joseph E. Johnston looked longingly at "Kirby Smithdom" as it was coming to be called. Much of the state of Mississippi enjoyed a bumper harvest in 1863. If Johnston could control the commissaries and quartermasters in his territory as Kirby Smith controlled his, his army would be self-sufficient in all but meat. So Johnston began another lengthy, complaining correspondence with and about the Subsistence Bureau: it lasted all the autumn.[62]

Three hundred miles northeast of Johnston, his Subordinate General Bragg had the Army of Tennessee encamped near the southern border of that state at Chattanooga. His had been a rapid retreat. In July 1863 Bragg had allowed a Federal force under Rosecrans to push him south out of Tullahoma. Thereupon Bragg decided that the whole of middle Tennessee was untenable; he pulled back to Chattanooga. Rosecrans moved forward to threaten him again, and Bragg prepared another retreat—all the while pointing to small successes. "Damn this way of beating the Yankees and then running away from them!" said one of Bragg's demoralized soldiers. Asked where they were retreating to this time, another exclaimed: "To Cuba—if old Bragg can get a bridge built across from Florida."[63] The Tennessee lands which Bragg was in the process of finally losing had been the Confederacy's best remaining source of bacon. From late August 1863 Bragg was drawing more bacon than ever from the Atlanta reserves.

On August 25 Bragg's commissary, Major Giles Hillyer, reported on his current stocks. However short they might appear in meat, they still made a

---

[60]   The author of the standard work, Robert C. Black, confesses that he does not understand Wadley's dismissal (*The Railroads of the Confederacy*, 122-23).

[61]   October 23; 1863 to Quartermaster General (*OR* ser. IV, vol. 2, 881-83).

[62]   Johnston's first letter in this series was dated September 20, 1863 (*OR* ser. I, vol. 30, pt. 4, 673). Further letters will be found in Ibid., 702; and Ser. I, vol. 31, pt. 3, 587, 598-99, 613-14, 682-83, 714.

[63]   Digby Gordon Seymour, *Divided Loyalties: Fort Sanders and the Civil War in East Tennessee* (University of Tennessee, 1963), 74.

telling contrast to the scarecrow commissariat of Lee. After feeding his men on the last day of August, Hillyer would have on hand:

Breadstuffs	1,100,000	rations.	I have no fear...
Rice and Peas	3,000,000	rations.	No probable difficulty...large stores still remaining in the rear.
Vinegar	1,200,000	rations.	No probable difficulty ...
Soap	3,000,000	rations.	" " "
Salt	4,500,000	rations.	" " "
Sugar	150,000	pounds.	
Molasses	300,000	rations.	
Fresh beef	None.		
Bacon, salt beef, lard	900,000	rations.	... Only 15 days' supply...

Hillyer enclosed sub-reports from Cummings in Atlanta and R. T. Wilson (now Chief Commissary at Loudon, Tenn.) from whom he was drawing meat. Wilson could promise no more than 100,000 pounds of fresh beef and 20,000 pounds of bacon twice a month. He wrote: "There is no use of shutting our eyes to the fact that there is no bacon worth speaking of in the country, and that if it can't be had from beyond the limits of this state, the armies can't be supplied." Cummings reported to Hillyer from Atlanta:

> ... I have not to-day exceeding 800,000 pounds [of bacon] all told on hand, and my shipments to Richmond average over 50,000 pounds per day, and my orders from Richmond are to ship all bacon on hand as rapidly as possible.
>
> In addition to my shipments to Richmond, I am making daily shipments to other points: therefore I estimate that within twenty days—thirty at the outside—from this time I will be entirely out of bacon.

Cummings could supply Hillyer with breadstuffs, he said, "unless I am peremptorily ordered to ship to Richmond."

> Only a few days since I received an order from the Commissary General of Subsistence directing me to ship as quietly and rapidly as possible all the wheat I had on hand or could accumulate to Richmond, over and above the absolute wants of the armies that were dependent upon me. I answered I could barely supply the requisitions of flour for the armies in my immediate neighborhood, therefore could not make shipments to Richmond unless specially ordered.

As to beef cattle, he promised to have his entire stock in west Georgia driven to Hillyer. Cummings said he had more in southwest Georgia, but lacked reliable transport to get them out:

> My agents in Southwest Georgia report that the principal part of the transportation is being taken for the use of the Army of Virginia in transporting corn, therefore I conclude that the prospect of feeding the Army of Tennessee is quite gloomy.[64]

---

[64]   *OR* ser. I, vol. 30, pt. 4, 547-52.

When Commissary Hillyer sent in these reports to his chief, Bragg endorsed to the Secretary of War: "The morale of this army is being seriously injured by this cause principally, and desertions, some to the enemy, are not uncommon."[65] But Northrop, who had already lived through Lee's worry about starvation when starvation did not turn up, and equally aware of the soldiers' despair under Bragg's leadership, rejoined: "General Bragg admits serious demoralization in his army; he attributes it to the prospect of impending want of subsistence one month ahead... An army with far less rations than his army has had, if operating actively, will not become demoralized."[66] That was another Northrop endorsement which would gain his Bureau no friends.

Cummings's report had alluded to one possible new source for beef: "My agents in Florida write me that there is an abundance of cattle there, but the people are indisposed to sell them for our currency and drivers cannot be had." The existence of herds in Florida had been well known from the beginning of the war. Northrop had tried unsuccessfully in 1861-62 to get them, but was opposed by Florida's States' Rights Governor Milton. Now better counsels seemed to prevail, but the difficulties remained formidable.

Florida's long peninsula was in many places a honeycomb of seacoast and swamp. Its one useful port, Pensacola, had been abandoned to the Federals by Bragg when he moved to concentrate in the West. The Federals also held various offshore Florida forts, from which their navy raked up and down the coasts with some regularity. Railroads were almost non-existent: two lonely lines wandered across the extreme north of the state, neither connecting with the main network in Georgia and beyond. The only way to get Florida cattle to the Confederate armies, therefore, was to drive them over many miles.

Florida's population numbered fewer than 150,000. Half were slaves, and a considerable number were Indians. None of them had much reason to favor the Confederacy, and the Indians were likely to be hostile to any incursion. Into their vast and trackless swamps whole herds could be made to vanish in an hour. And the semi-wild cattle themselves were often stampeded by snakes or the sudden tearing storms that blew up with tropic ferocity. Florida humidity produced malaria more threatening than anywhere else in North America. And many places where the ground was less swampy were covered with endless stretches of sawgrass capable of cutting man or beast to ribbons if they tried to pass through.

Yet one event more than any other had put Florida on the Confederate subsistence map: the fall of Vicksburg. With the loss of the last Confederate control on the Mississippi, it seemed unlikely that they would be able to swim many more cattle from the west. At the same moment Beauregard, in

---

[65]   Ibid., August 26, 1863, 547.

[66]   Ibid., September 4, 1863, 550.

Charleston harbor, faced the beginning of the Federal siege he had long anticipated. His troops were chronically under-supplied with meat, so he too looked to Florida.

The recent laws enacting Bureau impressment and the tithing tax-in-kind had now produced a Chief Commissary for each state. In Florida the man was Brevet Major Pleasant W. White—chosen, Northrop wrote, "after much deliberation & much consultation with the leading men of that State. He was considered a man of great energy & capacity for business, & of high character. This reputation he has fully sustained since his appointment, as will be shown by the records of this Bureau."[67] As with virtually all of the state Chief Commissaries appointed in 1863, the choice of White proved again Northrop's ability to select a good man. Everybody agreed about White, including the generals.[68]

White had his work cut out for him. His biggest problem was manpower. Only a very few experienced natives, who happened to be sympathetic to the Confederate cause, could be trusted to drive Florida cattle over the many miles of danger-ridden paths that would bring them to any useful railhead. And those few were relentlessly pursued by conscripting officers anxious to fill quotas. Nonetheless by August 1863 White was organizing large drives, though he could never achieve the 3,000 head per week called for by Northrop's Bureau and the generals. His drovers began in north Florida, where distances were shortest. When they did reach a railhead, bad track and trains requisitioned elsewhere often forced them to drive the beasts all the way to Savannah in the East or Atlanta in the West—distances of two and three hundred miles. As cattle in north Florida were exhausted, the drovers moved south down the peninsula: every such move increased the length of drives.

The season for cattle driving in Florida was from early spring—as early as February, when new grass extended grazing northwards—to August, when the fierce summer sun had parched all but the swamps to tinder for forest fires. Yet August was still months ahead of curing time for new bacon, and Confederate armies were living off the last old bacon. So the pressing need for Florida cattle came just when the regular driving season was at an end. To drive the cattle beyond August was to risk starving them on the long marches. Still throughout the autumn of 1863 the clamor for them increased on all sides. Cummings in Atlanta actually persuaded White to accept a special agent to come to Florida with the brief of getting cattle for the commands he fed.[69] Chief Commissary Guerin of South Carolina dispatched an officer of his own to check up on White and find out why he was sending no more than one-third of his diminishing cattle stock to Charleston. He too found a good officer working at full stretch.[70]

---

[67] December 7, 1863 to Adjt. Gen. Cooper (NYPL: Northrop Papers).

[68] That would not prevent J. E. Johnston from perpetrating a particularly nasty snipe against those who fed him under Northrop's Subsistance Bureau—"officers who have not been thought by the Government competent to the duties of high military grades" (Quoted in Johnston, *Narrative of Military Operations*, 266).

[69] Much of the above information is indebted to Robert A. Taylor, "Rebel Beef: Florida Cattle and the Confederate Army, 1862-1864", in *Florida Historical Quarterly*, vol. 67, no. 1 (July 1988), 15-31.

[70] Major C. McClenaghan to Guerin, October 29, 1863 (*OR* ser. I, vol. 28, pt. 2, 459-62).

Major White, his energies at breaking point, wrote to Northrop on October 5 of his personal searches for cattle right down into south Florida—of having "ridden through mud and water by day and night among alligators and insects".[71] What he found was not encouraging, and people everywhere less and less willing to sell for Confederate money. White summarized the position in a semi-private circular addressed only to leading Floridians and dated November 2, 1863. He quoted from begging letters sent to him during October—from Guerin in Charleston; from Major Locke, the Chief Commissary of Georgia; from Cummings in Atlanta; from Major Millen in Savannah. Every one expressed utmost urgency and near-complete dependence on Florida cattle. The production of bacon throughout the Confederacy during the coming winter was expected to be inadequate: "This makes it the duty of every man to economize as much as possible, to sell not a pound to anyone else while there is any danger of our army suffering, and to pledge at schedule rates his entire surplus bacon, beef, sugar, and syrup to the Government. I solemnly believe our cause is hopeless unless our people can be brought to this point. ... You are especially requested not to allow this circular to go out of your possession, but to read it to such persons as you know to be true and prudent, and to begin the work contemplated immediately."[72]

In the event White and his men gave the Confederate armies a large proportion of their meat throughout the autumn of 1863—right outside the driving season.[73] But by December White's men everywhere in Florida were reporting that they no longer had any cattle capable of surviving the immense length of drives north on trails without any real grazing at that season. Impressment played an ever larger role. Before the end of the year Governor Milton was receiving anguished protests from his citizenry that every milch cow in the state was being driven away by impressors: families of serving soldiers were being stripped.[74] At the end of 1863, Major White estimated that 30,000 head of cattle had been driven out of Florida by properly constituted officers. How many more had gone to private parties under color of impressment no one could say.

The late months of 1863 saw a final defeat of Confederate arms in most of Tennessee. After the Federals under Rosecrans had pushed Bragg over the border into Georgia, everybody realized that something must be done. In early September, Davis had detached Longstreet's forces from Lee and sent them west to assist Bragg. That large movement revealed the state of Southern railroads mercilessly. Longstreet's Assistant Adjutant General Gilbert Moxley Sorrel recalled: "Never before were so many troops moved over such worn-out railways... Never before were so many crazy cars—passenger, baggage, mail, coal, box, platform, all and every sort, wobbling on

---

[71]   Robert Taylor, "Rebel Beef", 21.

[72]   *OR* ser. I, vol. 28, pt. 2, 471-74.

[73]   See Northrop's endorsement of March 15, 1864 on a complaint from Governor Milton: "This circular of Maj. White's was productive of the most material results." (M-437, r 135, f 317).

[74]   *OR* ser. IV, vol. 3, 47.

the jumping strap iron—used for hauling good soldiers. But we got there, nevertheless."[75] Longstreet's men were indeed good soldiers and their commander saw chances that Bragg could not or would not recognize. Together they managed to smash the Federals at Chickmauga—Bragg's greatest victory, if it was Bragg's—and retake Chattanooga.

Longstreet found what everyone else found west of the Atlantic coast states—that western Confederates ate better than Lee. Longstreet's only trouble came from Georgia's being a "dry" state. Preparing for the battle of Chickmauga, Longstreet had positioned his artillery: "... and then I rode away to enjoy my spread of Nassau bacon and Georgia sweet potatoes. We were not accustomed to potatoes of any kind in Virginia, and we thought we had a luxury, but it was very dry, as the river was a mile and more from us, and other liquids were over the border."[76]

Nothing followed the Confederate victory at Chickmauga, though Longstreet pleaded with Bragg to use the whole Southern force against Knoxville. Bragg refused. A month later Bragg, with much ill will and only at the special request of Davis, detached Longstreet to lay siege to Knoxville by himself with an insufficient force. When Longstreet went there, he found no provisions—because Bragg had ordered them all, together with the Confederate troops already near Knoxville, back on the same train that had brought Longstreet.[77] Then it was the turn of Longstreet's men to be demoralized: they did no good at Knoxville and soon had to retreat.

Bragg meanwhile allowed Grant, who had replaced Rosecrans, to lever him out of Chattanooga once more and back over the Georgia border. Then at last, at the end of 1863 and at Bragg's own request, he was replaced as commander of the Army of Tennessee by Joseph E. Johnston. General Joe had not wanted the job at all. He had been rusticating in the rich commissary district of Mississippi. As soon as he had to join Bragg's army at Dalton, Georgia in December 1863, the picture changed. The Dalton district was poor. So Johnston would now have to depend on Northrop's system of one district aiding another—the system he had spent his time in Mississippi complaining about and trying to overthrow.

---

[75] Recollections of a Confederate Staff Officer (New York: Neale, 1905), 189.
[76] Longstreet, From Manassas to Appomattox (Philadelphia: Lippincott, 1896), 451.
[77] Ibid., 486.

CHAPTER 18

PRISONERS OF INFLATION

At the beginning of the war neither side had large facilities for holding prisoners of war. They were routinely exchanged with little formality. As attitudes hardened, prisons were laid out or converted from old forts and city
warehouses. An elaborately drafted formal convention for exchanging prisoners was agreed upon after much negotiation in July 1862. It did not prevent continuous misunderstandings and some bad faith on either side. Federal authorities appeared to interrupt the exchanges whenever they found
they held more Confederate prisoners than the Confederates held of theirs.
Confederate authorities retaliated, and by the summer of 1863, amid mutual recrimination, the exchanges practically ground to a halt.[1]

In and about Richmond were 13,000 Federal prisoners, held there in
hopes of renewed exchanges. They were nominally in charge of the Confederate Quartermaster General, but actually controlled by the Provost Marshal
and Commandant of Prisons, Brigadier General John H. Winder.[2] The divided authority worked because Quartermaster General Myers basically left
the job to Winder and his own commissary, Captain Jackson Warner.

Warner operated a budget for feeding the prisoners of war that was
out of control—not only of the Subsistence Bureau but of government price
schedules. One measure of the abuse emerged in an offer to Winder from a
Richmond speculator to furnish beef cattle to the prisoners at 80 cents a
pound—"providing you can protect them from the Government agents."[3]

---

[1] The best history of these matters is W. B. Hesseltine, *Civil War Prisons* (Columbus, Ohio State
University, 1930): see especially 7-34, 69-114, 254 ff. The numbers of prisoners held on either side and
the quality of their lives have always been contentious issues. Summaries from Southern and Northern
viewpoints respectively can be found in E. Merton Coulter, *The Confederate States of America* (LSU,
1950) 470-81; and James M. McPherson, *Battle Cry of Freedom* (OUP, 1988) 792-802. They agree in
dismissing charges of calculated cruelty on either side.

[2] See Arch Fredric Blakey, *General John H. Winder C.S.A.* (Gainesville: Univ. of Florida, 1990).
Blakey's book is a major piece of difficult research, on the whole triumphantly brought off. He makes the
plausible suggestion that Winder and Northrop were similar personalities. Unfortunately his apparent
failure to grasp the fact that feeding prisoners of war was the responsibility of the Quartermaster General
until 1863 renders vague several of his accounts of Northrop, Jackson Warner, and their quarrels. In
peripheral matters his book offers much information not easily available elsewhere.

[3] October 28, 1863 (*OR* ser. II, vol. 6, 440).

The schedule-price for beef in Virginia then was 25 cents.[4] With prices like that, Winder and Warner could buy what they liked. So they drove up prices and competition against Subsistence Bureau agents trying to buy food for Lee's army in the same markets at schedule-prices. The result was that the prisoners fared much better than Confederate soldiers in the field.

The volume of food for prisoners also made a heavy tax on the more and more inadequate transport system of railroads, wagons, and even boats near the capital. One officer's recollection is graphic. He had just returned from Lee's camps, where they had no meat. Now he was to visit the Richmond prisoner of war camp at Belle Isle: "To my astonishment, when I reached the little wharf where I was to be boated across the river, I saw more meat awaiting transportation there than I had seen for months in or near Richmond. Captain Jackson Warner ... was in the act of transferring to them beef enough to feed them for days."[5]

Northrop knew all this. He had tried repeatedly without success to equalize the rations between prison and field. That equality was laid down in the army regulations of both sides. But Provost Marshal Winder was a tough man, determined to protect his bailiwick: he insisted on procuring as much as possible of the full ideal ration prescribed by Regulations, whatever the shortages on the Confederate field. The resulting quarrels often reached Secretary Seddon. Winder evidently got his way repeatedly—to Northrop's outrage.[6]

Fuel was added to the fire in the summer of 1863 by reports of conditions among Confederate prisoners of war locked up in Fort Delaware, a marshy island building recently designated by the Federals as a permanent prison. Confederates were crammed into the fort until there were eight thousand. The Federal Surgeon General warned that the place was dangerously overcrowded. His recommendations for relief were ignored by the Federal Commissary General of Prisons. Scurvy broke out, then smallpox. When the news reached Richmond, Robert Kean wrote in his diary of "the diabolism of this *policy*, for such it undoubtedly is, to destroy our soldiers by the most miserable of deaths. The devilish malignity of that people passes belief and comprehension...".[7] It was a rhetoric which the Federals would return with interest.

In August 1863 Quartermaster General Myers was dismissed by the President. Davis had particularly wished to get rid of Myers before the next session of Congress. Myers had friends in Congress who wanted him promoted to brigadier general—and who had managed in their previous session to get it enacted that the office of Quartermaster General should carry

---

[4]   September 30, 1853 (*OR* ser. IV, vol. 2, 836).

[5]   "Col. C. S. Armee" (identified by William C. Davis as Charles Stuart), "Rummaging through Rebeldom" No. 16, in *The New York Citizen*, July 27, 1867.

[6]   Seddon to Winder's son, December 29, 1875 (*SHSP*, I, 206).

[7]   *Inside the Confederate Government* (entry for August 2, 1863), 89.

a brigadier's rank. Davis seized on that (between sessions of Congress) as a means for dismissing Myers—since he had not yet attained the now-pre-scribed rank—in favor of someone more to his own liking. His choice fell on Alexander Lawton of Georgia, an able field officer just recovering from serious wounds.[8]

Northrop quickly met with Lawton in Secretary Seddon's office over the prisoner of war rations. They decided:

1. that the Commissary General should henceforth assume the duty of subsisting prisoners of war.

2. that prisoners of war should be subsisted as Confederate soldiers so long as supplies held out; if it became necessary to subsist Confederate soldiers at posts on less than those in the field, the prisoners should feed as soldiers at posts; "and if at any time or finally it unhappily became impossible to furnish even reduced rates of meat to both the soldiers and the prisoners, the soldiers should be preferred."[9]

Northrop repeatedly urged Seddon to move the prisoners away from Richmond. The Commissary General wanted them to be sent south, where winters were warmer and food supplies available that would not subtract directly from Lee.[10] Lee supported Northrop with two further reasons: the tax the prisoners' presence imposed on transport around Richmond, and the potential danger their large numbers would pose in the event of enemy attack on the capital.[11]

Lee suggested Danville, southwest of Richmond and close to the North Carolina border, as a site for keeping the Richmond prisoners. Northrop did not really like the choice, as Seddon recalled: "I did not understand the Commissary General to insist exactly against the selection of Danville ... but while I was considering the propriety of sending them there he certainly urged, as a consideration against it, that it would be difficult to subsist them, both because some of the counties around were believed to have had a deficient crop and because there was no direct railroad communication from the south [i.e., from anywhere in the Confederate food chain but Richmond]. Other considerations, however, left me, I thought, no other reasonable alternative, and a limited number were sent there."[12] Again Seddon rejected Northrop's appeal to move the bulk of the prisoners out of Richmond, because he kept hoping to resuscitate the exchange cartel.

Meanwhile Winder's commissary, Captain Warner, was raising every obstacle to the Commissary General's control. In September 1863 the new Quartermaster General had to order Warner to comply. Then within a fortnight supplies of beef for the prisoners began running short. The Subsistence butcher was ordered by Northrop to fill meat requisitions for hospi-

---

[8] A useful background summary appears in Goff, *Confederate Supply*, 142-44.

[9] Summarized by Seddon in *OR* ser. II, vol. 6, 821.

[10] Statement by Ruffin, Seth Barton French, and Burr Noland, July 25, 1865 (Copy certified correct by French, now in Georgetown archives).

[11] October 28, 1863 to Seddon (*OR* ser. II, vol. 6, 438-39).

[12] *OR* ser. II, vol. 6, 821.

tals before those of Confederate soldiers at posts or prisoners. When meat was short, soldiers at posts and prisoners were given double rations of bread and vegetables.[13]

Warner and Winder made a terrific fuss. Poor Quartermaster General Lawton endorsed on October 28: "The Commissary Department and General Winder never seem to agree, and I respectfully ask the interposition of the Secretary of War."[14] Winder also refused to recognize Northrop's authority until ordered to do so by Seddon.[15] Then Winder told Seddon that the prisoners were close to revolt: " ... No force under my command can prove adequate to the control of 13,000 hungry prisoners."[16] How real was that threat? Northerners were accustomed to more quantity and quality than Confederates, so it would need less deprivation to set their hunger on the rampage. Yet in the event the Yankee prisoners never did revolt.

The prison commissary Warner retailed his own complaints to all and sundry. They were picked up by the anti-Davis press. The *Richmond Examiner* editor Pollard was to use material developed from that time in several books written after the war. Pollard then drew a picture of Warner as almost without food for his prisoners:

> The next day Captain Warner represented to General Winder ... that they were in the actual pangs of hunger. He was directed at once to make a requisition on Colonel Northrop, the cross-grained and eccentric Commissary General—an officer whose idea of importance was to have a fit of insolence whenever he was approached, and who was either gruff or hysterical in his official intercourses.
> "I know nothing of Yankee prisoners," he said; "throw them all into the James River!"
> "At least," said Captain Warner, "tell me how I am to keep my accounts for the prisoners' subsistence."
> "Sir," said Northrop, slightly inclining his eyes to the anxious inquirer, "I have not the will or the time to speak with you. Chuck the scoundrels into the river!"
> Here was a quandary. There was no law to charge the Commissary General with the subsistence of prisoners; he insisted that it belonged to the quartermaster's department; the latter denied it, and, in a dead-lock of quibbles the prisoners might be left to starve.[17]

The final paragraph shows the confusion engendered by the divided authority over prisoners. Pollard's (and presumably Warner's, for Pollard cites no other source) chronology is garbled. Northrop could not have denied his responsibility to feed his prisoners of war after the convention approved in August 1863: so this part of the story could only relate to a time before then. Yet the account of Winder sending Warner to the Commissary General could

---

[13] Ibid., 951.

[14] Ibid., 439.

[15] Ibid., 457.

[16] Ibid., 439.

[17] Pollard, *Life of Jefferson Davis, with a Secret History of the Southern Confederacy* (*rpr* Freeport, N.Y.: Books for Libraries Press, 1969), 338-40.

not have taken place before October 31, 1863, when Seddon ordered Winder to look to the Commissary General for prisoners' food.

The point should be carefully noted, because of what was later made of those words attributed to Northrop. In view of his short temper and the continual harassment he was under by 1863, it is conceivable that Northrop might have uttered some such words when the prisoners' feeding was not in his control. If he said them after he achieved that control, they can only have been a momentary by-product of anger at Winder's and Warner's continued attempts to get the prisoners better food than Lee's soldiers could have.

Clearly, from Northrop's repeated attempts to have the prisoners sent away from Richmond to the South so they could be better fed, it would have been farthest from his mind seriously to advocate their extermination. Moreover any deliberate attempt to starve prisoners of war would fly in the face of every regulation ever laid down for any modern western army; and Northrop was a famous stickler for regulations. Yet the notion that he wished to impair the lives of Federal prisoners of war was claimed after the war by outraged Northerners—who basically cited Pollard for their evidence.[18]

It is perhaps a part of the evidence that Northrop had previously declined to appoint Warner to the Subsistence Bureau. That might have given Warner a grudge. Northrop was to set down his own view in a letter written to Davis in later years: "The only wrong ever done to prisoners by a Confederate officer was by Capt Warner, Gnl Winder's commissary. He was from Ohio. [Assistant Secretary of War A. T.] Bledsoe wanted me to appoint him; I would not. He got the commission [for prison commissary]. ... He sent off a batch of prisoners once without food enough; they suffered. It was raked up & I found that this fellow had deliberately sent them off unsupplied though he was offered precisely the provisions then issued to the troops in Richmond."[19] The only conceivable object of such an action would have been to embarrass the Commissary General.

* * *

Through the autumn of 1863 Northrop stayed in the forefront of every endeavor to reform the railroads. He pleaded with the government to repair road and rail bridges vital to supplying Lee from south of Richmond.[20] He was still trying to have cattle swum across from the Trans-Mississippi, despite the Confederate loss of the river.[21] Occasionally he could even find a little humor in some "new" suggestion. One was the notion of establishing government fisheries, sent from Georgia with overflowing Biblical rhetoric:

> The infamous enemy who invades our country threatens to starve us into submission. God said: "Let the waters bring forth abundantly," and it was done. He gave to man dominion over the fish of the sea. In

---

[18]   See Northrop's later views of such a notion, quote below pp. 286, 289, 301.

[19]   May 9, 1878 (Rowland, VII, 271, where it is mistakenly assigned to 1870).

[20]   *OR* ser. I, vol. 29, pt. 2, 364-66.

[21]   On November 19 Northrop had Seddon point out to both Kirby Smith and J. E. Johnston the present low stage of the river, and urge them to cooperate over cattle (*OR* ser. I, vol. 53, 914; vol. 31, pt. 3, 714).

our rivers, lakes, and bays there is an inexhaustible supply of fish, which in our abundance we have never resorted to.

Could they not turn their invalids and wounded soldiers into gentle fishermen? Northrop endorsed:

> The writer has not shown from Scripture that the promised dominion over the waters and the fishes therein will confer on the 10,000 Confederate invalids and exempts the skill to fabricate all the appliances necessary to catch the fish or the judgment, perseverance, and hardihood requisite to use them successfully, even if the vast amount of cord needed was obtainable.
>
> Nor has it been shown that in the absence of these facilities and endowments the promised dominion will cause in the fish a due avidity to be caught ...
>
> It must also be shown that the promised dominion over the waters will be admitted by Mr. Lincoln in favor of the Confederates, and induce him to prohibit hereafter the boat expeditions which have been used with great activity heretofore to break up the fisheries in the waters of Virginia and North Carolina.
>
> This whole subject has long ago been carefully considered, and but little fish has been secured ...[22]

One hope for more meat remained in importation from England. The Erlanger loan had produced £262,500 as the War Department's share, and in October 1863 Seddon divided it up thus:

Quartermaster's Department	£85,000
Ordnance Department	55,500
Commissary Department	40,000
Medical Department	30,000
Nitre and Mining Department	40,000
Engineer Department	12,000.[23]

Unfortunately the blockade-running ships commissioned by William Crenshaw were dogged with misfortune. One of the five had been chased onto North Carolina sands while attempting to sail into Wilmington harbor in August, and destroyed. Another met a similar fate in October. Yet some meat was entering the country. Crenshaw had meanwhile formed a new company, with which Northrop signed a contract in November to import 3 million pounds of meat.[24]

A month earlier Northrop made another contract with the Wilmington firm of Power, Low & Co. These importers, granted high profits, were to use British ships of the Liverpool firm Edward Lawrence & Co. "They all went to work with promptness and fidelity," wrote Frank Ruffin.[25] The Power, Low contract was to produce the greatest supply of bacon for the Confederate army from any single source in 1864.

---

[22] October 24, 1863 (*OR* ser. IV, vol. 2, 916-18).

[23] *OR* ser. IV, vol. 3, 241.

[24] Wise, *Lifeline of the Confederacy*, 144. See also a MS memorandum from Lewis Crenshaw (Va. Hist. Soc.: Ruffin Papers R 8386a, 57-58).

[25] *The New York Herald*, July 21, 1865, 3.

At home, however, all the efforts of Northrop and his Bureau were beginning to be neutralized. There were two basic linked causes—inflation and increasing shortages of every useful thing throughout the Confederacy. The results could be seen in the cost per ration of army food. In 1861 it had been 25 cents. By 1863 it was $1.12 and rising by the month, with many more soldiers to feed.

When the new Acts of Impressment and Tithes-in-Kind demanded the publication of official price-schedules, it had been decided to fix the schedule-prices well below market values to try to put a brake on inflation. At the end of May 1863 in Richmond, the War Department clerk Jones (one of the hordes of government workers struggling harder and harder to support a family on government wages) copied into his diary a comparison of actual market prices from a local newspaper with the Virginia schedule-prices published then. It showed the schedule-prices ranging from 70 percent all the way down to 20 percent of market prices. That was assuming the articles were for sale in the market at all; some were not.[26]

The people hated it. As soon as the new Subsistence Bureau impressments were applied, they set up a sustained bellow of rage. The limitations on Bureau impressment did nothing to prevent popular opinion (with some expert guidance from the anti-Davis press) from attributing every high-handed impressment of food to Subsistence Bureau officers. During the summer and autumn of 1863 the name of the Bureau became odious everywhere. One editorial published in *The Daily Mississippian* and sent to the Secretary of War may stand for all: "In many counties it has been quite common for pert, insolent, and not unfrequently [*sic*] self-constituted officials to pounce upon every thing they may happen to fancy... Heads of families with several small children to feed are in the habit of hiding their scanty supplies of bacon, corn and salt—sometimes burying it in the ground—to save it from impressment. ... The effect of indiscriminate impressments without, as it is very often the case, any payment whatever, is a widespread feeling of insecurity—a dread of Confederate cavalry, second only to the dread of Yankee robbers, and a slow but certain alienation of the people from the Government."[27]

Although that clearly involved more than the Subsistence Bureau, Secretary Seddon sent it straight to Northrop. The Commissary General "splutters over it in his angular chirography at a furious rate" (in the observation of Jones).[28] Northrop's endorsement drew yet again the distinction laid down in law between Bureau impressment and field impressment powers, and reassured the Secretary that his men observed it scrupulously.[29]

Yet nothing Northrop did or said could quell the rising tide of accusation, reaching into the government itself. Jones wrote in his diary: "Everywhere the people are clamorous against the sweeping impressments of crops,

---

[26]   *Diary*, I, 335-37. Up the government roster, Kean of the War Bureau was finding the same difficulties (*Inside the Confederate Government*, 108).

[27]   September 18, 1863 (M-437, r 105, ff 917-18).

[28]   *Diary*, II, 56.

[29]   September 28, 1863: quoted above p. 201.

horses, etc. And at the same time we have accounts of corn, and hay, and potatoes rotting at various depots! Such is the management of the bureaus."[30] Such, if he had stopped to think about it, was the management of Confederate transport. Yet if a clerk privy to War Department papers could think such things, it was a measure of what was being concluded by those who knew less. The story was the same among those who knew more, or should have done. War Bureau chief Kean (who had been up to that time consistently friendly to Northrop) wrote on October 4 of "the persistent folly of the commissariat, which systematically seizes everything which in any quantity starts to market."[31]

On November 2 Northrop was driven to ask Seddon to retract the power of the Richmond City Council to purchase food for its poor. Seddon refused. Northrop tried to get Kean to back him up: the time had arrived, said the Commissary General, to choose between people and army. Kean went to Seddon—to be told that the only real problem was the recovery of Tennessee, and "that Colonel Northrop's statements were exaggerated to make an impression for his present purpose...".[32]

Protests against the new impressment came in from the Governors of North Carolina, South Carolina, Florida, and Georgia. Georgia's Governor Brown went so far as to question the central government's right to impress anything in his state. When Secretary Seddon assured him of the existence of that right, the Governor pleaded for "the absolute importance and necessity" of revising schedule-prices to match market values.[33] From Georgia also came a letter to Northrop written by the commissary of the Savannah district, Major M. B. Millen, charged with driving cattle to Atlanta. Major Millen was being ground between the protests of Governor Brown and the depredations of conscripting officers hungry to fill their ever-expanding draft quotas with his expert cattle drovers impossible to replace:

> From one third to a half of my time has lately been taken up in endeavoring to retain my men until something can be decided upon.
> ... We are now about at a stand still in our purchases. These delays and difficulties will result in empty depots in a few months and an army in the field without food, and of course the people will say it is all the fault of an *in*-efficient commissariat.
> I expect before the war closes that all commissaries will be hung as high as Hamaan—on which occasion the order I presume will be the higher the Grade the more lofty the limb.[34]

As the disparities between real and schedule-prices produced more and more speculation, black markets and hoarding, the effects reached into the Confederate army. On November 20, 1863 Jones recorded: "A private soldier writes the Secretary to-day that his mother is in danger of starving—

---

[30]   *Diary*, II, 103.
[31]   *Inside the Confederate Government*, 106.
[32]   Ibid., 117.
[33]   November 9, 1863 (*OR* ser. IV, vol. 2, 943-44).
[34]   October 5, 1863 (M-437, r 109, ff 729-30).

as she failed to get flour in Richmond at $100 per barrel. He says that if the Government has no remedy for this, he and his comrades will throw down their arms and fly to some other country with their families, where a subsistence may be obtained."[35]

The same price-disparities fuelling inflation were also withdrawing supplies from Lee's soldiers. At nearly the same moment Jones made his diary entry, Virginia Chief Commissary Burr Noland was reporting to Northrop a rise in actual prices of all the prime foods by a hundred percent in a month. The publication of schedule-prices was actually preventing Subsistence Bureau impressment, since Bureau men were prohibited from impressing food in transit to markets, or for immediate consumption. Noland begged Northrop to find some way to get those limitations lifted:

> The [popular] construction given to that Order has filled the land with purchasers—private individuals—R. Road companies—manufacturers of all kinds—corporations of every class—Relief Associations of cities, towns, & counties, all personally, or by their agents in the market, buying a *year's* supply; unlimited as to price, & protected from impressment.
>
> Speculators are also at work; whose purchases are, of course, always *in transitu*, & *thus* also rrotected.
>
> This sudden influx of purchasers into the market has stimulated the cupidity of producers & holders of the necessaries of life; and has induced them to withhold their supplies (under the expectation of higher prices) ...
>
> Our officers can't buy—nor is it reasonable to expect parties to sell to the Govt at schedule prices, when double that price is offered at their door by others—they can't impress, for holders have, with great promptness, contracted for all their surplus to parties who pay these higher prices...[36]

Where could Northrop turn? Secretary Seddon had no power to alter the laws of impressment: only Congress could do that, and they were still in recess. In desperation Northrop turned to Lee, who as a general had the broad impressing powers the Bureau needed to acquire. Could Lee be persuaded by his own act to extend the powers of field impressment to Northrop's Bureau? Northrop begged him to do it. But Lee did not think he could: if such a crisis then existed, he wrote, Northrop should get his power from the Secretary of War.[37] Northrop answered: "The troops will be in want before the tithe meat comes in [in February 1864] sufficient (if it ever will be) to meet the want". Then he voiced something like a last hope. If Lee would only make the impressing order invoking field conditions, "such action will rouse the nation to a sense of its real condition, brought on or allowed by the timidity of the political leaders in Congress and the [State] Legislatures."[38] Out of loyalty he did not mention the President who proved no more able or willing to help Northrop out of that blind alley than Seddon or Lee.

---

[35] *Diary*, II, 100-01.

[36] November 14, 1863 (NYPL: Northrop Papers).

[37] November 19, 1863 (*OR* ser. I, vol. 29, pt. 2, 838).

[38] Ibid., November 20 and 22, 1863, 838-39, 843-44.

A fortnight later harbingers of Northrop's long foreseen meat famine came in. On December 5, 1863 Noland reported that there remained only four days' rations of fresh beef—reduced rations—for Lee's men. To remedy the shortage, Noland had to resort to buying uncured pork from Virginia farmers in advance of the curing season; it was borrowing from a thin future. Three days earlier Seddon had been forced to allow Northrop to sign a contract to buy beef behind enemy lines. There was no indication that Davis was even consulted.

So the most vital of Northrop's plans to circumvent the shortage of food was implemented without debate. It was a full year late, and the amount available was no longer enough. What followed was recalled by Frank Ruffin: "By the 8th of January [1864] the Secretary of War was compelled to order the purchase of meat without regard to impressment rates (which were renewed when a small surplus had been obtained)."[39] But the rampart of price-schedules had been breached by the government which promulgated them, and everyone knew it.

* * *

In preparation for a new session of Congress the Bureau chiefs, Department Secretaries and the President planned a pyramid of reports. Before them came the Bureau estimates for the first six months of 1864. Northrop's contained something rare indeed—a statement that less money was needed than expected. The reason was unhappy: the last estimates had been raised high on hopes of receipts from William Crenshaw's blockade runners, but actual importations had been curtailed by the Bureau's inability to get enough government cotton to trade for gold to support Crenshaw's ship-building to the utmost. As ships had been wanting to bring in purchases, therefore a part of the purchase-money granted by Congress was left unexpended.

Not all the appropriation could be ploughed back, Northrop warned. Some was needed to settle outstanding heavy debts contracted by his men on credit when the Treasury would not disgorge appropriated cash for home purchases. Also his men were now buying up as much as they could of rice and corn crops in South Carolina and Georgia: they also must draw on those funds. Still the Commissary General was prepared to deduct $50 million from his current estimate, leaving the total demand at just under $58 million.[40]

On November 18, 1863 Northrop sent in his report to the Secretary of War. Beginning with meat, he enclosed a copy of the old "Comparative View" showing reserves in autumn 1861 and autumn 1862. With this he sent a new Comparative View: where in October 1862 he had more than 5 million pounds of bacon in store, now there were barely 2 million pounds. Of beef cattle in Virginia, there was actually a tiny increase: but stocks were minuscule. Beyond those facts, it was virtually impossible to make accurate estimates of

---

[39] *The New York Herald*, July 21, 1865, 3.

[40] *OR* ser. IV, vol. 2, 938-39. For some history of the government cotton supply to the bureaus later in the war, see Ruffin's testimony before the Confederate Congress, pp. 18-19 (Va. Hist. Soc.: Ruffin Papers R 8386a, 57-58: these paragraphs were not printed in *The New York Herald*).

beef purchases for the coming months. The largest numbers of cattle left in the Confederacy were in Mississippi—and a portion of them was claimed by the state government there. Florida reported a total stock of only 200 cattle remaining on October 15: that figure excluded direct reservations by Bragg's and Beauregard's agents, allowed to operate in the face of Northrop's stringent objections.

As to future bacon, prospects were as bleak. Inflation had almost eliminated hog purchasing by Bureau men working within the price schedules. Loss of territory, renewed hog cholera, ever weakening transport, hoarding and speculation had all played their parts. By the blackest irony, in a few areas threatened by the enemy it had become easier to buy because "people are afraid of losing all". But quantities available in such places were small, and transport nearly nonexistent. Of William Crenshaw's 3 million pound purchase of salt meat in England, much had not yet arrived—either because of delays in building new blockade-runners or lack of ready money to grease the wheels of transshipment from the Islands.

Except for European hopes, then, the prospect was quite empty. No more could rationally be looked for from the Trans-Mississippi; and sugar, once used to substitute for missing meat, was now so low that it could only be given to hospitals. Then Northrop spelled out precisely why his prospect was so bleak: "This Bureau has therefore to report its conviction that for the coming twelve months there will not be enough meat in the country for the people and the armies of the Confederate States: and as the people can, for the reasons above stated, obtain what there is more readily, and insist on having it without any regard to the wants of our soldiers, it is presumed they must bear the brunt of hunger as well as of arms." In other words, the government had failed, was failing, and would probably continue to fail to place their citizenry on a war footing.

The situation over bread might be less bad, but its evaluation was bedeviled by widespread concealment of flour from impressing officers. There might be enough wheat in the remaining Confederacy, but not in Virginia. Northrop pleaded for the completion of a forty-mile rail connection from Greensboro, North Carolina to Danville, Virginia: that would eliminate the worst bottle-neck in transferring food from the South to Lee.[41]

Northrop wanted a supply of whiskey "for issue under circumstances of great exposure and protracted fatigue". Only Georgia and Alabama produced enough grain to justify its diversion from bread-making—and Governor Brown and the Georgia Legislature had banned whiskey-making. That left Alabama; so again the supply lay far from Lee. An experiment to import whiskey from abroad had failed for want of ships. The Commissary General concluded by advertising his most recent recommendation to Seddon—that

---

[41]   The strategic promise of this rail link had been recognized from the outset of the war. Local opposition to the spectre of central government power yoking states had delayed its charter until 1862. Scarcity of materials further delayed its completion until May 1864—and then it was on the meanest terms. For the history of this penultimate rail achievement of the Confederacy, see Black, *The Railroads of the Confederacy*, 148-53, 227-29.

impressing powers for accumulation should be withdrawn from the field, and confined exclusively to his Bureau.[42]

Thus again the question arose: should not such a report of weakness at levels above the reporter be accompanied by resignation? Again the chivalric pride of the Old South returned the same answer: it was the answer of Davis himself—the "duty man". In the very week of Northrop's report, it was expressed another way by the Assistant Secretary of War, Judge John A. Campbell. Robert Kean noted in his diary on November 15, 1863: "The Judge told me he felt that in the present state of the country to resign looked like desertion, and this was the chief consideration which made him hesitate."[43]

On November 20 Secretary Seddon sent to the President his report, covering those of his Bureau Chiefs. On Northrop's request to forbid accumulation by army commissaries, Seddon hedged. He was embarrassed by such special appointments as Johnston's commissary Banks, and asked for a ruling from Congress or the President. (Neither would give one.) Seddon praised the Commissary and Quartermaster Bureaus for managing, in the face of manifold difficulties, "to keep the armies at all times moderately supplied". He recognized that "Bacon and beef must, in view of the needs of the Army and the people, be scarce during the coming year." Yet he still differed from the Commissary General on the question of actual shortage. He looked for great results from the Tithe-in-Kind.

Seddon utterly condemned impressment—"a harsh, unequal, and odious mode of supply" resorted to because of inflation. In its place he put forward the remedy which had for some time been the gossip of the War Department and many others—diminution of the currency by wholesale devaluation. He trod carefully here, but he trod: "... As the mischief weighs as a paralysis on the energies of this Department, I may be excused for saying that in my judgement the sole effective remedy is prompt reduction of the existing issues to the amount needed for currency by the people of the Confederacy, and the inflexible determination and pledge never to exceed it." (Seddon had reason for that plea. On September 30, 1863 the nation's debt had stood at just under $1,000 million, of which more than $700 million was unfunded. By January 1, 1864 the figures would be $1,221 million and $923 million. The entire rise was thus unfunded—money-printing.)[44]

Turning to transport, Seddon identified the railroads as a weak point, but would entertain no motion to condemn them; they had "rarely failed to meet the requirements of the Government with alacrity and zeal." (Northrop must have ground his teeth when he read that, and he would have had company among the Bureau chiefs.) Seddon concluded, "It has not been necessary during the year to exercise the large discretionary powers of control vested by Congress in the Executive over the railroads...". He opened that door a crack when he went on to say that the railroads would have to be

[42] *OR* ser. IV, vol. 2, 968-72.
[43] *Inside the Confederate Government*, 122-23.
[44] Schwab, *The Confederate States of America*, 56.

provided with more means for repair and maintenance, and those must come from the army (thus taking up Lee's hint of willingness to furnish mechanics). Then came a darker forecast: "Some of the minor roads will have to be sacrificed to keep up the tracks of the leading lines." It was a measure of how far the Confederacy had come down the road of centralization for a Secretary of War to feel able to write those words without fear of impeachment by Congress or editorial lynching by the business interests. With regard to Northrop's proposal (supported by Lee) to eliminate passenger trains whenever government freight was held up, Seddon at last gave his support in many qualifying words.

Finally in his section on supply, the Secretary sounded another warning: because the port of Charleston was effectively blockaded by the Federal capture of Morris Island in the outer harbor, the enemy were sure to increase blockading pressure on the one remaining major east-coast port of Wilmington.[45] In that, Seddon's forecast was dead accurate.

On December 7, the day Congress reconvened, President Davis sent them his own report synthesizing the others. His document was longer than Seddon's, but it said less than ever before about the Bureaus, merely endorsing the Secretary of War's remarks. Above all, Davis said, Congress must reform the currency: he adjured them to get on with this legislation as fast as they could.

Turning to the growing horror of war prisons on both sides, Davis condemned Federal attempts "to shield themselves from the execration excited by their own odious treatment of our officers and soldiers, now captive in their hands, by misstatements—such as that the prisoners held by us are deprived of food. ... In accordance with our law and the general orders of the Department, the rations of the prisoners are precisely the same, in quantity and quality, as those served out to our own gallant soldiers in the field, and which have been found sufficient to support them in their arduous campaigns—while it is not pretended by the enemy that they treat prisoners by the same generous rule."

Davis also had an ominous message for his own Bureaus. Conscription must be extended above the age of forty-five. Some of those new conscripts could replace younger men at present detailed in the Bureaus, allowing them to be sent up to the line.[46] So there would be further fights to preserve the trained and seasoned experts on whom all operations of supply—immensely hampered as they were—more and more heavily depended.

As soon as Congress reconvened, the anti-Davis elements went for the blood of the President's allies. On the opening day, December 7, 1863, Senator James Orr introduced a resolution demanding that the Committee on Military Affairs investigate "the arbitrary, unjust, and needless impressment

---

[45]   *OR* ser. IV, vol. 2, 1004, 1007-1015.
[46]   Ibid., 1039, 1041, 1043, 1045.

of provisions, under orders from the Commissary General".[47] A week later Orr served his friend Beauregard by persuading the Senate to call for all the President's papers covering Beauregard's failed attempt to dismiss Guerin early in the year—with the object of reopening the whole matter.[48]

Meanwhile Henry Foote was busy in the House of Representatives. The prison commissary Warner had complained of Northrop to Foote (who lodged in Warner's house during sessions).[49] Of course Foote fell on it. His verbiage made as good copy as ever. Having occupied the House's time on December 9 with wholesale abuse of the President, he turned again to abuse Northrop. The anti-Davis press retailed every succulent word:

> ... If the Yankee prisoners have not got enough, it is the fault of the Commissary General, Mr. Northrop, and his way of doing business. This man has been a curse to the country. Though he has injured the country more than the enemy, he is retained in office. He is a pepper doctor from South Carolina, and he looks more like a vegetarian than any man I ever saw.
>
> I have heard that he sent in an official document to the War Department to prove that the vegetable diet is by far the best for the sustenance of life. [Thus the gossip mills had distorted the terms agreed with Lawton and Seddon for emergencies: or had Foote's own imagination performed that feat?]
>
> Northrop should be dragged from his position. ... I intend to move his dismissal from office at a very early day.[50]

But not before the last potential for abusive publicity had been extracted.

The next day Foote regaled the House with a resolution demanding "that all quartermasters, commissaries and disbursing officers be required to hand in a statement, under oath, of all the property they possessed at the time of going into office; all that they now possess; and that all property which cannot be satisfactorily accounted for shall be seized by the Government... Surely no member would be unwilling to vote for my resolution. ... On what ground would any member dare to vote against it?"[51] Nine members of the House dared to vote against it, but the resolution passed handily.

The following day Foote proposed another resolution, demanding to know how many commissaries and quartermasters had been replaced in the Bureaus by disabled soldiers.[52] Informed of the present existence of a law covering the subject, Foote roared that the law was a dead letter because of nepotism, and called for investigation. To that also the House assented. He

---

[47] *Journal of Congress, III*, 453.

[48] Ibid., 487.

[49] Northrop's letter of July 7, 1865 to Rev. J. J. Early describes Warner as "H. S. Foote's friend and *host*" (Georgetown archives).

[50] *SHSP*, vol. 50, 23-24. The transcript above restores present tense in place of past, and past tense in place of past perfect.

[51] *SHSP*, vol. 50, 30.

[52] Ibid., 36-39. It is worth noting that many Subsistence Bureau clerks by this time were women. Some, like Frank Ruffin's cousin Mrs. Judith McGuire, were gentlewomen forced into employment by the need to supplement family income to meet rocketing prices. When Mrs. McGuire entered on her employment in the Bureau on January 3, 1864, she found thirty-five ladies already at work there. See her *Diary of a Southern Refugee During the War* (New York: E. J. Hale, 1867), 244, 250.

then demanded that the standing committee inquire "promptly and rigidly" into alleged corruption in the Commissary and Quartermaster Bureaus, and again the House agreed. Foote hoped it would be a replay of his previous year's resolution with more incriminating evidence. Through all the tearing rhetoric, he had still retailed nothing but hearsay.

The Congressmen had a lively session. They were far more "prompt and rigid" in pursuing the Subsistence and other alleged scandals than they were in addressing the matter which the President had defined as the highest priority—reform of the currency, the state of which was bleeding the country white and threatening to break down national law and order. But when Foote at last made his motion for Northrop's dismissal on January 25, 1864, it was defeated by a vote of 46 to 20.[53]

When the motion for Northrop's removal was lost, Foote declared that he had done with the question of the Commissary General forever.[54] Those of his colleagues inclined to doubt their good fortune were soon to be proved right. Yet at least one of the representatives voting against removing Northrop had done so partly because he doubted the legislature's power to remove Bureau chiefs. The congressional foes of Davis kept a resolve to do something.

Already the Senate had tried to assert some control over Presidential appointments by a bill requiring that all officers confirmed by the old Provisional Congress (up to February 1862) should be renominated to the present Senate. Senator Orr, professing eagerness that the law should not become a dead letter, proposed an amendment to the new appropriations bill that would withhold payment of salary to any officer not renominated and reconfirmed. When Semmes of Louisiana argued that the effects of such a measure would be uncontrollable, Orr acknowledged that his quarry was the Commissary General. Orr was supported by Wigfall of Texas—once the President's friend, now his enemy. But others persuaded Orr to withdraw the amendment: "Senators owned frankly that they were not ready to face the music." They passed the appropriations bill without riders.[55]

If Northrop had any political instincts, he would have taken steps to give the Senate better information. His soldier's training enjoined the bearing of contumely in silence. As at his confirmation by the Provisional Congress in early 1862, he ignored the noisemakers and went about his work. In the War Bureau, however, Robert Kean connected Orr's threat with the act of a year ago making the Quartermaster a Brigadier General: "The tender point is the case of the Commissary General. He is in the same situation; they have run him to the wall. If he is [re-]nominated he will certainly be rejected—a deep mortification to the President and himself; if he is not, the President

[53] SHSP, vol. 50, 302.

[54] SHSP, vol. 50, 302.

[55] This debate is not reported in the Senate Journal or in SHSP. I owe its documentation to Mary Dix, co-editor of The Papers of Jefferson Davis. She discovered that it had been leaked to The Charleston Mercury. Its report on February 13, 1864 has made it possible to reconstruct the story above, with information of Orr's withdrawal of his appropriation amendment from the Mercury issue of February 15.

will have put himself in a false position in order to save his friend. The true solution is for Colonel Northrop to resign."[56] But Colonel Northrop did no such thing: Foote's motion to remove him had failed barely a fortnight since.

For the congressional investigation into the charge of starving prisoners of war, Northrop asked Seddon to testify. The committee chairman suggested instead that the Commissary General address a series of questions to his superior for written answers. Northrop did so.[57] Having taken its testimony, the committee reported to the House on February 13, 1864: "... The complaint that the prisoners suffered from being deprived of a sufficiency of food is entirely without foundation." If the prisoners' meat ration was short, they said, it was basically due to the pressure of enemy action.[58] Four days later Congress signified its approval of the arrangement whereby the Commissary General fed the prisoners of war by removing the informality. On February 17 they enacted a law devolving the duty specifically upon the Commissary General.[59] It was the only sensible arrangement. Yet its responsibility was to weigh on Northrop's future and reputation more heavily than any other.

On the same day, the last of their session, Congress also got around to doing what the President had asked for first. The value of a dollar in gold was then $23 in Confederate money. The remedy enacted that day was to call in all Treasury notes over $5 value by April 1 (July 1 in Trans Mississippi). Holders of those notes could choose between a twenty-year bond paying 4 percent, and immediate funding in a new issue providing two new dollars for three old ones.[60] It remained to be seen how the people would react; if their government repudiated its own currency once, it might do so again.

That session of Congress had also brought in heavy new taxes on every source of private income, weighted to favor essential jobs and against luxury.[61] Two interlinked bills tightened and extended conscription everywhere, and created an "Invalid Corps" to replace drafted government employees with wounded soldiers.[62] There was much bureaucratic hand-wringing over this, but Northrop's public response was immaculate. He addressed a circular to all his commissaries of the rank of major and above. If they presented special cases among their staffs, he would look at them. For the rest: "It is no time to give up and say that ruin will follow on the removal of our trained men. Let us all do our best to comply with the law and call on the War Dept: to do its part as the cases are presented."[63]

Other legislation changed the balance between impressment and trading through enemy lines—at last. Impressment was curtailed: appraising officers were henceforth in every case to be local residents, and from their

---

56   *Inside the Confederate Government* (February 10, 1864), 136.

57   *OR* ser. II, vol. 6, 821-22, cited above, p. 227.

58   Ibid., 951-52.

59   Ibid., 1020: announced to the Army by General Order on March 5, 1864.

60   *OR* ser. IV, vol. 3, 159-61; Schwab, *The Confederate States*, 66, 68.

61   *OR* ser. IV, vol. 3, 140-52.

62   Ibid., 178-81, 214.

63   M-474, r 101, ff 478-79. For Northrop's continued cooperation, see *OR* ser. IV, vol. 3, 628-29.

decisions there was no military appeal; and all impressed goods must be paid for on the spot.[64] That last provision, combined with the new currency act, should sound the knell of wholesale impressment by impostors.

The complementary series of acts brought the legislation Northrop had so long looked for. These acts regulated importing, exporting, and dealing in foreign currency so as to reserve all three effectively to the government. The importing and exporting acts specified what portion of each ship's cargo must be devoted to government freight, what the rest of the cargo could and could not contain (under threat of confiscating the jewels and luxuries still so profitable to shippers), and what taxes the government would impose on any private freight it did allow.[65]

The foreign-trade legislation virtually recognized trading with the enemy. It was passed on February 6, 1864, and called on the Secretary of War to create military guidelines. Seddon did this so tardily and half-heartedly that his circular to the generals was not written until March 21: "When these supplies can be secured by the exportation of these articles [in particular cotton] into the country occupied by the enemy, the Department supposes that it would be prudent and lawful to do so; but great circumspection is necessary for the execution of any plan of the kind, and all such traffic must be subject to the inspection and control of the department commanders... ". He outlined elaborate procedures.[66] A separate letter to Lee placed the entire northern Virginia business in the hands of Burr Noland.[67]

In fact Northrop had quietly anticipated that legislation. Ever since he had supported William Crenshaw's mission to England at the end of 1862, the Commissary General had been making more and more direct foreign-trade arrangements of his own. All sorts of dodges had been used to feed Lee's army even partially. One was recalled by Frank Ruffin: "... But for the providence of this Bureau, without the privity of the Government, in accepting a suggestion of Mr. Crenshaw to import a large amount of coffee for sale [to any buyer willing to pay an inflated market price] for the express purpose of supplying the Army, it is doubtful if it could have been subsisted through the winter of 1863-64."[68] Lee's army had not enjoyed regular rations of coffee from early in the war, and the new supply was not really intended for their consumption (though evidence suggests they did receive some of it). It was simply that, after all the failures to secure prompt shipment from abroad and delivery of meat owing to its bulk and weight, no clean-handed shipper would refuse cases of coffee—dry, light, and densely profitable. The secret profits would secretly buy overpriced meat hidden close to the Army of Northern Virginia.

---

[64]   *OR* ser. IV, vol. 3, 198-99.

[65]   Ibid., 79-82, 187-89.

[66]   Ibid., 239-40. The generals addressed were Johnston, Beauregard, Longstreet, Polk, Pickett, Breckinridge, and Maury.

[67]   Ibid., 245-46.

[68]   *The New York Herald*, July 21, 1865, 2.

When the Commissary General was driven to dealing in food to feed the army, clearly the less said the better. Doubtless there were other such arrangements, whose threads Northrop kept in his own hands. The "contraband" trade is one of the least documented of Confederate subsistence operations. But a vivid outline has survived for one key area—the coastal counties of the Virginia-North Carolina border. Northrop wrote: "My agents were trading all around Virginia and North Carolina by my authority alone—*sub silentio*, and this became a very large business. There were nearly 30 little agencies around Virginia trading yams and tobacco for bacon, and on the Blackwater in North Carolina 1500-2000 bales of cotton I think were traded every month. The Secretary of War officially knew nothing about these latter arrangements, but they supplied Lee with meat. The chief manager of the North Carolina trade was Major Tannahill."[69]

Robert Tannahill, the commissary at Petersburg, Virginia, was to recall for Northrop:

> ... It is impossible even to approximate the magnitude of the business as it was done day and night. ... I was often down to supervise and confer with Capt White, ... a most valuable and efficient officer. Being a native of the county, he knew every one. His energy was remarkable—besides he had a turn for business and accomplished wonders.
> We had a fixed scale for exchanges. We gave

> 2 pounds of Cotton for 1 pound of Coffee
> 2   "   "   "   " 1   "   " Sugar
> 1 pound "   "   " 1   "   " Bacon. ...

> You may remember that parties arriving in Richmond on this business were referred to me when they approached the Scty of War or Genl Lee. I am sure that I had contracts booked for nearly 6,000 Bales of Cotton to be delivered in exchange for supplies a month before the evacuation [in 1865] and a prospect of doing at least 20,000 Bales more very soon.

Tannahill recalled an interview with Lee on the old subject of providing cavalry protection for Subsistence operations. Now at last better understanding prevailed:

> When I called on Genl Lee and asked him to detail a Company of Cavalry to report to Capt White, and explained the object was to protect supplies expected from the North in exchanges for Cotton, he appeared surprised and astonished. He had had no intimation of it, and remarked with much interest that he was afraid it could not be consummated, and then observed:
> "Certainly, Major, the order shall be given: those people must want Cotton bad."
> I told him that I was sanguine, and that the steamer expected was just the beginning of a large business. The ship did arrive, the

[69]   May 23, 1880 to Davis (Rowland, VIII, 458). For an outline of civilian trade over these borders, see Ludwell Johnson, "Contraband Trade in the Last Year of the Civil War", in *The Mississippi Valley Historical Review*, vol. 49, no. 4 (March, 1963), especially page 642.

cargo Bacon Sugar and Coffee discharged and Cotton put on board (some 200 Bales) during the night, and I think the Cotton must have sold at some $1.60 per lb or about $800 per Bale.

There Tannahill saw the hand of Benjamin Butler, placed in charge of the Federal Army of the James from November 1863:

> I of course cannot say that General Butler had any interest in the exchanges while he was in command at Norfolk.[70] All I know is that we had no difficulty in getting supplies when we gave Cotton...
>   We kept our stock of Cotton (some 3000 Bales) at Weldon and sent what we required down by Railroad every day or two. [After the enemy destroyed the line] the business was carried on for a long time by wagons and carts doing the transportation on a large scale.[71]

On a rare personal note, Northrop recalled giving Tannahill $50 (recently sent by Maria's uncle Dr. Steuart in Maryland) to buy bacon for his own family.[72] He would hardly have done this unless supplies for Lee from that source were ample. It was a solitary instance, so far as I know, of using his position—and not for his own consumption, as he was vegetarian. The Northrop household was seen thus by Charles Steuart: "... No one in all the South lived more like a 'Spartan in the storm of adversity'. For weeks his house was a stranger to meat—not even butter or eggs, and often not even milk, were used there. Tea or coffee—except the detestable native substitutes for both—he and his family forgot the taste of ... and not one cent's worth of what belonged to 'the common weal' was diverted by him from its public purpose. He had a large and most interesting family; and although holding one of the highest positions in the Government, there was no officer of it who lived in such a self-sacrificing way as he did."[73] The lesson of the Osage was with him yet.

[70] Ludwell Johnson makes no doubt of Buter's guilt: see his "Contraband Trade During the Last Year of the Civil War", in *The Mississippi Valley Historical Review*, 49 (1963), 641.

[71] March 12, 1880 to Northrop (NYPL: Northrop Papers).

[72] May 23, 1880 to Davis (Rowland, VIII, 458).

[73] 'Col. C. S. Armee', "Rummaging through Rebeldom" No. 16, in *The New York Citizen*, July 27, 1867, 1.

CHAPTER 19

1864: The Year of Nemesis

1863 had been the last year to offer large new remedies for the increasingly insoluble problem of Confederate food supply. 1864 was to be totally different. Though some projects started in 1863 would produce surprisingly well in view of the limitations now hedging every action, Northrop by this time could find nothing else to initiate—or almost nothing. Practically with the turn of the year, a new mood of despair began seeping through commissary reports from every direction. A look at the Commissary General's calendar for the first fortnight of the new year shows almost every day darker; by the end of the fortnight the darkness was visible.

January 1, 1864 was a Friday. On that day Northrop's order took effect withdrawing sugar from the troops and limiting its issue to hospitals.[1] On the same day Major Millen wrote from Savannah that he could no longer buy hogs with Confederate money nor expect any to come in by way of Tithe-in-Kind; all the animals were being made to disappear. He called, as Noland in Virginia had called before him, for an extension of Subsistence Bureau powers of impressment.[2]

Saturday, January 2 saw the writing of three letters from the military field. Johnston in his new command at Dalton, Georgia reported that he had only eight days' rations—apparently caused by a shortage of wood to run the trains. As trains then reaching him mostly brought beef cattle, Johnston wanted all his cattle driven from any distance to save the trains for other food.[3] He did not suggest how the cattle could survive long drives in winter without any grazing.

From Longstreet, isolated in his remaining corner of East Tennessee, came a letter dated the same day. Northrop had just warned Longstreet that he could not count on any supplies from Virginia. "If this is the case," wrote the general, "it cannot be expected to occupy here with any view to offen-

---

[1] M-437, r 135, ff 194-195.
[2] *OR* ser. I, vol. 32, pt. 2, 523.
[3] To Davis (Ibid., 510).

sive movements; and if no such purpose is contemplated it loses much of its importance, if not all."[4]

Gravest of all on that January 2 was a communication from Lee. The Army of Northern Virginia was practically out of meat. Despite the sharpest cold of a Virginia winter, Lee had been forced to cut his troops' meat ration to a quarter pound. He could learn of no meat on its way to him.[5]

From Subsistence Bureau stores on Sunday, January 3 came the statement that both bread and flour were totally exhausted throughout Richmond. It would thus be impossible for the present to respond to any requisition whatever. The writer was Major Seth Barton French, a former aide to the Governor of Virginia, seconded to the commissariat in the previous summer and already recognized as one of Northrop's ablest officers. Major French added that supplies were still reported from North Carolina, but were untransportable: the total number of available railroad cars had fallen below the day-to-day needs of the Subsistence Bureau alone.[6]

On Monday, January 4 Davis wrote directly to Northrop about Lee: "The case requires prompt attention, and it will be well for you to obtain from the Secretary of War any orders which will aid you to meet the emergency of the occasion." That had the appearance of a blank check. But Northrop did not fill it in. He wrote instead a long endorsement disputing Lee's ration figures (apparently Northrop did not understand that Lee had been forced to reduce) and rehearsing all his own warnings for a year past; beyond that he had nothing to suggest.[7] To anyone familiar with Northrop's old habits of tenacious fight, this was new indeed. Had he now concluded that it was useless to ask his immediate superior, the Secretary of War, for anything?

Below his endorsement, nonetheless, Northrop noted: "Not finding the Sec of War in I carried this to the President...". That interview produced results. The same afternoon Davis wired to Lee that Northrop had ordered 90,000 pounds of meat from Wilmington—presumably from stores for Whiting's forces there: nothing about railroad cars to bring it. For anything else, Davis wrote, Lee would have to impress in the short term from food stockpiled by private corporations for their year's consumption.[8]

Did Lee make impressments then? Possibly not, for the following day, January 5, he wrote to Northrop—ostensibly to answer Northrop's last letter to him (of as long ago as December 7) which had warned him that the supply of beef was nearly exhausted and that it was time to impress. Lee repeated

---

[4]   To Cooper (Ibid., 509).

[5]   *OR* ser. I, vol. 33, 1061.

[6]   *OR* ser. I, vol. 51, pt. 2, 808. *OR* ascribes Seth Barton French's Subsistence correspondence to S. Bassett French. That caused me to consult Glenn C. Oldaker, comp., *Centennial Tale: Memoirs of Colonel "Chester" S. Bassett French, Extra Aide-de-Camp to Generals Lee and Jackson ...* (N.Y.: Carlton Press, 1962). The book makes no mention of Subsistence, and shows Bassett French to have been elsewhere when Barton French (about whose second name all MS Subsistence records agree when they go beyond initials) was laboring for the Subsistence Bureau.

[7]   Univ. of Va. MSS Dept.: William J. Rucker coll.

[8]   *OR* ser. I, vol. 33, 1064.

his former objections and returned to the argument that Northrop should get extended impressment powers from the Secretary of War. He finished by complaining more bitterly than ever that all other Confederate commands were better provisioned than his own.[9] Northrop knew that only too well, and knew also his own powerlessness to stop it by orders to such generals as Johnston and Beauregard.

That same day, January 5, Beauregard's sub-commissary at Sullivan's Island in Charleston harbor reported his post out of bacon and fresh beef and unable to buy any. On this, Chief Commissary Guerin endorsed that the situation was due to government price-schedules making it impossible for Bureau officers to impress.[10] Soon another sub-commissary reported his depot out of meat. At that, Beauregard's Assistant Adjutant General Jordan wrote a deliberately offensive rejoinder to Guerin: "Middlemen can find supplies— can draw them out with the currency of the country—and it is believed that your department can do the same by sending the necessary number of energetic agents into the proper quarter." Jordan and Beauregard met Guerin's statement of impossibility with flat contradiction—based evidently on their choice to ignore the price-schedules.[11] Beauregard then wrote to Adjutant General Cooper demanding again that Guerin be replaced. When that reached Northrop's desk, his endorsement turned the accusation on the commander: "General Beauregard's writings and orders which have reached this Bureau indicate a want of information respecting the existing condition of the country, and the effect of the feelings and fears of the people for food, the influence of the laws and orders, the currency and limitation of prices for public purchases, and the condition of the railroads...".[12]

On January 6 Johnston telegraphed Northrop from Georgia. The contents of his wire underlined yet again the disparity of his rations with Lee's: "Our beeves are very lean [probably from over-lengthy driving out of season], so that the ration, three-fourths of a pound, gives very little meat. I therefore suggest to double the ration of rice." Northrop endorsed Johnston's wire: "Since this telegram was received, complaints have been received from Charleston and Wilmington of the inadequacy of transportation to produce breadstuffs for troops at those points. Rice will have to be substituted largely, and the double ration asked for [by Johnston] cannot be allowed."[13]

On Thursday, January 7 the president of the railroad in Mississippi informed General Polk (commanding there in succession to Johnston) that his line was so close to breakdown from government overuse that only an extraordinary permission to trade cotton with the enemy for vital replacement materials could save it.[14]

---

[9]　Ibid., 1064-65.

[10]　*OR* ser. I, vol. 35, pt. 2, 506-7, 510.

[11]　Ibid., 512-13.

[12]　Ibid., 507-8, 512-13, 520-22. The acrimony went on until March, when Davis confirmed again Northrop's power to appoint and control State Chief Commissaries (*OR* ser. I, vol. 14, 976-77; vol. 35, pt. 1, 543-45, 554-56, 566-73; vol. 53, 321-24).

[13]　To Seddon (*OR* ser. I, vol. 32, pt. 2, 522).

[14]　*OR* ser. IV, vol. 3, 9-10.

The next day, January 8, was that on which Secretary Seddon was compelled to authorize the purchase of meat for Lee without regard to price. That purchase was intended merely to meet a crisis; but it so rapidly became standard drill that Frank Ruffin would write a year later: "Since that time the supply of cattle for the Army of Northern Virginia, with the exception of about fifteen hundred obtained from southwestern Virginia, have all come from beyond our lines, as far as northwestern Virginia [i.e., almost certainly from the Union state of West Virginia]; and have in most cases been paid for in greenbacks or gold—both of which were obtained with difficulty and inadequate sums."[15]

On January 9 Lee's commissary Cole reported "every shipment of meat is robbed of from 8 to 15 hundred pounds."[16] In Richmond Major French wrote the same day that corn shipped from Subsistence Bureau stores in Georgia was now systematically waylaid by army quartermasters—presumably to feed their animals. French also renewed his own plea to regulate trains. Two passenger trains a day still ran over lines into Virginia on which, a month before, vital corn had been ordered up from the South and had never come. French concluded two things: that no reliance could be placed on anything said by the railroads, and that the next months of winter inactivity in army manoeuvers should be used to accumulate food stores with the railroads forced to cooperate. On the back of French's paper Northrop wrote: "After a conference with the Q'M Gnl [Lawton] on this subject we both conferred with the Secretary of War, who agreed to give such details from the Army—during the winter—as should be necessary to repair the rolling stock of the RR: and at the same time Gnl Lawton informed me that the arrangement—which for 12 months I have urged—was ordered that only one passenger train should be run per day."[17]

On Sunday, January 10 Northrop answered Lee with a renewed plea for Lee to extend the Bureau's impressment. Lee remained immovable: "I foresee nothing but evil and confusion", he wrote back, "if the armies are told to take care of themselves. The supplies must be obtained by a general system under a common control, so that there may be uniformity...". That enshrined precisely the policy Northrop had fought to establish at the outset. Near the end of his letter, Lee did hint that the real weakness lay above Northrop.[18]

On January 11 Senator Benjamin Hill introduced a bill to order district attorneys throughout the Confederacy to make comprehensive routine investigations of all disbursing officers in the army. The bill provided for trials of accused officers, with a ten percent commission for the prosecuting attorney on every sum collected. The measure quickly passed the Senate.[19]

---

[15]   *The New York Herald*, July 21, 1865, 3.
[16]   Northrop's summary in "Book No. 3" (Va. Hist. Soc.: Ruffin Papers R 8386).
[17]   NYPL: Northrop Papers.
[18]   *OR* ser. I, vol. 33, 1087-88.
[19]   *SHSP*, vol. 50, 211-14, 282-84.

On the same day Governor Milton of Florida reported that in several counties of his state there was not enough corn left to sustain families of soldiers serving at the front. Could not Colonel Northrop open his depots—which they knew were rich—to the tune of ten or twelve thousand bushels?[20] Yet those stores were still in Florida for only one reason: there was no transport to bring the food north to the soldiers themselves.

Still on January 11, Lee wrote to Davis about the losses turning up in railroad shipments of food from Richmond and Staunton to his army. Those losses in the past few days alone totalled 5,000 pounds of bacon. That equalled 20,000 rations at their present rate: "If the railroad agents will take no care of the safety of Government freight, Government agents had better be sent with each train of provisions."[21] It was already being done—with no effect.

The commissary at Columbus, Georgia reported that he could provide 75,000 bushels of corn a month—exactly what Lee needed—but could get no transport. Major French sent that to Northrop on January 12—with the horrendous totals of all that had gone missing from Subsistence rail shipments from the time he first noticed 50,000 bushels lacking in the previous September.[22]

The last day of this first fortnight in 1864, January 13, brought a conversation between the prisoner-of-war commissary Warner and the War Department clerk Jones. They were close friends: Warner had repeatedly subtracted food purchased for his prisoners to sell to Jones (and doubtless others of his friends) under market cost. From their talk that day Jones recorded an obscene fantasy: "Captain Warner says it is believed there will be a riot, perhaps, when Colonel Northrop, the Commissary General, may be immolated by the mob."[23]

* * *

With food running short in Richmond, there was talk of moving entire government departments away. One group of women clerks in the Treasury was sent to Columbia, South Carolina, and the Auditor's office moved back to Montgomery, Alabama. But sub-dividing the government, especially with communications breaking down, was clearly not the answer. A more practical remedy was to send away the thousands of prisoners of war still held in Richmond. It began at last in February 1864, after several open-air prison sites had been laid out in Georgia; many of the Richmond prisoners were sent to one near Andersonville. Progress was slow because only one train a day could be made available for their transport.

As the state of railroad repair declined, the owners seemed ever more eager to extract the last scraps of profit before a final breakdown. On February 8 Major French relayed to Northrop fresh reports of "the cupidity of

---

20 OR ser. IV, vol. 3, 14-15.
21 OR ser. I, vol. 33, 1076-78.
22 OR ser. I, vol. 46, pt. 2, 1224-25.
23 Diary, II, 128.

railroad companies and the corruption of agents and employés" continuing to prefer private freight: "We are now dependent on the south for bread... a line of communication between 600 and 700 miles in length. To-day we have not on hand rations for two days; and with no prospect of accumulations in [Virginia] from purchases, &c., it is impossible to foresee how forward movements can be made by the Army of Northern Virginia in the spring...".[24]

Northrop sent this to Seddon, and Seddon sent it to Quartermaster General Lawton. Lawton reported that government demands on the railroads had doubled in the past year—particularly Subsistence.[25] (So much for the old claim of the anti-Davis papers that Northrop was a do-nothing Commissary General—a claim repeated by lazy writers for a century afterwards.) With nearly every voice around Seddon howling for government control, the Secretary at last issued the order. It was dated March 12—more than a month after French's complaint: "The Quartermaster General is hereby authorized to stop passenger trains upon any line of railroad in which either forage or subsistence for the Army may be delayed, until the same or such portion thereof as may be necessary to the public service shall be removed."[26]

Two days later came the torch to light this bonfire. Burr Noland's brother Richard (also in the Virginia commissariat) was with Northrop late in the morning on March 14, and saw the beginning of it. Into the Commissary General's office came a telegram from Lee's commissary Cole reporting that he had no meat and only one day's rations of bread. Richard Noland recalled Northrop endorsing on it: "The condition of things which I predicted six weeks ago is upon us. Will the Secretary of War say how the army is to be fed?—or words to that effect, and sent (I think) Capt Dudley to the Secretary."[27]

Northrop's messenger arrived at Seddon's office when the clerk Jones was on duty. He wrote: "This I placed in the hands of the Secretary myself, and he seemed roused by it. Half an hour after, I saw Col. Northrop coming out of the department with a pale face and triumphant, compressed lips."[28] Within two days the government took control of the entire rail network between Augusta, Georgia and Charlotte, North Carolina, the great bottleneck in the transport of food from the south. Immediately after, it took over lines from the port of Wilmington to Richmond.[29]

The results were dramatic. By March 18 Quartermaster General Lawton was writing: "More Govt. stores have been transported from Wilmington & Charlotte to Richmond in the last five days than ever before during this war in the same space of time."[30] Richard Noland recalled hearing that in eight

---

[24]   *OR* ser. IV, vol. 3, 89-90.

[25]   Ibid., 91-92.

[26]   Ibid., 209.

[27]   Undated signed MS written perhaps at Northrop's request, now with his papers in NYPL. Richard William Noble Noland (1822-1886) was Burr Noland's junior by three and a half years. See *Tyler's Quarterly Historical and Genealogical Magazine*, vol. 2 (October 1920) 132-34.

[28]   *Diary*, II, 171.

[29]   Goff, *Confederate Supply*, 199.

[30]   Ibid., 199.

days the Subsistence Bureau had a thirty days' supply of food.[31] Frank Ruffin wrote: "... In two weeks we had more subsistence on hand than we had accumulated before in any one month."[32] The results convinced the Railroad Bureau chief Sims (who up to that time had claimed that only repair would make the trains run). Soon Sims recommended that the government takeover in North Carolina be made permanent "under one management and worked as one corporation... That the railroads should come under military control I am becoming every day more satisfied."[33]

The largesse was short-lived. By the end of March 1864, Northrop recalled, "... Members of Congress remonstrated, and the Secretary yielded."[34] Seddon made Lawton issue another order, returning to merely stopping passenger trains if there was a crisis. On April 5 Northrop attacked Seddon: unless all passenger trains were stopped, "the army could not be subsisted, and Richmond and all Virginia might have to be abandoned, and the country might be pillaged by our own soldiers."[35]

No result. On April 7 Northrop wrote to Adjutant General Cooper: "While General Lee's army has been for a long time on very short meat rations, there are now 1,000,000 pounds of meat [stranded] en route to this point. It cannot be said that there is such an actual deficiency in rolling-stock as to cause this difficulty...".[36] On April 12 Lee told Davis his supplies were so precarious that "any derangement in their arrival or disaster to the railroad would render it impossible for me to keep the army together, and might force a retreat into North Carolina. ... All pleasure travel should cease, and everything be devoted to necessary wants."[37]

Meanwhile Northrop's letter to Cooper had reached the President. Davis asked the views of his new military adviser—none other than General Braxton Bragg. After Bragg's failure in the West, Davis had brought him to Richmond to fill the post once held by Lee. Everyone foresaw trouble.[38] In this case Bragg supported Northrop: "... the necessity will justify an arrangement by military supervision [to] secure the passage of freight cars on all connected roads without breaking bulk...". ("Breaking bulk" was wholesale removal of cargo from the cars of one company to those of an ongoing carrier, always demanded as a condition of accepting the shipment even over lines of the same gauge.) Seddon himself concurred with Bragg. But Davis would not do it. He endorsed on April 23: "Due effort should be made to secure coopera-

31 Northrop Papers, NYPL.

32 *The New York Herald,* July 21, 1865, 3.

33 February 22, March 31, April 1, 1864 to Lawton (*OR* ser. IV, vol. 3, 92-93, 258, 228-29).

34 April 21, 1878 to Davis (Rowland, VIII, 182).

35 Northrop's MS not found; Jones saw it, and wrote this summary immediately afterwards (*Diary,* II, 182).

36 *OR* ser. I, vol. 51, pt. 2, 850-51.

37 *OR* ser. I, vol. 33, 1275.

38 The biographer H. J. Eckenrode offered an interesting view of Davis and Bragg as a symbiotic relationship: see *Jefferson Davis: President of the South* (London: Allen & Unwin, 1924), 249-51, 254-55, 278-81, 302-4.

tion of railroad companies in the most effective plan before proceeding to take possession of the railroads."[39]

Five days later Seddon, reporting to the President before a new session of Congress, spelt out the need he saw at last—three years late in Northrop's book—for draconian control. In return for lending skilled mechanics from the army for repair and new rail construction, Seddon wrote, the government should exert "full command over all the resources and means of transport possessed by the roads whenever needed... The roads should be run under unity of management, without reference to their local limits or separate schedules, and with the rolling-stock possessed by all...". Seddon castigated the private railroad interests as "too great to be acquiesced in". He concluded by warning that the Confederacy had gone too far in revolution to turn back; failure to concentrate resources would now bring nothing but the conqueror's yoke.[40]

Seddon's report was dated April 28, 1864. It frightened the wits out of the railroad men, who promptly promised that they would loyally transport 10,000 bushels of corn every day to Virginia.[41] That was enough for Davis. In the President's message to the new Congress convening on May 2, there was not a word about transport.[42]

All this time the wealth to buy anything lay everywhere still throughout the Deep South—in cotton. A letter from the Inspector of Field Transport for the state of Mississippi pushed hard for trading cotton through enemy lines against needed supplies. He described a "perfect mania" of private cotton trading going on every day through Yankee lines, while government cotton lay along the entire front being stolen if not ruined by weather. When this reached the Subsistence Bureau, Frank Ruffin endorsed wearily that he had heard it all before. He cited an instance when Northrop had tried to get 3,000 bales lying at Tuscaloosa—"with ropes burst and bagging rotted, preyed upon by thieves and eaten by cows"—from Treasury Secretary Memminger, who controlled all government cotton: Subsistence wanted it to pay an important food contract. "Mr. Memminger replied that he could not spare it; he wanted it himself; so I had to instruct my agent to buy cotton for his purpose. He has lately applied for funds for that purpose and I have none to send him." That endorsement, Ruffin remembered, did not even get a reply.[43]

The only response (if it was a response) was a request from Memminger next day to prohibit private shipments of government cotton altogether. That would close down all such contracts as William Crenshaw's and Power,

---

[39]   April 20 and 22, 1864 (*OR* ser. I, vol. 51, pt. 2, 851-52).

[40]   *OR* ser. IV, vol. 3, 339-44.

[41]   Reported in Jones (*Diary*, II, 196), April 30, 1864.

[42]   Richard Goff (*Confederate Supply*, 202), went so far as to write: "The Army of Northern Virginia might have been adequately fed if Davis had allowed it." I am not sure about "adequately"; "better" without a doubt.

[43]   A. M. Paxton, April 11, 1864 (*OR* ser. IV, vol. 3, 282-83); Ruffin in *The New York Herald*, July 21, 1865, 2.

Low's, which were still feeding Lee from abroad when the blockade-runners (mostly private) were allowed to take cotton out to the Islands of Bermuda and Nassau—to pay for shipment of the meats purchased for Northrop almost a year ago and now beginning to rot from want of transport to Wilmington, Richmond and Lee.

Memminger it was who had devised the currency devaluation passed by Congress in February. A judgment on his entire performance was to be rendered by the distinguished old scholar of Confederate finance, J. C. Schwab: "As soon as the government began to exchange new notes for old ones at the established ratio of $2 for $3, their value fell, and both kinds circulated side by side, were equally discredited and continued to depreciate together... We miss in [Memminger] the ability to foresee the inevitable consequences of the measures he proposed...".[44]

From the beginning of April 1864 the Confederate Treasury's failure to pay Subsistence (and other bureau) requisitions became endemic.[45] Northrop had accordingly agreed with his best flour supplier in Richmond, Haxall, Crensaw, to pay their milling costs in kind—a percentage toll of the flour they ground. Thus the company accumulated a stock of its own. That stock they were now laying out in two loyal ways: selling it to the poor of Richmond at about half the current market price, and actually advancing it to the government as a loan whenever trains from the South failed to bring any flour for populace or soldiers.

Then someone—was it Bragg?—questioned the toll payment of flour to Haxall, Crenshaw, charging that it was a tax on the army's food. Very well, said the firm, may we then be paid in cash? So Northrop gave Seddon "the alternative of buying, or returning in kind, what had been borrowed by the government from Haxall & Crenshaw". Seddon decided to return the flour in kind, and the Quartermaster General directed that it be sent "as soon as supply permitted". That decision was instantly second-guessed by Bragg.[46]

Not only was Bragg's memo a delaying tactic; but it looked as if Bragg was trying to supersede the Secretary of War and establish hegemony over the Bureau chiefs. According to Army Regulations, Bureau chiefs reported to the Secretary of War and only to him. Northrop had, as he freely admitted, corresponded with Bragg—"it having been long my determination to interest every one who I thought could in any way press some measures which would increase transportation."[47] Northrop answered Bragg that the matter had been settled by the Secretary of War.

Back came Bragg's rejoinder: "I have the honor to inform you that it is the desire of the President that the present arrangement of paying toll, in grain, to the mills for grinding our meal in the Department of Henrico [the

---

[44] Schwab, *The Confederate States*, 68-70. Schwab's judgment is more than confirmed by Douglas Ball in *Financial Failure and Confederate Defeat* (Univ. of Illinois, 1991).

[45] *OR* ser. IV, vol. 3, 931; *The New York Herald*, July 21, 1865, 2.

[46] Undated, untitled, unsigned endorsement by Northrop, ca. April 29, 1864 (NYPL: Northrop Papers). The text, headed "Subsistence Department", begins: "The paper marked 'A', dated 4 April ...".

[47] Ibid.

Richmond area] be discontinued immediately; and that the whole of the supplies received shall be devoted to the use of the troops. ... This note is addressed to you as immediate information. An appropriate order as your authority will be issued to you from the Adjutant and Inspector General's Office."[48]

That placed Northrop in an impossible position, as it removed any means whatever for settling the debt to his major suppliers. To make matters worse, it was (according to Bragg) the wish of Davis himself. Northrop shared his confidence with the clerk Jones, as Jones had just published an open letter to Davis on the subject of supplies which met Northrop's approval. Jones wrote that Northrop "showed me another order from Bragg (through the Adjutant General) to take possession of the toll meal at Crenshaw's mills. This [Northrop] says is contrary to contract, and he was going to the Secretary to have it withdrawn. 'Besides,' he said, 'and truly, it would do no good. The people must eat, whether they get meal from Crenshaw or not. If not, they will get it elsewhere, and what they do get will be so much diverted from the commissariat.' "[49]

Davis backed up Bragg. Jones saw the endorsement on April 19: "The President says that Gen B. certainly has the right to give orders—being assigned to duty here, and I presume, representing the President himself... Col. N. says that don't satisfy him; and that no general has a right to issue orders to him!"[50] Basically it upset and made ambiguous the chain of command responsibility. No army can afford that—least of all one placed as the Confederate army found itself placed for subsistence now.

It appears that Northrop then tried indirection. Four days later, on April 23, came a letter to Northrop from Captain P. A. Wellford, a commissary with much experience of the Richmond markets, actually stationed at the Haxall, Crenshaw mills to receive Tax-in-Kind wheat in Richmond. Captain Wellford summarized his experience—which was that paying the flour toll to Haxall, Crenshaw had significantly dampened inflation: "The dealers throughout the city, being aware of the supply passing over to Messrs H & C, have been considerably restrained in their charges in consequence. The toll thus paid has been, I consider, indirectly returned to the Government in great part by the effect it has had in keeping down prices here & elsewhere." As soon as Bragg's order was known, said Wellford, the price of flour shot up. On the other hand, the money had not yet actually been paid over; could there not be a reconsideration?[51]

---

[48]   April 14, 1864 (*OR* ser. IV, vol. 3, 300). The day before this, Bragg had tried to impose authority on Northrop in another matter. The clerk Jones saw the papers (now missing)—and failed to grasp the real issue: "Gen. Bragg received a dispatch yesterday, requesting that commissary stores for Longstreet be sent to Charlottesville, and he ordered his military secretary to direct the Commissary General accordingly. To this Col. Northrop, C.G.S., took exceptions, and returned the paper, calling the attention of Gen. B.'s secretary to the Rules and Regulations, involving a matter of red tape etiquette. The C.G.S. can only be *ordered* or *directed* by the Secretary of War." (*Diary*, II, 186).

[49]   Jones, *Diary*, II, 187.

[50]   Ibid., 188.

[51]   April 23, 1864 to Northrop (Huntington Library: Eldridge Coll., Box 63).

However Wellford's letter came to be written, it offered Northrop a separate reason to reopen the whole matter of command structure with the President. One case in point had just come to hand in the appeal of a Mrs. Boatwright for a barrel of Government Tithe-in-Kind flour or corn meal to relieve her family; that appeal the President was inclined to allow.[52] So Northrop sent Wellford's letter, accompanied by an urgent endorsement of his own, to Secretary Seddon with the request that he resubmit to the President. Northrop's language was not diplomatic but straightforward. He quickly summarized the questions leading up to Seddon's decision that Haxall, Crenshaw be paid in kind. Then:

> It appears that an appeal was taken from his decision in some irregular way, and it was decided against this Bureau & the War Department, that toll should no longer be paid in grain. It must now be paid for at about $200,000 more than it could have been bought for on the 4th April. ...
>
> This morning Mrs. Boatwright's case is sent in by the President for relief. The order of the President about this toll corn will create more & worse cases of the same kind, and I ask the Secretary of War to review the subject & have a reconsideration of a decision the full fruits of which are yet to come.[53]

Seddon read this and endorsed: "Respectfully resubmitted to the President at the special request of the Commissary General 27 Apl 64."

Davis was furious. He returned the whole lot direct to Northrop with a scorching endorsement:

> To what does the foregoing refer, in the expression "the President's desire on the subject"? [They were practically the words of Bragg's order.] I do not know what is regarded as an appeal made in an irregular way, but can see that some one must have been in error to produce the result described as a heavy pecuniary loss to the Govt.
>
> The deficient supply of grain, embarrassing as it has done the Army of Northern Virginia, should have suggested to all concerned that debts had better be paid in some other way than by drawing on that insufficient store.

(How then did Davis expect to pay Haxall, Crenshaw for milling Lee's flour? The contract, approved by the War Department, had specified payment in kind because the Treasury was so unwilling to release cash to settle government bills.) At the end of Davis's endorsement came a sharpness Northrop could never have looked for from his old friend:

> I must also inquire what order of the President is the subject of the closing criticism, and in what manner the President sent to you for relief of Mrs. Boatwright.[54]

---

52   NA, RG 109, B 364 (Letters rec'd., Records of the Sec. of War): endorsement only, April 18, 1864.

53   Ibid., April 26, 1864.

54   Ibid., April 28, 1864.

Northrop returned a patient and level answer, a copy of which was kept in his own possession for the rest of his life. The copy is without date, heading, address, or signature—suggesting how sensitive and private he considered it:

> ... I have, to my own mind, sufficiently demonstrated in endorsement of paper "B" [Bragg's order of April 14] that the deficient supply of grain for the Army of Virginia will not be increased by taking the toll of the mill—for an amount of grain, equivalent to the tolls intended to be sold to the public, must come by rail from the south for that purpose, or be abstracted from Virginia in other directions— which would be available to the Army if not sent to Richmond [for the populace].
>
> Consequently I consider that the measure indicated in Genl. Bragg's letter "B" (stated to be in accordance with the desire of the President...), was in no way calculated to reach the difficulty—and was one that would do no good.
>
> The paper marked "C" responds to the enquiry respecting Mrs. Boatwright, who applied to the President for relief. The Secretary of War (the representative of the President to the Bureau of War) forwards it for my consideration.[55]

The pressures of the Confederate presidency were by now overwhelming. It was understandable that Davis should turn to his old friend Bragg for advice and support. But when that advice made a still older friend's task impossible, it could only suggest that Davis was beginning to crack. He might have remembered that he himself had imposed the Commissary General's office on Northrop against Northrop's wish, and that for three years Northrop had tried his best to serve him.

Anything that might have followed was interrupted by the cruellest private blow. Davis was so raddled by his duties and pressures that he could hardly eat. On April 30 his wife brought a small lunch into his office to try and tempt him. Her back was turned only a moment when "the most beautiful and brightest of my children, Joseph Amory, had, in play, climbed over the connecting angle of a bannister and fallen to the brick payment below. He died a few minutes after we reached his side."[56] The Northrops' younger son Frank had been at the President's mansion playing with the Davis children earlier that morning.[57]

* * *

In the face of all his discouragements, Northrop kept on his job through sheer military rigor. But rigor and willed hardness in the end form a process. That process was stopping the Commissary General's ears against a rising tide of complaints. Major General John C. Breckinridge in western Virginia had felt himself forced to send out his own agents to purchase cattle for his men—at higher prices than schedule rates, and in opposition to Subsistence

---

55   Ca. April 29, 1864 (NYPL: Northrop Papers).

56   *Jefferson Davis: A Memoir by his Wife*, II, 496-97.

57   Information in January 1991 from Mrs. Mary Hunt, who had it from her grandfather, Frank Northrop.

Bureau men working his district. When Northrop protested, Breckinridge replied that the Commissary General's men did not fill his requisitions, yet were always sending food out of his district to Richmond: "I have tried every other mode prescribed by law and order. ... I know the great difficulties the Commissary General has to encounter in feeding the armies, and nothing could induce me to interpose an illegal or factious obstacle." [58]

Many of the complaints addressed to Northrop in the past had been frivolous or politically motivated; some still were. Perhaps Northrop hardly had the will to distinguish those that were not so motivated—and their increasing weight. That emerged in a new report he sent to Seddon on May 4, 1864: "Under the comparative scarcity of subsistence the Army has been reduced, as is known, to much less than what is called the regulation rations —but it is believed, with much less discomfort or suffering to the troops than was anticipated; with but little dissatisfaction on their part; and, it is hoped, with a better effect on their health than was produced by the wasteful issue of full rations." (Tell that to Sergeant John Worsham, whose Virginia company had just come through their worst winter in Virginia, and who wrote: "For months we had not had a full ration, and the rations became more scanty as the war continued, and after this time we never received as much as we wanted to eat unless we captured it from the enemy.") [59]

The conclusion of Northrop's report was unrelieved pessimism. To furnish the army any vegetables beyond occasional rice and peas, said the Commissary General, had been rendered "obviously impossible" by the state of the currency and slow transport—the vegetables would have rotted *en route*. (This he was able to improve upon considerably within a fortnight; but no hope lit the present report.) He saw the army's future food coming more and more from Europe through the blockade, but there again he found a check.

Subsistence Bureau purchasing agents abroad had been placed under control of a new Bureau of Foreign Supplies. Its chief was Thomas L. Bayne, brother-in-law of the Ordnance Chief Gorgas. Bayne had in fact run the Ordnance Bureau shipping operations earlier in the war, and Northrop expected him to favor that Bureau still. [60] Yet centralization of all the diffuse Confederate supply efforts abroad was itself right in line with Northrop's own philosophy. Moreover Bayne's new Bureau, assisted by the recent legislation, began to show some success in getting the old meat shipped in from the Islands at last. It seemed, however, that Northrop's instinct by this time was to resist every initiative not his own. His report finished in a weary rehearsal of Subsistence initiatives frustrated by his superiors. [61]

---

[58]   April 17, 1864 to Cooper (*OR* ser. I, vol. 33, 1289-90). See also Breckinridge to Northrop, May 4, 1864 (*OR* ser. I, vol. 37, pt. 1, 712).

[59]   Worsham, *One of Jackson's Foot Cavalry*, 195.

[60]   For Northrop's later and still unfavorable views on Bayne, see his letter of May 23, 1880 to Davis (Rowland, VIII, 458).

[61]   May 4, 1864 to Seddon (*OR* ser. IV, vol. 3, 379-80).

The date of Northrop's report, May 4, 1864, was the day the new Federal commander-in-chief Ulysses S. Grant began to move on Richmond. The campaign had been long in the planning. Grant had, as he wrote, two choices. One was to use Virginia's coastal rivers as highways to provision himself, and attack Richmond from the north and east. The disadvantage of that lay in Lee's interposing placements: the Confederates could then move north and east to oppose Grant on lines interior to his own. The alternative was to move on Richmond from the northwest: that would obviate Lee's geographical advantage, but would force Grant to carry all his provisions with him, as the country there was so exhausted of food and forage. So he must come from the east: longer marches on disadvantageous lines were nothing in the scale with inadequate provisions.[62]

Thus the contending armies would almost retrace the succession of the Seven Days' Battles fought around Richmond two years earlier. Only in 1864 Lee would be forced to react and retreat, while the Northern commander drove the offensive. Grant's wagon train was sixty-five miles long, and he could call on support from every direction. To the Virginia Peninsula southeast of Richmond, Grant brought Benjamin Butler and his army to attack Petersburg and cut vital rail lines connecting Richmond with the South. Southwest he had Brigadier General George Crook along the Tennessee-Virginia Railroad, destroying the line behind him as he came on to Richmond. In the Valley of Virginia, Grant planned to place the ruthless Philip Sheridan in command of 12,500 cavalry armed with new repeating carbine rifles and well mounted. Their charge would be to terrorize and lay waste all the farms with their crops maturing toward another harvest. Before that Sheridan's cavalry was to help Grant soften Richmond. And there was still Burnside with 20,000 troops kept as a reserve in Maryland.

Federal forces in the Richmond area alone outnumbered Lee's entire army more than two to one. Grant used his giant strength as a bludgeon: in six weeks he would lose more men than Lee commanded altogether. Lee no longer had the force for openly offensive strategy, so he took to thickly wooded lands above Richmond. But there, though his skill won victory after victory in the forests, the Confederates were always relentlessly pushed closer to Richmond as Grant swung southeast in a clockwise narrowing spiral.

Forests are impossible country through which to send large supplies. In normal circumstances, an army about to enter such places would call on their reserve supplies to cook and take with them enough food for several days ahead. But Lee's army had for months been unable to accumulate reserves of anything. When Lee knew he was going into the woods, he persuaded Northrop to send two trains laden with food to Beaver Dam Station, up on the Virginia Central line towards Louisa Court House and Gordonsville. Northrop did it against his better judgment. The trains contained over half a million rations of bread and nearly a million (reduced rations) of meat: to produce them Northrop had had to strip his cupboards to the walls, using

---

[62]   Grant, "Preparing for the Campaigns of '64", in *Battles and Leaders*, IV, 102-7.

every scrap still remaining from the largesse of March when the government ran the trains for a fortnight. On May 9 Sheridan's cavalry cut the railroad and burnt both trains with all the supplies.

Next day, May 10, Secretary Seddon gave authority for Burr Noland, as Chief Commissary of Virginia, to issue an emergency circular to all Subsistence men in the district. They had now no choice but to appeal to the populace or impress from them—even though such impressment had now been made illegal: "Impress freely if necessary. Give receipts for these supplies, to be paid for in cash or to be returned hereafter in kind, at the option of the party. ... Act with promptness, as the exigency is great."[63]

Through it all Lee's men put up such a show of strength in battle after bloody battle in the Spotsylvania Wilderness that their enemy greatly overestimated their numbers. In fact injury, death, and desertion were thinning Lee's ranks every day. Before the end of May, Grant had driven them so close in upon Richmond that they had no need of railroads. On May 29 the clerk Jones saw a full train of provisions standing in the center of the city at Broad Street, "visited hourly by wagons for the army now in the immediate vicinity."[64]

The Confederate ration was not enough for men going through what Lee's men were enduring. Their plight on June 1 at Cold Harbor (barely five miles out of Richmond) was to make a permanent nightmare for George Eggleston of Lamkin's Battery: "In my own battery three hard biscuits and one very meager slice of fat pork were issued to each man on arrival, and that was the first food that any of us had seen since our halt at the North Anna River, two days before. The next supply did not come till two days later, and it consisted of a single cracker per man, with no meat at all."[65]

Lee's own staff saw the results for themselves: "... the General received by mail a very small slice of salt pork, carefully packed between two oak chips, and accompanied by a letter saying that this was the daily ration of meat, and that the writer having found it impossible to live on it had been, though he was a gentleman, reduced by the cravings of hunger to the necessity of stealing. The incident gave the commanding general great pain and anxiety, and led to some strong interviews and correspondence with the Commissary Department."[66]

Northrop ransacked his cupboards again, and somehow managed to put together enough to raise the meat ration for Lee's troops to half a pound. Northrop wrote: "On the 1st of June, the twenty-sixth day of the fighting, application was made for whiskey to be issued to them, on the ground that they were broken down and needed the stimulant. It being impossible to issue whiskey [as Georgia's Governor Brown had prevented its making from the only nearby grain source large enough], coffee and sugar were given in lieu of it as an extra issue." And some fresh vegetables were now coming

[63]   OR ser. I, vol. 51, pt. 2, 910.

[64]   Diary, H, 222.

[65]   "Notes on Cold Harbor", in Battles and Leaders, IV, 231-32.

[66]   Charles C. Venable, "General Lee in the Wilderness Campaign", Ibid., 240.

through. That supply, wrote Lee on June 10, "greatly promotes the health and comfort of the men".[67] Northrop resumed: "On the 11th June, when the army had enjoyed a little rest and had to some extent recovered from the effect of continuous marching and fighting, the meat ration was reduced to one-third pound. The extra issue of coffee and sugar was and is continued on the ground that it is absolutely necessary..."[68]

Northrop had been forced to reduce Lee's meat ration again because Major General Robert Ransom, in charge of local Richmond troops participating with Beauregard in the defence of Petersburg, had heard of Lee's "very much larger" ration, and promptly complained to the Adjutant General: "It very naturally and justly produces discontent."[69] Ransom's men had homes in the area, to which they could return at least every few days for a bath and a feed and perhaps a night's sleep in a bed; so the comparison with Lee's veterans was odious. But as there were simply not the resources to feed the entire eastern army at half a pound a day, Ransom's complaint had the result of reducing his own commander-in-chief.

Even that, with its entire history, did not satisfy General Bragg, when he received the papers from Seddon with an approving endorsement. Bragg, determined to meddle, said that Ransom (and Archibald Gracie with his brigade for good measure) "had done and were still doing the same service as the Army of Northern Virginia...": so Bragg demanded that Ransom's and Gracie's men also be given coffee and sugar. Northrop, powerless to stop it, added another enemy-making endorsement: "It being presumed that the Secretary of War does not concur in the comments of General Bragg, no remark upon the inaccuracy is deemed necessary. The troops are now all upon the same footing."[70]

By then, late in June 1864, Grant's campaign against Richmond had ground to a halt. But Lee, in miraculously achieving stalemate, was forced into what he had always most dreaded—a siege at Petersburg, lying south on the railroad from Richmond. On June 26 he wrote to Davis of his fear that Grant would cut the railroad line bringing food to his troops. In that case Lee would have no option but to attack the entrenched Federals—"which I should not hesitate to do but for the loss it will inevitably entail. A want of success would in my opinion be almost fatal" to Richmond.[71] The Federals did indeed cut the line, but Lee was able to bring up supplies from trains stalled to the south by means of wagons.[72]

In July Lee agreed to let Jubal Early undertake the only true offensive the Confederates mounted in Virginia in 1864. Early took a small force (all Lee could spare, and probably more than he could spare) northwards down the Valley of Virginia into enemy territory. Early met with astounding suc-

---

[67] *Wartime Papers*, 773.
[68] Endorsement of June 16, 1864 on Ransom to Cooper, June 12 (*OR* ser. I, vol. 36, pt. 3, 899).
[69] Ibid., June 12, 1864, 898.
[70] Ibid., June 20 and 23, 1864, 899-900.
[71] *Wartime Papers*, 807.
[72] Ibid., June 25, 1864 to Davis, 811.

cess, and marched up to the gates of Washington. With an adequate force, he might have had a chance of taking the Federal capital, and thereby of unstringing the Federal campaign against Richmond. As it was, he was soon driven back up the Valley, where he gradually lost ground to Sheridan through the autumn.

The same attrition haunted Lee. On August 18 the Federals captured and cut a big section of the vital Weldon Railroad south of Petersburg. That line had been Lee's main food channel from the South. He tried repeatedly to dislodge the enemy and retake the railroad, but his forces were too weak. After that, supplies from the South could only come over the rackety Greensboro-Danville line, barely completed through the Piedmont by cannibalizing other lines in late spring.

To try to replenish Lee's failing ranks, Bragg ordered conscription so savage that no man between 15 and 55 was safe to walk the streets of Richmond without a military pass; not even to church. Stories were rife of large-scale entrapments and pitchforkings into the army. "No wonder there are so many deserters," wrote Jones in October; "no wonder men become indifferent as to which side shall prevail... They say now such a despotism is quite as bad as a Stanton [U. S. Secretary of War] despotism, and there is not a toss-up between the rule of the United States and the Confederate States."[73]

Early in July 1864 Northrop had received information that the Navy Department and the Nitre and Mining Bureau both had agents moving through Virginia fields purchasing the new wheat at high prices, apparently with the object of providing a six months' stockpile for their own employees. Already they had snapped up some of the best crops in the Richmond vicinity by ignoring schedule-prices.[74] At that, Northrop caused the Secretary of War to order that food supplies for any branch of government had to come through the Subsistence Bureau, at the rates of current army rations. But then the Treasury refused to give Northrop any precedence in the lengthening queue for cash.[75] One way and another it kept the Subsistence Bureau from much of the Virginia wheat harvest for 1864.

As if that were not enough, the Virginia commissioners for schedule prices now made a disastrous mistake. Attempting at last to bring their impressing prices somewhere near current market levels, the commissioners raised prices across the board by about five fold.[76] From every quarter came vociferous protest.[77] The effects on Subsistence purchasing were reported by Northrop on July 21: where the estimates granted by the last Congress were based on $2 cost per ration, the actual cost had just trebled overnight—with cash requisitions for his Bureau unpaid by the Treasury

---

73   *Diary*, II, 343-44.

74   S. B. French, July 6 and 8, 1864 (*OR* ser. IV, vol. 3, 533 and 535).

75   August 5, 1864 to Seddon (M-437, r 137, ff 276-77).

76   Jones, *Diary*, II, 253.

77   See e.g. J. W. G. Smith to Major J. S. Calvert, July 16, 1864 (*OR* ser. IV, vol. , 538-39).

now topping $20 million. He wrote: "...The purchase of wheat and corn at $30 and $24 respectively, by the Virginia schedule, and the reflex action on the other States..., calls for an expenditure which astounds and defies calculation." By the last irony, Northrop had just learned that the railroad chiefs had been so frightened by Seddon's threat of nationalization that "the railroads now have no difficulty in bringing whatever is offered".[78] The Commissary General called for an instant revision of the new prices, and all Virginia called with him. At the beginning of August they were brought down somewhat, but not before inflation had been given another vicious twist.[79]

As a hedge against the perils of Confederate money, Northrop had in June received Seddon's authority "to purchase the paper currency of the United States for the use of his office as occasion may require".[80] Instantly the Commissary General's men began buying greenbacks from Northern prisoners of war at Andersonville and elsewhere—as many as they would sell—at (Confederate) $4.50 each: Northrop set that rate. Other bureaus quickly followed suit.[81]

Conditions among the prisoners of war were growing terrible. There was no money to do anything for them. So many Union prisoners had been sent to Andersonville that illness was rampant and deaths rose ominously with summer heat. In July General Winder succeeded in stopping the shipment there of any more men. On the 25th he reported that Andersonville held close to 30,000 prisoners, 2,650 troops, 500 blacks, "and not a ration at this post", though Winder had ordered at least ten days' rations to be kept ahead.[82] Northrop rejoined that Winder had no right to give any orders on the subject. As Federal troops in the West had cut the railroad from Alabama (which had been supplying Johnston's troops with corn), "the support of the Army of Tennessee is on Georgia—which must still furnish Virginia with stores. ...Meanwhile we have no money either to buy or impress provisions. ...General Winder thinks the prisoners should have ten days' ahead, while the army may be restricted to a day's ration."[83]

Then came another and sharper difference with Davis. The district of Southwest Mississippi and East Louisiana had a new commander, Brigadier General George B. Hodge. He found "great abuse" in the commissariat there and applied to Davis for "disbursing officers of character and capacity to command the confidence of the community...". Davis asked Northrop (through the presidential aide, Preston Johnston, for "a list of officers of such standing ... from whom a commissary might be selected". Northrop protested that such a request again violated the command structure; the

[78] OR ser. IV, vol. 3, 549-50.

[79] Mrs. McGuire, a grandmother forced by inflation to clerk in the Subsistence Bureau, encountered the state of things in Richmond shops on August 22, 1864: "Just been on a shopping expedition for my sister and niece, and spent $1,500 in about an hour. I gave $110 for ladies' morocco boots; $22 per yard for linen; $5 apiece for spools of cotton; $5 for a paper of pins, etc." (Diary of a Southern Refugee, 292).

[80] June 8, 1864 (OR ser. IV, vol. 3, 477).

[81] Captain R. B. Winder to Major W. L. Bailey, July 9, 1864 (OR ser. II, vol. 7, 451; see also vol. 8, 312).

[82] OR ser. II, vol. 7, 499.

[83] Ibid., July 23, 1864, 499-500.

request should be put to the Chief Commissary of the district, the long-serving and highly trusted W. H. Dameron. The President's request had the effect of casting doubt on Dameron's "suitableness" for his post.

On August 5 Preston Johnston attacked Northrop in writing: did his words carry the accents of Davis himself? "As you are unwilling to receive or unable to comprehend the verbal communication I attempted to deliver you from the President, I have the honor to submit it to you in writing." Northrop sent that letter direct to Davis next day with a lengthy endorsement beginning:

> The enclosed paper is respectfully returned to His Excellency the President. All communications from him are entertained by me with willingness; but when they propose action, must be definitely apprehended by me. When the action proposed—to my understanding —conflicts with existing arrangements of the War Department for the management of the Commissariat, I consider it my duty to present this incompatibility for your consideration.

Any ambiguity in the command structure at that point threatened Subsistence operations over the entire district: it would instantly bring back the bad old days of generals and their field commissaries competing against the Bureau. Any officer charged with auditing claims from the public should certainly be under control of the Subsistence Bureau. "With these remarks, I herewith furnish a list of the principal officers of this Bureau now on duty in Mississippi."[84]

When Davis read that, he descended into cold rage. He called Northrop into his office, delivered himself of "severe remarks", forbade response, and sent him away. Apparently Davis came up to the threshold of sacking his Commissary General on the spot. There was in fact no rational way to disagree with what Northrop had written.

Before long, Davis thought better of his sharpness. That evening he left a private note in Northrop's office. (With the continuing enemy threat to Richmond, all the Bureau offices were being kept staffed night and day against emergencies.)[85] Davis's note has not been found: evidently he expressed the view that in several recent matters "a change" had "been wrought" in Northrop. It reached Northrop on returning to his office after supper. He responded instantly with a private letter that was both generous and unswervingly loyal:

> Augt 6th 64
> Dear Davis
>
> Your note of this evening left at the office has just been handed to me.
> Before leaving my house the bell rang several times, each time I hoped it was a message from you for me to go to you.
> I received in silence your severe remarks to day—involving your opinion that I had tried to mystify a simple point by a labored argument—not to the purpose—and that I had treated you badly. You had previously excluded discussion.

84 NA, RG 109, Officers: Herbert, R.G.
85 Adjt. Gen.'s order of May 12, 1864 (OR ser. I, vol. 36 pt. 2, 993).

> I then stated that I could not accept your opinion without dissent. Your response left me nothing but to accept the opinion you had expressed.

Northrop took this chance to defend his own actions in writing:

> I consider that justice to Major Dameron in the discharge of the duties imposed on him, and justice to myself in the discharge of the duties of my position, required what I did. I consider that my endorsement was to the point and appropriate to the message and letter to which it was affixed.
>
> I do not now desire you to examine, to concur, or to respond to this; I inform you what was in my mind in respect to the transaction.

What he wished to convey to Davis with the greatest clarity, however, was his own unaltered and ongoing sense of loyalty to his old friend. If Davis thought differently, he was wrong:

> No change has been wrought in me towards you, none can be in my feelings, for I know, that *deliberately unjust*, you can *never* become; and I am attached to you from your intrinsic qualities, and because you have ever been ready to do for me all that you could.
>
> I have steadily, from duty to Almighty God, tried to perform all my duties, and since you have held your present position, I have felt that the truest service I could render you was to do my official duty industriously, consistently and impartially.
>
> Of all men with whom I have ever had to deal, you and John Bellinger have seemed to me to be the most faithful in friendship. With him I have had serious differences on points of duty—on one occasion lasting long. This separation has never occurred with you before, and your letter of to night is most welcome to me.

Then Northrop encouraged his friend to take the long view:

> If circumstances permitted us to enter on the points which you think indicate that a change has been wrought in me, you might perceive that while our judgments differ, *mine* have seemed to me logical and proper. When this war is over and we can review matters advisedly, you may perceive that the animus of my acts has ever been to consult the interest of the cause and of my "Dept", and that perhaps my judgments have been correct, when it was supposed I was indifferent to the latter.

It proved an accurate forecast, as Davis's big book on the war was clearly to show when it appeared in later years (see above, p. 51 and below, p. 304). But the end of Northrop's letter turned back to the present:

> Your official position cannot sever the attachment which a true man has to you, although it may diminish the intercourse between you and your friends. Our duties occupy us fully, and while for the same ends, they seldom bring us together except for me to render explanations and to meet difficulties which are naturally prone to give rise to irritation. Meanwhile I have always intended to be faithful to you.
>
> Yours as ever
> L Northrop [86]

---

[86]   Harvard University: Dearborn Coll.

That letter to his old friend, written under the greatest provocation, gave fresh evidence of Northrop's self-control and perspicacity. The old intimacy, however, was not so easily regained. The two friends were to keep their distance for more than a dozen years.

By September 1864 there was not enough money in the Confederate Treasury to pay the soldiers' wages, let alone buy food for them. Northrop issued a new circular summarizing the rules of impressment, and adjuring his commissaries to apply them as rigorously as ever they could.[87] The real quarry of Northrop's circular was the new Secretary of the Treasury, George Trenholm. Treasury arrears to the Subsistence Bureau now topped $30 million.[88] Commissaries were receiving little cash to finance impressments anywhere. As soon as the circular was printed, Northrop took Frank Ruffin and headed for Trenholm's office. Together they read it to him, and told him that the fate of the country depended on him. Trenholm listened, sympathized, held out hopes.

On September 15 Major French reported to Northrop that their last month's collection of meat from all sources would not feed Lee's army alone for a week. People would not sell because they had begun to doubt their government's ability to "liquidate accrued indebtedness".[89] A month later, on October 18, French reported "the alarming condition of the commissariat" state by state:

> Georgia, Alabama, and Mississippi are the only States where we have an accumulation, and from these all the armies of the Confederacy are now subsisting, to say nothing of the prisoners.
>
> The Chief Commissary of Georgia telegraphs that he cannot send forward another pound.
>
> Alabama, under the most urgent call, has recently shipped 125,000 pounds, but cannot ship more.
>
> Mississippi is rendering all the aid possible to the command of General Beauregard [recently transferred west again], in supplying beef. She is without bacon.
>
> Florida is exhausted, and can only respond to the local demand.
>
> South Carolina is scarcely able to subsist the troops at Charleston and the prisoners in the interior of the State.
>
> During my late trip to North Carolina, I visited every section of the State for the purpose of ascertaining the true condition of affairs and, under your orders, to send forward every pound of meat possible to the Army of Northern Virginia, and to supply the forts at Wilmington. After a thorough and careful examination, I was unable to ship one pound to either Virginia or Wilmington ...

Northrop submitted the report first to the Secretary of War and then to the President, with his endorsement pointing out the $30 million owed the Bu-

---

[87]   September 5, 1864 (*OR* ser. IV, vol. 3, 622-23).

[88]   Ibid., 720.

[89]   Ibid., 653-54.

reau in unpaid requisitions by the Treasury. Davis sent back the briefest endorsement: "Returned to C.G.S. I have noticed the remarks on requirements, and learn that they have probably been delayed by absence of clerks" to sign new Treasury issues.[90]

The real situation was reported a few weeks later by Ruffin. On November 16, as Ruffin wrote, Major French had gone to Wilmington, on what both he and Ruffin both understood to be Secretary Trenholm's assurance that he would make available English "sterling bills" to pay for meat and coffee at that moment expected to be run through the blockade. But when French arrived and the cargoes came in, Trenholm said he had no recollection of such a promise and no money to give. With Northrop's blessing, Ruffin addressed the Secretary of War:

> What is material is that we now need £65,000 sterling, including £27,500 already drawn for, but including what we some time ago requested to be furnished Mr. W. G. Crenshaw in Liverpool.
>
> The intimation of a deferred payment in sterling has repelled our largest contractor, who only waits your and Mr. Trenholm's action to continue or cancel his orders. And others, if they have not preceded, will certainly follow him; whilst I am assured by Major French, whom I deem every way competent to the conclusion, that if he had the funds he could import all bacon necessary to meet our wants.
>
> I regret to find the credit of the Government so low, but I deal with facts; and knowing that the offer of sterling at an uncertain future period will prevent our getting meat from abroad at once— without which the Army must suffer—I respectfully ask that cotton (which the Government can give) shall be furnished in lieu of sterling which it cannot give.[91]

But the Treasury would not release cotton either.

When the Subsistence Bureau blockade-running contracts with Crenshaw and Power, Low came up for renewal, both Trenholm and Colonel Bayne from the Bureau of Foreign Supplies opposed it (as Ruffin reported) "on the ground that it will absorb, as they say it has absorbed, all the cotton they can carry out ...".[92] Northrop fought hard for the contract renewals.[93] He knew perfectly well the merchants were making 650 percent profit by the contract: such were the risks and losses of blockade-running against an encircling enemy. But Power, Low and Crenshaw between them had been responsible for the greatest importation of the army's meat.

Of course Bayne wanted to get all the contracts into his own hands. Bayne pointed to the fact that his Bureau of Foreign Supplies had by then

---

[90]   *The New York Herald*, July 21, 1865, 3. French's tabulation of the minuscule amounts of meat held at the various Army posts is with Ruffin's Papers (Va. Hist. Soc. R 8386a, 56).

[91]   *OR* ser. IV, vol. 3, 899-901. A full account is given in Ruffin's testimony before the Confederate Congress in January 1865 (pp. 23-29 in Va. Hist. Soc. transcript; omitted in *The New York Herald*).

[92]   *The New York Herald*, July 21, 1865, 2.

[93]   See the letter of October 16, 1864 from the Wilmington commissary Major S.V. Reid to Ruffin praising the achievements of Power, Low and testifying that the quality of food they brought in was excellent and superior to that of any other blockade-running firm; and correspondence between Lewis Crenshaw and Bayne (Va. Hist. Soc: Ruffin Papers).

imported 7 million pounds of meat. Ruffin retorted that that was "one-twelfth of what we consume".[94] But he and Northrop lost their fight to renew. In December 1864, by special order, all power to make foreign contracts was confided to Bayne's bureau. The same order covered trading through enemy lines as well.[95] Control of what had latterly proved the Subsistence Bureau's two chief sources for meat was thus taken away.

It could not have come at a worse time. Lee's army, engaged as they had been for months in the bloody and unequal struggle about Richmond, were again without adequate food. On October 21 Lee had reported his men getting bacon only one day in four. At the same time he ordered all the garrisoned forts below Wilmington to be provisioned for thirty days in case they were cut off by the enemy.[96] The Subsistence Bureau was able to carry that out through sheer luck, as French reported: " ... But for the timely arrival of the steamer *Banshee* at Wilmington, General Lee's order for thirty days' reserve at the forts could not have been furnished."[97] The *Banshee* and her sister ships would bring no more under those contracts.

The state of Lee's commissariat was seen by a blockade-running captain, John Wilkinson. After an absence at sea of only a few weeks, Wilkinson found himself on Confederate land again in the last weeks of 1864:

> The half starved and ill clad Army of Northern Virginia was in the trenches around Petersburg ... I was summoned again, and for the last time during the war, to Richmond. It was in the early part of December. There now remained to the Confederacy only the single line of rail communication from Wilmington, via Greensborough and Danville, to Richmond.
>
> The progress of demoralization was too evident at every step of my journey. And nowhere were the poverty and the straits to which the country was reduced more visible than in the rickety, windowless, filthy cars, travelling six or eight miles an hour over the worn out rails and decaying road-bed. We were eighteen hours in making the distance (about one hundred and twenty miles) from Danville to Richmond.
>
> As we passed the rear of General Lee's lines, and I saw the scare-crow cattle there being slaughtered for the troops, the game seemed to be at last growing desperate. We were detained for perhaps an hour at the station where the cattle were being slaughtered. Several soldiers who were on the train left us there; and as soon as they alighted from the cars, they seized portions of the offal, kindled a fire, charred the scraps upon the points of their ramrods, and devoured the unclean food with the avidity of famished tigers.[98]

Joseph E. Johnston's Army of Tennessee had remained relatively well fed for much of 1864. They ate the beef cattle still being swum across the

[94] *OR* ser. IV, vol. 3, 900.

[95] *The New York Herald*, July 21, 1865, 3.

[96] *OR* ser. I, vol. 42 pt. 3, 1056.

[97] *The New York Herald*, July 21, 1865, 3.

[98] John Wilkinson, *The Narrative of a Blockade-Runner* (N.Y.: Sheldon, 1877), 225-27.

Mississippi in their thousands.[99] They ate so continuously from Cummings's Subsistence Bureau stores in Atlanta that Johnston himself would remember Cummings as "one of the most intelligent and zealous agents of the Commissary General that I encountered during the war".[100] And they consumed nearly the whole of a fresh supply of cattle extracted from the Florida swamps during the first half of 1864 and driven up with the protection of a new "Cow Cavalry" under the command of former Congressman Charles Munnerlyn.[101] (Northrop thought so highly of Munnerlyn's men that he petitioned Secretary Seddon to exempt them from the ever more voracious conscription: and Seddon did it.[102])

Johnston had spent the entire spring and half the summer of 1864 falling back before the Union armies under Major General William T. Sherman — retreating cleverly, with skill and judgment, but retreating. Repeated calls from Davis and Bragg to attack the Federals were ignored or rejected. Reading between the few lines Johnston did write to them, it looked as if he was deciding to give up Atlanta. When Johnston said anything, he said he was badly outnumbered. He was; but his odds were better than Lee's in Virginia.[103]

Southern railroad lines after four years of war.

The light rails are almost fracturing, and ties are rotting from direct exposure to the ground. Appomattox Station, 1865.

Plate 97 in A. Gardner's Photograpic Sketchbook of the War.

[99] Northrop to Breckinridge, February 9, 1865 (*OR* ser. I, vol. 46 pt. 2, 1222).

[100] *Narrative of Military Operations*, 351.

[101] See Robert A. Taylor, "Cow Cavalry: Munnerlyn's Battalion in Florida", in *Florida Historical Quarterly*, vol. 65, no. 2 (October 1986), 196-214.

[102] *OR* ser. IV, vol. 3, 730-31.

[103] Eckenrode, *Jefferson Davis*, 284, 293.

On July 17 Davis removed Johnston from command of the Army of Tennessee, and replaced him with 33-year-old General John B. Hood. Hood was, as Lee observed, a born fighter; but there was a question about his other qualities needed for such a command. At the beginning of September Hood lost Atlanta to Sherman. (Just before the city burned, Cummings got a good part of his Subsistence stores away to Augusta.)

Then Hood convinced Davis to let him invade Tennessee. The object was to cut Sherman's supply lines behind him, and so force him to retreat. A year ago, under someone other than Bragg, it might have worked. (Even four months ago Johnston had tried to get support in Richmond for sending Major General Nathan B. Forrest's cavalry to do that job. But Bragg used his position as the President's adviser to oppose the plan—it was said because he did not want any chance of success there to cast odious comparison on his own late generalship.) Now the huge Federal machine was invincible: Sherman paid little heed to Hood's diversion, leaving him to the tender mercies of Major General George Thomas, "the Rock of Chickmauga". Thomas dealt Hood a smashing defeat at Nashville in December. That was the virtual end of the Confederate Army of Tennessee, and of significant Confederate opposition west of the Atlantic coastal states.

104

SHERMAN'S FORAGERS ON A GEORGIA PLANTATION.

---

[104]   *Battles and Leaders*, IV, 674.

Hood's departure from Georgia, meanwhile, had opened a broad avenue for Sherman to march unopposed through Georgia. He promptly took it, cutting a sixty-mile wide swathe through the best remaining Confederate farmlands—gorging, burning, laying waste everything public or private that came within his reach. It was a new notion of "total war", Sherman told his soldiers. Their job was not to fight, but to consume. Later he wrote: "Each mile of advance swept aside all opposition, consumed the very food on which Lee's army depended for life ...".[105]

On December 20 the first goal of Sherman's march was evacuated by the Confederates. It was Georgia's port city of Savannah—which Sherman presented to Lincoln as a "Christmas present". At the same moment in Virginia, Sheridan's cavalry was moving in to destroy the great Confederate resource for salt—all the mines around Saltville.

---

[105]　Ibid., 259; see also 675.

CHAPTER 20

HEADHUNTING

When Congress reconvened on November 7, 1864 the mood was murderous. Despite all their objurgations, investigations, rhetoric and new laws, Lee's army still lacked food. And the condition of much of what did reach the soldiers was horrible. When meat came in from the Islands now, it was often half rotten from protracted storage waiting for transport. Yet if it was even conceivably edible, the commissariat had no choice but to send it up as better than nothing. When the Congressmen heard that army rations were not only short but rotting, even friends of the Davis Government gave ear to the headhunters.

Henry Foote led the pack in new investigations throughout late November. One day, as Northrop was being supported by Congressman T. B. Hanly of Arkansas, Foote ridiculed Hanly with loud laughter. They immediately came to blows on the floor of the House. Hanly savagely pounded Foote. Foote responded by "tearing off Hanly's shirt bosom and knocking Commissary General Lucius B. Northrop [who tried to separate them] into a corner".[1] When *The Richmond Examiner* called on the House to expel Foote, Foote challenged the editor to a duel. The editor's second was Foote's fellow Congressman from Tennessee (but bitter enemy) W. G. Swan. Foote insulted Swan as "no gentleman"; Swan hit him over the head with an umbrella; Foote picked up a gun and tried to shoot Swan; and both Congressmen and the editor found themselves in the Richmond City Court severely reprimanded and bound over to keep the peace.[2]

(It proved to be the virtual end of Foote's Confederate career. In January 1865, claiming a one-man peace initiative to Washington, he absconded through enemy lines. Refused a hearing by Lincoln and threatened with imprisonment, Foote took ship for Europe and disported himself in Paris and Italy through the last days of the Confederacy. On returning to New York, he was expelled to Canada and lived there as a refugee until permitted to go back to Tennessee, perhaps as a part of carpetbagging Reconstruction.)

---

[1] T. R. Hay, "Lucius B. Northrop", 18.
[2] E. M. Coulter, *The Confederate States*, 143.

270

On November 30, 1864 Northrop responded to a Senate enquiry as to whether he had stopped meat rations for prisoners of war. Northrop stated that he had, on October 1, because of the grave shortage of meat for the Confederate army: the prisoners were given sorghum as a substitute. But then supplies of sorghum failed, and the prisoners were returned to eating just what Confederate soldiers ate.[3]

On December 12 Northrop answered the Senate's enquiry over rations for the army. At the end of a detailed summary of all the existing difficulties, he cited a new one. Major Tannahill, just back from North Carolina, reported that the state government there was buying corn and wheat for their employees at double the schedule rates. Other state governments would be sure to follow. Northrop's conclusion was bleak: "... Nothing seems left to us but to yield to the demand, and appeal to the people to supply the Army on the terms they exact." Nobody outside the Subsistence Bureau believed that moment was actually upon them. Northrop knew they didn't believe him, and finished his report with a quick summary of the influences that defeated him: "If the Army is not as well fed as the condition of the country will allow, or if at any time it should be without food, it will be the result of these influences in overruling an efficient and comprehensive system which has proved and maintained itself against constant and potent opposition."[4] If the Senators saw themselves included in that opposition, they were welcome to do so.

Writing a few days later to Secretary Seddon about the failures of blockade-running management, Northrop rendered something like a final personal judgement on the entire Confederate war effort: "... If all Government agents were ruled by comprehensive principles and a single eye to the general weal, and not influenced by special interests or inclinations—if these agents would inflexibly carry out orders, and not be swayed by the representations of ship owners or captains seeking preferable freight:—in other words, if the War Department could be a center of unity, & if the Government could be a unit, the theory of the regulations would be universally applicable. I am however satisfied that results have shown what will always be the case—that the supplies of this Bureau will be the last to get in."[5]

On December 3 Frank Ruffin reported that they had only nine days' rations in store for Lee. As no more came in during the ensuing nine days, the crisis overtook them on December 13 when Subsistence stores ran out of salt meat.[6] Disaster was averted by luck and begging. The luck was a timely arrival at Wilmington of several Crenshaw and Power, Low ships— probably the last of their kind as contracts lapsed. The begging was Northrop's going hat in hand to the navy and the state of North Carolina—both of whom had beaten him out of the 1864 wheat market by offering more than sched-

---

[3]   November 30, 1864 to Seddon (NA, RG 109, Presidential Messages: filed with Davis's Message to Congress of December 6, 1864).

[4]   *OR* ser. IV, vol. 3, 930-32.

[5]   December 20, 1864 (Ibid., 473; MS copy in Ruffin Papers, Va. Hist. Soc. 8386a, 18-36).

[6]   Lee to Davis, December 14, 1864 (*Wartime Papers*, 877).

ule-prices. Both now responded to his appeal for Lee's starving army. These combined actions would put off the next food crisis for nearly a month.[7]

In late December Northrop's reflection on the failed chances for unified action was ironically underlined. From the columns of *The Richmond Examiner* (whose editor had been smelling the Commissary General's blood for months) wafted a recipe for giving Lee's army one gigantic feed on New Year's Day, 1865. It could be done, said the paper, by public contributions of food and money. And its success showed just how much still remained' hidden by the Southern people. Government employees high and low, well-to-do farmers and their wives, leading citizens of every stripe salved their consciences by bringing forth piles of food and wealth. Secretary Trenholm of the Treasury gave $2,000 of his own money. The Richmond Theatre raised $15,000 with a benefit performance. And *The Examiner* regaled its readers by reporting "the biggest barbecue ever gotten up on this continent", served to the troops on a twenty-mile front—"a table twenty miles long".[8] Then they all went back to business as usual.

By the end of December 1864 the money brokers in Richmond were offering $50 Confederate for $1 in gold.[9] Subsistence Bureau requisitions unpaid by the Treasury exceeded $34 million. Other bureaus were suffering similarly, as total Treasury arrears topped $320 million.[10] Trenholm demanded authority to impose an across-the-board tax of 16 percent on the net worth of every Confederate citizen. His proposal left Congress "weak in the knees".[11] By January 11, 1865 gold was selling in Richmond at $66 Confederate.[12]

The turn of the year brought two railroad measures for which Northrop had long pleaded. One was the stoppage of all private freight from Georgia into Virginia. The other was the wholesale impressment of the Piedmont Railroad. Then nature intervened. Floods washed out a section of the scratchily built line, leaving a gap which would take weeks to repair—if men could be found and detailed. And that promptly brought on the next food crisis for Lee. When Seddon told the general he must impress, Lee telegraphed back on January 11: "There is nothing within reach of this army to be impressed."[13]

---

[7]   Ruffin in *The New York Herald*, July 21, 1865. At this moment Lee's soldiers received not only staples but the occasional "luxury" not seen since early in the war. Captain James Hunter, stationed six miles below Richmond, wrote to his sister on December 17: "Flour, sometimes [corn]meal, bacon, occasionally beef, rice, sugar, coffee, vinegar, salt, pepper, soap and yesterday and occasionally cabbage, turnips and potatoes are the issues we get. We don't get very much but by being very careful we do well on it and are healthier than if we got more" (*The Confederate Veteran*, November-December 1991, 36).

[8]   G. F. J. O'Brien, "James A. Seddon, Statesman of the Old South" (Ph.D. thesis, Univ. of Maryland, 1963, 480), quoting *The Richmond Examiner* between December 20, 1864 and January 4, 1865.

[9]   Jones, *Diary*, II, 368.

[10]   *OR* ser. IV, vol. 3, 974-75.

[11]   Kean, *Inside the Confederate Government*, 188.

[12]   Jones, *Diary*, II, 383.

[13]   *Wartime Papers*, 881.

That day Northrop summarized the position for Seddon. If the Piedmont Railroad could be restored at all, it would take two months. During that time Lee's food could come only from southwestern Virginia and the Carolinas. For that, three things were needed: "funds, wagon transportation, and co-operation of the people".[14] Northrop recognized that he himself was not the man to make this appeal, damaged as he was by persistent congressional investigations, press rhetoric, and public anger over impressments. The only man to galvanize the people, Northrop told Seddon, was Lee himself. Seddon sent the idea to Lee with heavily qualified endorsement.[15] Lee took Northrop's advice. He addressed a circular "to the farmers, millers, and other citizens to furnish, with all possible promptness, whatever breadstuffs, meat (fresh or salt) or molasses they can spare".

Lee's circular concluded: "Arrangements have been made to pay promptly for all supplies delivered under this appeal, or to return the same in kind as soon as possible."[16] What were these arrangements? Unless the Treasury was prepared to withdraw all limitations imposed on Northrop and other Bureau chiefs and supply unlimited cash, Lee's last sentence came down to a promise to return the supplies in kind at an early date. As Lee's circular appeared on January 12, 1865, Seddon was writing a special order in Richmond, concluding: "It is expected that the present emergency will be of short duration...".[17]

As soon as he saw that, Northrop pointed out that such promises were futile. Seddon's claim that the food crisis in Virginia would be brief was sure to be read as information from Northrop's Bureau. Northrop contradicted: "I have therefore to state that the exigency for food has been on us for weeks —that it has been long foreseen and announced—and I see no prospect of its passing away. The feeding from hand to mouth is our permanent condition... I cannot authorize officers to hold out the expectation that the provisions, impressed, will or can be restored in kind. This Bureau will, as it has ever done, exert every means to collect supplies—but cannot hold out expectations which it sees no prospect of fulfilling, nor to allow to pass unnoticed the order to make arrangements to lighten burdens on the people, when it well knows that it is powerless to make such arrangements."[18]

On January 16 Lee told Seddon the popular appeal had succeeded: "... I am glad to say that so far as I know, the crisis in relation to this matter is now past."[19] But of course it was not past at all. Hardly a week later a letter came in from Captain Thomas Foster, one of Northrop's longest serving and most skilled Virginia cattle agents, in the Potomac Valley: "I know the Government needs every hoof in my division, yet I do not feel that I would be

---

[14] *OR* ser. I, vol. 46, pt. 2, 1035.

[15] Ibid., 1039-40.

[16] *Wartime Papers*, 883.

[17] *OR* ser. I, vol. 46, pt. 2, 1041.

[18] Northrop to Cooper, January 12, 1865 (M-474, r 154, ff 632-33). Northrop or his clerk mistakenly dated it January 11, and Cooper himself corrected it.

[19] *Wartime Papers*, 882.

doing the farmers justice to take their stock unless I knew where or when the pay would come. I now owe the people $40,000 or $50,000 in gold and greenbacks." Foster's letter was addressed to Richard Noland, who endorsed that he had sent all the gold and greenbacks he had, and they were not enough. Noland sent the letter to his brother Burr, Chief Commissary of Virginia: Burr Noland reported to Northrop that he had no more gold either.[20] Northrop sent it all to Seddon, together with a letter from a Charlottesville commissary who stated that he owed $1,200,000—much of it outstanding since the spring of 1864.[21]

Seddon passed the lot to the Secretary of Treasury, who duly informed Northrop that "the resources of the Treasury do not admit of the payment of specie in satisfaction of requisitions". Northrop then asked Secretary Trenholm to send the whole file to the President as of "vital and immediate importance".[22] Davis did nothing effective.

Congress meanwhile had been busy. Since the departure of Foote, the joint committee of investigation had been chaired by John B. Baldwin. He and his fellow Virginians forced the broadening of the Subsistence inquiry to cover the entire spectrum not only of War Department Bureaus, but all the executive appointments and officers right up to the existing cabinet. Richmond rocked with rumors that Congress was going to unstring Davis's Presidency and undertake its own peace overtures to Washington.

The Congressional imputation upon Cabinet officers so distressed Secretary Seddon that on January 18, 1865 he sent in his resignation. One of his reasons, he told Robert Kean privately, was that he had been "deeply pained" at the testimony of Northrop and Ruffin, "attacking" him (as he thought) before Congress instead of resigning themselves.[23] There is nothing in their surviving testimony suggesting any special wish to attack Seddon: Northrop and Ruffin had simply told the truth as they saw it.[24]

Through it all a significant element in Congress pursued Northrop as their chief quarry. ("The Commissary General's head is to go off," wrote Kean on January 23: "this is settled.")[25] The way Congress found to attack Northrop was to enact a new law that the office of Commissary General, like that of Quartermaster General, should carry the military rank of Brigadier General. The Senate passed that law on January 26, the House followed on February 8. It would force the President to send them a nomination—whether

---

[20]   *OR* ser. IV, vol. 3, 1031-32.

[21]   Ibid., January 6, Charles Taylor to Richard Noland, 1865, 1005.

[22]   Ibid., January 30, Trenholm to Davis, 1865, 1045.

[23]   *Inside the Confederate Government*, 193.

[24]   MS copy, apparently complete, given by Ruffin to Va. Hist. Soc. (Much of the testimony was printed in *The New York Herald*, July 21, 1865.) The Ordnance chief Gorgas wrote in his diary on January 15, 1865: "... Those about Northrop abuse the President grossly, from which I infer that their principal has changed his tone" (165). The inference was almost certainly wrong. If Ruffin and others behaved differently, it would have been from outraged loyalty to their Bureau chief.

[25]   *Inside the Confederate Government*, 191.

of Northrop or someone else—on which they could act. The feeling against Northrop was not unanimous. When Congressman Miles admitted openly "the object was to remove Col. Northrop", Baldwin protested that the Bureau had been well run. Miles rejoined: "In these times the test of merit must be success."[26]

It could be thought that Davis had anticipated Northrop's removal when in November 1864 he directed Seddon to send in Northrop's nomination as Brigadier General. Seddon had sent the nomination on November 26 to Adjutant General Cooper. If it reached the Senate, they did not act on it. Davis had not spoken to his old friend since the dressing down in the presidential office in August.[27]

Lee joined the clamor for Northrop's removal. On January 27, 1865 he reported alarming levels of desertion caused by non-payment of the troops' wages for months, and insufficient food: "I do not see why the supplies that are collected from day to day could not, by intelligent effort, be collected in such a manner as to have more on hand at a given time. The fact that they are collected at all is proof that they exist...".[28] Of course they existed. They only wanted buying and transporting. At the time of Lee's last food crisis a fortnight ago, Northrop had called again for sixty wagon trains in lieu of the broken railroad.[29] But that was no longer realistic either, for Lee had not the forces to spare from fighting.

Davis did not accept Seddon's resignation until February 1, when he wrote him a long and generous letter.[30] It was another six days before a new Secretary of War came on duty. He was General John C. Breckinridge, and gossip was that one of his conditions for accepting the post was that Northrop must go. Breckinridge immediately called for reports from all the Bureau chiefs of their resources and needs.

Northrop's report to Breckinridge was dated February 9, but the assemblage of necessary documents delayed its submission until February 13. It covered a broad range: statements of meat stranded *en route* to Richmond from points inland and through the blockade; breadstuffs *en route* to Richmond; the history of supplies from the Trans-Mississippi; statements of long-term debts unfunded by the Treasury, of widespread currency and transportation failures; continuous attempts to get supplies from beyond enemy lines in the teeth of government opposition; the sabotage of successful blockade-running contracts by Bayne's Bureau of Foreign Supplies and the Treasury; harassment by conscription officials until all his best Subsistence officers were distracted with half their time taken up trying to retain irreplaceable experts; repeated Congressional investigations, full of insulting imputations but always vindicating his policies—until now. Then at last Northrop offered his resignation:

---

[26]   Jones, *Diary*, II, 416.
[27]   Northrop to Davis, March 31, 1878 (Rowland, VIII, 145).
[28]   Lee to Seddon (*Wartime Papers*, 886-87).
[29]   January 11, 1865 to Seddon (*OR* ser. I, vol. 46, pt. 2, 1035).
[30]   *OR* ser. IV, vol. 3, 1046-48.

If the chief of the bureau cannot be trusted to do all in his power to put men in the field consistently with his duty of feeding the army, then he had better be substituted by some one who can.

... Unless suitable men, unembarrassed by fears of removal (except for inefficiency), ample funds, and (for the present) coin in sufficient quantity to keep the Army of Virginia in beeves (which, being at present driven from beyond our lines, can be obtained by coin alone) are furnished, this bureau cannot perform its functions.

And this brings me finally to the inquiry you make—as to the ability of a chief of this bureau to effect the purposes for which it was created. I observe, then: that, in my judgement, it cannot be done, except under an administration of the other branches of service (whose operations underlie those of this bureau) different from the past.[31]

On February 8 Lee had written that his ragged, hungry army was now kept so constantly at full stretch without adequate food or clothing that they could not continue: "Yesterday, the most inclement day of the winter, they had to be retained in line of battle, having been in the same condition the two previous days and nights. I regret to be obliged to state that under these circumstances, heightened by assaults and fire of the enemy, some of the men had been without meat for three days, and all were suffering from reduced rations and scant clothing, exposed to battle, cold, hail, and sleet. ... Taking these facts in connection with the paucity of our numbers, you must not be surprised if calamity befalls us."[32]

When that came into Breckinridge's office, Northrop was with him, and apparently Robert Kean also. Kean recorded that Breckinridge showed it to Northrop—who then could conceal no longer his own utter weariness of the whole unequal struggle. Kean recorded Northrop's responses as follows:

"Yes," the old stoic remarked, "It is just what I predicted long ago." And he went on to rehearse the record without a single suggestion of relief.

General Breckinridge inquired, "But Colonel, what shall we do?"

"Well, I don't know. If my plans had been carried out instead of thwarted etc., etc."

The Secretary sent [Lee's] letter up to the President, who presently returned it with a very sharp endorsement...[33]

It was perhaps the most ungenerous and ultimately selfish endorsement of Davis's Presidency. But his words were a speaking likeness—especially the tell-tale adverb "patiently": "This is too sad to be patiently considered, and cannot have occurred without criminal neglect or gross incapacity. Let supplies be had by purchase, or borrowing, or other possible mode."[34]

"Soon after," Kean recorded, "the President wrote the Secretary a note that meat and whiskey must be borrowed, or impressed, and should be sent over before the commissary officers slept that night."

---

31   *OR* ser. I, vol. 46, pt. 2, 1211-26.

32   Ibid., 1209-10.

33   *Inside the Confederate Government*, 200.

34   *OR* ser. I, vol. 46, pt. 2, 1210.

This too Colonel Northrop saw but laid coolly aside, remarking to [Quartermaster General] Lawton *sotto voce* that it was "sensational"; to the Secretary that he could not borrow because he had already borrowed more than could be returned, nor impress because by the law money had to be tendered...

This probably hastens his fate, which was sealed before.[35]

Clearly Northrop intended it so. His resignation was accepted by Breckinridge, and on February 16 he was succeeded by Brigadier General Isaac St. John, the chief of the Nitre and Mining Bureau who had competed against Northrop to buy into the Confederate harvest of 1864 for his own Bureau.

Northrop spent some days instructing his successor in the duties of Commissary General. He introduced the Bureau subordinates, all of whom were staying on except Frank Ruffin. Northrop also took the precaution of having copies made of many important documents, to keep privately in case of future need.[36] (It is well he did so; without those copies, scattered though they now are, reconstructing the history of his Bureau would have been nearly impossible.) Then as he was clearly no longer wanted, he made arrangements to leave Richmond. There was no point in returning to Charleston, which fell to the Federals on February 18, 1865 after a siege of years. The old city's capture was part of a "March through the Carolinas" by Sherman.

The Federal idea now was to "punish" South Carolina in particular as "the seat of the rebellion". While one wing of Sherman's army occupied Charleston, another sacked and burned the state capital city of Columbia, a hundred and fifty miles to the northwest. From Columbia the Federals headed towards Wilmington and Richmond. On the way their cavalry came to the quiet little county town of Lancaster near the North Carolina border. There Lucius Northrop's brother Claudian had been living for nearly four years. His law practice in Charleston decimated by the approach of war, Claudian had found happiness in the love of a beautiful woman thirty years his junior, who had become his second wife in April 1861. Together they had come to Lancaster to supervise a plantation left to the Catholic Diocese of Charleston. As soon as Columbia burned, Claudian made his will. On February 26 the foraging "bummers" who regularly preceded the main body of Sherman's army reached the plantation, demanding family silver and much else. Claudian protested he had nothing for them. They killed him and burned the house.

Lucius, with his insider's knowledge and military training, was better equipped to anticipate the Federals. When he finished in Richmond, he reverted to the plan he had formed in 1860 as war approached—to get away and establish his family on a quiet farm. His choice now fell on an obscure place forty miles southwest of Raleigh, in the center of North Carolina. It lay beside the Deep River at a place called "Egypt" (so named by travellers re-

---

[35]   *Inside the Confederate Government*, 200.

[36]   July 31, 1885 to Davis (Museum of the Confederacy: Davis Coll.). Northrop's use of his document copies informs many of his late letters to Davis. After Northrop's death the copies were dispersed; not all have yet been located.

turning from the Nile, where corn grew as richly as at the North Carolina river).[37] Near the farm lands lay open-pit coal mines, working to produce fuel for blockade-runners and government iron foundries. There had grown up shops and huts for workers.

Northrop had learned of the place through an agent of Bishop Lynch's —James Browne, a hard man, but seemingly trustworthy. The area had never seen any fighting. Northrop had already sent some of his slaves there for safety, but they found it a rough place (as Lucius had reported to Bishop Lynch at Charleston in the previous November): "... My negroes dread the Yankees. Nannie, Cuffie's wife (Belly's child you know) wrote me a letter from 'Egypt' Chatham Co, N Ca—this is with Jas Browne at the mine—complaining of the man & the nature of affairs generally. The culminating evil was that she was surrounded by white people of the lowest class, such as she was not accustomed to and had never before been among...".[38]

Rough or not, Lucius Northrop went down in March 1865 and rented the plantation house with some farm land. He returned to Richmond, vacated his house there, sold the furniture, took his family of six with six servants, and started for "Egypt" on March 29 or 30. Their departure was in the nick of time. Grant was closing in, with Sherman not far behind. Confederate archives were being boxed for removal. The creaky trains still ran, and it proved not impossible to get places for them all in a train leaving the city.

Arrived at "Egypt" on the evening of March 30, they found their large house occupied by hospital patients from Fayetteville, to the south. Sherman had just sacked Fayetteville, and the authorities there had pitched on the mansion at "Egypt" as a place to send their patients. Smallpox had broken out among the patients, rendering the house uninhabitable without fumigation, even if the Northrops could get it back. The alternative was grim: "I had to put my family in a little tenement of three diminutive rooms, the other half occupied by a coal miner and family. Since then we have lived there surrounded by those whom we could not associate with and therefore soon became unfriendly." When the Federals arrived there, they burned the farm fences and took the horses. Northrop offered his people their choice: "I had caused my negroes always to be instructed; therefore they could think, take care of themselves, and they left me—except the house servants—to return to [South] Carolina."[39] That left the man of 53 to work his fenceless hired fields with only his ten-year-old younger son to help him. The Northrops' elder son was away in the Confederate Navy, which he had joined at sixteen.

*   *   *

Back in Richmond, Commissary General St. John and Secretary of War Breckinridge began their offices in agreement with the general derogation of Northrop and all his works. Very quickly St. John came to a different

---

[37]   William S. Powell, *The North Carolina Gazetteer: A Dictionary of Tar Heel Places* (UNC, 1968), 131. The place (since 1907 in Lee County) is still known as "Little Egypt".

[38]   November 1, 1864 (CDA 31 R 3).

[39]   July 7, 1865 to Rev. J. J. Early (Georgetown archives).

understanding, as he wrote: "Beyond the most trusted confidential officers of the Executive and the War Department, few knew how far military events and hostile pressure had come to control the power of the Subsistence Bureau to execute its ordinary duties." He found Northrop's staff excellent and very helpful.[40] When in later years he asked them for recollections, Burr Noland would write to St. John: "I think the plan adopted by your predecessor, Colonel Northrop (which was continued by you), for obtaining for the use of the army the products of the country, was as perfect and worked as effectively as any that could have been devised. ... Your action was prompt, energetic and efficient."[41]

It was indeed—enabled to be so by a number of factors. Early 1865 found St. John a vigorous 37, as opposed to Northrop's 53 (the verge of old age as they counted things then). St. John was a Yale graduate, trained for both civil engineering and the law. Several years as a journalist had given him an ability to organize his thoughts tersely, and ease of expression on paper. Then St. John had acquired an experience of railroad administration in the half dozen years before the war. From 1862 he had run the Confederate Nitre and Mining Bureau with great success.

St. John had not wanted the commissariat any more than his predecessor had done. Yet he took a hand with a vigor and imagination to recall the Northrop of early 1861. He too realized that the only chance to feed Lee's army now lay in a general appeal to the people. But for his appeal, St. John evolved an ingenious scheme. Within days of taking office, he asked each farmer or miller or planter to subsist an individual soldier for six months. The plan met an enthusiastic response, and in a few more days food of every description began rolling into Subsistence depots everywhere in the Confederate states. An appeal to Governor Vance of North Carolina produced a further significant amount. St. John also asked his own successor at Nitre and Mining to turn over reserves of food (which St. John himself had bought over Northrop's price in 1864)—thus opening a source apparently closed to Northrop.[42]

By March 10, 1865 St. John would give Breckinridge his opinion that supplies sufficient to feed Lee's army could be collected "with adequate military protection ... and with a prompt supply of suitable funds. ... A great effort will be required, but with funds it can be done."[43] That was the refreshing note St. John struck. Northrop had been saying the same thing for years, but he had come to say it negatively: without cavalry and funds, food could not be collected. St. John, beginning with a clean slate, cheered up everybody immensely. The appearance of a new Commissary General after four years, moreover, made everyone realize at last the desperate position of food supply in the South. St. John also was a centralizer; but now finally the Confederates had learnt that lesson.

---

[40]   July 14, 1873 to Davis (*SHSP*, vol. 3, no. 3, 97 and 99).

[41]   Ibid., April 16, 1874 to St. John, 107-8.

[42]   Ibid., July 14, 1873 to Davis, 98.

[43]   *OR* ser. IV, vol. 3, 1137.

The most powerful of St. John's advantages was the new Secretary of War under whom he served. Breckinridge was not only a clear military thinker with field experience of commissary privation and self-catering; he also had governmental experience running right up to the Vice Presidency of the United States before the war (under James Buchanan). Breckinridge understood exactly what his Commissary General needed, and was utterly determined to give it to him.

First, he had St. John into his office every day to report progress and make his needs known.[44] Breckinridge backed St. John to the hilt. On February 16, 1865, St. John's first day in office, Breckinridge telegraphed to Beauregard at Columbia, South Carolina: "Our necessities here are great. Why interfere with provisions at Charlotte Junction, ordered here by the Commissary General?"[45] A fortnight later Joseph E. Johnston was served with the same message. Their protests were overridden.[46] Almost overnight, with such help as this, St. John was able to reverse the long-standing pattern of Beauregard and Johnston feeding at the expense of Lee in Virginia.

Nowhere was the influence of Breckinridge more palpable than in the courage it gave his assistants to tell him the truth. On March 5 a letter was addressed to him by his Assistant Secretary John Campbell—full of home truths the like of which had never crossed Seddon's desk from any pen but Northrop's:

> This Department is in debt from $400,000,000 to $500,000,000. The service of all its bureaus is paralyzed by the want of money and credit. ...
> Subsistence for the army ... has been attended with difficulty since the commencement of the war, in consequence of the want of efficient control over the transportation and difficulty of funds. There were abundant supplies in the country at that time, and the transportation was fully adequate, but these were not under control. The Treasury has never answered the full demands of the Commissary Department with promptitude.
> ... These embarrassments have become so much accumulated that the late Commissary General pronounces the problem of subsistence of the Army of Northern Virginia, in its present position, insoluble; and the present Commissary General requires the fulfillment of conditions, though not unreasonable, nearly impossible.[47]

Nearly but not quite. Why hadn't Campbell sent such a letter to Seddon in Northrop's years? Because Seddon would have done nothing much. Breckinridge now seized the reins of both Treasury and the railroads. "The damaged roads were speedily repaired," wrote Noland.[48] And by using the new orders, Breckinridge really did make the trains run for the government and not for the profiteers.

---

[44]　Breckinridge to St. John (May 16, 1871 (*SHSP*, vol. 3, no. 3, 105).

[45]　*OR* ser. I, vol. 47, pt. 2, 1202.

[46]　Ibid., 1326, 1330.

[47]　*OR* ser. I, vol. 51, pt. 2, 1065-66.

[48]　April 16, 1874 to St. John (*SHSP*, vol. 3, no. 3, 108).

Then they had a windfall of sorts. Both the Richmond & Danville and Piedmont lines (scrappily repaired again) were able to add to their rolling stock of engines and cars from lines being lost in the West. It was Breckinridge who had moved that rolling stock east just in time. The difference it made to food collection was to form a permanent memory for the railroad president Lewis Harvie:

> No one who witnessed can ever forget the result. Contribution was universal, and supplies of food sufficient to meet the wants of the army at the time were at once sent to the depots on the road, until they were packed and groaned under their weight... And from the increased motive power above referred to, they could have been delivered as fast as they were required.
>
> Moreover, sufficient means—not in Confederate currency, but in *specie* ... had been furnished me by Mr. Trenholm, Secretary of the Treasury, to meet the exigency and pay all pressing demands of the company.[49]

However had that happened?

It happened because everybody realized at long last the need for draconian controls over money. For Subsistence, the process of forcing that realization was as follows. When Breckinridge received Judge Campbell's letter of March 5 on the parlous state of things, he had St. John get from his chief assistants (French, T. G. Williams, and Claiborne—Northrop's officers) specific statements of their needs.[50] Treasury Secretary Trenholm had meanwhile been persuaded to support the Confederate currency—which had dropped to 100 to 1—by buying Confederate notes at $60 in exchange for the Treasury's remaining stocks of gold.[51]

The linch-pin was a new act which Congress was persuaded to pass—without any apparent prompting from Davis or Trenholm. This too was almost certainly to a considerable extent the work of Breckinridge. Its title told all: "An act to raise coin for the purpose of furnishing necessary supplies for the Army." Coin. The act empowered the Treasury "to borrow from any bank, banking company, corporation, association, or person, any sum or sums in coin" up to $3 million in gold value, repayable in cotton or tobacco which the lender could freely export from the Confederacy for profit. If that did not suffice to raise enough food money, the Treasury Secretary was empowered to levy a tax of 25 percent on all gold, silver, and foreign currency held in the Confederate States: the tax would be due and collectible on April 1.[52]

The results, even in advance, were spectacular. Before the act was passed on March 17, word went out that the Confederacy was finally taking control of its finances. Now there was a real prospect that food for sale could be paid for in a currency capable of retaining its value; and that all

---

[49] Ibid., 110.
[50] *OR* ser. I, vol. 46, pt. 2, 1297-99.
[51] Campbell's letter of March 5, 1865 referred to this (*OR* ser. I, vol. 51, pt. 2, 1065).
[52] *OR* ser. IV, vol. 3, 1155-56.

food sold or given to the army, and placed in depots near railroads which actually collected things and took them on, would really reach the mouths of Lee's hungry soldiers.

Thus at last, by pressure of war and experience of privation, the Confederate government had been brought to implement virtually every one of Northrop's stipulations for feeding their army. The irony was that by the time they did it, there was very little army left. And that became the St. John commissariat's final advantage over Northrop's—the saddest of all. By the time St. John took over as Commissary General, the territory to be provisioned had been quartered. With Sherman advancing through the Carolinas, it was quickly coming down to no more than western North Carolina and southern Virginia. Desertions from Lee's ranks increased: between February 18 and March 15 nearly 3,000 disappeared—almost a tenth of what Lee had left. So every day there were fewer mouths to feed, and those few closer to Richmond. On April 1, 1865 St. John had 300,000 rations in Richmond and others close by: it was enough to feed Lee comfortably for ten days.[53]

They did not have ten days left. On that April 1 Lee's brave line of defending soldiers, stretched thinner and thinner by Grant's inexorable reinforcements and endlessly extending deployments, finally broke. On Sunday morning, April 2 Lee telegraphed to Davis that he could not hold the rail line from Petersburg into Richmond beyond nightfall. That day the city was evacuated by the government. Davis and most of his Cabinet took a special train west to Danville. By the time orders arrived for army provisions, all the trains were commandeered elsewhere.

St. John remained in Richmond overnight with Breckinridge, loading trains of wagons and sending them southwest in the general direction indicated by Lee: "the military situation" (as Lee expressed it) precluded any specific destination. Early on the morning of April 3, St. John and Breckinridge left Richmond with the Federal guns thundering in their ears.

Among the citizenry left in Richmond was Mrs. McGuire, who clerked in the Subsistence Bureau. She and her elderly husband had stayed for the simplest of reasons: they had nowhere else to go. Throughout the night of April 2-3 the house where they lodged had rocked with explosions as arriving Federal troops blew up Confederate ammunition stores and set the lower city alight. She wrote: "About seven o'clock I set off to go to the central depot to see if the [railroad] cars would go out. ... Women, both white and coloured, were walking in multitudes from the Commissary offices and burning stores with bags of flour, meal, coffee, sugar, rolls of cotton cloth, etc. ... I turned to come home, but what was my horror, when I reached Ninth Street, to see a regiment of Yankee cavalry come dashing up, yelling, shouting, hallooing, screaming! All Bedlam let loose could not have vied with them in their diabolical roarings. ... The Federal soldiers were roaming about the streets; either whisky or the excess of joy had given some of them the appearance of being beside themselves." Mrs. McGuire went to seek the

    [53] Williams to St. John, September 1865 (*SHSP*, vol. 3, no. 3, 105); Ibid., May 16, 1871, Breckinridge to St. John, 104.

Federal Provost Marshal's office to get a military guard for her house. Her return home with the Union soldier showed the progress of the fire through what had been the Confederate capital: "The War Department was falling in; burning papers were being wafted about the streets. The Commissary Department, with our desks and papers, was consumed already."[54]

At Danville the brave, obstinate Davis struggled to keep up the motions of government with a rump of his Cabinet. On April 7 he sent a telegram to Northrop well-nigh incredible in the circumstances. It was uneasily poised between solicitude and rigor:

> Mr. Mallory informed me of your embarrassment [over housing], which I hope may be removed.
>   Are you not aware that your commission remains in force, making you assignable to duty anywhere in the Subsistence Department? I ask because the records of the War Office are not now accessible, and it has been intimated to me that you regard yourself as out of service.
>
> Jeff'n Davis[55]

Two days later, on April 9, Lee surrendered the Army of Northern Virginia to Grant at Appomattox. When Lee asked to be allowed to feed his men from St. John's wagon train which had been captured by the Federals, Grant immediately ordered high-quality Union rations sent over to the literally starving Confederates. Would 25,000 rations be enough? "Plenty; plenty; an abundance," answered Lee. It was probably more than the total number of soldiers Lee had left. [56]

Davis tried still to carry on, moving from place to place as one after another became unsafe. His "Cabinet" were leaving him one by one. At Greensborough, North Carolina on April 15 Davis gave grudging assent for Joseph E. Johnston to negotiate with Sherman. Four days later at Charlotte, news reached the Davis party of Lincoln's assassination. By May they were in Georgia. In the woods near Irwinville early on the morning of May 10, 1865, Davis with his wife and half a dozen others were surprised by Federal troops and captured. The Southern Confederacy was at an end.

*   *   *

The first business of the conquering Federals was to liberate their fellows held in Confederate prisons throughout the South. The liberators were appalled at the squalor, disease, starvation and death they found. The great majority of liberating Federals had never seen the inside of any prison, including the ones their side kept.

Confederate authorities had tried to feed prisoners of war as they fed their own soldiers: if they failed, it was due basically to the famine in food transport inflicted in large part by their enemies. Federal prisons for Confederates, by contrast, were mostly far from any fighting and with full re-

---

[54]   *Diary of a Southern Refugee*, 335-39.

[55]   *OR* ser. I, vol. 46, pt. 3, 1387.

[56]   Marshall, *An Aide-de-Camp of Lee*, 272; Freeman, *R. E. Lee*, IV, 141.

sources available; yet the Federals had never made any pretense of trying to give their Confederate prisoners of war the same as their own soldiers. As a result there had been nearly as large a percentage of prisoner deaths in their camps as in the Confederate camps.[57]

None of this, if they knew it, carried any weight with the conquering Federals or the national press they now entirely controlled. When news came out of how their boys had starved in Rebel prisons, Yankee outrage knew no bounds. A fair sample can be read in the diary of George Templeton Strong, an otherwise kindly and cultivated New Yorker serving on the Sanitary Commission charged with oversight of Federal military hospitals. On March 29, 1865 (nine days before Lee's surrender but with many prison camps in the South already liberated) Strong recorded his reaction to the report of a fellow commissioner just returned from North Carolina:

> His account of the condition of hundreds of returned prisoners, founded on personal inspection, is fearful. They have been starved into idiocy—do not know their own names, or where they are, or where their home is. ... The disembowelment and decapitation of all men, women, and children of a Chinese city convicted of rebel sympathies is an act of mercy compared with the politic, slow torture Davis and Lee have been inflicting on their prisoners with the intent of making them unfit for service when exchanged.
>
> I almost hope this war may last till it become a war of extermination. Southrons who could endure the knowledge that human creatures were undergoing this torture within their own borders, and who did not actively protest against it, deserve to be killed.[58]

The violence of these remarks shows that Strong's Sanitary Commission (in receipt of thousands of dollars in private contributions for the comfort of U.S. soldiery over and above the official army medical staff and hospitals) had not the smallest idea of the virtually equal conditions endured by Confederates in Yankee prisons. Strong heard of Sherman's and other Federals' ravaging of Southern agriculture, and his reflections were smug.[59] He seemed unable to connect that "scourging" with the South's failure to feed and house prisoners of war in satisfactory conditions. When Lincoln was assassinated on April 14, 1865 by a Southerner, Strong wrote: "Grant's generous dealing with Lee was a blunder... Let us henceforth deal with the rebels as they deserve."[60]

Lincoln's successor Andrew Johnson set mild terms for the "Reconstruction" of the South, following Lincoln's own ideas of amnesty. Radical Republicans roared so loudly for a hard peace that they laid the foundations of an impeachment against Johnson's Presidency. Johnson's proclamation of May 29, 1865, offering amnesty to a broad range of Confederates up

---

[57]   This statement is based on figures given by a recent historian in no way sympathetic to the South, James M. McPherson (*Battle Cry of Freedom*, 802).

[58]   *The Diary of George Templeton Strong*, ed. Allan Nevins and Milton Halsey Thomas, *abr* T. J. Pressly (Univ. of Washington, 1988), 282.

[59]   Ibid., 294.

[60]   Ibid., 296.

through the rank of colonel on the signing of a U.S. loyalty oath, so angered the Washington Congress that they would make a Constitutional Amendment to limit the power of Presidential pardon.

United States Secretary of War Edwin Stanton, who had a passionate devotion to his army, read the columns of horror that filled the Northern press day after day, week after week with experiences of Federals who had suffered in Southern prisons. Who was responsible? Who could be brought to book? Winder, the commandant of those prisons, had died at his post in February 1865. Commissary General St. John had surrendered in May and was soon to take the oath for amnesty; in any case, he had held his office only during the last few weeks of war. Who remained of those chiefly responsible for feeding (or not feeding) Federal prisoners of war? Northrop.

On June 13, 1865 Stanton caused an order to be sent to the Union commander in Virginia: "The Secretary of War directs the immediate arrest of L. B. Northrop, rebel commissary general of subsistence. Is he in Richmond?"[61] He was not. He was reported to be in North Carolina; searches at Raleigh and Wilmington proved negative. Federal commanders at Richmond and in South Carolina sent negative reports. Then on June 26 the sub-commander at Raleigh realized that Northrop was farming at "Egypt". A Federal party was ordered out to make the arrest.

Northrop had been there all the spring. He was not in hiding: apparently it never occurred to him that he might be the object of any search. He was working in the open fields to harvest crops for his family. Cultivation of corn and potatoes was anything but easy for a lame man in his fifty-fourth year: "... I tried to plough but my limb would not stand it; when I hoed long it swelled—although hoeing can be done chiefly on one leg, relieving the other of much. My attempts finally effected a break down...".[62] It had taken the form of fever and ophthalmia, added to the hemorrhoids which had plagued him for years. The eye condition confined him to a darkened room for a fortnight in late spring.

During that dark fortnight news of the Federal amnesty reached him. Northrop had never been a political animal. The slowly accumulating nightmare of Confederate Army subsistence over which he had presided through four years had left a burden of frustration and resentment. He found no hesitation in wishing to get the amnesty, as the clearest way to get on with his own life.

On June 29, 1865, before he could hear any result of his application for amnesty, the Federal soldiers arrived at "Egypt", arrested him on the spot, and marched him away—leaving Maria, ten-year-old Frank, and the four girls aged seven to fifteen without protection in that lonely and ambiguous place. The soldiers took him to Raleigh, and on to Richmond on Sunday, July 2. They locked him up in one of the former Confederate prisons (converted from a tobacco warehouse) called Castle Thunder, which

---

[61] *OR* ser. I, vol. 46, pt. 3, 1276.
[62] July 7, 1865 to Rev. J. J. Early (Georgetown archives).

was where they were putting Confederates accused of war crimes. Yet in Northrop's case no charge was made or suggested.

Conditions in the prison were uncomfortable enough, especially for a man with his physical problems. Northrop was later to tell his son Frank about having to place the legs of his iron bedstead in pools of coal oil to keep off the vermin.[63] Yet from the following Sunday, July 9, he was permitted under guard to attend mass at St. Peter's, Richmond.[64] To his imprisonment also belongs the one photograph of him known to exist: he hated photography, and might never otherwise have permitted his image to be thus recorded. The photograph shows him well dressed and groomed, with a clean collar, necktie, frock coat, and watchchain.

His captors did not prohibit the writing of letters. From almost the moment of his arrival at Castle Thunder, Northrop started a campaign of letters addressed to those who might help his release. One of the first was an epistle of ten pages to the President of Georgetown College, Rev. John J. Early, SJ. Northrop's letter rehearsed his own upbringing in Southern ways, his politics (such as they were), Federal and Confederate Army service, his departure from Richmond and difficulties at "Egypt", his arrest and imprisonment. A parole, he wrote, "will not prevent criminal proceedings if I have done anything special". In the continued absence of charges, he could only speculate. To dereliction of duty from the United States Army in 1861, he would answer that he was effectively out of service on account of the old wound. To a charge of being fit for farm work, he would confirm details of recent illness by medical examination. As to Federal outrage over prisoners of war, Northrop pointed out that they had been fed as Confederate soldiers according to Regulations: "They drew alike on requisitions, and even if I had been capable of vindictive feelings against bodies of common ignorant men, and had been base enough to gratify this malice by misusing my position, I could not have effected my purpose." With this long letter to Father Early he enclosed an appeal to President Johnson.[65]

The entire packet went to Early through a mutual friend and former Confederate Assistant Adjutant General, Major William Barton. Barton's covering note read in part: "Of course his confinement is very irksome, & the anxiety as to the future of his family weighs heavily upon him—though he bears all with the composure of a philosopher & the resignation of a Christian...".[66]

The Northern press busied itself with preparing a case against Northrop based on the treatment of prisoners of war. That case seemed at first to rest on a statement published by G. T. Strong's Sanitary Commission—to the effect that the starvation of Northern prisoners had been deliberate policy with the Confederate Government.[67] Who had put forward that idea? None

---

[63]   Information from Frank Northrop's granddaughter Mary Hunt, 1991.

[64]   July 8-9, 1865 (NA, RG 109, Officers).

[65]   *The Papers of Andrew Johnson*, VIII (Univ. of Tennessee, 1989), 388-89.

[66]   July 7, 1865 (Georgetown archives).

[67]   Cited in a denying report issued by a committee of the Confederate Congress in March 1865: a copy of this report had been obtained by Horace Greeley's *New York Tribune*, which published it *in extenso* on June 29, the day of Northrop's arrest.

other than Henry Foote: so asserted *The New York Herald* on June 30, the day after Northrop's arrest. That elicited a long letter from Foote himself, dated from Montreal. Outrage at the treatment of Northern prisoners, Foote now claimed, had prompted his own departure from the Confederacy in January. It was not the Confederate Cabinet who had decided to starve the prisoners but (as his friend Commissary Warner had assured Foote) Commissary General Northrop—"a most wicked and heartless wretch" who had persuaded his superiors to give the prisoners "nothing but bread and vegetables". Foote finished off with professions of ignorance, as well as hatred, of all the works of Davis and his cohorts.[68] On this *The Herald* editorialized:

> It appears that Mr. Northrup [*sic*], a Southern vegetarian philosopher, who believes in feeding the human family on grass and hay, used his position as Commissary to put his theories in practice on the Union prisoners. Obtaining the sanction of the chief of the rebel War Department, who endorsed the scheme for the purpose of retaliation, as he claimed, the experiment was tried and was followed by horrible results.

To anyone who knew the facts, the picture of Northrop as demonic vegetarian philosopher bent on using the Southern commissariat as a castle of Frankenstein experiment was laughable. To any reader who did not know the facts, there was a case to answer. What did the arresting authorities themselves make of it? Two days earlier *The Herald* had reported Northrop's arrest and imprisonment: "The charges against this man Northrop are not known, but are supposed to be of a grave character, from the fact that he was consigned to Castle Thunder."

On July 21 *The Herald* published nearly the whole of Frank Ruffin's testimony to the Confederate Congressional committee in January 1865. It filled more than six full-length columns of the paper's fine print. They made sober reading for the North, as the editor James Gordon Bennett admitted in the same issue:

> This report ... shows that it was utterly impossible for the rebel States to produce supplies enough to sustain the rebel armies, and that they never did so; and it also shows that many attempts made to feed those armies by meats that ran the blockade were all crippled by the blundering stupidity of Jeff. Davis and his associates.
>
> This report, moreover, makes some remarkable disclosures of the operations of men on our side of the lines. It shows that there were on our side, in 1862, a great many men ready to furnish the rebels with all necessary army supplies, and that these men had sufficient influence with our government to be able to get their boat loads of stores through the lines...

There was not a word now about Northrop.

Four days later, on July 25, 1865, Ruffin, French, and Noland addressed a formal petition to President Johnson: "The undersigned were officers of the Bureau of Subsistence of the Confederate States... Our duties kept all of

---

[68]   *The New York Herald*, July 8, 1865.

us stationed in the office of the Commissary General, & made us familiar with the acts of the Bureau." They rehearsed the facts surrounding the change of responsibility for feeding prisoners of war to the Commissary General in 1863, the prison commissary Warner's complaints, the Confederate Congressional investigation and Northrop's acquittal of his charges. They insisted that the prisoners had at least the same rations as Confederate soldiers in camps "so far as we & the Commissary General knew". Northrop's idea for a vegetable diet "of *equal nutrient value*", they said, had been rejected by Secretary Seddon:

> That paper had been preceded, & was followed, by frequent and earnest appeals from the Commissary General to the Secretary of War, to remove the prisoners of war to the south—where it was thought a warm climate would ensure less suffering from cold—and an abundance of food on the spot would guarantee immunity from hunger, as well as diminish the danger of shortening Genl. Lee's supplies—a course of proceeding inconsistent with any plan or wish to starve or maltreat the prisoners. ...
>
> It is understood here, that the Archives of Congress were captured by the Federal Army, upon its entrance into Richmond. If so, the papers in the case under discussion will be found among them—and to them reference is confidently made, for the result of the investigation & the character of the prosecutors...[69]

And there, for the time being, the matter stopped.

On July 26 Northrop wrote to Bishop Lynch in Charleston about the Federal myth-making already begun at Castle Thunder: "Three weeks ago last Sunday I reached this Chateau Celebre which patriotic Yankees visit to bear away relics, as memorials of Yankee martyrs in the Southern Crusade for the Christian liberty of Hamite or Cushite or Canaanite or whatever other type of brethren have been made free. I do not know how Flora and Mom Hannah [his former slaves] will like it."[70]

A month later, on August 28, he made another application release. Eight weeks in prison had brought a recurrence of the eye problem and a skin rash developing into eczema. His family had gone to the Steuarts in Maryland, but he worried about them. He addressed this appeal to the commander in Virginia, Brigadier General Alfred Terry: "I will give my parole to keep you informed of my locality, and to respond to any summons; or I will give bond to the same effect with any security you may require."[71] The Provost Marshal replied that as Northrop's arrest had been on orders from Secretary Stanton, only Stanton could effect a release: "General Terry has forwarded your application to the Secretary of War for his action."[72]

A month after that, on September 29, Northrop wrote again to Father Early:

[69]　MS copy in Georgetown archives, certified correct by French.

[70]　Wight, 476-77.

[71]　MS copy in Georgetown archives.

[72]　August 30, 1865 (NYPL: Northrop Papers).

Near three months have elapsed & no charge is alleged. This is as unfair as for a man to practice in secret with the view of challenging another when he gets ready. Who knows what evidence may have been available that may not be when a trial is sprung on a man, on charges unknown to him previously.

(That fear was real. For weeks Federal authorities had been conducting a trial of Henry Wirz, the commandant at Andersonville Prison. The Military Commission in Washington summoned many people to appear—whether as witnesses or defendants was not always clear.[73] Wirz was condemned to death. Just before his execution he was offered a reprieve in exchange for a statement to convict Jefferson Davis of cruelty to Federal prisoners of war. Wirz refused and was hanged.)

Northrop continued his letter to Early:

As for the charges of starving prisoners, I told the Provost Marshal General here that I held them in utter scorn, that shutting up masses of men—that is shutting up *any* men—i.e. shutting up *humanity*—to starve *it*, was an act beyond creditability.[74]

Letters of sympathy and offers of help came from several directions. One was the commissary R. J. Moses, who at the end of the war had been chief commissary of Georgia: "I only heard a few days ago that you were in prison, charged with cruelty to the Andersonville prisoners. Heaven knows that if there was ever such a charge without a shadow of foundation, this is such. Major Allen can prove, and so can I, that the Andersonville prisoners were supplied from this post with precisely the same rations as our army in the field, and the details here."[75] Another letter came from former Confederate Congressman John B. Baldwin (then recently elected to the Virginia General Assembly): "I always regarded you as the worst treated man in the Confederacy, and it would be truly hard to be the most severely dealt with by the United States."[76]

At last, after four months in Castle Thunder and still without any formal charges brought, a parole was offered. It confined Northrop to the state of Virginia, but his request was accepted for extension to Maryland. He must report all his movements to the Federal authorities, and hold himself "ready to appear at any time hereafter at such place as may be required to answer any charges...". On November 2, 1865 Northrop signed the parole.[77] The door of Castle Thunder swung open, and he limped out into the autumn air.

---

[73] One so summoned was Robert Kean of the Confederate War Bureau. He wrote: "The Commission got in the habit of *revoking* the subpoenas of witnesses for the defense, whose testimony they did not wish to hear. Thus was *suppressed* Mr. Seddon's defense [Seddon was also imprisoned], which would have put the sufferings at Andersonville where they belonged, on the shoulders of E. M. Stanton." (*Inside the Confederate Government*, 230)

[74] Georgetown archives.

[75] October 17, 1865 (Huntington Library: quoted in Didier, "Scape-Goat", II, 10).

[76] Quoted in Didier, "Scape-Goat", II, 9.

[77] NA, RG 109; Officers: Parole reports of his movements now preserved extend only a few months into 1866.

CHAPTER 21

"A TICKET-OF-LEAVE MAN"

That was Northrop's description of himself in the aftermath of war, defeat, imprisonment, and parole.[1] On emerging from Castle Thunder, his attention was called to an article just published by Beauregard's Assistant Adjutant General Thomas Jordan. The subject was "Jefferson Davis": Davis (still in prison and unable to defend himself) was pictured as a fanatic bordering on instability, the true author of the South's woes. But Jordan nursed a particular animus against Davis's old friend Northrop for exposing the irregularity of Jordan's commission as brigadier general.[2] Accordingly Jordan described Northrop as "so eccentric and full of mental crotchets as to be generally regarded in Charleston as of unsound intellect, and unfit for the management of his own small affairs."[3]

People who knew the truth saw that for what it was. Captain Edward Palfrey, formerly of the New Orleans commissariat, wrote to his old commanding officer: "I should like to contribute my mite, if possible, to warding off the assassin blow aimed at the imprisoned gentlemen by Tom Jordan, & neither of whose shoe latches is he worthy to tie."[4] Other friends worried at the danger to Northrop's reputation, as he himself would recall: "After my release Judge Campbell wrote advising that I should prepare an account of my administration ...". But Northrop was so occupied in getting his life together that it was easier to ignore the whole thing. Thinking about the Confederate past could only remind him of Southerners' ingratitude to him after four years of hardest work—as well as the unpalatable new order emerging in the Reconstructed South. A dozen years later he would write: "Having no respect for the judgment of the people, I was indifferent to their opinions

---

[1] December 15, 1879 to Davis (Rowland, VIII, 434). The passage is quoted below, p 303.

[2] See Northrop to Davis, April 29, 1879 (Rowland, VIII, 387).

[3] *Harper's New Monthly Magazine*, October 31, 1865, 611. When Jordan's proofs were shown to Beauregard, the general was horrified and tried unsuccessfully to stop the publication (Williams, *Napoleon in Gray*, 304).

[4] Quoted in John Riely to Northrop, November 30, 1865 (NYPL: Northrop Papers).

of me, and replied accordingly to Judge C."[5] In fact he was never to take any loyalty oath to the United States. He would write to Bishop Lynch: "You have been to Rome and seen the only sovereign I recognize *now*."[6]

For his children, he sought Catholic schooling. Father Early at Georgetown offered their Jesuit education free to Bernabeu, in settlement of an old debt.[7] So Bernabeu, at a loose end as he approached his nineteenth birthday, had entered Georgetown in October, while his father was still in Castle Thunder. The younger son Frank was sent to school at Emmittsburg, Maryland, where he was expected to prepare for priesthood. But Frank himself wanted to study medicine—an idea apparently abetted by Dr. Steuart (on whose estate south of Baltimore Maria and the children were still staying). Lucius is reported to have been so angered at the change of plan that he went up to Emmittsburg and removed Frank on the spot.[8] The girls were sent to the Convent of the Visitation Academy at Frederick, Maryland. The school's musical life fostered Louise's talents as soprano singer and pianist.[9] For Isabel, study at the Academy focussed a religious vocation. It gave the third daughter, Claudia, a sophisticated finish to equip her for married life as a New York hostess. The youngest daughter, Clara, was educated later at the expense of Maria's Aunt Clara de Bernabeu.[10]

Lucius Northrop spent Christmas 1865 with his family at Dr. Steuart's house. Northrop thought of settling close to the Steuarts in Maryland, but land prices in the victorious United States were too high. His own house in Charleston was rented: he did not want to sell it then, as property prices in South Carolina (undergoing a notoriously corrupt Reconstruction) were depressed. The 320 acres in Arkansas remained uncleared, and so would require an effort no longer practical for him even if he could get his parole extended so far. So his choice fell on Virginia.

To accumulate funds for a purchase, he asked Bishop Lynch and Henry Guerin in Charleston to help him collect old debts and sell stock. Northrop's papers had gone for safekeeping to the bishop's sister at the Ursuline Convent in Columbia, which was then burnt by Sherman. Getting the papers reconstituted was a slow, costly, and ultimately imperfect process. At least one of his debtors, hearing that the papers were burnt, refused payment until Northrop brought suit. As he worked to get his money together for a farm, Northrop wrote to Bishop Lynch on March 22, 1866:

> I have brains but do not see how they can be converted into bread, so I must turn clodhopper & deal with free negroes. ... See Flora & let me know if that family wish to cast their fortunes with me & mine; if so I will, when I fix myself, arrange for them.[11]

---

5   April 21, 1878 to Davis (Roland, VIII, 180-81).

6   November 18, 1867 (CDA 41 P 6).

7   August 11, 1867 to Early's successor, Reverend B. A. Maguire, SJ (Georgetown Archives).

8   Information from Frank Northrop's granddaughter Mary Hunt, 1991.

9   The Academy Prize-Day programs of 1867 and 1868 show Louise performing challenging solos and duets in both categories.

10   June 28, 1878 to Davis (Rowland, VIII, 220).

11   CDA 35 B 1.

He was to wait another ten months before purchasing. On January 23, 1867 he wrote to Bishop Lynch that he had secured a farm just south of Charlottesville.[12] Set well back from the road to Lynchburg, the tall brick farmhouse faced south. It rose two stories over high cellars. Each floor was laid out on the same symmetrical plan: central staircase hall with a single large, classically proportioned room on either side. Each of the rooms had windows front and back, with a fireplace centered in the end-wall opposite the door into the room. The cellar rooms were stone flagged for hanging meat and keeping food. The kitchen was a detached square brick structure at the back, with servant cabins west of the house and a small family cemetery on the edge of woods to the east.

The farm of 234 acres and the house had once belonged to the family of Colonel John S. Mosby, the famous Confederate raider, and it had been named "Tudor Grove". Northrop re-named it after Orcus, the abode of the dead in ancient Roman religion: he called his place "Minor Orcus". Writing a dozen years later to Jefferson Davis on the subject of Purgatory, Northrop forecast: "... It would not be consistent to expect you to escape and I am *certain* I won't. I gave my place a name, admonishing me of my future or next abode, when I leave this."[13]

Because of his parole and the attendant possibility of confiscation, the farm was bought in the name of James Steuart, Dr. Steuart's eldest son and Maria's cousin, in trust for Maria. The purchase price of $5,000 was met by a cash payment of $2,100 and a note for the balance due in a year.[14] The deed was signed on April 1, 1867.[15] The officiating Justice of the Peace was Edward Coles of Biscuit Run, close by. Coles and his family were to become Northrop's intimate friends in the years to come. Before the end of the month Lucius Northrop was settling into his latest and last career, as he wrote to Bishop Lynch: "I get up any morning at 4 o clock and work all day, relieving my leg as much as possible. I am so stiff & sore sometimes that motion is often labour. I feel with comfort the *'rest'* of Sunday."[16] Conditions in the house were spartan: they still had very little furniture.

In June the family were joined by Bernabeu, but for an unhappy reason. Bernabeu had been expelled from Georgetown: the cause was represented as trouble with the school's young prefects (students for priesthood serving as supervisors). But enough hostility had been shown to Bernabeu by Father Early's successor as President, Rev. B. A. Maguire SJ, to suggest that the lack of school fees might be at the bottom of it. It took Lucius Northrop several weeks to gather his energies to answer the expelling President: when he did, he laid out Maguire in a seven-page epistle.

---

[12]   CDA 38 T 7.

[13]   October 7, 1879 (Rowland, VIII, 422).

[14]   CDA 43 P 2.

[15]   Albemarle County Deed Book 62, 320-21.

[16]   CDA 40 C 6.

Minor Orcus, near Charlottesville, Va, ca. 1950.

Minor Orcus with cabin, ca. 1950.

Dear Sir

    I have received my son's report for the quarter ending June 67, on which you have affixed the stigma of expelling him on account of his "*unhappy temper*" which has caused "*much complaint during the past year*"—"*insulting the gentlemen of the College on several occasions*".

    Nothing could be more disgraceful as a *gentleman*, than to insult, where there is no liability of collision, or as a Catholic to wrong those who are priests or aspirants to Holy Orders. Unless your judgment in the cases alluded to has been justly reached, *he* is much wronged, and *I* also, by your proceeding.

The college reports of Bernabeu's academic achievements and conduct, sent with the expulsion, were more than satisfactory: Lucius quoted them. Then:

    Bernabeu is bold and *plain spoken*, but in *critical times* has proved himself trustworthy. He acts, on what he *thinks* good reason, and he is generally logical: when otherwise, I have never failed to obtain contrition and submission by calm reason. I hear of no such effort having been made by you as President of the College. ...

    I further say that when a boy of 16 [Bernabeu's age on joining the Confederate Navy in 1863] has for two years of war been thrown among men *alone*—and has been compelled to be the custodian of his own honor and rights, and been highly commended for his conduct, *his* account of difficulties is as likely to be correct as young men who have had no such stern schooling, viz. your Prefects.[17]

None of those points served to restore Bernabeu's Georgetown education.

    When the time came to pay off the farm in the following spring, the money was not forthcoming. Northrop had entrusted Bishop Lynch's man at "Egypt", James Browne, to collect the money on which he relied; Browne proved unreliable and finally dishonest. Northrop turned to Bishop Lynch, who after much effort was able to bring the worst of the trouble to some solution so the debt could be paid.[18] Returning his thanks on June 21, 1868, Northrop sent a little picture of his household: "I began here like Robinson Crusoe, and have got along by unremitting labour and endurance. At present we have become quite like other people, Maria's Aunt having sent her a present of furniture—which arrived with your letter. ... I have confidence now in my ability to manage a farm and improve it."[19]

    At Christmas 1868 the United States Government announced an unconditional pardon for most former Confederates. It meant little to Northrop. Jefferson Davis was apparently experiencing similar emotions. Released from his prison in 1867, Davis took his family for protracted stays in Canada and Europe. Contact was renewed briefly when, following their return, the Davises lost the younger of their two remaining sons to diphtheria in October 1872. Northrop wrote a brief note of condolence, excluding any mention of the Confederacy.[20]

---

[17]   Copy, marked by Northrop "Duplicate" and mostly in another hand (possibly that of a daughter), but annotated and signed by him (Georgetown archives).

[18]   September 11, 1867 (CDA 41 C 2); November 18, 1867 (CDA 41 P 6); May 15, 1868 (CDA 43 P 2).

[19]   CDA 44 B 7.

[20]   October 23, 1872 (Rowland, VII, 332).

By the 1870s the American push westward was reaching upper California. Indians were dislocated, their reservations routinely violated. A band of Modocs under their leader "Captain Jack" rose in bloody rebellion in early 1873. Northrop was interested to read that entire detachments of the United States Army seemed powerless to subdue them. When Captain Jack and his men killed the commanding general at a peace conference, the army brought an overwhelming force to capture, try, and hang Captain Jack. Northrop sent his reflections to Bishop Lynch; they included an implied comparison of the besieged Indians with the defeated South:

> Do you find any consolation from Capt Jack and the Modocs? They have no newspapers to tell their side. I know enough to induce the belief that the Whites are always wrong. ...
> Whenever my heart burns, I thank Capt Jack for inflicting disgrace on the U. S. Army. [John Wilkes] Booth & Capt Jack teach a good lesson: God permits evil but lets the evil instruments have a lesson admonitory.
> The U. S. Govt, having no use for the Modocs, will destroy them—they keep us for slow consumption—if it can be slow.[21]

The proximity of the University of Virginia in Charlottesville offered some intellectual interest, but there were limits. Anticipating a visit from Bishop Lynch, Northrop wrote: "Your old friend Mrs. Holmes will be most glad to see you, and I wish you could stay a short time with her at the University. It would do the polite conceited professors some good to meet one whose reading & knowledge is not limited to heretical theories and histories by modern scientists."[22] Mrs. Holmes, a daughter of Confederate Brigadier General John B. Floyd, was the wife of George Frederick Holmes, Professor of History and General Literature. Holmes had a particular interest in the War. At its beginning in 1861 he had urged the University to collect every scrap of evidence—in vain. He did apparently ask Northrop and others to lecture on their experiences to the University students.[23]

Two other friends of Northrop on the faculty were John Randolph Page, Professor of Agriculture and supervisor of the University's experimental farm, and Francis H. Smith (1829-1928), Professor of Natural Philosophy. Smith's term as professor lasted more than fifty years, interrupted only by Confederate service as Commissioner of Weights and Measures. It would be fascinating to know more of Northrop's associations with those men, but the University archives are silent and all the witnesses long dead. One benefit was a session at the University for Bernabeu, who studied mathematics, engineering, and natural philosophy from 1869 to 1871.[24]

Northrop remained nonetheless a private man, as jealous of privacy as of honor. This was recalled in later years by his son Frank in conversation

---

[21] May 3, 1873 (CDA 55 B 1). See Keith A. Murray, *The Modocs and their War* (Univ. of Oklahoma, 1959).

[22] January 27, 1878 (CDA 64 Y 6).

[23] Information from Mary Hunt, 1991. An article on Holmes by Henry E. Shepherd appears in *The Library of Southern Literature* (Atlanta: Martin & Hoyt, 1907), VI, 2467.

[24] University of Virginia archives.

with his own daughter, who wrote: "Soon after General Northrop settled near Charlottesville, a Connecticut Insurance Company offered him a large sum, several thousands per annum, for his name as President, requiring no service from him. Notwithstanding General Northrop was in very straitened circumstances, he refused (just as General Robert E. Lee did a similar offer) as he feared his name might be used to defraud the people of the South. ... My grandfather hated publicity in any form, and was opposed to even having his picture taken. On one occasion while sitting on his horse in the streets of Charlottesville, a local photographer endeavored to secure a photograph unawares, but my grandfather detected him in time to foil his attempt by cutting his horse and riding away."[25]

In 1873 Northrop passed his sixty-second birthday. In November of that year his eldest daughter Louise married a writer, Eugene Didier. Didier was gaining fame as an expert on the life and work of Edgar Allan Poe, while he practised the craft of journalist.[26] The newlyweds made their home in his city, Baltimore. Northrop's second daughter Isabel was already in Baltimore preparing to take her vows as a nun. Unfortunately in 1874 she developed rapid tuberculosis. Her father, whose physical troubles had begun to make travelling far from home uncomfortable, went on a painful journey to bring her home to die—"which she did in my arms."[27] The third daughter Claudia was married in March 1875 to James Henry Martin, a New York businessman; they would make their life in the North.

In 1876 Bernabeu entered a drug and chemical business in St. Louis. (An earlier business venture in Memphis had failed; the only consolation had been that the young man's trouble had elicited signal help from Jefferson Davis—with whom Lucius Northrop was still on distant terms.)[28] To start Bernabeu in his new shop, his parents sold $5,000 worth of stock which Maria had held for twenty years.[29] Bernabeu was to pay them interest at the rate of the stock's dividends.

The next years brought little happiness. In May 1877 both of Louise Didier's baby daughters, the Northrops' first grandchildren, died in Baltimore within days of each other. The end of that year presaged a loss closer to home. His own youngest daughter Clara (called "Clement" in the family) fell ill with a virulent ear infection. Her father could do nothing for her. By December poor Clement was so disoriented that she had to be taken to the Mount Hope Asylum for the Insane near Baltimore. Six months later she died there, just after her twentieth birthday. The grieving father wrote: "She was without exception the most beautiful and graceful creature I have ever seen, and in soul the most noble and elevated. ... I have never dealt with any other

---

[25] Marie Floyd Northrop to Dr. L. W. Payne, Jr., September 13, 1909 (NYPL: Walter Fleming Papers, Box 6, f 65).

[26] See the article on Didier in the *Dictionary of American Biography* (New York: Scribner, 1943), V, 307.

[27] May 9, 1878 to Davis (Rowland, VII, 269: misdated 1870).

[28] Northrop to Davis, March 31, 1878 (Rowland, VIII, 145). No details appear to survive.

[29] The date of the loan was given by Lucius Northrop as "about 25th February 1876" (Albemarle County Will Book 30, 168-69).

person in life towards whom there would not be some fluctuations of feeling consequent on human impulse. ... I am content, for she is blessed. No heavier blow can fall...".[30]

Earlier in 1878 Northrop had added another 46½ acres to the farm. Yet he felt himself far down the vale of years as he wrote to Bishop Lynch: "I have never lost sight of the past, and remember the night when I drove you from the Seminary to my mother's bed. You brought One who remained. May I be thus guided to my end, as our end approaches, griefs & sufferings assail us, as friendly monitors." Increasing physical debility forced him to depend more and more on servants and hands. And that led him on in the same letter to a rare lively picture of the household at "Minor Orcus":

> I have just broken up a nest of thieves which has been with us for over two years, getting into trunks & closets, eating up our poultry and distributing our clothing. I could not dismiss or arrest them until other servants were available—this has always controlled me, for my wife can't work & needs attention. So she prayed to God to send her a good woman with three children—a boy & two girls— fearing that unless a boy came I would not take them. Behold the family came, the very thing wanted. An old-time set, and we shall try to keep them by showing them where their interests lie.—My wife is like old Cousin Susan Bellinger—prays for what she wants— with precision.[31]

Later letters to Bishop Lynch continued the themes of age and loss. In December 1878 Northrop wrote: "I am deep into my 68th year—older than my mother or her parent, and I know of but one of my predecessors who exceeded 68."[32] Then he injured his crippled knee, which stopped all his own work at planting for weeks. In February 1879 he wrote: "The farm don't pay expenses—never has, and this year will not pay my small grocery bill, excluding wages."[33]

Even his thirty-year friendship with Bishop Lynch was coming to an end. The cause was the Bishop's brother, who had helped Northrop reclaim some railroad bonds burnt at Columbia but then kept the certificates and collected the interest himself. The Bishop offered to stand security for his brother, and even to sell a house and lot of his own in Charleston to refund the money. Northrop would have nothing but the bonds: his insistence fomented only distress, embarrassment, and at last disengagement.[34] It repeated exactly the hardness shown to his own brother Claudian twenty years earlier. Recently Lucius had written to Claudian's son: "I pray every night for your father...".[35] It was sad that his concern in such a case seemed to appear so slowly.

---

[30]   June 28, 1878 to Davis (Rowland, VIII, 220-21).

[31]   CDA 64 Y 6. Susannah Bellinger (d. 1865), a first cousin of Northrop's mother, had been the earliest of all the family to be converted to Catholicism, around 1830. See O'Connell, *Catholicity in the Carolinas and Georgia*, 181.

[32]   CDA 67 C 1.

[33]   February 25, 1879 (CDA 67 S 6).

[34]   CDA 64 M 6, 64 W 1, 64 Y 6, 66 H 7, 66 M 3, 66 M 7, 66 R 3, 67 S 6, 68 S 1.

[35]   December 7, 1877 to Claudian Northrop the younger (CDA 64 N 4).

A new trouble had come from Bernabeu's enterprise in St. Louis. The young man had been married in May 1878, and a son was born in February 1879. But just then Bernabeu's second business failed through the dishonesty of his partner.[36] The elder Northrops' money was lost, and there was a year and more of anxiety before Bernabeu could find a new career. Once again, however, he was helped by Jefferson Davis.[37]

* * *

When Davis had returned finally to Mississippi in 1877, he determined to write a comprehensive history of the Confederate Government. Others, including his enemies, were publishing their views. As Davis was approaching his three-score-and-ten, it was time to begin his own account if that account was to exist. He would call it *The Rise and Fall of the Confederate Government.*

The chief problem was source material. Much had been destroyed in the burning of Richmond. Much more had been taken into the United States archives in Washington, where it was unavailable to Davis. And so, early in 1878, he had carefully approached Northrop. With his letter Davis sent the draft of a short description he proposed to include about the Subsistence Bureau and Northrop's good administration of it. Northrop responded on March 31, 1878:

> My dear Davis,
>
> I am very glad to receive the assurance of your confidence in the perpetuity of my friendship for you. The estrangement to which you allude was anterior to my removal from office, by the act of Congress cunningly devised to gratify spite, by bringing my name before it for confirmation [as Brigadier General in November 1864]. You believed that the cause [of the South] was not hopeless, and therefore desired to avoid useless contest with Congress. ...
>
> Your noble treatment of my son in Memphis was conclusive of the matter.

He began to answer Davis's questions. There was the Battle of Drewry's Bluff, fought near Richmond in May 1864. Both Davis and Northrop had witnessed parts of it. Beauregard, commanding the Confederates, had appeared to accomplish less than he might have done. Northrop wrote:

> ... That failure confirmed my opinion that our cause was lost, and that with such a Congress and such generals, you could accomplish nothing. ...
>
> Last night after going to bed, I began thinking over these things and was so disgusted by the picture which arose to my vision, that I could not dismiss it, and lay awake till near daybreak. I very much fear that your undertaking will worry you to death. ...
>
> What you say of my Dept. is true, but it will be attributed to partiality unless you sustain it by adding [the evidence and results

---

[36]   Lucius Northrop to Bishop Lynch, February 25, 1879 (CDA S 6).

[37]   J. B. Northrop to Davis (Rowland, VIII, 348).

of congressional investigations]. I am indifferent about the matter. I did my part from no love of the people or any patriotic ardour, but from duty. ...

Will you rejoin [i.e. answer this letter]? My wife sends love. I pray God speed you. I admired your fortitude in enduring as well as your fidelity.

Affectionately yours,
L. B. Northrop[38]

Davis did reply on April 11, 1878. He was disturbed by the tone of a recent article by his second Secretary of State, Robert Hunter, on "The Peace Commission of 1865". But he promised to send Northrop an orange wood cane of his own fashioning and polishing in token of their friendship. Northrop responded:

Yours of the 11th brings your image back to my heart. I wish it could have been answered at once. Only on Sunday had I leisure to hunt over all old papers, and last Sunday we had mass at Charlottesville.

Your letter is an accurate mirror, and with the orange cane shall be left to Bernabeu as a souvenir of the last of the Chevaliers of the south,—for whose soul we will pray if he goes before us.

The letter covered a wide spectrum. Northrop's memory, aided by his copy documents, provided facts and views preserved nowhere else. But he set down his details in such haphazard order, as they tumbled out of his recollection, that it would have been anything but easy for Davis to make a connected account of them. Northrop himself was aware of it when he began to wind up his long letter:

It is late, I have to rise at daylight every morning: if I have forgotten any thing or can furnish you any information let me know, and what I can do, I will. I have tried since the war to avoid dwelling on a period of life which was most harassing...

Hunter's attack indicates I think that your book will be assailed by details, calculated to divert from a calm comprehensive estimate.[39]

Davis's answer sought to set Northrop's mind at rest about the Presidential role in the Commissary General's forced resignation: "I no more doubted your sincerity than I did your existence...". The Senate, said Davis, had really been after them both. He then asked about the source of a Subsistence paper which had appeared in the Richmond newspaper editor E. A. Pollard's book *The Lost Cause* since the war. And he asked Northrop to visit him in Mississippi to renew their old friendship face to face.[40]

Northrop, nursing his sick wife, had to reply: "Much would I enjoy a trip south, and very much the pleasure of being with you, but circumstances exclude all ideas of pleasure this side of the grave. My daily presence is essential here." There was also his own poor health. He recalled the terrible

---

[38] Rowland, VIII, 145-47.
[39] April 21, 1878 (Rowland, VIII, 179-84).
[40] Ibid., April 29, 1878, 187.

journey to Baltimore in 1874 to bring back the dying Isabel: "The trip was made in 40 hours. 12 hours from home is too long, so my friend I cannot travel." Another budget of recollections brought further bitterness, but the letter ended gently: "My wife sends 'her love to you and says she hopes my letters satisfy you.' She still views you as chief of the Confederates—not understanding that failure should engender incrimination."[41] A week later Northrop wrote again: he had searched for the paper quoted by Pollard without success. "A little farm is like housekeeping; I am called on perpetually, and every time I begin to look for papers, am called off."[42]

Davis sent no fewer than three orange canes—one for Northrop and one for each of his sons. But the letter and package arrived on the day of "Clement"'s death, and inevitably much of Northrop's response was taken up with her. He promised to try to send Davis a copy of Pollard's book.[43] He sent it on September 12, 1878 with another letter: "I wish you had never undertaken to write a book without any foundation but memory and conscious rectitude in past action. ... I have never read [Pollard's] book but knowing its source can estimate its tone."[44]

Early in 1879 the question of responsibility for supply failures after First Manassas was looming once more. Joseph E. Johnston had excoriated both Davis and Northrop in his memoirs published in 1874. Now Beauregard, who had learned of Davis's project, was threatening to do the same if he was criticized. Northrop, at the turn of the year, had had a visit from a former captain of the Albemarle Cavalry at Manassas, Eugene Davis. Northrop wrote: "He is a gentleman every inch of him—confirms the fact that *all the* [Confederate] *forces* were ordered to pull back instead of pursuing—that a sort of alarmed anxiety arose to recall the troops—he scouts the idea that either provisions or transportation were objects to be considered...". Northrop also told his old friend about the blow to his wounded knee in December.[45]

Davis, unwell himself, responded with a renewed invitation to visit his "soft climate... How happy I should be to nurse you and talk to you of things common to us and unknown to none [sic] others. For I believe there is not one of our associates in the Arkansas Squadron of Dragoons who are yet living." He asked whether Eugene Davis would write out a memorandum of his experience at Manassas.[46]

Northrop persuaded the captain to do this, and enclosed it with a new letter of his own: "Your allusions to me penetrate my heart, and your condition of health distresses me. Get a light active horse of gliding motion, of blood and long pasterns and strong muscle and ride every day...". He offered to send P. V. Daniel's paper about the generals' misuse of railroads,

---

[41] "May 9th, 78" Museum of the Confederacy: Davis Coll. Rowland's transcript (VII, 269-71) is mis-dated 1870.

[42] May 17, 1878 (Rowland, VIII, 200-201).

[43] Ibid., June 28, 1878, 220-21.

[44] Ibid., 278-79.

[45] January 7, 1879 (Tulane, r 22, ff 407-8).

[46] January 19, 1879 (Rowland, VIII, 337-38).

and to obtain from Burr Noland the details of his attempts to save the meat at Thoroughfare Gap.[47] Clearly Northrop himself was becoming interested.

On March 17, 1879 Davis urged Northrop to write his own account of Confederate Subsistence.[48] Davis already had such a paper from Josiah Gorgas on the Ordnance Bureau. He was right to urge Northrop to do the same. The existence of Gorgas's paper has unquestionably helped his later reputation, and had Northrop written similarly, his own appearance in many histories might have been different. But Gorgas was several years younger than Northrop at a time of life when vigor was beginning to be a critical factor; and Gorgas had an academic mind.

Northrop's response showed him apparently ready to write something. But writing about subsistence inevitably led to broader issues. It was hard to know, in sessions of thought and review snatched from the work of the farm, where to stop: "I have been quite content for 14 years to remain silent, but once in I want to write effectively if not elegantly." Did Davis wish to hear about the only case of Confederate officer mistreating Yankee prisoners? It was Warner, the commissary of prisons.[49]

Davis asked for the information: "That old buzzard Warner met me since the war, and stated that the prisoners he had seen denied the statements about their ill-treatment and expressed much gratitude to him... It would unquestionably be well for you to bring in the whole matter."[50] Warner, though a Confederate, had come from Ohio. When an acquaintance of Davis had recently raised the subject of alleged Southern cruelty to prisoners, Northrop told Davis: "... I edified him with the respect which the possession of slaves caused white people to hold for their own race,—cruelty to prisoners was impossible to southerners."[51]

In April 1879 Northrop wrote to tell Davis of reading extracts from General Richard Taylor's newly published memoir, *Destruction and Reconstruction*.[52] Six days later Northrop sent news of Taylor's death just a week after his book was published: "... Though I never met him I had imbibed great admiration of his abilities on Red River. He overcame the dislike I felt for his father [Zachary Taylor], due chiefly to your narration of scenes at Jefferson Barracks. ... We grow wiser as age advances, and I suspect your haughty and sarcastic style of younger days may have given the old general cause of antagonism to you."[53]

Davis responded: "I hope you are right in the supposition that with age I have gained wisdom and lost hauteur and sarcasm. If I have not acquired the 'greatest of all, charity', better appreciation of my own weakness has probably given me more forbearance towards others than existed in the

---

47 Ibid., January 29, 1879, enclosing Eugene Davis to Northrop, January 27, 340-42.
48 Ibid., 368-70.
49 March 26, 1879 (Tulane, r 22, ff 501-5).
50 April 24, 1879 (Rowland, VIII, 380-83).
51 Ibid., May 14, 1879, 390.
52 Rowland, VIII, 377-78.
53 Ibid., 378-80.

pride and self-confidence of youth." He sent further reminiscences of their time in the Dragoons, and added: "I like such a horse as Genl. Z. Taylor described as his preference, a horse that was 'big when lying down'. He was a man of very strong common sense and honest as the magnetic needle."[54]

Northrop replied in May 29: "My wife this morning asked me what I had been laughing at after daybreak, we sleep in the same room during the winter. I remembered revolving your reminiscences about Ed.ᵈ Nowland & his mustang. I always had a tenderness for his idiosyncracies, & therefore for his big headed steed 'Saded el Keress'—and think that the motto 'Honi soit qui mal y pense' would have prevented my answering the laudation of his delicate muscle by a comparison of his rump—as both fitting a 'pint cup'."[55]

Northrop wrote again on his sixty-eighth birthday, September 8, 1879. He sent further plans for a pamphlet on Confederate subsistence, and added: "If you can spare time, think a little and let me have the benefit of your superior controversial experience."[56] Davis answered: "I give it to you in a sentence: Severe facts, but gentle words." He wished Northrop could relieve his lameness by a visit to Mississippi. Then he raised again the subject of Beauregard at Drewry's Bluff, recalling that Northrop had been there too.[57]

Northrop responded with his own eyewitness account of that field:

> ... Late in the day, long after the enemy had been for two hours flying towards Proctor's Creek, I became convinced that Beauregard was very uneasy and would do nothing, so I started for Richmond, met [Major General Robert] Hoke, told him that we were remaining idle, "checked by one sentinal" and "a few flankers in the woods, while the enemy were flying by us." He replied, "We are waiting for Whiting." I answered W. is not coming, or he would have been up, the prey is before you and you are letting it escape. He repeated, "We are waiting for Whiting."—I said, handing him a biscuit—"Here is a piece of hard bread for you: nothing more is coming off here."...
>
> Beauregard you say was "inexact". I doubt if he ever had distinct ideas about anything during the whole war, except the vision of making himself appear a hero...[58]

Davis answered: "My dear Northrop, what the world denounces as impracticable, crabbed men are the only ones who never look at the rack to see [if] there is fodder in it or not; they are not blessed in this world, and I have come to think that the apothegm in regard to the eternity of truth and its final prevalence, must find its fulfillment in the future state." Davis and his wife both grieved that Northrop could not visit them: "Our home has a name [Beauvoir] less significant than yours, and was given by its former possessor to express a beautiful prospect. The air is soft. In winter especially the sea breeze is invigorating. The oranges are shining golden on the

---

    54   Ibid., April 25, 1879, 383-84.

    55   Tulane, r 26, ff 227-30. Rowland's transcript (VIII, 393-95) contains inaccuracies. For Edward Nowland, see above p. 46 n.13.

    56   Rowland, VIII, 410-11.

    57   Ibid., September 25, 1879, 415-19.

    58   Ibid., October 7, 1879, 420-22.

trees, and our pine knot fires soar in the chimneys, in their light I try to bury my unhappiness."[59]

Northrop responded on December 15, 1879:

> My dear friend,
>
>   ... Thanks for your last and kind wishes, and invitation to the bright oranges and balmy air,—contrasting with the cold of this region; let the rascally Confederate politicians say what they did, you *are* a practical man.

As for himself, Northrop could no longer resist something like total disillusion with the post-war United States:

> There is no room for love of country, all this talk of virtue and honor of States and paying their debts is stuff. Such [State] constitutions as now are said to exist with universal suffrage and an elective judiciary, are incapable of making contracts, and can't bind their successors. ...
>
>   I am not a Virginian and now care for no State. I am a "Ticket of leave man" bound by my parole to appear for trial whenever called upon by the President of the U.S. and laugh at the praters of State honour—"Patriot candidate for an office"; "Patriotism the last refuge of scoundrels" as old Dr. Johnson asserted.[60]

A few days later Northrop wrote again, condemning the generalship of Joseph E. Johnston, and finding fault with Albert Sidney Johnston's strategy at Bowling Green: did Davis agree? And he sent his advice for treating Davis's sciatica: "Have a good fire made in your room, double a blanket to lay on, and toast your whole back and body just as long as you can stand it... My wife would die before doing it; she thinks it an unbecoming position, but as we have lived some little in the woods it is not unsuitable. ... My wife is shut up with cold; on my reading your kind messages she mused and said, 'Ah, what a handsome man he was when I first saw him,—the very man to captivate woman,' so your message must have been agreeable to her."[61]

Davis replied that Northrop had been "quite right in your apprehensions about Bowling Green, and as a consequence, the danger of making Nashville a main depot". But the thin ice of Davis's office was revealed in another consideration that bound him then: "It would not have been proper in me to reveal a distrust which might have created a panic and especially while I was hoping for the arrival of arms... I am much obliged to you for your suggestions as to the treatment of my ailments. I have lived longer than the period allotted to man, and have suffered more than is often man's fate."[62]

> Minor Orcus
> Feby. 2nd,1880.
> My dear friend,
>   The severity of winter is on us. I have a sore throat, have to keep in and watch the fire.

[59]   Ibid., November 1, 1879, 423-26.
[60]   Ibid., December 15, 1879, 432-34.
[61]   Ibid., December 20, 1879, 435-37.
[62]   Ibid., January 14, 1880, 437-39.

We have mass in Charlottesville semi-monthly. I could not go. My signora did, and astounded me just now by taking up her prayerbook to look over the epistle read yesterday, for me to help her understand it, but in vain. I consoled her by St. Peter's declaration that it was hard to understand, and as St. Paul in the case in question says he "speaks foolishly", we had better give it up and humbly confess that we speak a great deal of foolishness habitually.

So you will please consider compassionately whatever I may write now. I prefer to write just now to my last living contemporary friend than to attempt enlightening my wife on an author always too difficult for me.[63]

In a further letter nine days later, Northrop told of turning out a closet in search of some leaf tobacco—and finding instead a pile of papers about Beauregard's commissariat in the West in 1862: "this is the *only* benefit I have ever derived from wanting a smoke."[64] But the discovery of those papers would be certain to complicate, and so delay, his own writing.

Nearly a year passed before Northrop sent a new plan for his article on the commissariat; it was far from the comprehensive statement Davis had requested, and Northrop knew it.[65] Davis's reply sought to calm his old friend's fears about his own book which was now finished:

I have in writing twice referred to you in terms which were just—therefore complimentary.

I dare say if we had had more electioneering talent, or had tried to conciliate the selfish, rather than rigidly to perform our duty, we might have gained approval where we met criticism; but now when old and broken in fortune, we should have been without that which to such as you are is worth more than all else—the consciousness of rectitude.

Davis finished by asking whether Northrop had a photograph of himself for engraving in Davis's book.[66]

But Northrop, thinking of the book's prospective audience, did not want them to see him: "Sincerely I contemn the American people,—though liking good people everywhere. Furnishing my portrait makes me concurrent in presenting myself to their notice. It will not add any force to your book, so there is no reason for my doing what is not agreeable, when merely personal. ... I am as God sees me, and I try not to care what man thinks. I never was more contented, and never will be fully contented, until thoroughly indifferent to human respect—an aim not fully attainable I know."[67]

---

[63] Ibid., 439-41. Sunday February 1, 1880 was Sexagesima. The Epistle for that day in the Douai Missal (in use until 1963) was from the Second Epistle of Paul to the Corinthians, from XI.19 to XII.9. Paul's claims to speak foolishly (XI.21 and 23) were probably ironic; but beginning in the midst of his statement, as this Epistle does, increases its difficulty. Many of Paul's contemporaries found him hard to understand. (This note owes its content to the kindness of the Rev. John Gibb and of Martin Haines.)

[64] February 11, 180 (Tulane, r 22, ff 747-52).

[65] January 26, 1881 (Rowland, VIII, 580-86).

[66] Ibid., February 1, 1881, 586-87.

[67] February 6, 1881 (Tulane, r 22, ff 1007-10).

In July 1881 Davis's *The Rise and Fall of the Confederate Government* was published in New York in two large volumes. One of the author's presentation copies went to Northrop, who responded on July 25: "Though incompetent to estimate such a work, I am sufficiently informed to say, that no man *has ever lived* who had such a problem as you undertook... America has never produced another man who could simultaneously have comprehended the problem of organising, supplying, and directing internally civil and military, while conducting all external relations, in a people where minorities rule by corrupting majorities. ... If I had not appreciated your genius and character *before* it had been proven, I should be afraid to go near you, for your penetration made you always hard to talk with. ... There is a marvellous unity in your character, manifested in this work."[68]

A year later, in July 1882, Davis wrote to learn how his old friend was faring. Northrop began with news of his family, prefaced by a wish: "May your young daughter love you as I did my mother, and be convinced that your love is inestimable, and can never be equalled by that of any other being but God. My wife is a lovable person, but nothing but Perfection can satisfy the cravings of an upright soul. I am resigned, but nothing on earth will ever content me—and should not. ... Bernabeu ... is now a division engineer on the Texas & St. Louis R.Rwy...". Frank, at twenty-seven, was still at home helping his father on the farm. "My two sweetest daughters [now dead] are I believe happy, though I pray for them daily. The other two are what is called settled in life by becoming wives and mothers—which means being entangled inextricably with consuming cares, added to the most difficult of all, the control of themselves." Then Northrop enlarged on his own outlook in the wake of Davis's grand book:

> It is *natural* that one who has produced such a book—evincing such knowledge and logic, with military and civil qualities surpassing all other americans, combined with integrity and heart—*should* have a "hope" in *the forces of reason* to bring back a return to sound principles and honest practices in other men.
>
> Our cause, as I viewed it, depended not on written constitutions or received rights; it was the natural and indestructible right of self-defense, demanded by past conspiracies... The practices of the Northern people and government before, during, and after the war, and the subsequent assimilation for the Southern people, excluded all hope. Experience, history, and "a priori" considerations satisfy me that no people, who have lost the generating principles of public and private life, can return to them.
>
> Men are *not* governed by reason, but by desires passions lusts... The present era is worse than the pagan: *now* the philosophers teach that man has no free will, therefore no responsibility, and no future life, or hope of compensation for inequalities here—hence everything is destructive, and *present desires* the law of life...[69]

---

[68] Rowland, IX, 4-6.
[69] Ibid., 179-81.

JEFFERSON DAVIS AFTER THE WAR:

FRONTISPIECE TO VOLUME II OF DAVIS'S THE RISE AND FALL OF THE
CONFEDERATE GOVERNMENT. WHEN DAVIS SENT A COPY TO NORTHROP
ON PUBLICATION, NORTHROP RESPONDED ON JULY 25, 1881:

"...the old man in the 2d volume has fattened and looks dour;
all previous ones since the war were caricatures."

Three months later Davis tried again to persuade him to write about the Southern commissariat: "It would constitute a record for a generation whose ears are more open to truth than the time-servers of to-day."[70] Northrop answered that he was too old and occupied with the farm and his sick wife.[71] It was to be another two years before events occurred to change his mind.

In 1884 Beauregard carried out his threat to rejoin the argument after the appearance of Davis's book. First there was a two-volume work entitled *The Military Operations of General Beauregard*, ghost-written by his friend Alfred Roman at the general's dictation. Then in November 1884 *The Century Magazine* published a sharp article on First Manassas over Beauregard's name (but with covert help from Thomas Jordan). Davis wrote to Northrop on November 6, 1884, enclosing a favorable review of Beauregard's book. That increased the urgency of Davis's plea:

> To puff Beauregard is one motive, to gratify malignity to me another, and you, as my especial friend—and who in your official capacity could be made a shelter for his own incapacity—come in for a share of his misrepresentations. ...
>
> When you and I and your official aides are no more, these printed stories will remain as the cause of our people's misfortune, unless an antidote is provided for the poison. .... Years ago I urged you to write a memoir of your administration of the C.S. Commissariat, because you deserved credit for well performing a herculean labor, and the achievement was part of the common glory of our people; and however little you may care personally for your due share of it, to your children and your children's children, the inheritance is not to be disregarded.[72]

Northrop responded a month later. He would try to get up a rebuttal for *The Century Magazine*, though domestic and farm duties distracted his elderly energies: "If I had your diction and fluency of language, it would be easier...".[73] By late February 1885 he had written enough to occupy six pages in *The Century*, he reckoned.[74] He offered it to the magazine, but there was not much enthusiasm. Another magazine editor was equally dilatory. Meanwhile in May 1885 *The Century* published an article by Joseph E. Johnston replying to Davis's book, and another by John Imboden recalling the rump court that Johnston had convened to sit on subsistence problems after First Manassas. That was the first Northrop had ever heard of it. By the time Davis called his attention to these renewed accusations, *The Century* had returned Northrop's article with regrets. The unstated fact was that his name would not attract a readership sure to follow the words of former eminent generals in the field.

Northrop wrote another long letter to Davis retailing a wealth of facts—many new—but laced with the refrain "Who cares now?"[75] He also protested

70   Ibid., October 15, 1882, 189.
71   Ibid., November 13, 1882, 190-91.
72   Ibid., 301-2.
73   Ibid., December 6, 1884, 310-13.
74   Ibid., 346-47.
75   July 31, 1885 (Museum of the Confederacy: Davis Coll.).

vigorously to the *Century* editor that he had been slandered again, and sent a sketched rebuttal with demands for fair play. At last the editor offered to set up that sketch in type. Northrop rejoined that his sketch was barely more than a third of the length given by the magazine to specific accusations against him. It was impossible in such a space "to state the charges intelligibly to your readers, and then refute them. You write courteously, and I reciprocate, but your conception surpasses possibility. You have circulated libellous writings against me among your readers. I have a moral right to undeceive them...".[76] The editor yielded only to the extent of an extra seventy words—and then cut out some of them—before the little piece was allowed to appear, occupying three-quarters of a page among Miscellaneous Correspondence Arising in the April 1886 number.[77]

The compression was too severe. Each of Northrop's facts and sentences was true in itself, but there was so little explanation or chronology remaining to interconnect them that an average reader would find difficulty in making much of the arguments. (I well remember my own first reading of the article years ago, and my feeling that Northrop was unable to express himself clearly—undeceived later by reading his letters.) So it was that the Commissary General's only published explanation of his Subsistence policies and experience gained little notice against his more glamorous adversaries.

The two old friends had three years left to them. Their letters, mostly shorter now, trickled on with two or three exchanges in 1887: largely they went over old ground, with an occasional flash of fresh recollection. In the spring of 1888 Northrop's wife began to fail. She lingered for another year. Northrop described the last scene in a letter written to Davis afterwards:

> She had been dying 13 months, but life was indefinite, her innervation [sic] seemed indestructible.
>
> *Shortly* before the *end* it was made apparent to me. I was answering a statement which was a mistake, she simply repeated it, I more fully showed the error, this had no effect, and I muttered to myself "damnation" and said no more; she simply remarked "don't curse". I then repeated the whole scene, very affectionately, and that her apparent immobility had distracted me; she simply said, "I can't help it." The truth flashed on me—the heart and goodwill are immoveable, but the brain is congesting and becoming dusky.
>
> In the morning of May 16 [1889] I thought she was dying. I rallied her with repeated sips of old whisky; in the afternoon that again became necessary and she rallied again, and I laid by her side— "I will lay down for a while," I said to her, "I must rest for the night."

---

[76] December 16, 1885 (Huntington Library: EG Box 43).

[77] It was however included with small verbal changes in the great four-volume permanent edition of the most significant articles published later by The Century Company as *Battles and Leaders of the Civil War*. They then gave it the title "The Confederate Commissariat at Manassas", though it covered a wider field. (Vol. I, 261).

(I had been nursing her 6 days and nights,—by myself.) In a short time, she tried to turn to me; I aided her, she put one hand to my left shoulder and the other on my right shoulder, and spoke an unbroken tissue of words, but unintelligibly articulated, with a steady look into my face and eyes, she finished it, and then her face instantly fell a little; and she was gone.

We had been married 48 years before. Few people are known by others; God alone knows us well—she was 75.[78]

It is the last letter now remaining in the files. Davis endorsed it to the effect that he answered five days later; but the whereabouts of that answer are not known—nor any further exchanges between the two old men whose friendship reached back sixty years to West Point. There could not have been much more, for in November 1889 Davis developed bronchitis while visiting a plantation on an island in the Mississippi River. His condition worsened, and he died on December 6. Thus the second pillar of Northrop's life fell seven months after the first.

On February 4, 1890 Northrop suffered a stroke which paralyzed the whole of his right side. His son Frank came immediately. On February 24 the old man managed to dictate and sign a new will—necessary since the death of Maria. Frank was to be executor, with no legal accountability to anyone (recalling Lucius's own position as his mother's executor). Frank would inherit the farm, and also some lands his father had acquired in Texas. The elder son Bernabeu had already received $5,000—"all that could reasonably have been expected from me to one of my heirs". His younger daughter, Claudia Martin, was to have the house and property in Charleston, and further land in Texas. The elder daughter, Louise Didier, was made residuary legatee.[79]

The legacy to Louise included many of his papers. Perhaps he made that provision in view of the fact that her husband was the only scholar in the family. It was also decided that Northrop, now unable to continue at the farm, should go to live with the Didiers and their children in Baltimore. There Louise was to write a few months later: "Mr. Davis' letters, papa keeps among his treasured papers,—letters from his own Mother, Sister etc. ... Papa would not part with one of them & never speaks of Mr. Davis without emotion."[80]

Gradually he weakened and finally became helpless. In the spring of 1893 the Didiers were expecting a seventh child. Lucius Northrop, at eighty-one, was moved to a Home for Confederate Veterans at Pikesville, near Baltimore, on April 18. The Home's register records a single visit to him—from Louise and her niece Isabel Martin on the following January 18. They must have seen then that he was close to the end. It came peacefully at six o'clock

---

[78]   September 15, 1889 (Rowland, X, 136-38). In fact Maria had just entered her seventy-fourth year.

[79]   Albemarle County Will Book 30, 168-69.

[80]   August 17, 1890 to Mrs. Jefferson Davis. On June 22, 1890 Didier had published a selection from the Davis letters in *The New York Sun*—apparently without Northrop's knowledge or approval (Tulane: Davis Papers, r 23, ff 1056-57, 1059-60, 1078-84, 1106-9). In 1907 Didier published further extracts from Northrop's papers in a small magazine, *Spare Moments*.

in the evening of February 9, 1894. The funeral took place three days later from the Didiers' house, with a requiem mass at St. Ignatius' Church followed by burial in the Catholic cemetery of Bonnie Brae. On his gravestone was carved a line from the English poet Alexander Pope: "An honest man is the noblest work of God."

So ended a life which had begun when the American Republic was just thirty-five years old, and its independence younger than that. Lucius Northrop had witnessed the American hunger for exploration and possession. He had reacted strongly against the savage treatment of the American Indian, but had matured in the acceptance of black slavery. At a time of life when he thought himself retired by an old and painful wound, he had been called to bring his best intelligence to bear on a central problem in the great but unavailing struggle to gain a second freedom for his homeland. It was a life lived much in sorrow and hope. In his world and time, he had sought for duty—for what his greatest friend identified as "the consciousness of rectitude".

AFTERWORD

Eugene Didier died in 1913, and his wife Louise followed in January 1915. Of their seven surviving children, only one married; but she had nine children, and there are many descendants.

John Bernabeu Northrop and his wife retired to Tampa, Florida, where he died in November 1923. Their son also left many children, and some of his descendants still live in Florida.

Claudia Martin had two children, but neither married. After her first husband's death, she married John Lawsche Bailey, who survived her. She died in January 1940, the last of all Lucius Northrop's children.

Frank Northrop and his wife, Lydia Coles, raised six children, of whom four have living descendants. After Lydia's death in 1929, Frank married in 1931 Mary Ficklin, a schoolteacher nearly thirty years his junior. He died in October 1938, but she lived to see her hundredth year in 1982.

311

BIBLIOGRAPHY

Printed Books

Abbott, Susan Woodruff, comp. *Early Families of Milford, Connecticut*. Edited and prepared for publication by Jacquelyn L. Ricker. Baltimore: Genealogical Publishing Co., 1979.

Agnew, Brad. *Fort Gibson: Terminal on the Trail of Tears*. Norman: University of Oklahoma Press, 1980.

Alderman, Edwin Anderson, Joel Chandler Harris, and Charles William Kent, eds. *Library of Southern Literature*. 12 vols. Atlanta: The Martin and Hoyt Company, 1908. Henry E. Shepherd, "George Frederick Holmes", 6, 2467.

Alfriend, Frank. *The Life of Jefferson Davis*. Cincinnati: Caxton Publishing House, 1868.

Anderson, Carter S. *Train Running for the Confederacy 1861-1865: An Eyewitness Memoir*, ed. Walbrook D. Swank. Shippensburg, Pa.: White Mane Publishing Co., 1992.

Appleton's Cyclopedia of American Biography, ed. James Grant Wilson and John Fiske. New York: Appleton, 1888.

Ball, Douglas B. *Financial Failure and Confederate Defeat*. University of Illinois Press, 1991.

Ballard, Michael B. *Pemberton: A Biography*. Jackson: University of Mississippi Press, 1991.

Barrett, John G. *Sherman's March Through the Carolinas*. Chapel Hill: University of North Carolina Press, 1956.

B[artow], E[velyn]. *Bartow Genealogy*. Baltimore: Innes & Co., [1878].

Battles and Leaders of the Civil War: Being for the most part Contributions by Union and Confederate Officers. Based upon "The Century War Series". Ed. Robert Underwood Johnson and Clarence Clough Buel. 4 vols. New York: The Century Co., 1884-87.

Bearss, Edwin C. *The Vicksburg Campaign*, vol. 1. Dayton, Ohio: Morningside Press, 1985.

[Beauregard, Pierre Gustave Toutant, co-author]. *The Military Operations of General Beauregard. See* Roman, Alfred.

Beers, H. P. *The Confederacy: A Guide to the Archives of the Government of the Confederate States of America*. Atlanta: National Archives Trust Fund Board, 1986.

Bethel, Elizabeth. *Preliminary Inventory of the War Department Collection of Confederate Records (Record Group 109)*. Washington: National Archives, 1957.

Black, Robert C., III. *The Railroads of the Confederacy*. Chapel Hill: University of North Carolina Press, 1952; reprint, Wilmington, N.C.: Broadfoot, 1987.

Blakey, Arch Fredric. *General John H. Winder C.S.A.* Gainesville: University of Florida Press, 1990.

[Brock, Sallie, later Mrs. Richard F. Putnam]. *Richmond During the War: Four Years of Personal Observation*. By a Richmond Lady. New York: G. W. Carleton & Co., 1867.

[Caffey, Thomas E., pseud.: "An English Combatant"]. *Battle-Fields of the South*. New York: Bradburn, 1864.

Caldwell, James FitzJames. *The History of a Brigade of South Carolinians, First Known as "Gregg's" and Subsequently as "McGowan's Brigade"*. Philadelphia: King & Baird, 1866; reprint, ed. with an Introduction, Notes, and Index by Lee A. Wallace, Jr. Dayton, Ohio: Morningside Press, 1984.

Catlin, George. *Letters and Notes on the Manners, Customs and Conditions of the North American Indians*. 2 vols. Reprint, New York: Dover Press, n.d.

Channing, Steven A. et al. *The Civil War. Confederate Ordeal: The Southern Home Front*. Alexandria, Va.: Time-Life Books, 1984.

Chesnut's Civil War, Mary, ed. C. Vann Woodward. New Haven, Conn.: Yale University Press, 1981.

Christian, Frances Archer, and Susanne Williams Massie. *Homes and Gardens of Old Virginia*, with an Introduction by Douglas Southall Freeman. Richmond: Garrett and Massie, 1931.

Clemons, Harry. *Notes on the Professors for whom the University of Virginia Halls and Residence Houses are Named*. Charlottesville: University of Virginia Press, 1961.

Cohn, David L. *The Life and Times of King Cotton*. New York: Oxford University Press, 1956.

Congress of the Confederate States of America 1861-1865, Journal of the. 7 vols. Washington: Government Printing Office, 1904-05.

Cooke, Philip St. George. *Scenes and Adventures in the Army.* Philadelphia: Lindsay & Blakiston, 1859.

Cormier, Steven A. *The Siege of Suffolk.* Lynchburg, Va.: H. E. Howard, 1989.

Coulter, E. Merton. *A History of the South.* Vol. 7, *The Confederate States of America 1861-1865.* Baton Rouge: Louisiana State University Press, 1950.

Cullum, George Washington. *Biographical Register of the Officers and Graduates of the U.S. Military Academy, at West Point, N.Y., from its Establishment, March 16, 1802 to the Army Re-Organization of 1866-67.* 7 vols. in 8. New York: D. van Nostrand, 1868.

Daly, Louise Haskell. *Alexander Cheves Haskell: The Portrait of a Man.* Norwood, Mass.: The Plimpton Press, 1934; reprint, with a New Introduction by Lee A. Wallace, Jr. Wilmington, N.C.: Broadfoot, 1989.

Davis, Jefferson, Constitutionalist, ed. Dunbar Rowland. *See* Rowland.

Davis, Jefferson, The Papers of. Vols. 1-7 (all published by 1993), ed. Haskell M. Monroe, Jr., James T. McIntosh, Lynda Lasswell Crist et al. Baton Rouge: Louisiana State University Press, 1971 ff.

Davis, Jefferson. *The Rise and Fall of the Confederate Government.* 2 vols. New York: Appleton, 1881.

[Davis, Varina Howell]. *Jefferson Davis: A Memoir by His Wife.* 2 vols. New York: Belford Co., 1890.

Davis, William C. *Jefferson Davis: The Man and his Hour.* New York: Harper Collins, 1991.

Davis, William C., ed. *The Confederate General*, Vol. 4. Washington: National Historical Society, 1991.

Davis, William C., ed. *The Image of War 1861-1865.* 6 vols. Garden City, N.Y.: Doubleday, 1981-84.

DeLeon, Thomas Cooper. *Belles, Beaux and Brains of the 60's.* New York: G. W. Dillingham Co., 1907.

DeLeon, Thomas Cooper. *Four Years in Rebel Capitals.* Mobile, Ala.: Gossip Printing Co., 1890.

Dictionary of American Biography. New York: Scribner, 1943. "Eugene Lemoine Didier", 5, 307; "Lucius Bellinger Northrop", 7, 567-68.

Divine, John, Wilbur C. Hall, Marshall Andrews, and Penelope Andrews. *Loudoun County and the Civil War*, ed. Fitzhugh Turner, with a Foreword by George A. Hocken, Jr. Leesburg, Va.: Potomac Press, for the Loudoun County Civil War Centennial Commission and the Loudoun County Board of Supervisors, 1961.

Dufour, Charles L. *Nine Men in Grey.* Garden City, N.Y.: Doubleday, 1963.

Eckenrode, H. J. *Jefferson Davis: President of the South.* London: George Allen & Unwin, 1924.

Edgar, Walter B., N. Louise Bailey, et al. *Biographical Directory of the South Carolina House of Representatives.* Vols. 1-4 (all published). Columbia: University of South Carolina Press, 1974-1984.

Eggleston, George Cary. *A Rebel's Recollections.* New York: Putnam, 1905.

Ehle, John. *Trail of Tears: The Rise and Fall of the Cherokee Nation.* New York: Doubleday, 1988.

Ellsworth, Henry Leavitt. *Washington Irving on the Prairie, or A Narrative of a Tour of the Southwest in the Year 1832,* ed. Stanley T. Williams and B. D. Simison. New York: American Book Co., 1937.

"English Combatant, An", pseud. of Caffey, Thomas E., q.v.

Faust, Patricia L., ed. *Historical Times Illustrated Encyclopedia of the Civil War.* New York: Harper & Row, 1986.

Federal Writers' Project. *History of Milford, Connecticut 1639-1939.* Bridgeport, Conn: Braunworth & Co., for The Milford Tercentenary Committee, 1939.

Foote, Henry S. *Casket of Reminiscences.* Washington: Chronicle Publishing Co., 1874.

Freeman, Douglas Southall. *Lee's Lieutenants.* 3 vols. New York: Scribner, 1942.

Freeman, Douglas Southall. *R. E. Lee.* 4 vols. New York: Scribner, 1934.

Freeman, Douglas Southall. *The South to Posterity: An Introduction to the Writing of Confederate History.* New York: Scribner, 1951; reprint, Wilmington, N.C.: Broadfoot, 1983.

Fremantle, Arthur James Lyon. *Three Months in the Southern States: April-June 1863.* Edinburgh and London: William Blackwood and Sons, 1868.

Furse, George Armand, C.P. *Provisioning Armies in the Field.* London: William Clowes & Sons Ltd., 1899.

Gardner, Alexander. *Gardner's Photographic Sketch Book of the Civil War.* Reprint, New York: Dover, 1959.

Gates, Paul W. *Agriculture and the Civil War.* New York: Knopf, 1965.

Goff, Richard D. *Confederate Supply.* Durham, N.C.: Duke University Press, 1969.

Gorgas, The Civil War Diary of General Josiah, ed. Frank E. Vandiver. University of Alabama Press, 1947.

Hagerman, Edward. *The American Civil War and the Origins of Modern Warfare.* Bloomington: University of Indiana Press, 1988.

Haskell, Alexander Cheves. *See* Daly, Louise Haskell.

Haskell, John Cheves. *The Haskell Memoirs*, ed. Gilbert E. Govan and James W. Livingood. New York: Putnam, 1960.

Hattaway, Herman, and Archer Jones. *How the North Won: A Military History of the Civil War*. University of Georgia Press, 1983.

Hattaway, Herman, and Archer Jones. *Why the South Lost the Civil War*. Athens: University of Georgia Press, 1986.

Hendrick, Burton J. *Statesmen of the Lost Cause*. New York: Literary Guild, 1939.

Hesseltine, W. B. *Civil War Prisons*. Ohio State University Press, 1930.

Irving, Washington. *A Tour on the Prairies*. New ed., with a Foreword by Richard Batman, and Editor's Preface and Introductory Essay by John Francis McDermott. Norman: University of Oklahoma Press, 1956.

Jervey, Theodore D. *Robert Y. Hayne and his Times*. New York: Macmillan, 1909.

Johnson, Andrew, The Papers of, 8. Knoxville: University of Tennessee Press, 1989.

Johnson, Robert Underwood, and Clarence Clough Buel, ed. *Battles and Leaders of the Civil War. See under title*.

Johnston, Joseph Eggleston. *Narrative of Military Operations...* New York: Appleton, 1874.

Jones, John Beauchamp. *A Rebel War Clerk's Diary*. 2 vols. Philadelphia: Lippincott, 1866.

Kane, Harnett T. *Gone Are the Days: An Illustrated History of the Old South*. New York: Bramhall House, 1960.

Kean, Robert Garlick Hill, Inside the Confederate Government: The Diary of, ed. Edward Younger. New York: Oxford University Press, 1957.

Kingsley, William L., ed. *Yale College: Sketch of its History*. 2 vols. New York: Holt, 1879.

Kunhardt, Dorothy Meserve, and Philip B. Kunhardt, Jr. *Matthew Brady and his World: ...from Pictures in the Meserve Collection*. Alexandria, Va.: Time-Life Books, 1977.

Lambert, Edward R. *History of the Colony of New Haven, Before and After the Union with Connecticut, Containing a Particular Description of the Towns that Composed That Government, viz., New Haven, Milford...* New Haven, Conn.: Hitchcock & Stafford, 1838; reprinted by The Rotary Club of Milford, Connecticut, 1976.

Land, Aubrey C., ed. *Bases of Plantation Society*. Columbia: University of South Carolina Press, 1969.

Lash, Jeffrey N. *Destroyer of the Iron Horse: General Joseph E. Johnston and Confederate Rail Transport, 1861-1865*. Kent, Ohio: Kent State University Press, 1991.

Lee, Richard M. *General Lee's City*. McLean, Va.: EPM Publications, 1987.

Lee, Robert E. *Lee's Dispatches: Unpublished Letters of General Robert E. Lee, C.S.A., to Jefferson Davis and the War Department of the Confederate States of America 1862-1865*. From the Private Collection of Wymberley Jones de Renne, of Wormsloe, Georgia. Ed., with an Introduction and Notes by Douglas Southall Freeman. New ed., with Additional Dispatches and Foreword by Grady McWhiney. New York: Putnam, 1957.

Lee, Robert E., The Wartime Papers of, ed. Clifford Dowdey and Louis H. Manarin. New York: Bramhall House, 1961.

Lester, Richard L. *Confederate Finance and Purchasing in Great Britain*. Charlottesville: University of Virginia Press, 1975.

Long, E. B., and Barbara Long. *The Civil War Day By Day: An Almanac 1861-1865*. Garden City, N.Y.: Doubleday, 1971.

Longstreet, James. *From Manassas to Appomattox*. Philadelphia: Lippincott, 1896.

Lonn, Ella. *Salt as a Factor in the Confederacy*. New York: Walter Neale, 1933; reprint, University of Alabama Press, 1965.

Ludmerer, Kenneth M. *Learning to Heal: The Development of American Medical Education*. New York: Basic Books, n.d.

Marshall, Charles, An Aide-de-Camp of Lee: Being the Papers of Colonel, ed. Sir Frederick Maurice. Boston: Little, Brown, 1927.

McCarthy, Carlton. *Detailed Minutiae of Soldier Life in the Army of Northern Virginia 1861-1865*. Richmond, Va.: Carlton McCarthy & Co., 1882.

[McGuire, Judith]. *Diary of a Southern Refugee During the War*. New York: E. J. Hale, 1867.

McKim, Randolph H. *A Soldier's Recollections*. New York: Longmans, Green, 1910.

McPherson, James. *Battle Cry of Freedom*. New York: Oxford University Press, 1988.

Meredith, Roy. *Mr. Lincoln's Camera Man: Matthew B. Brady*. New York: Scribner, 1946.

Miller, Francis Trevelyan, ed. *The Photographic History of the Civil War*. 10 vols. New York: The Review of Reviews Co., 1912.

Moore, Edward A. *The Story of a Cannoneer under Stonewall Jackson*. New York: William Neale, 1907.

Moore, Samuel J. T., Jr. *Moore's Complete Civil War Guide to Richmond*. [Richmond, Va.]: The author, 1973.

Morton, Thomas G., and Frank Woodbury. *The History of the Pennsylvania Hospital 1751-1895*. Philadelphia: Times Printing House, 1895.

Murray, Keith A. *The Modocs and Their War*. Norman: University of Oklahoma Press, 1959.

Nevins, Allan. *The War for The Union.* 8 vols. New York: Scribner, 1947-1971.

Nichols, James L. *The Confederate Quartermaster in the Trans-Mississippi.* Austin: University of Texas Press, 1964.

Northrup, A. Judd. *The Northrup-Northrop Genealogy.* New York: Grafton Press, 1908.

O'Connell, Jeremiah Joseph, OSB. *Catholicity in the Carolinas and Georgia: Leaves of its History.* New York: D. & J. Sadlier, 1879; reprint, Spartanburg, S.C.: The Reprint Co., 1972.

Official Records of the Union and Confederate Armies [OR]. See: War of the Rebellion, The: A Compilation of the Official Records of the Union and Confederate Armies.

Olmstead, Frederick Law. *The Cotton Kingdom.* 2 vols. New York: Mason Brothers, 1861; reprint in one vol. New York: Knopf, 1953.

Orcutt, Samuel. *History of the Towns of New Milford and Bridgewater, Connecticut, 1703-1882.* Hartford, Conn.: Case, Lockwood and Brainard, 1882.

Papers of Jefferson Davis, The. See: Davis, Jefferson, The Papers of.

Patterson, Isabel, Mrs. William Hatcher Jones, and Laura Bellinger Jones. *Builders of Freedom: A Genealogy of Related Families Whose Ancestors Were Champions of Liberty and Among the Early Settlers of America.* Augusta, Ga.: Walton Printing Co., 1953.

Pollard, Edward A. *Life of Jefferson Davis, with a Secret History of the Southern Confederacy.* Reprint: Freeport, N.Y.: Books for Libraries Press, 1969.

Pollard, Edward A. *The Lost Cause.* Reprint, [n.p.]: Fairfax Press, 1974.

Pollard, Edward A. *Southern History of the War.* 2 vols. New York: C. B. Richardson, 1866; reprint in one vol., [n.p.]: Fairfax Press, 1977.

Powell, William S. *The North Carolina Gazetteer: A Dictionary of Tar-Heel Places.* Chapel Hill: University of North Carolina Press, 1968.

Powell, William S., ed. *Dictionary of North Carolina Biography*, vol. 1. Chapel Hill: University of North Carolina Press, 1979: "William Sheppard Ashe", by James M. Clifton.

Putnam, Sallie B. *Richmond During the War. See under* Brock.

Ramey, Emily G., and John K. Gott. *The Years of Anguish: Fauquier County, Virginia 1861-1865.* Warrenton, Va.: Printing Shop of The Fauquier Democrat, for the Fauquier County Civil War Centennial Committee and the Fauquier County Board of Supervisors, 1961; reprint, Annandale, Va.: Bacon Race Books, 1987.

Ramsdell, Charles W. *Behind the Lines in the Southern Confederacy.* The Walter Lynwood Fleming Lectures in Southern History, 1937. Edited with a Foreword by Wendell H. Stephenson. Baton Rouge: Louisiana State University Press, 1944; reprint, New York: Greenwood Press, 1969.

Richmond, The Stranger's Guide to the City of Richmond, Va.: G. P. Evans, Oct. 1863.

Roman, Alfred, [with the silent collaboration of P. G. T. Beauregard]. *The Military Operations of General Beauregard.* 2 vols. New York: Harper, 1884.

Rosengarten, Theodore. *Tombee: Portrait of a Cotton Planter.* New York: Morrow, 1986.

Rowland, Dunbar. *Jefferson Davis: Constitutionalist. His Letters, Papers and Speeches.* Collected and Edited by. 10 vols. Jackson, Miss.: Printed for the Mississippi Department of Archives and History, 1923.

Schwab, John Christopher. *The Confederate States of America 1861-1865: A Financial and Industrial History of the South During the Civil War.* Yale Bicentennial Publications Series. New Haven, Conn.: Yale University Press, 1913.

Sellers, John R., comp. *Civil War Manuscripts: A Guide to the Collections in the Manuscript Division of the Library of Congress.* Washington: Government Printing Office, 1986.

Seymour, Digby Gordon. *Divided Loyalties: Fort Sanders and the Civil War in East Tennessee.* Knoxville: University of Tennessee Press, 1963.

Shackelford, George Green. *George Wythe Randolph and the Confederate Elite.* Athens: University of Georgia Press, 1988.

Sims, James Marion. *The Story of My Life.* New York: Appleton, 1884.

Sorrel, G. Moxley. *Recollections of a Confederate Staff Officer.* New York: William Neale, 1905.

Southern Historical Society Papers. See under Newspapers and Serials.

Stevenson, William G. *Thirteen Months in the Rebel Army.* Reprint, New York: A. S. Barnes & Co., 1959.

Stoney, Samuel Gaillard. *This is Charleston: A Survey of the Architectural Heritage of a Unique American City.* Charleston, S.C.: Carolina Art Association, 1960.

Stranger's Guide to the City of Richmond. See under Richmond.

Strong, The Diary of George Templeton, ed. Allan Nevins and Milton Halsey Thomas, abridged by T. J. Pressly. University of Washington Press, 1988.

Symonds, Craig L. *Joseph E. Johnston: A Civil War Biography.* New York: Norton, 1990.

Taylor, Richard. *Destruction and Reconstruction.* New York: Appleton, 1879.

Thompson, Samuel Bernard. *Confederate Purchasing Operations Abroad.* Chapel Hill: University of North Carolina Press, 1935; reprint, Gloucester, Mass.: Peter Smith, 1973.

Todd, Richard C. *Confederate Finance.* Athens: University of Georgia Press, 1954.

Vandiver, Frank. *Confederate Blockade Running Through Bermuda 1861-1865*. Austin: University of Texas Press, 1947.

Van Every, Dale. *Disinherited: The Lost Birthright of the American Indian*. New York: Morrow, 1966.

Wagner, Frederick B., Jr., ed. *Thomas Jefferson University: Tradition and Heritage*. Philadelphia: Lea & Febiger, 1989.

Waklyn, Jon L. *Biographical Dictionary of the Confederacy*. Westport, Conn.: Greenwood Press, 1977.

Waring, Joseph Ioor. *A History of Medicine in South Carolina 1825-1900*, with a Preface by Richard H. Shryock. Columbia: South Carolina Medical Association, 1967.

War of the Rebellion, The: A Compilation of the Official Records of the Union and Confederate Armies. 4 series, comprising 70 vols. in 128. Washington; Government Printing Office, 1880-1901. Approximately one-third of the volumes have been used directly in this book: see footnotes for details.

Warner, Ezra J. *Generals in Grey*. Baton Rouge: Louisiana State University Press, 1959.

Warner, Ezra J., and W. Buck Yearns. *Biographical Register of the Confederate Congress*. Baton Rouge: Louisiana State University Press, 1975.

Watson, William. *Life in the Confederate Army*. New York: Scribner & Welford, 1888.

Wilkins, Thurman. *The Ridge Family and the Decimation of a People*. 2nd ed., revised. Norman: University of Oklahoma Press, 1986.

Wilkinson, John. *The Narrative of a Blockade-Runner*. New York: Sheldon & Co., 1877.

Williams, T. Harry. *P. G. T. Beauregard: Napoleon in Gray*. Baton Rouge: Louisiana State University Press, 1955.

Wise, Stephen R. *Lifeline of the Confederacy: Blockade Running During the Civil War*. University of South Carolina Press, 1988.

Worsham, John. *One of Jackson's Foot Cavalry*. New York: William Neale, 1912.

Articles, pamphlets, monographs, and theses

Beardsley, E. E. "The Parsonage of the 'Blue Meeting House' ", in *New Haven Colony Historical Society Papers*, 1 (1877), 105-119.

Benner, Judith Ann. *Fraudulent Finance: Counterfeiting and the Confederate States, 1861-1865*. Hill Junior College Monograph No. 3, 1970.

Bronson, Henry. "Medical History and Biography: Joel Northrop", in *New Haven Colony Historical Society Papers*, 2 (1878), 378-80.

Crist, Lynda Lasswell, "A 'Duty Man': Jefferson Davis as Senator", in *Journal of Mississippi History*, 50 (November 1989), 281-95.

Diamond, William, "Imports of the Confederate Government from Europe and Mexico", in *Journal of Southern History*, 6 (1940), 470-503.

Didier, Eugene Lemoine, "Jefferson Davis Speaks", in *The New York Sun*, June 22, 1890.

Didier, Eugene Lemoine, "The Scape-Goat of the Confederacy", in *Spare Moments*, October and November 1907.

Felt, Jeremy P. "Lucius B. Northrop and the Confederacy's Subsistence Department", in *Virginia Magazine of History and Biography*, 69 (1961), 181-93.

Gonzales, John Edmond. "The Public Career of Henry Stuart Foote (1804-1880)". Ph.D. thesis, University of North Carolina, Chapel Hill, 1957.

Hay, Thomas Robson. "Lucius B. Northrop: Commissary General of the Confederacy", in *Civil War History*, 9 (1963), 5-23.

Herndon, John W., comp. "A Genealogy of the Herndon Family", in *Virginia Magazine of History and Biography*, 11 (1904), 334 ff.

Hillman, E. Haviland. "The Brisbanes", in *South Carolina Historical and Genealogical Magazine*, 14 (1913), 179 ff.

Hunter, James. Letter of December 17, 1864 to his sister. Printed in *The Confederate Veteran*, November-December 1991, 36.

Johnson, Ludwell H. "Contraband Trade in the Last Year of the Civil War", in *Mississippi Valley Historical Review*, 49 (1963), 635-52.

Johnson, Ludwell H. "Trading with the Union: the Evolution of Confederate Policy", in *Virginia Magazine of History and Biography*, 78 (1970), 308-325.

Jones, Mrs. J. O. et al. "Beauvoir: Jefferson Davis Shrine". Gulfport, Miss.: Dixie Press for United Daughters of the Confederacy, 1976.

Jordan, Thomas. "Jefferson Davis", in *Harper's New Monthly Magazine*, October 31, 1865, 610-620.

N[orthrop, Claudian Bird]. "Political Remarks by N.": Nos. 9-11. Charleston: Evans & Cogswell, 1861.

[Northrop, Claudian Bird], "Southern Odes by the Outcast". Charleston: Harper & Calvo, 1861.

O'Brien, G. F. J. "James A. Seddon, Statesman of the Old South". Ph.D. thesis, University of Maryland, 1963.

"Porcher, The Memoirs of Frederick Augustus", in *South Carolina Historical and Genealogical Magazine*, 46 (1945), 21 ff.

Rankin, Frank G. "Eli Metcalfe Bruce", TS ca. 1980. Copy in possession of the writer.

Ruffin, Frank. "A Chapter in Confederate History", in *The North American Review*, 134 (1882), 97-110.

Skoch, George. "Cantankerous Carolinian: The Man Who Fed the South", in *Civil War Times*, 22 (1983), 40-44.

Smith, John Gilmore. "The Passing of Bishop Northrop", a series of eight articles in *The Charleston Sunday News*, August-September 1920.

Taylor, Robert A. "Cow Cavalry: Munnerlyn's Battalion in Florida 1864-1865", in *Florida Historical Quarterly*, 65 (1986), 196-214.

Taylor, Robert A. "Rebel Beef: Florida Cattle and the Confederate Army 1862-1864", in *Florida Historical Quarterly*, 67 (1988), 15-31.

Thompson, James West. "Beauvoir: A Walk Through History". Biloxi, Miss.: Beauvoir Press, 1988.

Tyler's Quarterly Historical and Genealogical Magazine, "The Noland Family", 2 (1920), 132-34.

Wight, Willard E., ed. "Some Letters of Lucius Bellinger Northrop, 1860-1865", in *Virginia Magazine of History and Biography*, 68 (1960), 456-477.

Newspapers and serials

Baltimore Sun, The. February 10, 1894. Obit. of L. B. Northrop by Gen. Bradley Johnson.

Baltimore Sunday Herald, The. July 8, 1887. Jefferson Davis interview with J. Thomas Sharf.

Charleston Daily Courier, The. September 6, 1861.

Charleston Mercury, The. One of the great Southern papers of record. I have made particular use of the issues of October 18, 1862; and February 13 and 15, 1864.

Charleston Sunday News, The. See under *Articles*, etc., Smith, John Gilmore.

Charleston Times, The. September 29, 1812. Obit. of Amos Northrop.

New York Citizen, The. "Rummaging through Rebeldom, by Col. C. S. Armee" [prob. Charles E. L. Stuart]. No. 3: April 20, 1867; No. 16: July 27, 1867.

New York Herald, The. July 21, 1865. Frank Ruffin's Testimony Before the Confederate Congress, January 1865 (slightly abridged), pages 2-3. A major printed source for Confederate Subsistence policy and action. See also June 30, July 8 and 25.

New York Sun, The. June 22, 1890. See under *Articles*, etc., Didier, Eugene Lemoine.

New York Tribune, The. June 29, 1865.

Pittsburg Dispatch, The. December 19, 1889. Anon. recollections of Jefferson Davis at West Point.

Richmond Enquirer, The. February 24, 1863. Ruffin's self-defense against Foote's attacks.

Richmond Examiner, The. The leading anti-administration paper of the Confederacy. Amongst much else, I have made special use of October 2, 1861; and December 20, 1864 through January 4, 1865.

Richmond Whig, The. May 30, 1861: Account of Davis's arrival in Richmond. August 3, 1861: Account of Davis family's move into the presidential mansion.

Southern Historical Society Papers. Richmond: Virginia Historical Society, 1876-1959. Vols. 1-38 (1876-1910); vols. 39-52 [New Series 1-14] (1914-1959).

Manuscript sources

Charleston, S.C. Cathedral of St. Mary and St. John. Baptismal records, 1845-1860.

Charleston, S.C. Cathedral of St. Mary and St. John. Diocesan records.

Fielding, Mr. and Mrs. Geoffrey, Baltimore. Family papers.

Frederick, Maryland. Convent of the Visitation Academy. Archives.

Georgetown University, Washington, D.C. Archives.

Georgia. Irwin County. Deed Book 3 (1844), 336-339.

Harvard University, Cambridge, Mass. Dearborn Collection.

Huntington Library, San Marino, Calif. Brock Coll., Box 284; Eldridge Coll., Box 76.

National Archives, Washington, D.C. etc.:

Record Group 94:

Adjutant General's Office. U.S. Military Academy. Cadet Applications, 1823/29. Northrop. L. B.

Adjutant General's Office. Letters Received. 56-N-1860.

Applications for Appointment, Civilian. Maryland, No. 2. Northrop, L. B., recommendation for John Steuart.

Record Group 109. Confederate Records.

General and Staff Officers Files: Broadwell, William A.
Dameron, William H.
Guerin, Henry C.
Herbert, R. G.
Johnston, Theodore H.
Lee, Richard Bland.
Northrop, Lucius Bellinger.

Letters Received by the Confederate Adjutant and Inspector General. Microfilm publication M-474 (164 reels).

Letters Received by the Confederate Secretary of War. Microfilm publication M-437 (151 reels).

Letters Sent by the Confederate Secretary of War. Vols. 1-3.

Letters Sent by the Confederate Secretary of War to the President.

Presidential Messages.

Telegrams Received by the Confederate Secretary of War. Microfilm publication M-618 (19 reels).

Telegrams Sent by the Confederate Secretary of War. Microfilm publication M-524 (1 reel).

New York Public Library. Civil War Collection. Northrop papers.
     Century Collection.
     Fleming, Walter, papers.
North Carolina, University of. Cooper Papers #2482. Northrop, L. B.
     Moses, Raphael J. Autobiography (MS).

Richmond, Va. Museum of the Confederacy. Jefferson Davis Coll.
     Valentine Museum.
     Virginia Historical Society. F. G. Ruffin papers.

South Carolina. Charleston Court of Common Pleas. Judgment Rolls.
     Box 70, Roll 14.
     Charleston Probate Office. Will Book L, 319, Box 94 #9.

South Carolina Historical Society, Charleston. Northrop, Amos, Agreement with Langdon Cheves, December 5, 1809. MS 12-44-2.

Steuart, Arthur B., Baltimore. Family papers.

Tulane University, New Orleans. Louisiana Historical Association. Jefferson Davis Papers, reel 22. Letters from L. B. Northrop.

Virginia. Albemarle County. Deed Book 62 (1867).
     Will Book 30, 168-9.

Virginia, University of. University archives.
     William J. Rucker Coll.

INDEX

Wayne, U.S. Fort, Oklahoma Territory, 22, 24

Webster, Daniel, 3

Wellford, P. A. (CS Capt & Commissary), 253, 254

West Point, U.S. Military Academy at, Northrop as applicant, 6-7; as student and graduate, 8ff.

Whaley, William, 41

White, George W. (CS cattle agent in Texas), 141 & n. 36

White, Pleasant W. (CS Maj, Florida Chief Commissary), 222-23 & n. 73

White family, 27

Whiting, William C. (CS Maj & Gen), 96, 167 n. 8, 180 n. 13, 213 n. 39, 302

Wigfall, Louis T. (CS Congressman), 94, 239

Wilkinson, John (CS blockade runner), quoted, 266

Wilson, R. T. (Tenn. meat packer, CS cattle agent), 77, 133-34

Winchester RR, *see* Railroads

Winder, John H. (CS Gen), Provost Marshal of Richmond, 144; Commandant of Prisons, 225 & n. 2, 226-29, 261

Wirz, Henry (CS Maj), 289

Wise, Henry (CS Gen), 115-16

Withers, William T. (CS Col), 82

Woodruff, William, 44; Northrop's letters to, 44-46

Worsham, John (CS volunteer), quoted, 62-63, 115, 130, 151, 256

Z

Zollicoffer, Felix (CS Gen), 136